Critical Survey of Long Fiction

English Novelists

Editor

Carl Rollyson

Baruch College, City University of New York

Salem Press

Ipswich, Massachusetts • Hackensack, New Jersey

Cover photo:
Emily Brontë (© Lebrecht Authors/Lebrecht Music & Arts/Corbis)

978-1-4298-3689-0

CONTENTS

CONTRIBUTORS

Todd K. Bender
Original Contributor

Cynthia A. Bily
Adrian, Michigan

C. F. Burgess
Original Contributor

John J. Conlon
Original Contributor

Deborah Core
Original Contributor

Robert P. Ellis
Original Contributor

Kristine Ottesen Garrigan
Original Contributor

Peter W. Graham
Original Contributor

Erwin Hester
Original Contributor

John R. Holmes
Franciscan University of Steubenville

Rebecca Kuzins
Pasadena, California

Lawrence F. Laban
Original Contributor

Fred B. McEwen
Original Contributor

Charles E. May
California State University, Long Beach

Laurence W. Mazzeno
Alvernia College

Carole Moses
Original Contributor

Allan Nelson
Caldwell College

K. Bhaskara Rao
Original Contributor

Samuel J. Rogal
Original Contributor

John C. Shields
Original Contributor

Scott D. Vander Ploeg
Madisonville Community College

Ronald G. Walker
Original Contributor

The English Novel

To a greater extent than any other literary form, the novel is consistently and directly engaged with the society in which the writer lives and feels compelled to explain, extol, or criticize. The English novel, from its disparate origins to its development in the eighteenth century, from its rise in the nineteenth century to its present state, has been strongly influenced by the social, political, economic, scientific, and cultural histories of England. In fact, English writers dominated the novel genre in its earliest stages of development and continued to do so through much of its history. As a realistic form, the novel not only reflects but also helps define and focus society's sense of itself, and as the novel reflects the growth of England first into a United Kingdom, then into an empire, and its decline to its present role in the Commonwealth of Nations, it does so predominantly through the eyes of the middle class.

Indeed, the origins and development of the English novel are most profitably examined in relation to the increasing growth and eventual dominance of the middle class in the course of several hundred years. Typically concerned with middle-class characters in a world largely of their making, the novel sometimes features excursions into the upper reaches of English society; with more frequency, it presents incursions by members of the upper class into the familiar world of the solid middle class. As a form of realistic literature intended primarily for the middle class, often for their instruction and edification (or excoriation), the novel frequently depicts the worlds of the lower orders of society—not only the exotic cultures subjugated by Imperial Britain but also the familiarly strange domestic worlds of the "criminal classes," a subculture with its own hierarchies, vocabulary, customs, and occupations.

As distinguished from allegory and romance, the English novel has for its primary focus the individual situated in society and his or her emotions, thoughts, actions, choices, and relationships to others in complex and often bewildering environments. Set against backgrounds that realistically reflect all facets of the English experience, the "histories" or "lives" of the novels' protagonists must hold a necessary interest for readers who, in turn, seek to make sense of, master, cope with, escape from, or become fully assimilated into the society in which they, like their heroes and heroines, find themselves. While any attempt to trace with great particularity the multiple relationships between the history of the English novel and the larger patterns of English society remains necessarily imperfect, the general outlines of those relationships can be sketched.

Origins of the English novel

Although long-standing debates about the origin of the English novel and the first English novel continue, it is both convenient and just to state that it is with the fiction of Daniel Defoe (1660-1731) that the first novel appeared, especially in the sense that term came to have in the late eighteenth century and continues to have today. Without considerable injustice it may be said that the novel first developed out of a series of false starts in the seventeenth century and a series of accidents in the eighteenth. The reading public, having been exposed to large amounts of novelistic material, fictions of various lengths, epics, and prose romances, appears to have been ready to receive a form that went beyond Aphra Behn's *Oroonoko: Or, The History of the Royal Slave* (1688), John Bunyan's *The Pilgrim's Progress* (1678, 1684), and the prose works of earlier masters such as Sir Thomas Malory, John Mandeville, Robert Greene, Thomas Dekker, and Thomas Nashe. Such a form would emphasize unified action of some plausibility, individualized and articulate characters, and stories presented with such verisimilitude that the readers could find in them highly wrought illusions of the realities they knew best.

The literary children of the eighteenth century, the novel and its sibling the short story, created a taste for fiction of all varieties in a middle-class readership whose ranks were swollen by a newly literate mercantile class. This readership appears to have wanted and certainly received a literary medium of their own, filled with practically minded characters who spoke the same middle-class English language and prized the same middle-class English goals (financial and familial success) as they themselves did. In general, the novel helped make the position of the individual in new, expanding, and increasingly urban social contexts more intelligible; frequently addressed directly to the "dear reader," the novel presented unified visions of individuals in society, reflected the cultural and social conditions of that society, and supported the presumed rationalist psychology endemic to the age, which was fostered by Francis Bacon, Thomas Hobbes, and John Locke.

The novel was influenced by historic events and societal developments, especially tidal changes that involved the class structure of English society. The merchant class had existed for centuries and had steadily grown in the Age of Discovery and during colonization in the seventeenth century. In that century, a number of events conspired to begin the disestablishment of the feudal, medieval world, a disestablishment that would become final in the early nineteenth century. The beginning of the English Civil War (1642) marked the most noteworthy outbreak of religious and class strife England had yet seen. The subsequent regicide of Charles I in 1649 and the abolition of monarchy and the House of Lords by the House of Commons in that year signaled the formation of the Puritan Commonwealth (1649-1660) and the first rise to political dominance of the middle class, a much-contested context. In the Glorious Revolution of 1688, Parliament invited William of Orange and his wife, Mary, the Protestant daughter of the Catholic James II, to rule England. James II (the "Old Pretender") fled to France with his son Charles (the "Young Pretender" or Bonnie Prince Charlie), established himself in exile, and began plotting a return to power that would eventuate in the Scottish rebellions of 1715, 1719, and 1745-1746 on behalf of the Stuart monarchy. The Glorious Revolution may, in part, be seen as establishing the principle that the English middle class, through Parliament, could choose their own ruler; it may also be seen as another phase in the growth of power of that middle class.

A war with France (1689-1697) saw the beginning of the national debt, but the late seventeenth and early eighteenth centuries (especially during the reign of Queen Anne, 1702-1714) were marked by material progress, increased mercantilism, drastically increased population, and a rapid and irreversible shift of population from the country to the city. Apart from two major trade monopolies (the Hudson Bay Company in Canada and the East India Company in the Indian subcontinent), trade was open to all after 1689. Free enterprise flourished and with it the middle class, as early eighteenth century England became a mercantile society teetering on the brink of the Industrial Revolution and the concurrent scientific revolution that abetted it. While the governance of England still rested with a relatively small number of families, the hereditary landowners of England had to share power with the new merchant princes of the era.

From this milieu of class conflict emerged the earliest English novels. Rooted both in the picaresque tradition stemming from the anonymous Spanish *Lazarillo de Tormes* (1554; English translation, 1576) and Miguel de Cervantes' *Don Quixote de la Mancha* (1605, 1615) and in the pseudohistorical tradition, Daniel Defoe's novels present their fictions as fact, as the "histories" or "lives" of characters such as Robinson Crusoe, Colonel Newport, and Moll Flanders. Defoe's novels are distinguished by a realism that employs minute and concerted observations, as well as a morality that—despite lapses, an occasional blind eye to folly, and some ambiguous presentations of vice—fits well with the morality of the middle class, especially when erstwhile sinners repent and exemplify the Protestant virtues of seriousness, usefulness, social responsibility, and thrift. Like their many literary descendants, Defoe's characters evince a cheerful triumph of person over place and situation, an eventual mastery of the world and its too-familiar snares in the common and the uncommon adventures that form their educative encounters with the world and with themselves.

Even more obviously in line with middle-class Puritan ethics is the work of Samuel Richardson (1689-1761), whose epistolary novels of personality, sensibility, and moral conflict present the first multidimensional characters in English prose fiction. *Pamela: Or, Virtue Rewarded* (1740-1741) began by accident what Walter Allen calls the "first great flowering of the English novel." Commissioned to compose and print *Familiar Letters* as models of correspondence, moral guides, and repositories of advice to "handsome girls," Richardson expanded the project until it became *Pamela*. The particular virtue rewarded is chastity, in the face of assaults from a member of the Squirearchy, Mr. B., who is, ironically, a justice of the peace. One important artistic concern in the novel is the power of the written word to effect the conversion of wayward characters. One could take the view that Pamela's epistles reinforce traditionally Christian, or social, or merely prudential morality and that they also represent the generally desirable triumph of a member of the lower-middle class over representatives of the upper-middle class and the titled upper class. Virtue is, Richardson suggests, its own reward; it is all the better if it brings other rewards prized by the middle class. The novel's themes of moral courage and virtue reaffirmed bourgeois values and thus helped create an avid reading public.

Following Defoe, whose fiction offered a journalistic facticity, and Richardson, who wrote transparent moral sermons, Henry Fielding (1707-1754) was the first to write avowed novels and depict ordinary English life and the panorama of his age. Like Richardson, Fielding's beginning as a novelist was fortuitous. Sir Robert Walpole served George I and George II as prime minister from 1721 to 1742, and for much of that time he was the object of satire at the hands of several playwrights, Fielding among them. With Walpole's successful introduction of the Licensing Act of 1737, Fielding's career as a dramatist ended, and he turned his ironic and satiric vision to the new prose form, the novel, perfecting that form, many argue, in *The History of Tom Jones, a Foundling* (1749). Before that accomplishment, however, Fielding began his prose efforts by writing a broad satire of Richardson's title character, Pamela Andrews, which he titled *An Apology for the Life of Mrs. Shamela Andrews* (1741). He followed this success with *The History of the Adventures of Joseph Andrews, and of His Friend Mr. Abraham Adams* (1742), concerning Pamela's imagined brother, but took the story in new directions at midnovel. His *Amelia* (1751) is the first novel of social reform and thus was a point of reference for Charles Dickens and the many contributors to the "Newgate novel" in the nineteenth century. In *Amelia*, Fielding clearly exposes social wrongs and provides possible remedies for them. His portrayal of gambling dens, prison life, and the omnipresent Hogarthian gin mills foreshadows the excessive realism (or naturalism) of Honoré de Balzac and Émile Zola in France and George Moore in late Victorian England.

Two other great eighteenth century novelists, Tobias Smollett (1721-1771) and Laurence Sterne (1713-1768), added various dimensions of eighteenth century English life to the novel's inventory. In *The Adventures of Roderick Random* (1748), Smollett brought to the novel the first extended account of one fundament of English trade, prosperity, and adventure: seafaring life. Like Fielding and Defoe, he used English military history as background material for some of the finest English picaresque novels. Sterne, in *Tristram Shandy* (1759-1767), departed from the norm that his contemporaries had established, introducing a stream-of-consciousness technique to refract society through the prism of an individual mind, a technique that would not be further developed until the early twentieth century in the novels of James Joyce and Virginia Woolf.

THE GOTHIC NOVEL

By the end of the eighteenth century, both the novel of sentiment and the gothic novel had appeared in *The Vicar of Wakefield* (1766) by Oliver Goldsmith (1728 or 1730-1774) and *The Castle of Otranto* (1765) by Horace Walpole (1717-1797). While Goldsmith's work and others like it continue in prose the situations and characteristics of the highly popular sentimental domestic drama of middle-class life, Walpole's novel exists outside of the conventions of eighteenth century thought and fiction. His is the only novel of those already mentioned that does not take as its premise the world as it exists, society in the country or city, and the generally agreed upon concept of the possible as coextensive with the real. Premised, then, on questions of epistemology and radical uncertainty, one can ascribe to *The Castle of Otranto* the beginnings of gothic traditions in the novel.

An emphasis on shared, common experience and consensus unified society and its conception of itself intellectually, philosophically, and psychologically. This society, in many respects the first truly modern society, emerged near the end of the seventeenth century into the era of Enlightenment and took for its tenets common sense, secular reason, science, and gentility. One fundamental emphasis of this era was upon the necessity to treat life and its problems in the spirit of reason and scientific empiricism rather than in the traditional spirit of appeal to authority and dogma. In this era, the landed gentry and not a few of the merchant princes regarded themselves as "Augustans" and sought to imitate the values and beliefs of the Roman patricians of the age of Augustus. In so doing, they set the intellectual tone of their times by asserting rationalism (and skepticism) as the primary focus of thought and by insisting on symmetry in all phases of life as well as of art, artificial ornament and the preference of artifice to "nature," reserved dignity in preference to any form of enthusiasm, and expansive, urbane sophistication instead of narrow, superstitious thought. It comes, then, as an extraordinary incongruity to find not only Walpole's work but also other novels of horror written, avidly read, and widely praised in this neoclassical Age of Reason.

Nevertheless, Walpole's gothic story was immensely successful, quite probably so in reaction to the restraint of the age, the dominion exercised by the Protestant ethic, and the evangelicalism of the century born in the advent of Wesleyanism and Methodism. In his conscious outlandishness, Walpole set a new course for fiction. His horrific pseudo-medieval tale was followed by the gothic novels of Clara Reeve (1729-1807), Ann Radcliffe (1764-1823)—especially *The Mysteries of Udolpho* (1794)—and Matthew Gregory Lewis (1775-1818), and by numerous novels of the Romantic period. The success of this kind of imaginative, experimental writing is most probably what allowed for later development of novels based on fantasy, including science fantasy and science fiction. Mary Wollstonecraft Shelley's *Frankenstein* (1818) continued the gothic strain in the nineteenth century and became the preeminent novel of experimental science.

THE LATE EIGHTEENTH CENTURY

The last quarter of the eighteenth century, a period that saw the beginnings of Romanticism, featured the remarkable first ministry of William Pitt, the Younger (1759-1806), a ministry that laid the foundation for much of the reform movement in the nineteenth century. The intellectual tenets of the Augustan Age, already called into question by the gothic novelists and several poets of the age, were about to suffer a sea change in the triumph of individualism that characterized Romanticism. Economically, however, England maintained rather than altered its newfound tradition of progress, legitimatized by the writings of David Ricardo and Adam Smith. The advances of industry and capitalism begun early in the Augustan Age continued and ensured an economic boom that, with few setbacks, was to characterize the nineteenth century and fuel the expansion of the empire. Culturally, the pre-Romantic period was marked by an extraordinary growth in literacy, helped in great part by the growth of charity schools, the drive to regularize and teach English (if only for commercial purposes), the increasing new opportunities for the education of women, and the establishment and development of circulating libraries.

Two writers of this transitional period—the era, roughly speaking, between the outbreak of unrest in the American colonies in the early 1770's and the accession of Queen Victoria (1837)—stand apart from the mainstream of the rapidly changing world in which they lived. One, Jane Austen (1775-1817), epitomized an age that had already passed; the other, Sir Walter Scott (1771-1832), eschewed his own world except to the extent that he could translate some of its characteristics to other times. Austen's works, unpublished until the second decade of the nineteenth century, are the last novels of the Enlightenment. Unlike those of the other great eighteenth century novels, the characters presented by "the great feminine Augustan" are drawn almost exclusively from the landed gentry. In her novels she presents minute descriptions of the members of that class, their characters, beliefs, aspirations, and hopes in a period marked by a strong desire for stability on the part of the gentry despite the fact that they were surrounded by the armies of change. A supremely accomplished novelist, Jane Austen set the pattern for all subsequent novels of manners and family. Her characters interest themselves in issues of importance only to themselves—social position, socially and financially advantageous marriages, and the orderly passage of property from one generation to the next. The portraits that emerge are absolutely dissimilar to those of Fielding and his fellows and are essentially those of the placid, insulated upper class; as such, they present not only highly wrought pictures of the gentry but also invaluable insights into a social stratum that utterly vanished in the twentieth century.

Scott's Romantic novels, unlike Austen's works, deal with the world as it might have been rather than as it then was. His novels transplant nineteenth century heroes of sense, sensibility, and virtue to remote places or historically distant times. Moreover, his pioneer work in shaping the historical consciousness and national identity of Scotland while recounting its seventeenth century and eighteenth century history, and his novels of medieval and Renaissance Britain won him a place as a universally respected novelist of his century.

Both Austen and Scott are anomalies. Austen clearly summarizes the Augustan Age and its concerns, and Scott is surely the spokesman of a movement that grew in the last decades of the eighteenth century and took hold as the dominant intellectual mode of subsequent centuries, Romanticism. Though his novels rarely treat the world in which he lived, Scott's perceptions were conditioned by the growing intellectual and emotional tenets of Romanticism. Although he sought to explore the political and social conditions of earlier times in English and Scottish history, he consistently chose not to recognize the inescapable facts of the Industrial Revolution, the expensive (both in money and in lives) wars England waged in his own time, and the bloodless social revolution that saw the gentry finally replaced by the middle class as the political and economic rulers of England. The largest element of Scott's Romanticism is a studied medievalism that may be viewed as an escapist alternative (of considerable psychological necessity) to the pervasive and turbulent revolutions in every sector of society and as a reassertion of fundamental and traditional values. One benefit Scott gained by focusing upon Romantic medievalism as his chief fictional concern is that he thereby escaped the social censure and ostracism other Romantics experienced. Not only did he achieve personal respectability as a poet-turned-novelist, but he also created such a large and insatiable reading public for his and others' novels that the novel became the most popular form of literature.

THE VICTORIAN NOVEL

The Victorian novelists—Charles Dickens was arguably the greatest of them—mark a new era in the novel, an era in which the primary middle-class emphasis on its own place in society and the reformation of society in its own image came to the fore. Society itself expanded in the Victorian Age to include not only England and the United Kingdom but also an empire upon which, proverbially, the sun never set. In consequence, novelists, in their characters, backgrounds, and plots, often surveyed an empire that extended geographically to all continents, covering fully one-tenth of the earth's surface, and financially to the entire populated world. Trade and tradesmen literally moved the empire, opened Australia and Canada to colonization, brought India into the fold (first via the East India Company and then, in 1857, under the Crown), and brought about the foundation of the corporate world with the Companies' Act of 1862.

The reform movement, in part attributable to the Romantic rebellion and in larger part to the middle-class redefinition of societal ideals, came to partial fruition in the 1820's and flourished in the 1830's and in subsequent decades. The hated and inflationary measure of 1815 prohibiting grain imports, the Corn Law, was modified in 1828; the Combination Acts of the era illustrate the pronounced middle-class opposition to trade unionism; the repeal of the Test Act (1828) and the passage of the Catholic Emancipation Bill (1829) brought about a liberalization of attitudes toward Roman Catholics and extended political franchise to a large number of men; the Third Reform Bill (1832) abolished slavery in the empire; the Factory Act (1833) regulated working hours and required two hours of schooling daily for children under the age of thirteen; and the New Poor Law (1834) represented another phase of regularizing governmental services and social programs. These reforms typify, without nearly exhausting, the great social legislation of this era. Reform was the byword of the early decades of the nineteenth century and the hallmark of the entire Victorian era as English society evolved. Subsequent reforms in suffrage, for example, seem to have moved at a glacial pace and only included women in 1928, but each new enfranchisement under the ministerial guidance of Benjamin Disraeli and William Gladstone added appreciably to the power of the middle class. It was quite natural, then, for the English novel to add social reform to its repertoire of themes.

Conditions for novelists also improved in nineteenth century England. As the eighteenth century marked the end of patronage as the primary support of artists and writers, so the explosion of periodicals, the multiplication of newspapers, the growth of publishing firms, and the extension of consumerism to literary works in the nineteenth century made it possible for more writers to try to live by and from the pen. "Grub Street" had meant, since the mid-eighteenth century, hard times for writers such as Samuel Johnson and Oliver Goldsmith, and in the eighteenth century the supply of writers far exceeded the demand. This, too, was the case in the nineteenth century, but less severely so, and it would remain the case despite the paperback, magazine, and other media revolutions of the twentieth century. It has often been suggested that Dickens,William Makepeace Thackeray, and most popular novelists of the century whose novels were first serialized in journals and magazines wrote at such length because they were paid by the line of print; while padding is one possible consequence of such a method of publication and payment, the leisurely pace of the novel, its descriptiveness and its length, date from the eighteenth century and grew without regard to such payment schedules. Serial publication no doubt influenced how authors arranged their plot developments. Authors provided rising action toward the end of each installment rather than solely toward the end of the entire novel. These suspenseful moments became known as "cliffhangers" for their ability to tease readers into purchasing the next issue.

The Victorian novel as exemplified in the works of Charles Dickens (1812-1870) not only describes life but competes with it as well. Here one finds a verisimilitude so persuasive that the swarming complexities of Victorian life seem fixed in the novels. While carrying on the traditional celebration of middle-class values, Dickens also tried to make sense of the complex variety of choices open to his readers, of the fabric of society (by explaining, exposing, and mythologizing the middle class), of the ills of his society (by exposing them and calling for their reform), and of the patent injustices of capitalist society (by emphasizing their consequences, the plight of the victims of injustice, and the dehumanization of its perpetrators). To all of these concerns Dickens added a sense of comedy that suffused his early and some of his middle work but that changed to ferocity in his last complete novel, arguably his best after *Bleak House* (1852-1853, serial; 1853, book), *Our Mutual Friend* (1864-1865, serial; 1865, book).

Like Scott and many of his own contemporaries, Dickens is not above providing in his fiction a psychological escape from the mechanized world of his readers, as in *Pickwick Papers* (1836-1837, serial; 1837, book), a genteel picaresque work set in the period before the Age of Steam. Little else but artificially contrived escape exists for the reader and the protagonist of *Oliver Twist* (1837-1839, serial; 1838, book), an intense (and in its initial chapters unrelieved) examination of the workhouse system, one of the more depressing phenomena of the reform movement. Similarly, his descriptions of the criminal classes (so severely criticized, especially in regard to his depiction of prostitutes and child criminals, that he felt compelled to document his observations in the preface to the novel's second edition) illustrate the predatory relationship of this class to all other classes and form an indictment of the society that spawned and neglected them, an indictment that Dickens reiterated in *Bleak House* and elsewhere. Dickens the social reformer achieves some of his most enduring effects by indulging in the sentimentalism inherent in the sort of melodrama popular in the Victorian Age and still popular in some sectors today.

The Chancery Court and the legal system are the objects of Dickens's satiric wrath in *Bleak House*, a novel that amply illustrates that "the Law is a Ass," while in few other novels has the middle-class Gospel of Wealth been so soundly condemned as in *Dombey and Son* (1846-1848, serial; 1848, book). It is significant that in this novel the railway appears for the first time in Dickens's works. Dickens cast a cold eye on another English social institution, debtors' prison, in *Little Dorrit* (1855-1857, serial; 1857, book), in which London's Marshalsea Prison is the primary setting. On a smaller canvas in *Hard Times* (1854), he took on the educational abuses favored by the Gradgrinds of British industrial Coketowns, complete with their belief in the dullest of "facts."

Similar social issues and notions of reform appear in the Newgate novels (picaresque tales of crime and punishment by incarceration in Newgate Prison) and in the important work of the novelist Elizabeth Gaskell (1810-1865). Both Gaskell and Charles Kingsley (*Alton Locke*, 1850) did much to introduce the working-class or proletarian figure as a central focus of fiction, a focus Thomas Hardy would further sharpen late in the century.

William Makepeace Thackeray (1811-1863), a contemporary and sometime friend of Dickens, presented the world of the upper-middle class and limited his novels to that sphere. His *Vanity Fair: A Novel Without a Hero* (1847-1848) eschewed the conventional novel of intrigue and focused on the steady social climb of Becky Sharp from the position of governess to the ranks of the leisured gentry, a new class only possible to the England of empire and Industrial Revolution. Thackeray is at pains to glorify the virtues of the upper-middle class and to bolster them through his fiction: Marriage, home, and children constitute the proper society he portrays. Surely it is still possible to see in these ideals the safe harbors they had become for Victorians: It is also possible to view them as indicative of the societal dichotomy present in nearly every aspect of Victorian thought, a dichotomy that, in this case, emphasized an intense desire for security while positing the need for the adventurous life of acquisition. Like many of his predecessors and contemporaries, Thackeray turned his hand to the historical novel to explore from a nineteenth century perspective the social and literary life of the Queen Anne era, the Jacobite plots to return the Stuarts to monarchy, and the campaigns of the Duke of Marlborough.

Anthony Trollope (1815-1882) brought to the novel two new subject areas drawn from Victorian life: In his Barsetshire novels he introduced the first accurate portraits of English clerics; in his political or parliamentary novels he presented accurate descriptions of English politicians and political life rivaled only by those of Benjamin Disraeli (1804-1881), the first earl of Beaconsfield and twice prime minister of England (1867-1868; 1874-1880). In the novels of Trollope and Disraeli the vast and intricate world of ministries and parliaments, political intrigue, and the multifarious activities of empire in relation to the political process achieve a place in the novelistic tradition of England.

The religious controversies of the era, notably the Oxford Movement and the Anglo-Catholicism it induced, are present as background to Trollope's Barsetshire novels. The controversies are the concerns of several characters in the works of George Eliot (Mary Ann Evans, 1819-1880), and enter into *Sartor Resartus* (1833-1834, serial; 1836, book) by Thomas Carlyle (1795-1881) as well as into numerous other novels of the era, many of which use the historical convention of setting stories in Roman times to explore the religious question. Eliot's explorations of the internal motivations of her characters, in *Middlemarch* (1871-1872), for example, led to a brand of novel sometimes described as "psychological," although the full manifestation of this inside story would be independently delivered by Virginia Woolf (1882-1941) and James Joyce (1882-1941) after the turn of the century. The scientific basis for certain religious controversies, such as the influx of German higher criticism, the use of evidence from the expanding science of geology, and the introduction of the theory of evolution by Charles Darwin (1809-1882), also find their way into the novels of the period. The religious question and its attendant fideist, agnostic, and atheistic responses find novelistic expression in the works of such writers as Trollope; Charles Kingsley (1819-1875), the exponent of "Muscular Christianity"; Edmund Gosse (1849-1928), especially in *Father and Son* (1907); and Samuel Butler (1835-1902), particularly in *Erewhon* (1872), *Erewhon Revisited* (1901), *The Fair Haven* (1873), and *The Way of All Flesh* (1903).

Both abrupt and gradual changes in the religious climate are reflected in many Victorian novels, particularly in the otherwise quite dissimilar works of George Meredith (1829-1909) and Thomas Hardy (1840-1928). Meredith's championing of "advanced ideas" generally and his particular advocacy of woman suffrage, free thought, political radicalism, and evolutionary theory (optimistically considered) combine to form a vision of the Comic Spirit that suffuses his works. Hardy was differently affected by the multiplicity of Victorian controversies and conflicting claims; in his works one finds not comedy but a tragic vision of human life dominated by an inexorable sense that the evolutionary process has produced in man a kind of alien species against which the permanent forces of nature are constantly arrayed. Nowhere is this more evident than in *Jude the Obscure* (1895), a novel so universally condemned by churchmen and the conservative literary establishment that Hardy turned away from the novel to become a poet of considerable importance.

Another element in the continuing debate that the Victorians carried on with themselves springs from the social reform movements of the era and collides with the positivistic thought of Auguste Comte (1798-1857), who coined the term "sociology." This element surfaced in some of Dickens's work (*Bleak House*; *Martin Chuzzlewit*, 1843-1844 [serial], 1844 [book]; *Our Mutual Friend*; and the unfinished *The Mystery of Edwin Drood*, 1870), rose to a different plane in the novels of Wilkie Collins (*The Woman in White*, 1860; *The Moonstone*, 1868), and formed much of the matter of "yellowback" or pulp novels as "shilling shockers" and "penny dreadfuls." It reached its logical Victorian zenith in the accounts of the world's greatest private consulting detective, Sherlock Holmes, by Arthur Conan Doyle (1859-1930), narratives that range from *A Study in Scarlet* (1887) to *The Case-Book of Sherlock Holmes* (1927).

THE DETECTIVE AND SPY NOVELS

The phenomenon of detective fiction captured the interest and imagination of the Victorian public at all levels of society. Organized police forces were first created in the nineteenth century, the science of criminology was born, and ingenious threats to life and, especially, property from the criminal classes grew apace with the unremitting urbanization of England. The steady progress of the fictional criminal, from the endearing rogues of sentimental fiction to the personification of social evil created by Conan Doyle in his Napoleon of Crime, Professor Moriarty, is directly related to the growth of the propertied middle class, to the swelling population of the "undeserving poor" (in George Bernard Shaw's phrase), to the ample opportunities for anonymity which urban centers and clear class divisions afforded, to the inevitable lure of easy money, and to the multiple examples of corrupt politicians on a national scale. Crime fiction kept pace with developments in crime and in criminal investigation, and in some cases the fiction anticipated developments in criminal science. The crime thriller, mystery story, and detective novel are still staple items of English fiction and have been so for more than a century, thanks to the efforts of Conan Doyle and the prodigious work of such writers as Agatha Christie (1890-1976) and John Creasey (1908-1973).

Still another subgenre linked to the detective novel was born of the armies of empire, international political events, and the information and communication explosions of the nineteenth century—the spy novel. Espionage had run through several Romantic and Victorian novels, but the Secret Service—John le Carré's "Circus" in his novels of the 1960's and 1970's—first came to prominence in *Kim* (1901) by Rudyard Kipling (1865-1936), and revolutionary espionage and anarchy came to the fore in *The Secret Agent* (1907) by Joseph Conrad (1857-1924). The spy novel in the twentieth century had great impetus from the events of World War I and World War II (in *The Third Man: An Entertainment*, 1950, for example, by Graham Greene) but is most closely associated with the post-1945 Cold War.

Both the detective novel of the Victorian Age and the spy novel born in its last days came to emphasize, of necessity, plot and action over character development and so tended to evolve into forms that do not fully coincide with the mainstream novel as the Victorians established it for themselves and their successors. A primary example of this is Ian Fleming's (1908-1964) character James Bond; a notable exception is John le Carré's (born 1931) George Smiley: Both writers and their characters face each other across an abyss. Yet the impulse to both sorts of fiction is historically rooted in the Romantic fiction of Scott and in the Romantic revival of the late nineteenth century, a revival sparked by an ever more urgent necessity to seek in fiction an escape from the complexities and difficulties of the present, and to find in fiction the disordered world set right, a finer or more exotic world, an adventurous world providing a chivalrous alternative to and a definite release from mercantile and corporate life.

In the Romantic revival of the late Victorian era, Robert Louis Stevenson (1850-1894) provided the best and most enduring fictional alternatives to the everyday life of Edinburgh, London, and the great industrial cities of the United Kingdom. Stevenson's novels of Scotland (*Kidnapped*, 1886; *The Master of Ballantrae*, 1889; *David Balfour*, 1893; *Weir of Hermiston*, 1896), *Treasure Island* (1881-1882), and *The Strange Case of Dr. Jekyll and Mr. Hyde* (1886) set a new fashion for tales of adventure and terror with such prime ingredients as soldiers, rebellions, pirates, and a monstrous transmogrification. His example was followed by H. Rider Haggard (1856-1925) in *King Solomon's Mines* (1885), Anthony Hope (1863-1933) in *The Prisoner of Zenda* (1894), Bram Stoker (1847-1912) in *Dracula* (1897), and P. C. Wren (1885-1941) in *Beau Geste* (1924), and by the writers of "best sellers" in succeeding generations. The novels of Alistair MacLean (1922-1987), Frederick Forsyth (born 1938), Jack Higgins (Harry Patterson, born 1929), and the hundreds of novels about World War II continue the Scott-Stevenson tradition, mixing reality with escapism. Further other-world fiction was provided by authors such as H. G. Wells (1866-1946) who, in science fantasies such as *The Time Machine: An Invention* (1895) offered readers hypothetical realities in novels that were sometimes classified as "speculative fiction."

THE TWENTIETH CENTURY NOVEL AND BEYOND

The end of Queen Victoria's reign and the accession of Edward VII (1901) truly marked the end of an age and of a century in which the novel rose to literary supremacy. On the eve of the twentieth century, England had passed several relatively peaceful decades since the Napoleonic era. The military excursions of the Crimean War (1854-1856), the Sepoy Rebellion in India (1857), a war with China (1857-1858), and the Boer War in South Africa (1899-1902) in no way prepared the empire for the global struggle that began in 1914 in the reign of George V and lasted as the Great War (now, World War I), until 1918. This and other military conflicts of the twentieth century left clearly discernible marks upon the development of the English novel. World War II (1939-1945), the most cataclysmic for England, is also the most notable of the conflicts but not the longest. Wars, "police actions," and skirmishes in the distant corners of the empire, from Suez (1956) or Palestine (1949) to the Falkland Islands (1982), and extending temporally from the Boer War to the Argentinian conflict, may have matched in sporadic intensity but not in overall bitterness the continuing Anglo-Irish struggle, begun many centuries ago and marked in the twentieth century by the Easter Rising (1918), the partition of Ireland (1922), and the move to Commonwealth status (1937) and to Republic (1949) for the South.

World War II, however, justly overshadowed all other military events of the twentieth century and exerted such an influence on the course of the English novel that the number of fictional works about Britain's "finest hour" has grown astronomically since 1945. World War II may have passed into cultural memory, but it remained, for whole generations, a recent event of personal history that also marks the beginning of the "postmodern" world. Shortly after the war, beginning around 1947, the empire was virtually dismantled, and more than one billion people throughout the world gained political independence.

THE PROLETARIAN NOVEL AND THE NOVEL OF SOCIAL CRITICISM

The British economy was sapped by expensive modern warfare, the rapid dissolution of the empire, and the immigration of large numbers of the middle class; it was plagued by taxation (marked by the establishment of the first modern social security system, in 1912, and later by the socialistic British welfare state, 1945-1951), devastated by the Great Depression of 1929 and the wholesale destruction of property in the Battle of Britain and the subsequent saturation bombing of London, and eroded by massive unemployment and the steady devaluation of the pound sterling. These events and their economic effects form a background for the rise of the proletarian novel and the novel of social criticism of the 1950's and subsequent decades, including works by Kingsley Amis (1922-1995), John Braine (1922-1986), John Wain (1925-1994), and Alan Sillitoe (born 1928), who are now known as the Angry Young Men.

Social issues that occasioned the protests of the Victorian novelists were largely resolved during the last decades of Victoria's reign, ceased to have the same importance in the years when Edward VII was monarch (1901-1910), and, except for the extension of the voting franchise to women (1928), became legally moot in the early years of George V's reign. A divergent set of social issues replaced them for twentieth century novelists such as John Galsworthy (1867-1933), H. G. Wells (1866-1946), Arnold Bennett (1867-1931), and George Moore (1852-1933). Galsworthy, for example, captured the decline and disintegration of Victorian/Edwardian pillars of the middle class into the "lost generation" of the 1920's, and in so doing raised lapsarian questions that contribute to a "modernist" sensibility. Wells, apart from his socialist propaganda, also examined the possibilities of dehumanization and the inevitable destructiveness of the retrograde evolution of English class, social, and scientific structures. Bennett and Moore, like Galsworthy, pilloried the bourgeoisie and Victorianism generally, and both imported techniques from the French naturalistic novel to do so. Although French and other Continental writers exerted considerable influence on the cultural development of the English novel from roughly the mid-nineteenth century onward (one finds such influences extending from the novels of George Eliot to those of Henry James), it is noteworthy that the anti-Victorian writers should employ the naturalistic technique of Balzac and Zola in their novelistic experiments.

The form of the novel, as established in the eighteenth century, had evolved but had not drastically changed throughout the nineteenth century. With the influx of the French aesthetic, symbolist, and decadent literature in the 1890's, and the experiments of Bennett and Moore, the stage was set for more radical experiments with the English novel, experiments that centered primarily on the traditional focus of the novel, character, and subordinated all else to it. One must look to the Anglicized American, Henry James (1843-1916), as a primary source for the experimental novel, even if James did remain clearly within the confines of the English novelistic tradition. By emphasizing such elements as angle of narration, the capturing of actual experience and the way people are, the primacy of individual psychology, and the disappearance of the traditional hero, James prepared the way for further experiments by Joseph Conrad, James Joyce (1882-1941), Virginia Woolf (1882-1941), D. H. Lawrence (1885-1930), and Lawrence Durrell (1912-1990), among others. In their fiction variations on the modernist questions of ultimate meaning, individual responsibility, and elemental issues of guilt, moral alienation and dehumanization, and atonement find enduring expression as each writer searches for individual answers to similar questions. Whether the scope of the search is global, as in Conrad's settings throughout the empire, or intensely local, as in Joyce's Dublin, Lawrence's Nottinghamshire, or the mind of Woolf's Mrs. Dalloway, it is the same inner search. In the light of the experimental novels of the twentieth century, *Tristram Shandy* no longer seems the oddity it once appeared to be.

Differing from the vast quantity of twentieth century English novels written in the authorized veins of bourgeois or antibourgeois traditions, the abundant novels of adventure, detection, mystery, romance (in all senses), espionage and humor—all forms in which society is reflected and sees itself—the experimental novel provided a different sort of novelistic focus, the novel of social criticism and satire in which the protagonist is no longer concerned with a place in society but is, as his or her American cousins have been since the days of Nathaniel Hawthorne and Herman Melville, most frequently an outsider who seeks to preserve and justify alienation from a disordered and dissolving society and culture. Set adrift from intellectual, social, religious, and cultural stability and identity, the interbellum generation (1918-1939) and the postwar or postmodern generations consistently emphasize the futility of human community under the social contract. Not only the Angry Young Men but also their predecessors, successors, and contemporaries such as Ronald Firbank (1886-1926), Aldous Huxley (1894-1963), Evelyn Waugh (1903-1966), George Orwell (1903-1950), William Golding (1911-1993), Graham Greene, and John le Carré engage in social criticism and satire that ranges from assailing the societal, mechanistic, technocratic trivializing of human dignity to asserting the necessity of a solitary quest for personal ethics in an era that lacks an ethical superstructure and in which organized religion is one among many residual elements of limited use.

Multiculturalism in the novel

Beginning in the last half of the twentieth century, a reinvigorated strain of fiction came to reflect the growing ethnic diversity of England's people and their multicultural character and global concerns, as many Commonwealth writers and expatriates chose England as their residence and principal forum. In addition, the growing genre of postcolonial fiction gave writers from the former British colonies new themes, genres, and readers. Three writers of the 1980's amply illustrate this diversity. Kazuo Ishiguro was born in Nagasaki in 1954; his family moved to England in 1960. Ishiguro's first novel, *A Pale View of Hills* (1982), is narrated by a Japanese widow, a survivor of the atomic bombing of Nagasaki, who is living in England. *An Artist of the Floating World* (1986) is the story of an old Japanese painter oppressed by guilt over the prostitution of his art in the service of Japanese imperialism. With his universally acclaimed third novel, *The Remains of the Day* (1989), winner of the Booker Prize, Ishiguro made a bold leap; here his first-person narrator is an English butler in the mid-1950's, a figure at once comic and poignant. The first-person narrator of *When We Were Orphans* (2000) is also an Englishman, but one who grew up in colonial Shanghai in the 1930's. *The Unconsoled* (1995) is Ishiguro's exploration of a dreamscape so ambiguous that it thoroughly upsets traditional narrative concepts. The main character, Mr. Ryder, finds that his conflicted past and his insecurities about his future transform everything he encounters into a surreal dream of reality. This defamiliarization from the real is one of the universal themes that Ishiguro gravitated toward in rejection of the earlier emphasis on the lapse between Japanese and English cultural identities. In either case, his fiction cautions that "we tend to think we're in far more control than we are." This confusion about identity and lack of control is fully realized in Ishiguro's dystopian novel *Never Let Me Go* (2005), which won the Arthur C. Clarke Award for the best British science fiction novel of the year.

Salman Rushdie, born in Bombay (now Mumbai) in 1947, was educated in England. His novel *Midnight's Children* (1981) views the partition of India and the creation of the independent Muslim state of Pakistan through the lens of Magical Realism. The novel was chosen, on the fortieth anniversary of the Booker Prize, as the Best of the Booker, the best of the novels ever to have won the coveted prize. *Shame* (1983) covers much of the same territory. Rushdie achieved international notoriety with his Joycean novel, *The Satanic Verses* (1988), a great wheel of a book that was condemned by Muslim fundamentalists for what they considered blasphemous treatment of the Qur'ān and of the life of Muḥammad. In *Haroun and the Sea of Stories* (1990), a children's book written for adults as well, Rushdie, threatened with death and forced into hiding, answers his critics with a celebration of storytelling and the unconstrained imagination. His return to the context of improbable reality in *The Moor's Last Sigh* (1995) offers readers a heightened emphasis on storytelling as a theme. Rushdie returned to the theme of partition with *Shalimar the Clown* (2005), set in Kashmir, but he set *The Enchantress of Florence* (2008) squarely in the fifteenth century, in Italy, and in the realm of fantasy.

V. S. Naipaul (born 1932), a Trinidadian-born British writer whose heritage is Indian, is a leading figure in postcolonial literature and the winner of the 2001 Nobel Prize in Literature. His novella, *In a Free State* (1971), the first book by a writer of Indian descent to win the Booker Prize, is set in a newly independent East African country, modeled on Kenya, which became independent from Great Britain in 1963. *A Bend in the River* (1979), also set in Africa, is narrated by an Indian shopkeeper who fits in neither with the Africans nor with their former colonizers. In *Half a Life* (2001) and its sequel *Magic Seeds* (2004), Naipaul depicts an Indian writer who moves to London and then to Africa. Naipaul has been criticized by postcolonial theorists for his apparent sympathies with the colonizers rather than with the colonized, but his Nobel citation praised him "for having united perceptive narrative and incorruptible scrutiny in works that compel us to see the presence of suppressed histories."

Women writers have used fiction to tell neglected stories in multicultural Great Britain. Beryl Gilroy (1924-2001) was born in what was then British Guyana, now the independent nation of Guyana. She traveled to Great Britain to study at the University of London, and she became a teacher, a psychotherapist specializing in the needs of black women and children, and a writer. Her first novel for adults, *Frangipani House* (1986), is set among the elderly in Guyana, and *Boy-Sandwich* (1989) depicts the experiences of young black boys in Great Britain's large cities. Bangladeshi British author Monica Ali (born 1967) shows the struggles faced by women in London's Bangladeshi neighborhoods in *Brick Lane* (2003), which was adapted as a feature film in 2007. *White Teeth* (2000), by Zadie Smith (born 1975), is about the moral and psychological struggles of immigrants, and her *On Beauty* (2005) explores the life of a mixed-race family.

Less emphatically concerned with diversity issues, A. S. Byatt (born 1936) and Julian Barnes (born 1946) seem to have inherited the position of authorial status occupied by the writers of the 1950's through the 1970's. Their novels exhibit such sophisticated strategies that in some cases, such as Barnes's *Flaubert's Parrot* (1984) and *Arthur and George* (2005), they are considered "post-postmodern." Byatt's works tend to focus on intellectual problems characteristic of past eras, such as allegorical representation common to the Renaissance, evidenced in *The Virgin in the Garden* (1978), and deistic wrangling over biblical stories, in *Babel Tower* (1996). Byatt translates these pedantic puzzles into contemporary English life, providing relevance for both the society she writes about and the history of ideas that influences them. She often combines modern and historical characters in one novel, as in the Booker Prize-winning *Possession* (1990) and *The Biographer's Tale* (2000), both of which tell the stories of intellectual figures from history and the scholars who study them.

At the beginning of the twenty-first century, Ian McEwan (born 1948) emerged as one of the leading writers of the English novel. The author of several novels as well as short stories, screenplays, poetry, a play, an opera, and books for children, he won the Booker Prize for *Amsterdam* (1998), a novel about a composer and a newspaper editor struggling with moral questions, hatred, and vengeance. A feature film adaptation of *Atonement* (2002), McEwan's most popular work, was released in 2007. This novel also deals with the consequences of making moral missteps.

The English novel, then, to paraphrase William Shakespeare's Hamlet, holds the mirror up to society and shows the very age and body of the time, its form and pressure. Even a brief sketch of the varied patterns of societal influences on the development of the English novel demonstrates that the novel is of all literary forms the most responsive to the changing emphases of an evolving society. Whether in overt reaction to the values of a society, in praise of them or in criticism of them, the novel consistently presents the society as the individual must confront it, explains that society to itself, and helps society to define itself.

John J. Conlon; Scott D. Vander Ploeg
Updated by Cynthia A. Bily

BIBLIOGRAPHY

Adams, Percy G. *Travel Literature and the Evolution of the Novel.* Lexington: University Press of Kentucky, 1983. Suggests a correlation between deception in travel stories and the essential (un)trustworthiness of the narrator.

Bradbury, Malcolm. *The Modern British Novel.* London: Penguin Books, 1994. Explores the great variety of twentieth century British literature.

Cavaliero, Glen. *The Supernatural and English Fiction: From "The Castle of Otranto" to "Hawksmoor."* New York: Oxford University Press, 1995. Wide-ranging discussion of the supernatural in English fiction is valuable for its discussion not only of well-known authors such as Ann Radcliffe and Horace Walpole but also of less-familiar writers and novels.

David, Dierdre, ed. *Cambridge Companion to the Victorian Novel.* New York: Cambridge University Press, 2001. Collection of eleven essays covers topics such as gender, sexuality, economy, and science as explored in the Victorian novel. Includes an extensive bibliography.

Horsman, Alan. *The Victorian Novel.* New York: Clarendon Press, 1990. Offers insightful and comprehensive treatment of both the major Victorian authors and many minor authors of the period. Includes a helpful chronology.

Kiely, Robert. *The Romantic Novel in England.* Cambridge, Mass.: Harvard University Press, 1972. Presents an overview of a dozen of the most commonly discussed Romantic and gothic novels published between 1764 and 1847.

McKee, Patricia. *Public and Private: Gender, Class, and the British Novel, 1764-1878.* Minneapolis: University of Minnesota Press, 1997. Surveys the sociological implications of changing roles represented in novels from the early period into the Victorian era.

McKeon, Michael. *The Origins of the English Novel, 1600-1740.* Baltimore: Johns Hopkins University Press, 1987. Provides an aggressive exploration of the philosophical and religious underpinnings of the early English novel.

Parrinder, Patrick. *Nation and Novel: The English Novel from Its Origins to the Present*

Day. New York: Oxford University Press, 2006. Examines the development of the British novel from 1485, with an emphasis on political and economic influences.

Richetti, John, et al., eds. *The Columbia History of the British Novel.* New York: Columbia University Press, 1994. A good standard of critical opinion on matters pertaining to the novel.

Roberts, Andrew Michael, ed. *The Novel: A Guide to the Novel from Its Origins to the Present Day.* London: Bloomsbury, 1994. Handy primer on the novel presents informative discussion of contemporary critical trends.

JANE AUSTEN

Born: Steventon, Hampshire, England; December 16, 1775
Died: Winchester, Hampshire, England; July 18, 1817

PRINCIPAL LONG FICTION

Sense and Sensibility, 1811
Pride and Prejudice, 1813
Mansfield Park, 1814
Emma, 1816
Northanger Abbey, 1818
Persuasion, 1818
Lady Susan, 1871 (novella)
The Watsons, 1871 (fragment)
Sanditon, 1925 (fragment), 1975 (completed by Anne Telscombe)

OTHER LITERARY FORMS

In addition to writing novels, Jane Austen (AWS-tuhn) was the author of various short juvenile pieces, most of them literary burlesques mocking the conventions of the eighteenth century novel. Her other works are *Lady Susan*, a story told in letters (written c. 1805); *The Watsons*, a fragment of a novel written about the same time; and *Sanditon*, another fragmentary novel begun in 1817. All these pieces appear in *Minor Works* (volume 6 of the *Oxford Illustrated Jane Austen*, 1954), edited by R. W. Chapman. Jane Austen's surviving letters have also been edited and published by Chapman.

ACHIEVEMENTS

Jane Austen, who published her novels anonymously, was not a writer famous in her time, nor did she wish to be. From the first, however, her novels, written in and largely for her own family circle, gained the notice and esteem of a wider audience. Among her early admirers were the Prince Regent and the foremost novelist of the day, Sir Walter Scott, who deprecated his own aptitude for the "big Bow-Wow" and praised Austen as possessing a "talent for describing the involvements and feelings and characters of ordinary life which is to me the most wonderful I ever met with." The critical consensus now places Jane Austen in what F. R. Leavis has termed the "Great Tradition" of the English novel. Her talent was the first to forge, from the eighteenth century novel of external incident and internal sensibility, an art form that fully and faithfully presented a vision of real life in a specific segment of the real world. Austen's particular excellences—the elegant economy of her prose, the strength and delicacy of her judgment and moral discrimination, the subtlety of her wit, the imaginative vividness of her character drawing—have been emulated but not surpassed by subsequent writers.

Biography

Jane Austen's life contained little in the way of outward event. Born in 1775, she was the seventh of eight children. Her father, the Reverend George Austen, was a scholarly clergyman, the rector of Steventon in rural Hampshire, England. Mrs. Austen shared her husband's intelligence and intellectual interests, and the home they provided for their children was a happy and comfortable one, replete with the pleasures of country life, genteel society, perpetual reading, and lively discussion of ideas serious and frivolous. Jane Austen, who never married, was devoted throughout her life to her brothers and their families, but her closest relationship was with her older sister Cassandra, who likewise remained unmarried. Austen relied on Cassandra as her chief critic, cherished her as a confidant, and admired her as the ideal of feminine virtue.

On the rector's retirement in 1801, Austen moved with her parents and Cassandra to Bath. After the Reverend George Austen's death in 1804, the women continued to live for some time in that city. In 1806, the Austens moved to Southampton, where they shared a house with Captain Francis Austen, Jane's older brother, and his wife. In 1808, Edward Austen (who subsequently adopted the surname Knight from the relations whose two estates he inherited) provided his mother and sisters with a permanent residence, Chawton Cottage, in the Hampshire village of the same name. At this house, Austen was to revise her manuscripts that became *Sense and Sensibility*, *Pride and Prejudice*, and *Northanger Abbey* and to write *Mansfield Park*, *Emma*, and *Persuasion*. In 1817, it became evident that she was ill with a serious complaint whose symptoms seem to have been those of Addison's disease. To be near medical help, she and Cassandra moved to lodgings in Winchester in May, 1817. Austen died there less than two months later.

Analysis

Jane Austen's novels—her "bits of ivory," as she modestly and perhaps half-playfully termed them—are unrivaled for their success in combining two sorts of excellence that all too seldom coexist. Meticulously conscious of her artistry (as, for example, is Henry James), Austen is also unremittingly attentive to the realities of ordinary human existence (as is, among others, Anthony Trollope). From the first, her works unite subtlety and common sense, good humor and acute moral judgment, charm and conciseness, deftly marshaled incident and carefully rounded character.

Austen's detractors have spoken of her as a "limited" novelist, one who, writing in an age of great men and important events, portrays small towns and petty concerns, who knows (or reveals) nothing of masculine occupations and ideas, and who reduces the range of feminine thought and deed to matrimonial scheming and social pleasantry. Though one merit of the first-rate novelist is the way his or her talent transmutes all it touches and thereby creates a distinctive and consistent world, it is true that the settings, characters, events, and ideas of Austen's novels are more than usually homogeneous. Her tales, like her own life, are set in country villages and at rural seats from which the deni-

Jane Austen
(Library of Congress)

zens venture forth to watering places or to London. True, her characters tend to be members of her own order, that prosperous and courteous segment of the middle class called the gentry. Unlike her novel-writing peers, Austen introduces few aristocrats into the pages of her novels, and the lower ranks, though glimpsed from time to time, are never brought forward. The happenings of her novels would not have been newsworthy in her day. She depicts society at leisure rather than on the march, and in portraying pleasures her literary preference is modest: Architectural improvement involves the remodeling of a parsonage rather than the construction of Carlton House Terrace and Regent's Park; a ball is a gathering of country neighbors dancing to a harpsichord, not a crush at Almack's or the duchess of Richmond's glittering fete on the eve of Waterloo.

These limitations are the self-drawn boundaries of a strong mind rather than the innate restrictions of a weak or parochial one. Austen was in a position to know a broad band of social classes, from the local lord of the manor to the retired laborer subsisting on the charity of the parish. Some aspects of life that she did not herself experience she could learn about firsthand without leaving the family circle. Her brothers could tell her of the university, the navy in the age of Horatio Nelson, or the world of finance and fashion in Regency London. Her cousin (and later sister-in-law) Eliza, who had lost her first husband, the comte de Feuillide, to the guillotine, could tell her of Paris during the last days of the Old Regime.

In focusing on the manners and morals of rural middle-class English life, particularly on the ordering dance of matrimony that gives shape to society and situation to young ladies, Austen emphasizes rather than evades reality. The microcosm she depicts is convincing because she understands, though seldom explicitly assesses, its connections to the larger order. Her characters have clear social positions but are not just social types; the genius of such comic creations as Mrs. Bennet, Mr. Woodhouse, and Miss Bates is that each is a sparkling refinement on a quality or set of qualities existing at all times and on all levels. A proof of Austen's power (no one questions her polish) is that she succeeds in making whole communities live in the reader's imagination with little recourse to the stock device of the mere novelist of manners: descriptive detail. If a sparely drawn likeness is to convince, every line must count. The artist must understand what is omitted as well as what is supplied.

The six novels that constitute the Austen canon did not evolve in a straightforward way. Austen was, memoirs relate, as mistrustful of her judgment as she was rapid in her composition. In the case of *Pride and Prejudice*, for example, readers can be grateful that when the Reverend George Austen's letter offering the book's first incarnation, titled "First Impressions" (1797), to a publisher met with a negative reply, she was content to put the book aside for more than a decade. *Sense and Sensibility* was likewise a revision of a much earlier work. If Austen was notably nonchalant about the process of getting her literary progeny into print, one publisher with whom she had dealings was yet more dilatory. In 1803, Austen had completed *Northanger Abbey* (then titled "Susan") and, through her brother Henry's agency, had sold it to Crosby and Sons for ten pounds. Having acquired the manuscript, the publisher did not think fit to make use of it, and in December, 1816, Henry Austen repurchased the novel. He made known the author's identity, so family tradition has it, only after closing the deal. For these various reasons, the chronology of Austen's novels can be set in different ways; here they are discussed in order of their dates of publication.

SENSE AND SENSIBILITY

Sense and Sensibility, Austen's first published novel, evolved from "Elinor and Marianne," an epistolary work completed between 1795 and 1797. The novel is generally considered her weakest, largely because, as Walton Litz convincingly argues, it strives but fails to resolve "that struggle between inherited form and fresh experience which so often marks the transitional works of a great artist." The "inherited form" of which Litz speaks is the eighteenth century antithetical pattern suggested in the novel's title. According to this formula, opposing qualities of temperament or mind are presented in characters (generally female, often sisters) who, despite their great differences, are sincerely attached to one another.

In *Sense and Sensibility*, the antithetical characters are Elinor and Marianne Dashwood, the respective embodiments of cool, collected sense and prodigal, exquisite sensibility. In the company of their mother and younger sister, these lovely young ladies have, on the death of their father and the succession to his estate of their half brother, retired in very modest circumstances to a small house in Devonshire. There the imprudent Marianne meets and melts for Willoughby, a fashionable gentleman as charming as he is unscrupulous. Having engaged the rash girl's affections, Willoughby proceeds to trifle with them by bolting for London. When chance once again brings the Dashwood sisters into Willoughby's circle, his manner toward Marianne is greatly altered. On hearing of his engagement to an heiress, the representative of sensibility swoons, weeps, and exhibits her grief to the utmost.

Meanwhile, the reasonable Elinor has been equally unlucky in love, though she bears her disappointment quite differently. Before the family's move to Devonshire, Elinor had met and come to cherish fond feelings for her sister-in-law's brother, Edward Ferrars, a rather tame fellow (at least in comparison with Willoughby) who returns her regard—but with a measure of unease. It soon becomes known that Ferrars's reluctance to press his suit with Elinor stems from an early and injudicious secret engagement he had contracted with shrewd, base Lucy Steele. Elinor high-mindedly conceals her knowledge of the engagement and her feelings on the matter. Mrs. Ferrars, however, is a lady of less impressive self-control; she furiously disinherits her elder son in favor of his younger brother, whom Lucy then proceeds to ensnare. Thus Edward, free and provided with a small church living that will suffice to support a sensible sort of wife, can marry Elinor. Marianne—perhaps because she has finally exhausted her fancies and discovered her latent reason, perhaps because her creator is determined to punish the sensibility that throughout the novel has been so much more attractive than Elinor's prudence—is also provided with a husband: the rich Colonel Brandon, who has long loved her but whom, on account of his flannel waistcoats and his advanced age of five-and-thirty, she has heretofore reckoned beyond the pale.

The great flaw of *Sense and Sensibility* is that the polarities presented in the persons of Elinor and Marianne are too genuinely antithetical to be plausible or dynamic portraits of human beings. Elinor has strong feelings, securely managed though they may be, and Marianne has some rational powers to supplement her overactive imagination and emotions, but the young ladies do not often show themselves to be more than mere embodiments of sense and sensibility. In her second published novel, *Pride and Prejudice*, Austen makes defter use of two sisters whose values are the same but whose minds and hearts function differently. This book, a complete revision of "First Impressions," the youthful effort that had, in 1797, been offered to and summarily rejected by the publisher Cadell, is, as numerous critics have observed, a paragon of "classic" literature in which the conventions and traditions of the eighteenth century novel come to full flowering yet are freshened and transformed by Austen's distinctive genius.

PRIDE AND PREJUDICE

The title *Pride and Prejudice*, with its balanced alliterative abstractions, might suggest a second experiment in schematic psychology, and indeed the book does show some resemblances to *Sense and Sensibility*. Here again the reader encounters a pair of sisters, the elder (Jane Bennet) serene, the younger (Elizabeth) volatile. Unlike the Dashwoods, however, these ladies both demonstrate deep feelings and perceptive minds. The qualities alluded to in the title refer not to a contrast between sisters but to double defects shared by Elizabeth and Fitzwilliam Darcy, a wealthy and well-born young man she meets when his easygoing friend Charles Bingley leases Netherfield, the estate next to the Bennets' Longbourn. If so rich and vital a comic masterpiece could be reduced to a formula, it might be appropriate to say that the main thread of *Pride and Prejudice* involves the twin correction of these faults. As Darcy learns to moderate his tradition-based view of society and to recognize individual excellence (such as Elizabeth's, Jane's, and their Aunt and Uncle Gardiner's) in ranks below his own, Elizabeth becomes less dogmatic in her judgments and, in particular, more aware of the real merits of Darcy, whom she initially dismisses as a haughty, unfeeling aristocrat.

The growing accord of Elizabeth and Darcy is one of the most perfectly satisfying courtships in English literature. Their persons, minds, tastes, and even phrases convince the reader that they are two people truly made for each other; their union confers fitness on the world around them. Lionel Trilling has observed that, because of this principal match, *Pride and Prejudice* "permits us to conceive of morality as style." Elizabeth and Darcy's slow-growing love may be *Pride and Prejudice*'s ideal alliance, but it is far from being the only one, and a host of finely drawn characters surround the heroine and hero. In Jane Bennet and Charles Bingley, whose early mutual attraction is temporarily suspended by Darcy and the Bingley sisters (who deplore, not without some cause, the vulgarity of the amiable Jane's family), Austen presents a less sparkling but eminently pleasing and well-matched pair.

William Collins, the half-pompous, half-obsequious, totally asinine cousin who, because of an entail, will inherit Longbourn and displace the Bennet females after Mr. Bennet's demise, aspires to marry Elizabeth but, when rejected, instead gains the hand of her plain and practical friend Charlotte Lucas. Aware of her suitor's absurdities, Charlotte is nevertheless alive to the advantages of the situation he can offer. Her calculated decision to marry gives a graver ring to the irony of the novel's famous opening sentence: "It is a truth universally acknowledged, that a single man in possession of a good fortune, must be in want of a wife."

The last of the matches made in *Pride and Prejudice* is yet more precariously based. A lively, charming, and amoral young officer, George Wickham, son of the former steward of Pemberley, Darcy's estate, and source of many of Elizabeth's prejudices against that scrupulous gentleman, first fascinates Elizabeth and then elopes with her youngest sister, the mindless, frivolous Lydia. Only through Darcy's personal and financial intervention is

Wickham persuaded to marry the ill-bred girl, who never properly understands her disgrace—a folly she shares with her mother. Mrs. Bennet, a woman deficient in good humor and good sense, is—along with her cynical, capricious husband, the ponderous Collins, and the tyrannical Lady Catherine De Bourgh—one of the great comic creations of literature. Most of these characters could have seemed odious if sketched by another pen, but so brilliant is the sunny intelligence playing over the world of *Pride and Prejudice* that even fools are golden.

MANSFIELD PARK

Mansfield Park, begun in 1811 and finished in 1813, is the first of Austen's novels to be a complete product of her maturity. The longest, most didactic, and least ironic of her books, it is the one critics generally have the most trouble reconciling with their prevailing ideas of the author. Although *Mansfield Park* was composed more or less at one stretch, its conception coincided with the final revisions of *Pride and Prejudice*. Indeed, the critics who offer the most satisfying studies of *Mansfield Park* tend to see it not as a piece of authorial bad faith or self-suppression, a temporary anomaly, but as what Walton Litz calls a "counter-truth" to its immediate predecessor.

Pleased with and proud of *Pride and Prejudice*, Austen nevertheless recorded her impression of its being "rather too light, and bright, and sparkling"—in need of shade. That darkness she found wanting is supplied in *Mansfield Park*, which offers, as Trilling observes in his well-known essay on the novel, the antithesis to *Pride and Prejudice*'s generous, humorous, spirited social vision. *Mansfield Park*, Trilling argues, condemns rather than forgives: "Its praise is not for social freedom but for social stasis. It takes full notice of spiritedness, vivacity, celerity, and lightness, only to reject them as having nothing to do with virtue and happiness, as being, indeed, deterrents to the good life."

Most of the action of *Mansfield Park* is set within the little world comprising the estate of that name, a country place resembling in large measure Godmersham, Edward Austen Knight's estate in Kent; but for her heroine and some interludes in which she figures, Austen dips into a milieu she has not previously frequented in her novels—the socially and financially precarious lower fringe of the middle class. Fanny Price, a frail, serious, modest girl, is one of nine children belonging to and inadequately supported by a feckless officer of marines and his lazy, self-centered wife. Mrs. Price's meddling sister, the widowed Mrs. Norris, arranges for Fanny to be reared in "poor relation" status at Mansfield Park, the seat of kindly but crusty Sir Thomas Bertram and his languid lady, the third of the sisters. At first awed by the splendor of her surroundings, the gruffness of the baronet, and the elegance, vigor, and high spirits of the young Bertrams—Tom, Edmund, Maria, and Julia—Fanny eventually wins a valued place in the household.

During Sir Thomas's absence to visit his property in Antigua, evidence of Fanny's moral fineness, and the various degrees in which her cousins fall short of her excellence, is presented through a device that proves to be one of Austen's most brilliant triumphs of plotting. Visiting the rectory at Mansfield are the younger brother and sister of the rector's wife, Henry and Mary Crawford, witty, worldly, and wealthy. At Mary's proposal, amateur theatricals are introduced to Mansfield Park, and in the process of this diversion the moral pollution of London's Great World begins to corrupt the bracing country air.

Just how the staging of a play—even though it be *Lovers' Vows*, a sloppy piece of romantic bathos, adultery rendered sympathetic—can be morally reprehensible is a bit unclear for most modern-day readers, especially those who realize that the Austens themselves reveled in theatricals at home. The problem as Austen presents it lies in the possible consequences of role-playing: coming to feel the emotions and attitudes one presents on the stage or, worse yet, expressing rather than suppressing genuine but socially unacceptable feelings in the guise of mere acting. In the course of the theatricals, where Fanny, who will not act, is relegated to the role of spectator and moral chorus, Maria Bertram, engaged to a bovine local heir, vies with her sister in striving to fascinate Henry Crawford, who in turn is all too ready to charm them. Mary Crawford, though it is "her way" to find eldest sons most agreeable, has the good taste to be attracted to Edmund, the second son, who plans to enter the clergy. Mary's vivacity, as evidenced by the theatricals, easily wins his heart.

Time passes and poor Fanny, who since childhood has adored her cousin Edmund, unintentionally interests Henry Crawford. Determined to gain the affections of this rare young woman who is indifferent to his charms, Crawford ends by succumbing to hers. He proposes. Fanny's unworldly refusal provokes the anger of her uncle. Then, while Fanny, still in disgrace with the baronet, is away from Mansfield Park and visiting her family at Portsmouth, the debacle of which *Lovers' Vows* was a harbinger comes about. The *homme fatal* Henry, at a loss for a woman to make love to, trains his charms on his old flirt Maria, now Mrs. Rushworth. She runs away with him; her sister, not to be outdone in bad behavior, elopes with an unsatisfactory suitor. Mary Crawford's moral coarseness becomes evident in her casual dismissal of these catastrophes. Edmund, now a clergyman, finds solace, then love, with the cousin whose sterling character shines brightly for him now that Mary's glitter has tarnished. Fanny gains all she could hope for in at last attaining the heart and hand of her clerical kinsman.

EMMA

Austen's next novel, *Emma*, might be thought of as harmonizing the two voices heard in *Pride and Prejudice* and *Mansfield Park*. For this book, Austen claimed to be creating "a heroine whom no one but myself will much like," an "imaginist" whose circumstances and qualities of mind make her the self-crowned queen of her country neighborhood. Austen was not entirely serious or accurate: Emma certainly has her partisans. Even those readers who do not like her tend to find her fascinating, for she is a spirited, imaginative, healthy young woman who, like Mary Crawford, has potential to do considerable harm to the fabric of society but on whom, like Elizabeth Bennet, her creator generously bestows life's greatest blessing: union with a man whose virtues, talents, and assets are the best complement for her own.

Emma's eventual marriage to Mr. Knightley of Donwell Abbey is the ultimate expression of one of Austen's key assumptions, that marriage is a young woman's supreme act of self-definition. Unlike any other Austen heroine, Emma has no pressing need to marry. As the opening sentence of the book implies, Emma's situation makes her acceptance or rejection of a suitor an act of unencumbered will: "Emma Woodhouse, handsome, clever, and rich, with a comfortable home and happy disposition, seemed to unite some of the best blessings of existence; and had lived nearly twenty-one years in the world with very little to distress or vex her."

Free though circumstance allows her to be, Emma has not been encouraged by her lot in life to acquire the discipline and self-knowledge that, augmenting her innate intelligence and taste, would help her to choose wisely. Brought up by a doting valetudinarian of a father and a perceptive but permissive governess, Emma has been encouraged to think too highly of herself. Far from vain about her beauty, Emma has—as Mr. Knightley, the only person who ventures to criticize her, observes—complete yet unfounded faith in her ability to judge people's characters and arrange their lives. The course of *Emma* is Miss Woodhouse's education in judgment, a process achieved through repeated mistakes and humiliations.

As the novel opens, the young mistress of Hartfield is at loose ends. Her beloved governess has just married Mr. Weston, of the neighboring property, Randalls. To fill the newly made gap in her life, Emma takes notice of Harriet Smith, a pretty, dim "natural daughter of somebody," and a parlor-boarder at the local school. Determined to settle her protégé into the sort of life she deems suitable, Emma detaches Harriet from Robert Martin, a young farmer who has proposed to her, and embarks on a campaign to conquer for Harriet the heart of Mr. Elton, Highbury's unmarried clergyman. Elton's attentiveness and excessive flattery convince Emma of her plan's success but at the same time show the reader what Emma is aghast to learn at the end of book 1: that Elton scorns the nobody and has designs on the heiress herself.

With the arrival of three new personages in Highbury, book 2 widens Emma's opportunities for misconception. The first newcomer is Jane Fairfax, an elegant and accomplished connection of the Bates family and a girl whose prospective fate, the "governess trade," shows how unreliable the situations of well-bred young ladies without fortunes or husbands tend to be. Next to arrive is the suave Mr. Frank Churchill, Mr. Weston's grown son, who has been adopted by wealthy relations of his mother and who has been long remiss in paying a visit to Highbury. Finally, Mr. Elton brings home a bride, the former Augusta Hawkins of Bristol, a pretentious and impertinent creature possessed of an independent fortune, a well-married sister, and a boundless fund of self-congratulation. Emma mistakenly flatters herself that the dashing Frank Churchill is in love with her and then settles on him as a husband for Harriet; she suspects the reserved Miss Fairfax, whose cultivation she rightly perceives as a reproach to her own untrained talents, of a clandestine relationship with a married man. She despises Mrs. Elton, as would any person of sense, but fails to see that the vulgar woman's offensiveness is an exaggerated version of her own officiousness and snobbery.

Thus the potential consequences of Emma's misplaced faith in her judgment intensify, and the evidence of her fallibility mounts. Thoroughly embarrassed to learn that Frank Churchill, with whom she has shared all her hypotheses regarding Jane Fairfax, has long been secretly engaged to that woman, Emma suffers the deathblow to her smug self-esteem when Harriet announces that the gentleman whose feelings she hopes to have aroused is not, as Emma supposes, Churchill but the squire of Donwell. Emma's moment of truth is devastating and complete, its importance marked by one of Jane Austen's rare uses of figurative language: "It darted through her, with the speed of an arrow, that Mr. Knightley must marry no one but herself!" Perhaps the greatest evidence of Emma's being a favorite of fortune is that Mr. Knightley feels the same as she does on this matter. Chastened by her series of bad judgments, paired with a gentleman who for years has loved and respected her enough to correct her and whom she can love and respect in return, Emma participates in the minuet of marriage with which Austen concludes the book, the other couples so united being Miss Fairfax and Mr. Churchill and Harriet Smith (ductile enough to form four attachments in a year) and Robert Martin (stalwart enough to persist in his original feeling).

Emma Woodhouse's gradual education, which parallels the reader's growing awareness of what a menace to the social order her circumstances, abilities, and weaknesses combine to make her, is one of Austen's finest pieces of plotting. The depiction of character is likewise superb. Among a gallery of memorable and distinctive characters are Mr. Woodhouse; Miss Bates, the stream-of-consciousness talker who inadvertently provokes Emma's famous rudeness on Box Hill; and the wonderfully detestable Mrs. Elton, with her self-contradictions and her fractured Italian, her endless allusions to Selina, Mr. Suckling, Maple Grove, and the *barouche landau*. Life at Hartfield, Donwell, and Highbury is portrayed with complexity and economy. Every word, expression, opinion, and activity—whether sketching a portrait, selecting a dancing partner, or planning a strawberry-picking party—becomes a gesture of self-revelation. *Emma* demonstrates how, in Austen's hands, the novel of manners can become a statement of moral philosophy.

NORTHANGER ABBEY

Northanger Abbey was published in a four-volume unit with *Persuasion* in 1818, after Austen's death, but the manuscript had been completed much earlier, in 1803. Austen wrote a preface for *Northanger Abbey* but did not do the sort of revising that had transformed "Elinor and Marianne" and "First Impressions" into *Sense and Sensibility* and *Pride and Prejudice*. The published form of *Northanger Abbey* can therefore be seen as the earliest of the six novels. It is also, with the possible exception of *Sense and Sensibility*, the most "literary." *Northanger Abbey,* like some of Austen's juvenile burlesques, confronts the conventions of the gothic novel or tale of terror. The incidents of her novel have been shown to parallel, with ironic difference, the principal lines of gothic romance, particularly as practiced by Ann Radcliffe, whose most famous works, *The Romance of the Forest* (1791) and *The Mysteries of Udolpho* (1794), had appeared several years before Austen began work on her burlesque.

Like *Emma, Northanger Abbey* is centrally concerned with tracing the growth of a young woman's mind and the cultivation of her judgment. In this less sophisticated work, however, the author accomplishes her goal through a rather schematic contrast. As an enthusiastic reader of tales of terror, Catherine Morland has gothic expectations of life despite a background most unsuitable for a heroine. Like the gothic heroines she admires, Catherine commences adventuring early in the novel. She is not, however, shipped to Venice or Dalmatia; rather, she is taken to Bath for a six-week stay. Her hosts are serenely amiable English folk, her pastimes the ordinary round of spa pleasures; the young man whose acquaintance she makes, Henry Tilney, is a witty clergyman rather than a misanthropic monk or dissolute rake. Toward this delightful, if far from gothic, young man, Catherine's feelings are early inclined. In turn, he, his sister, and even his father, the haughty, imperious General Tilney, are favorably disposed toward her. With the highest expectations, Catherine sets out to accompany them to their seat, the Abbey of the novel's title (which, like that of *Persuasion*, was selected not by the author but by Henry Austen, who handled the posthumous publication).

At Northanger, Catherine's education in the difference between literature and life continues. Despite its monastic origins, the Abbey proves a comfortable and well-maintained dwelling. When Catherine, like one of Radcliffe's protagonists, finds a mysterious document in a chest and spends a restless night wondering what lurid tale it might chronicle, she is again disappointed: "If the evidence of her sight might be trusted she held a washing-bill in her hand." Although Catherine's experience does not confirm the truth of Radcliffe's sensational horrors, it does not prove the world a straightforward, safe, cozy place. Catherine has already seen something of falseness and selfish vulgarity in the persons of Isabella Thorpe and her brother John, acquaintances formed at Bath. At Northanger, she learns that, though the general may not be the wife murderer she has fancied him, he is quite as cruel as she could imagine. On learning that Catherine is not the great heiress he has mistakenly supposed her to be, the furious general packs her off in disgrace and discomfort in a public coach.

With this proof that the world of fact can be as treacherous as that of fiction, Catherine returns, sadder and wiser, to the bosom of her family. She has not long to droop, however, for Henry Tilney, on hearing of his father's bad behavior, hurries after her and makes Catherine the proposal that he has long felt inclined to offer and that his father has until recently promoted. The approval of Catherine's parents is immediate, and the general is not overlong in coming to countenance the match. "To begin perfect happiness at the respective ages of twenty-six and eighteen is to do pretty well," observes the facetious narrator, striking a literary pose even in the novel's last sentence, "and . . . I leave it to be settled by whomsoever it may concern, whether the tendency of this work be altogether to recommend parental tyranny, or reward filial disobedience."

PERSUASION

Persuasion, many readers believe, signals Austen's literary move out of the eighteenth century and into the nineteenth. This novel, quite different from those that preceded it, draws not on the tradition of the novelists of the 1790's but on that of the lionized poets of the new century's second decade, Sir Walter Scott and Lord Byron. For the first time, Austen clearly seems the child of her time, susceptible to the charms of natural rather than improved landscapes, fields, and sea cliffs rather than gardens and shrubberies. The wistful, melancholy beauty of autumn that pervades the book is likewise romantic. The gaiety, vitality, and sparkling wit of *Pride and Prejudice* and *Emma* are muted. The stable social order represented by the great estate in *Mansfield Park* has become fluid in *Persuasion*: Here the principal country house, Kellynch Hall, must be let because the indigenous family cannot afford to inhabit it.

Most important, *Persuasion*'s heroine is unique in Jane Austen's gallery. Anne Elliott, uprooted from her ancestral home, spiritually isolated from her selfish and small-minded father and sisters, separated from the man she loves by a long-standing estrangement, is every bit as "alienated" as such later nineteenth century heroines as Esther Summerson, Jane Eyre, and Becky Sharp. Anne's story is very much the product of Austen's middle age. At twenty-seven, Anne is the only Austen heroine to be past her first youth. Furthermore, she is in no need of education. Her one great mistake—overriding the impulse of her heart and yielding to the persuasion of her friend Lady Russell in rejecting the proposal of Frederick Wentworth, a sanguine young naval officer with his fortune still to make and his character to prove—is some eight years in the past, and she clearly recognizes it for the error it was.

Persuasion is the story of how Anne and Frederick (now the eminent Captain) Wentworth rekindle the embers of their love. Chance throws them together when the vain, foolish Sir Walter Elliott, obliged to economize or rent his estate, resolves to move his household to Bath, where he can cut a fine figure at less cost, and leases Kellynch to Admiral and Mrs. Croft, who turn out to be the brother-in-law and sister of Captain Wentworth. Initially cool to his former love—or, rather, able to see the diminution of her beauty because he is unable to forgive her rejection—the captain flirts with the Musgrove girls; they are sisters to the husband of Anne's younger sister Mary and blooming belles with the youth and vigor Anne lacks. The captain's old appreciation of Anne's merits—her clear insight, kindness, high-mindedness, and modesty—soon reasserts itself, but not before fate and the captain's impetuosity have all but forced another engagement on him. Being "jumped down" from the Cobb at Lyme Regis, Louisa Musgrove misses his arms and falls unconscious on the pavement. Obliged by honor to declare himself hers if she should wish it, Wentworth is finally spared this self-sacrifice when the susceptible young lady and the sensitive Captain Benwick fall in love. Having discovered the intensity of his devotion to Anne by being on the point of having to abjure it, Wentworth hurries to Bath, there to declare his attachment in what is surely the most powerful engagement scene in the Austen canon.

Though the story of *Persuasion* belongs to Anne Elliott and Frederick Wentworth, Austen's skill at evoking characters is everywhere noticeable. As Elizabeth Jenkins observes, all of the supporting characters present different facets of the love theme. The heartless marital calculations of Mr. Elliott, Elizabeth Elliott, and Mrs. Clay, the domestic comforts of the senior Musgroves and the Crofts, and the half-fractious, half-amiable ménage of Charles and Mary Musgrove all permit the reader to discern more clearly how rare and true is the love Anne Elliott and her captain have come so close to losing. The mature, deeply grateful commitment they are able to make to each other is, if not the most charming, surely the most profound in the Austen world.

Peter W. Graham

OTHER MAJOR WORKS

SHORT FICTION: *Minor Works*, 1954 (volume 6 of the *Oxford Illustrated Jane Austen*; R. W. Chapman, editor).

NONFICTION: *Jane Austen's Letters to Her Sister Cassandra and Others*, 1932 (R. W. Chapman, editor).

CHILDREN'S LITERATURE: *The History of England*, wr. 1791 (published with Charles Dickens's *A Child's History of England* as *Two Histories of England*, 2006); *Catherine*, 1818; *Lesley Castle*, 1922; *Three Sisters*, 1933.

MISCELLANEOUS: *Love and Freindship, and Other Early Works*, 1922.

BIBLIOGRAPHY

Austen, Jane. *Jane Austen's Letters to Her Sister Cassandra and Others*. Edited by R. W. Chapman. 2 vols. Oxford, England: Clarendon Press, 1932. The first collection of surviving Austen letters is arranged chronologically in two volumes with appendixes that give summary identifications of anyone who is ambiguously mentioned in the text of the letters. With corrected spelling and punctuation. Includes a map of eighteenth century Berkshire and Surrey, England.

Brown, Julie Prewit. *Jane Austen's Novels*. Cambridge, Mass.: Harvard University Press, 1979. Provides a somewhat feminist perspective on Austen as a conscious artist who masterfully employed ironic comedy and satiric realism. Five chapters explore the purpose and subtleties of each novel. Includes an eye-opening chapter on the artist as a woman writer.

Copeland, Edward, and Juliet McMaster, eds. *The Cambridge Companion to Jane Austen*.

New York: Cambridge University Press, 1997. Collection of thirteen essays is divided between those concerning Austen's own world and those that address modern critical discourse, such as Claudia L. Johnson's "Austen Cults and Cultures." Some essays focus on Austen's novels, whereas others deal with broad issues, such as class consciousness, religion, and domestic economy. This excellent overview includes a chronology and concludes with an assessment of late twentieth century developments in Austen scholarship.

Galperin, William H. *The Historical Austen*. Philadelphia: University of Pennsylvania Press, 2003. Careful study provides a fresh explication of Austen's work. Examines how Austen used her fiction to serve as a "social and political" tool.

Halperin, John. *The Life of Jane Austen*. Baltimore: Johns Hopkins University Press, 1984. Biographical study focuses on the association between the life of the artist and the works she produced. Valuable for a realistic look at the life of a legendary figure. Includes illustrations.

Lambdin, Laura Cooner, and Robert Thomas Lambdin, eds. *A Companion to Jane Austen Studies*. New York: Greenwood Press, 2000. Collection of twenty-two essays devoted to Austen's works includes fourteen that examine her novels, including *Sanditon* and *The Watsons*—the two novels she left unfinished.

Lane, Maggie. *Jane Austen's England*. New York: St. Martin's Press, 1986. Fascinating volume is full of illustrations that give Austen's readers a look at the world of her novels. Arranged chronologically, taking the reader to the places Austen would have gone, usually through contemporary paintings. The first chapter, "The England of Jane Austen's Time," gives a good basic summary of social conditions around the beginning of the nineteenth century. Includes specific references to the novels; for example, a quote from the Box Hill episode in *Emma* is accompanied by a painting of Box Hill. Includes map, brief bibliography, and index.

Le Faye, Deirdre. *Jane Austen: A Family Record*. London: British Library, 1989. Revision of the 1913 edition of *Life and Letters of Jane Austen*, written by a descendant of Austen's nephew, James Edward. Thanks to additional extensive contemporary research, provides a thorough look at Austen's life and the close-knit family on which she was financially dependent. Includes illustrations and a thorough chronology of Austen's life.

Lynch, Deidre, ed. *Janeites: Austen's Disciples and Devotees*. Princeton, N.J.: Princeton University Press, 2000. Collection of nine essays explores the novelist as an enduring cultural phenomenon. Topics addressed include Austen's novels as works of Regency pop fiction, Austen's earliest readers and the reception of her work in the United States, and Austen and the discipline of novel studies.

Mooneyham, Laura G. *Romance, Language, and Education in Jane Austen's Novels*. New York: St. Martin's Press, 1986. Theorizes that a relationship exists among language, education, and romance in Austen's work. Asserts that the romance between heroine and hero is in itself educational for the heroine because romance offers the opportunity for open communication. This approach is provocative and useful, especially because it emphasizes Austen's own preoccupations. Covers all six of Austen's complete novels in individual chapters.

Nokes, David. *Jane Austen: A Life*. New York: Farrar, Straus and Giroux, 1997. Biography employs a broad perspective to explore the family in which Austen lived as well as the wider world in which the family belonged.

Selwyn, David. *Jane Austen and Leisure*. London: Hambledon Press, 1999. Examines the manners and customs of Austen's class in her era and how Austen portrays them in her works.

Todd, Janet M. *The Cambridge Introduction to Jane Austen*. New York: Cambridge University Press, 2006. Todd, an Austen scholar and editor of the author's work, provides an overview of Austen's life, her novels, the context in which they were written, and her works' reception. Includes a detailed discussion of each novel, providing a good starting point for the study of her major works.

Tomalin, Claire. *Jane Austen: A Life*. New York: Knopf, 1998. Compelling account of Austen's life is exceedingly well written and attempts to tell the story from the subject's own perspective. Proceeding in chronological order, the book concludes with a postscript on the fates of Austen's family members and two interesting appendixes: a note on Austen's final illness and an excerpt from the diary of Austen's niece Fanny.

APHRA BEHN

Born: Kent, England; July(?), 1640
Died: London, England; April 16, 1689
Also known as: Ayfara Amis; Aphara Amis; Astrea; Aphra Bayn; Aphra Johnson

PRINCIPAL LONG FICTION

Love Letters Between a Nobleman and His Sister, 1683-1687 (3 volumes)
Agnes de Castro, 1688
The Fair Jilt: Or, The History of Prince Tarquin and Miranda, 1688
Oroonoko: Or, The Royal Slave, a True History, 1688
The History of the Nun: Or, The Fair Vow-Breaker, 1689
The Lucky Mistake, 1689
The Nun: Or, The Perjured Beauty, 1697
The Adventure of the Black Lady, 1698
The Wandering Beauty, 1698

OTHER LITERARY FORMS

As a truly professional writer, perhaps the first British female to have written for profit, Aphra Behn (bayn) moved easily through the various literary genres and forms. Her plays include *The Forced Marriage: Or, The Jealous Bridegroom* (pr. 1670); *The Amorous Prince: Or, The Curious Husband* (pr., pb. 1671); *The Dutch Lover* (pr., pb. 1673); *The Town Fop: Or, Sir Timothy Tawdry* (pr. 1676); *Abdelazer: Or, the Moor's Revenge* (pr. 1676); *The Rover: Or, The Banished Cavaliers* (*Part I*, pr., pb. 1677; *Part II*, pr., pb. 1681); *Sir Patient Fancy* (pr., pb. 1678); *The Roundheads: Or, The Good Old Cause* (pr. 1681); *The City Heiress: Or, Sir Timothy Treat-All* (pr., pb. 1682); *The Lucky Chance: Or, An Alderman's Bargain* (pr. 1686); *The Emperor of the Moon* (pr., pb. 1687); *The Widow Ranter: Or, The History of Bacon of Virginia* (pr. 1689); and *The Younger Brother: Or, The Amorous Jilt* (pr., pb. 1696).

Although Behn enjoyed only mild success as a poet, her verse was probably no better or worse than that of a large number of second-rank versifiers of the Restoration. Behn's best poetry can be found in the song "Love in fantastic triumph sate" (1677), from her tragedy *Abdelazer*, and in a metrical "Paraphrase on Oenone to Paris" for Jacob Tonson's volume of Ovid's *Epistles* (1680). The remainder of her verse includes a long, amorous allegory, *A Voyage to the Isle of Love* (1684); an adaptation of Bernard de Fontenelle's epic that she titled *A Discovery of New Worlds* (1688); and two occasional pieces, "A Pindarick on the Death of Charles II" (1685) and "A Congratulatory Poem to Her Most Sacred Majesty" (1688).

Aphra Behn
(Library of Congress)

ACHIEVEMENTS

Aphra Behn's achievement as a novelist should be measured principally in terms of the modest gains made by the novel form in England during the seventeenth century. Prior to *Oroonoko*, the English novel lingered in the shadows of the theater. The small reading public contented itself with works such as John Lyly's *Euphues, the Anatomy of Wit* (1578), Sir Philip Sidney's *Arcadia* (1590), Thomas Lodge's *Rosalynde: Or, Euphues Golden Legacy* (1590), Thomas Nashe's *The Unfortunate Traveller: Or, The Life of Jack Wilton* (1594), and Thomas Deloney's *The Pleasant History of John Winchcomb in His Younger Days Called Jack of Newbery* (1597; better known as *Jack of Newbery*)—all long, episodic stories, sprinkled with overly dramatic characterization and improbable plot structures. In *Oroonoko*, however, Behn advanced the novel to the point where her more skilled successors in the eighteenth century could begin to shape it into an independent, recognizable form.

Behn possessed the natural gifts of the storyteller, and her narrative art can easily stand beside that of her male contemporaries. A frankly commercial writer, she simply had no time, in pursuit of pleasure and the pen, to find a place in her narratives for intellectual substance. Nevertheless, she told a story as few others could, and the force of her own personality contributed both reality and a sense of immediacy to the still inchoate form of seventeenth century British fiction.

BIOGRAPHY

The details of Aphra Behn's birth are not known. The parish register of the Sts. Gregory and Martin Church, Wye, England, contains an entry stating that Ayfara Amis, daughter of John and Amy Amis, was baptized on July 10, 1640. Apparently, John Johnson, related to Lord Francis Willoughby of Parham, adopted the girl, although no one seems to know exactly when. Ayfara Amis (some sources spell her first name as Aphara) accompanied her adoptive parents on a journey to Suriname (later Dutch Guiana) in 1658, Willoughby having appointed Johnson to serve as deputy governor of his extensive holdings there. Unfortunately, the new deputy died on the voyage; his widow and children proceeded to Suriname and took up residence at St. John's, one of Lord Willoughby's plantations. Exactly how long they remained is not clear, but certainly the details surrounding the time Behn spent at St. John's form the background for *Oroonoko*.

Biographers have established the summer of 1663 as the most probable date of Behn's return to England. By 1665, Behn was again in London and married to a wealthy merchant of Dutch extraction who may well have had connections in, or at least around, the court of Charles II. In 1665 came the Great Plague and the death of Behn's husband; the latter proved the more disastrous for her, specifically because (again for unknown reasons) the Dutch merchant left nothing of substance to her—nothing, that is, except his court connections. Charles II, in the midst of the first of his wars against Holland, hired Behn as a secret government agent to spy on the Dutch, for which purpose she proceeded to Antwerp, a Belgian city near the border with Holland. There she contacted another British agent, William Scott, from whom she obtained various pieces of military information, which she forwarded to London. Although she received little credit for her work, and even less money, Behn did conceive of the pseudonym Astrea, the name under which she published most of her poetry.

The entire adventure into espionage proved a dismal failure for Behn; she even had to borrow money and pawn her valuables to pay her debts and obtain passage back to England. Once home, early in 1667, she found no relief from her desperate financial situation. Her debtors threatened prison, and the government refused any payment for her services. Prison followed, although the time and the exact length of her term remain unknown. Some of Behn's biographers speculate that she was aided in her release by John Hale (d. 1692)—a lawyer of Gray's Inn, a wit, an intellectual, a homosexual, the principal subject of and reason for Behn's sonnets, and the man with whom she carried on a long romance.

When she did gain her release, she determined to dedicate the rest of her life to writing and to pleasure, to trust to her own devices rather than to rely on others who could not be trusted.

Behn launched her career as a dramatist in late December, 1670, at the new Duke's Theatre in Little Lincoln's Inn Fields, London. Her tragicomedy *The Forced Marriage* ran for six nights and included in the cast the nineteen-year-old Thomas Otway (1652-1685), the playwright-to-be only recently arrived from Oxford. Because of the length of the run, Behn, as was the practice, received the entire profit from the third performance, which meant that she could begin to function as an independent artist. She followed her first effort in the spring of 1671 with a comedy, *The Amorous Prince*, again at the Duke's; another comedy, *The Dutch Lover*, came to Drury Lane in February, 1673, and by the time of her anonymous comedy *The Rover*, in 1677, her reputation was secure. She mixed easily with the literati of her day, such as Thomas Killigrew, Edward Ravenscroft, John Wilmot, Earl of Rochester, Edmund Waller, and the poet laureate John Dryden, who published her rough translations from Ovid in 1683. With her reputation came offers to write witty prologues and epilogues for others' plays as well as what she wanted more than anything—money. A confrontation with the third earl of Shaftesbury and the newly emerged Whigs during the religious-political controversies of 1678, when Behn offended Charles II's opponents in a satiric prologue to an anonymous play, *Romulus and Hersilia*, brought her once again to the edge of financial hardship, as she was forced to abandon drama for the next five years.

Fortunately, Behn could fall back on her abilities as a writer of popular fiction and occasional verse, although those forms were not as profitable as the London stage. Her series *Love Letters Between a Nobleman and His Sister* and *Poems upon Several Occasions* (1684) were well received, but the meager financial returns from such projects could not keep pace with her personal expenses. When she did return to the stage in 1686 with her comedy *The Lucky Chance*, she met with only moderate success and some public abuse. *The Emperor of the Moon*, produced the following season, fared somewhat better, although by then the London audience had lost its stomach for a female playwright—and a Tory, at that. She continued to write fiction and verse, but sickness and the death of her friend Edmund Waller, both in October, 1688, discouraged her. Five days after the coronation of William III and Mary, on April 16, 1689, Behn died. She had risen high enough to merit burial in Westminster Abbey; John Hoyle provided the fitting epitaph: "Here lies proof that wit can never be/ Defense enough against mortality."

Analysis

In the early twentieth century, Vita Sackville-West, in trying to estimate Aphra Behn's contribution to English fiction, asked, "What has she left behind her that is of any real value?" Sackville-West bemoaned Behn's failure in her fiction to reflect fully London life, London characters, London scenes; her attention to exotic themes, settings, and characters merely debased and wasted her narrative gifts. Such a judgment, while plausible, fails to consider Behn's fiction in its historical and biographical context. Her tales abound with German princes, Spanish princesses, Portuguese kings, French counts, West Indian slaves, and various orders of bishops, priests, and nuns, yet Behn's *real* world was itself highly artificial, even fantastic: the intrigue of the Stuart court, the ribaldry of the London stage, the gossip of the drawing room, the masquerade, and the card parlor. Behn, in her real world, took in the same scenes as did John Dryden, Samuel Pepys, and the earl of Rochester. Thus it may be too hasty to assert that her fiction neglects her actual experience in favor of fantastic and faraway window dressing.

In *Agnes de Castro*, Behn lets loose various powers of love, with the result that her heroines' passions affect the fortunes of their lovers. Thus, Miranda (*The Fair Jilt*) reflects the raving, hypocritical enchantress whose very beauty drives her lovers mad, Ardelia (*The Nun*) plays the capricious lover whose passion carries her through a series of men as well as a nunnery, and Agnes de Castro presents a slight variation on these others in that she is a product of circumstance: She is loved by the husband of her mistress.

Another primary theme in Behn's work is that of the noble savage, which has traditionally been assigned to *Oroonoko*, as has the subordinate issue of antislavery in that same novel. In 1975, Professor George Guffey suggested a withdrawal from the feminist-biographical positions on Behn's work from which the noble savage/antislavery ideals spring and a movement toward "a hitherto unperceived level of political allusion." Guffey did not label *Oroonoko* a political allegory but did suggest that readers should look more closely at events in England between 1678 and 1688. Guffey maintained that the novelist deplores not the slavery of a black, noble savage but the bondage of a *royal prince*—again a reference to the political climate of the times. The interesting aspect of Guffey's analysis is that his approach lends substance to Behn's principal novel and to her overall reputation as a literary artist, and it parries the complaint that she failed to echo the sound and the sense of her own age.

In 1678, Sir Roger L'Estrange published *Five Love Letters from a Nun to a Cavalier*, a translation of some fictional correspondence by the minor French writer Guilleraques. Behn used the work as a model for at least three of her prose pieces: *Love Letters Between a Nobleman and His Sister*, *The History of the Nun*, and *The Nun*. For the latter two, the novelist took advantage, at least on the surface, of the current religious and political controversies and set forth the usual claims to truth.

THE HISTORY OF THE NUN

There may be some validity to the claim that *The History of the Nun* exists as one of the earliest examinations by a novelist into the psychology of crime and guilt. The events of the novel proceed reasonably enough at the outset but become less believable; by the conclusion, the events appear to be exceedingly unreal. Despite this difficulty, the novel does have some value. Behn demonstrates her ability to develop thoroughly the key aspects of the weaknesses and the resultant sufferings of the heroine, Isabella. Behn immediately exposes the concept that "Mother Church" can take care of a girl's problems, can easily eradicate the desires of the world from her heart and mind, and can readily transform a passionate maiden into a true, devoted sister of the faith. In addition, despite her wickedness, Isabella is very much a human being worthy of the reader's understanding. At every step, the girl pays something for what she does; with each violation against the Church and each crime of passion, she falls deeper into the darkness of her own guilt. What she does, and how, is certainly contrived, but how she reacts to her misdeeds reflects accurately the guilty conscience of a believable human being.

THE NUN

Behn's second "Nun" novel, not published until 1697, certainly leads the reader through a more complicated plot entanglement than the 1689 story, but it contains none of the virtue exhibited in the earlier work. The interesting aspect of *The Nun*'s plot is that Behn kills the heroine, Ardelia, first; only afterward do the principal rivals, Don Sebastian and Don Henriques, kill each other in a fight. The interest, however, is only fleeting, for those events do not occur until the end of the novel. All that remains of the bloody situation is Elvira, Don Sebastian's unfaithful sister. After weeping and calling for help, she is seized with a violent fever (in the final paragraph) and dies within twenty-four hours. Certainly, Behn's ingenuity in this piece demands some recognition, if for no reason other than her adeptness, as James Sutherland has put it, at "moving the pieces around the board."

AGNES DE CASTRO

Because of the relative sanity of its plot, in contrast to the two previous tragedies, *Agnes de Castro* comes close to what Behn's feminist supporters expect of her. In other words, in this piece, pure evil or a series of tragic events cannot be blamed entirely on love or on reckless female passion. Although Don Pedro genuinely loves his wife's maid of honor, Agnes, she, out of loyalty to her mistress, refuses to yield to his passion. Such action encourages the other characters to exhibit equal degrees of virtue. Constantia, Don Pedro's wife, seems to understand that the power of Agnes's charms, although innocent enough, is no match for her husband's frailty of heart over reason. Thus, she resents neither her husband nor her maid; in fact, she is willing to tolerate the presence of Agnes to keep her husband happy.

The novel, however, does not exist as a monument to reason. Something must always arise, either in politics or romance, to disrupt reasonable people's attempts at harmony. In the novel, a vengeful woman lies to Constantia and plants the idea in her mind that Agnes and Don Pedro are plotting against her. The woman's report breaks Constantia's trust in her husband and her maid, and the honest lady dies of a broken heart. The novel, however, remains believable, for Behn simply emphasizes the frailty of honor and trust in a world dominated by intrigue and pure hatred. Given the political and religious climates of the decade, the setting and the plot of *Agnes de Castro* are indeed flimsy facades for the court and coffeehouse of seventeenth century London.

THE FAIR JILT

Although in *The Fair Jilt* Behn continued to develop the conflict between love and reason, the novel has attracted critical attention because of its allusions to the writer's own experiences. Again, Behn lays claim to authenticity by maintaining that she witnessed parts of the events the novel relates and heard the rest from sources close to the action and the characters. In addition, the events occur in Antwerp, the very city to which the novelist had been assigned for the performance of her spying activities for Charles II's ministers.

From the outset of the novel, Behn establishes the wickedness of Miranda, who uses her beauty to enchant the unsuspecting and even tempts the weak into committing murder. Obviously, had Behn allowed her major character to succeed in her evil ways, nothing would have been gained from the novel. What results is the triumph of the hero's innate goodness; as weak as Prince Tarquin is, he endures. His loyalty and devotion outlast and, to a certain extent, conquer Miranda's wickedness.

OROONOKO

Behn's literary reputation today rests almost totally on a single work, *Oroonoko*. The novel succeeds as her most realistic work, principally because it recounts the specifics of seventeenth century Suriname with considerable detail and force. Behn installs her hero amid the splendor of a tropical setting, a Natural Man, a pure savage untouched by the vices of Christian Europe, unaware of the white man's inherent baseness and falsehood.

In lashing out at the weaknesses of her society, Behn does not forget about one of her major concerns—love. Oroonoko loves the beautiful Imoinda, a child of his own race, but the prince's grandfather demands her for his own harem. Afterward, the monarch sells the girl into slavery, and she finds herself in Suriname, where Oroonoko also is brought following his kidnapping. The prince embarks on a term of virtuous and powerful adventures in the name of freedom for himself and Imoinda, but his captors deceive him. Thereupon, he leads a slave revolt, only to be captured by the white scoundrels and tortured. Rather than see Imoinda suffer dishonor at the hands of the ruthless white planters and government officers, Oroonoko manages to kill her himself. At the end, he smokes his pipe—a habit learned from the Europeans—as his captors dismember his body and toss the pieces into the fire.

The final judgment on Behn's fiction may still remain to be formulated. Evaluations of her work have tended to extremes. Some critics assert that Behn's novels, even *Oroonoko*, had no significant influence on the development of the English novel, whereas others argue that the author's limited attempts at realism may well have influenced Daniel Defoe, Samuel Richardson, Henry Fielding, and others to begin to mold the ostensibly factual narrative into the novel as the form is recognized today. From Behn came the background against which fictional plots could go forward and fictional characters could function. Her problem, which her successors managed to surmount, was her inability (or refusal) to make her characters and events as real as their fictional environments. That fault (if it was a fault) lay with the tendencies and the demands of the era in which she wrote, not with the writer. Indeed, it is hardly a failure for a dramatist and a novelist to have given to her audiences exactly what they wanted. To have done less would have meant an even quicker exit from fame and an even more obscure niche in the literary history of her time.

Samuel J. Rogal

OTHER MAJOR WORKS

PLAYS: *The Forced Marriage: Or, The Jealous Bridegroom*, pr. 1670; *The Amorous Prince: Or, The Curious Husband*, pr., pb. 1671; *The Dutch Lover*, pr., pb. 1673; *Abdelazer: Or, The Moor's Revenge*, pr. 1676; *The Town Fop: Or, Sir Timothy Tawdry*, pr. 1676; *The Rover: Or, The Banished Cavaliers, Part I*, pr., pb. 1677, *Part II*, pr., pb. 1681; *Sir Patient Fancy*, pr., pb. 1678; *The Feigned Courtesans: Or, A Night's Intrigue*, pr., pb. 1679; *The Young King: Or, The Mistake*, pr. 1679; *The Roundheads: Or, The Good Old Cause*, pr. 1681; *The City Heiress: Or, Sir Timothy Treat-All*, pr., pb. 1682; *The Lucky Chance: Or, An Alderman's Bargain*, pr. 1686; *The Emperor of the Moon*, pr., pb. 1687; *The Widow Ranter: Or, The History of Bacon of Virginia*, pr. 1689; *The Younger Brother: Or, The Amorous Jilt*, pr., pb. 1696.

POETRY: *Poems upon Several Occasions, with "A Voyage to the Island of Love,"* 1684 (including adaptation of Abbé Paul Tallemant's *Le Voyage de l'isle d'amour*); *Miscellany: Being a Collection of Poems by Several Hands*, 1685 (includes works by others).

TRANSLATIONS: *Aesop's Fables*, 1687 (with Francis Barlow); *Of Trees*, 1689 (of book 6 of Abraham Cowley's poem *Sex libri plantarum*).

MISCELLANEOUS: *The Case for the Watch*, 1686 (prose and poetry); *La Montre: Or, The Lover's Watch*, 1686 (prose and poetry); *Lycidus: Or, The Lover in Fashion*, 1688 (prose and poetry; includes works by others); *The Lady's Looking-Glass, to Dress Herself By: Or, The Art of Charming*, 1697 (prose and poetry); *The Works of Aphra Behn*, 1915, 1967 (6 volumes; Montague Summers, editor).

BIBLIOGRAPHY

Altaba-Artal, Dolors. *Aphra Behn's English Feminism: Wit and Satire*. Cranbury, N.J.: Associated University Presses, 1999. Examines Behn's writings from the perspective of feminism. Includes bibliography and index.

Anderson, Emily Hodgson. "Novelty in Novels: A Look at What's New in Aphra Behn's *Oroonoko*." *Studies in the Novel* 39, no. 1 (Spring, 2007): 1-16. Explores the aspects of novelty in novels through a focused reading of *Oroonoko*. Argues that the novel demonstrates a concern for didacticism and its own newness that was characteristic of many eighteenth century novels.

Carnell, Rachel K. "Subverting Tragic Conventions: Aphra Behn's Turn to the Novel." *Studies in the Novel* 31, no. 2 (Summer, 1998): 133-151. Discusses Behn's experiments with the novel form and the strategies she employed to counter the blatantly misogynistic resistance to her participation in political exchange.

Hughes, Derek and Janet Todd, eds. *The Cambridge Companion to Aphra Behn.* New York: Cambridge University Press, 2004. Replete with tools for further research, this is an excellent aid to any study of Behn's life and work. Includes two essays discussing various aspects of her novel *Oroonoko.*

Link, Frederick M. *Aphra Behn.* New York: Twayne, 1968. Provides a comprehensive survey of Behn's novels, plays, poems, and translations, with the plays receiving the greatest attention. Includes a chronology, notes, bibliography, and index.

Rivero, Albert J. "Aphra Behn's *Oroonoko* and the 'Blank Spaces' of Colonial Fictions." *Studies in English Literature, 1500-1900* 39, no. 3 (Summer, 1999): 443-462. Discusses Joseph Conrad's *Heart of Darkness* (which first appeared as a serial in 1899 and was published in book form in 1902) and Behn's *Oroonoko.* Both works feature characters that begin as civilized and go spectacularly native, and both attempt to preserve hierarchies of race and class while representing the impossibility of doing so in chaotic colonial settings.

Sackville-West, Victoria. *Aphra Behn: The Incomparable Astrea.* New York: Russell & Russell, 1927. Brief study of Behn's life relies heavily on biographical passages in Behn's novels. Whereas Sackville-West finds her subject engaging as a woman, she does not wholeheartedly admire Behn's writing. An appendix lists Behn's works and production or publication dates.

Spencer, Jane. *Aphra Behn's Afterlife.* New York: Oxford University Press, 2000. Examination of Behn's works, including *Oroonoko*, emphasizes Behn's influence. Features a discussion of the author's reputation as a novelist. Includes bibliography and index.

Todd, Janet. *The Secret Life of Aphra Behn.* New Brunswick, N.J.: Rutgers University Press, 1996. Speculative biographical work includes an introduction that summarizes efforts to study Behn's work and life, her place in literature, her ability to write in so many different genres, and the biographer's efforts to overcome the paucity of facts available. Features bibliographies of works written before and after 1800.

_______, ed. *Aphra Behn Studies.* New York: Cambridge University Press, 1996. Collection of essays is divided into four parts: Part 1 concentrates on Behn's plays, part 2 on her poetry, part 3 on her fiction, and part 4 on her biography. Includes an introduction outlining Behn's career.

Wiseman, Susan. *Aphra Behn.* 2d ed. Tavistock, England: Northcote House, 2007. Biography examines Behn's life and work. Discusses her works in all genres, including her novels *Oroonoko* and *Love Letters Between a Nobleman and His Sister.*

EMILY BRONTË

Born: Thornton, Yorkshire, England; July 30, 1818
Died: Haworth, Yorkshire, England; December 19, 1848
Also known as: Emily Jane Brontë; Ellis Bell

PRINCIPAL LONG FICTION
Wuthering Heights, 1847

OTHER LITERARY FORMS

Poems by Emily Brontë and her sisters Charlotte and Anne are collected in the volume *Poems by Currer, Ellis, and Acton Bell* (1846). Juvenilia and early prose works by Brontë on the imaginary world of Gondal have all been lost.

ACHIEVEMENTS

Emily Brontë occupies a unique place in the annals of literature. Her reputation as a major novelist stands on the merits of one relatively short novel that was misunderstood and intensely disliked upon publication, yet no study of British fiction is complete without a discussion of *Wuthering Heights*. The names of the novel's settings and characters, particularly Heathcliff, have become part of the heritage of Western culture, familiar even to those who have neither read the novel nor know anything about its author's life and career. Several film and television versions, two of the most popular of which were released in 1939 and 1970, have helped perpetuate this familiarity.

The literary achievement of *Wuthering Heights* lies in its realistic portrayal of a specific place and time and in its examination of universal patterns of human behavior. Set in Yorkshire in the closing years of the eighteenth century, the novel delineates the quality of life in the remote moors of northern England and also reminds the reader of the growing pains of industrialization throughout the nation. In addition, more than any other novel of the period, *Wuthering Heights* presents in clear dialectic form the conflict between two opposing psychic forces, embodied in the settings of the Grange and the Heights and the people who inhabit them. Although modern readers often apply the theories of Sigmund Freud and Carl Jung to give names to these forces, Brontë illustrated their conflict long before psychologists pigeonholed them. *Wuthering Heights* is so true in its portrayal of human nature that it fits easily into many theoretical and critical molds, from the historical to the psychological. The novel may be most fully appreciated, however, as a study of the nature of human perception and its ultimate failure in understanding human behavior. This underlying theme, presented through the dialectic structure of human perception, unites many of the elements that are sometimes singled out or overemphasized in particular critical approaches to the novel.

Brontë's skill is not confined to representing the world and the human forces at work

Emily Brontë
(Library of Congress)

within her characters, great as that skill is. She has also created a complex narrative structure built on a series of interlocking memories and perceptions, spanning three generations and moving across several social classes. Told primarily from two often unreliable and sometimes ambiguous first-person points of view, the novel illustrates through its structure the limitations of human intelligence and imagination. Faced with choosing between Lockwood's and Nelly Dean's interpretations of Heathcliff's life, the reader can only ponder that human perception never allows a full understanding of another soul.

BIOGRAPHY

Emily Jane Brontë was born at Thornton, in Bradford Parish, Yorkshire, on July 30, 1818, the fifth child of the Reverend Patrick and Maria Brontë. Patrick Brontë had been born in county Down, Ireland, one of ten children, on March 17, 1777. He was a schoolteacher and tutor before he obtained his bachelor of arts degree from Cambridge in 1806, from where he was ordained to curacies, first in Essex and then in Hartshead, Yorkshire. He married Maria Branwell, of Penzance, in Hartshead on December 19, 1812, and in

1817, they moved to Thornton. The other children in the family at the time of Emily's birth were Maria, Elizabeth, Charlotte, and Patrick Branwell; another daughter, Anne, was born two years later. Charlotte and Anne Brontë also became writers.

In early 1820, the family moved to Haworth, four miles from the village of Keighley, where the Reverend Brontë was perpetual curate until his death in 1861. Maria Brontë died on September 15, 1821, and about a year later, her elder sister, Elizabeth Branwell, moved in to take care of the children and household. She remained with them until her own death in 1842.

Life at Haworth was spartan but not unpleasant. There was a close and devoted relationship among the children, especially between Charlotte and Emily. Reading was a favorite pastime, and a wide range of books, including the novels of Sir Walter Scott and the poetry of William Wordsworth and Robert Southey, as well as the more predictable classics, was available to the children. Outdoor activities included many hours of wandering through the moors and woods. Their father wanted the children to be hardy and independent, intellectually and physically, indifferent to the passing fashions of the world.

Maria, Elizabeth, and Charlotte had already been sent away to a school for clergymen's daughters, at Cowan Bridge, when Emily joined them in November, 1824. Emily was not happy in this confined and rigid environment and longed for home. Two of the sisters, Elizabeth and Maria, became ill and were taken home to die during 1825; in June, Charlotte and Emily returned home as well.

From 1825 to 1830, the remaining Brontë children lived at Haworth with their father and their aunt, Miss Branwell. In June, 1826, their father gave them a set of wooden toy soldiers, a seemingly insignificant gift that stimulated their imaginative and literary talents. The children devoted endless energy to creating an imaginary world for the soldiers. During these years, Charlotte and her brother Branwell created in their minds and on paper the land of "Angria," while Emily and Anne were at work on "Gondal." Although all of these early prose works have been lost, some of Emily's poetry contains references to aspects of the Gondal-Angria creations.

In July, 1835, Emily again joined Charlotte, already a teacher, at the Roe Head school. She remained only three months, returning home in October. Three years later, she accepted a position as governess in a school in Halifax for about six months but returned to Haworth in December; Charlotte joined her there early in the following year. During 1839 and 1840, the sisters were planning to establish their own school at Haworth, but the plan was never carried through.

Charlotte left home again to serve as a governess in 1841, and in February, 1842, she and Emily went to Mme Héger's school in Brussels to study languages. They returned to Haworth in November because of Miss Branwell's death. Charlotte went back to Brussels to teach in 1843, but Emily never left Yorkshire again.

From August, 1845, the Brontë children were again united at Haworth. They did not have much contact with neighbors, whose educational level and intellectual interests were much inferior to theirs. They kept busy reading and writing, both fiction and poetry. *Wuthering Heights* was probably begun in October, 1845, and completed sometime in 1846, although it was not published until December, 1847, after the success of Charlotte's *Jane Eyre* (1847).

Meanwhile, the sisters published *Poems by Currer, Ellis, and Acton Bell* in May, 1846. Finding a press was very difficult, and the sisters chose the pseudonyms to avoid personal publicity and to create the fiction of male authorship, more readily acceptable to the general public. The reaction was predictable, as Charlotte noted: "Neither we nor our poems were at all wanted." The sisters were not discouraged, however, and they continued to seek publishers for their novels.

The first edition of *Wuthering Heights* was published in 1847 by T. C. Newby, with Anne's *Agnes Grey* as the third volume. It was a sloppy edition and contained many errors. The second edition, published in 1850, after the author's death, was "corrected" by Charlotte. The public reaction to *Wuthering Heights* was decidedly negative; readers were disturbed by the "wickedness" of the characters and the "implausibility" of the action. Until Charlotte herself corrected the misconception, readers assumed that *Wuthering Heights* was an inferior production by the author of *Jane Eyre*.

In October, 1848, Emily became seriously ill with a cough and cold. She suffered quietly and patiently, even refusing to see the doctor who had been called. She died of tuberculosis at Haworth on December 19, 1848. She was buried in the church alongside her mother, her sisters Maria and Elizabeth, and her brother Branwell.

These facts about Emily Brontë's life and death are known, but her character will always remain a mystery. Her early prose works have been lost, only three personal letters survive, and her poems give little insight into her own life. Most information about the Brontë family life and background comes from Mrs. Elizabeth Gaskell's biography of Charlotte and the autobiographical comments on which she based her work. Charlotte comments that Emily was "not a person of demonstrative character" and that she was "stronger than a man, simpler than a child." She had a nature that "stood alone." The person behind this mystery is revealed only in a reading of *Wuthering Heights*.

ANALYSIS: WUTHERING HEIGHTS

Wuthering Heights is constructed around a series of dialectic motifs that interconnect and unify the elements of setting, character, and plot. An examination of these motifs will give the reader the clearest insight into the central meaning of the novel. Although *Wuthering Heights* is a "classic," as Frank Kermode has noted, precisely because it is open to many different critical methods and conducive to many levels of interpretation, the novel grows from a coherent imaginative vision that underlies all the motifs. That vision demonstrates that all human perception is limited and failed. The fullest approach to Emily Brontë's novel is through the basic patterns that support this vision.

Wuthering Heights concerns the interactions of two families, the Earnshaws and

Lintons, over three generations. The novel is set in the desolate moors of Yorkshire and covers the years from 1771 to 1803. The Earnshaws and Lintons are in harmony with their environment, but their lives are disrupted by an outsider and catalyst of change, the orphan Heathcliff. Heathcliff is, first of all, an emblem of the social problems of a nation entering the age of industrial expansion and urban growth. Although Brontë sets the action of the novel entirely within the locale familiar to her, she reminds the reader continually of the contrast between that world and the larger world outside.

Aside from Heathcliff's background as a child of the streets and the description of urban Liverpool, from which he is brought, the novel contains other reminders that Yorkshire, long insulated from change and susceptible only to the forces of nature, is no longer as remote as it once was. The servant Joseph's religious cant, the class distinctions obvious in the treatment of Nelly Dean as well as of Heathcliff, and Lockwood's pseudosophisticated urban values are all reminders that Wuthering Heights cannot remain as it has been, that religious, social, and economic change is rampant. Brontë clearly signifies in the courtship and marriage of young Cathy and Hareton that progress and enlightenment *will* come and the wilderness *will* be tamed. Heathcliff is both an embodiment of the force of this change and its victim. He brings about a change but cannot change himself. What he leaves behind, as Lockwood attests and the relationship of Cathy and Hareton verifies, is a new society, at peace with itself and its environment.

It is not necessary, however, to examine in depth the Victorian context of *Wuthering Heights* to sense the dialectic contrast of environments. Within the limited setting that the novel itself describes, society is divided between two opposing worlds: Wuthering Heights, ancestral home of the Earnshaws, and Thrushcross Grange, the Linton estate. Wuthering Heights is rustic and wild; it is open to the elements of nature and takes its name from "atmospheric tumult." The house is strong, built with narrow windows and jutting cornerstones, fortified to withstand the battering of external forces. It is identified with the outdoors and nature and with strong, "masculine" values. Its appearance, both inside and out, is wild, untamed, disordered, and hard. The Grange expresses a more civilized, controlled atmosphere. The house is neat and orderly, and there is always an abundance of light—to Brontë's mind, "feminine" values. It is not surprising that Lockwood is more comfortable at the Grange, since he takes pleasure in "feminine" behavior (gossip, vanity of appearance, adherence to social decorum, romantic self-delusion), while Heathcliff, entirely "masculine," is always out of place there.

Indeed, all of the characters reflect, to greater or lesser degrees, the masculine and feminine values of the places they inhabit. Hindley and Catherine Earnshaw are as wild and uncontrollable as the Heights: Catherine claims even to prefer her home to the pleasures of heaven. Edgar and Isabella Linton are as refined and civilized as the Grange. The marriage of Edgar and Catherine (as well as the marriage of Isabella and Heathcliff) is ill-fated from the start, not only because she does not love him, as her answers to Nelly Dean's catechism reveal, but also because both are so strongly associated with the values of their homes that they lack the opposing and necessary personality components. Catherine is too willful, wild, and strong; she expresses too much of the "masculine" side of her personality (the animus of Jungian psychology), while Edgar is weak and effeminate (the anima). They are unable to interact fully with each other because they are not complete individuals themselves. This lack leads to their failures to perceive each other's true needs.

Even Cathy's passionate cry for Heathcliff, "Nelly, I *am* Heathcliff," is less love for him as an individual than the deepest form of self-love. Cathy cannot exist without him, but a meaningful relationship is not possible because Cathy sees Heathcliff only as a reflection of herself. Heathcliff, too, has denied an important aspect of his personality. Archetypally masculine, Heathcliff acts out only the aggressive, violent parts of himself.

The settings and the characters are patterned against each other, and explosions are the only possible results. Only Hareton and young Cathy, each of whom embodies the psychological characteristics of both Heights and Grange, can successfully sustain a mutual relationship.

This dialectic structure extends into the roles of the narrators as well. The story is reflected through the words of Nelly Dean—an inmate of both houses, a participant in the events of the narrative, and a confidant of the major characters—and Lockwood, an outsider who witnesses only the results of the characters' interactions. Nelly is a companion and servant in the Earnshaw and Linton households, and she shares many of the values and perceptions of the families. Lockwood, an urban sophisticate on retreat, misunderstands his own character as well as the characters of others. His brief romantic "adventure" in Bath and his awkwardness when he arrives at the Heights (he thinks Cathy will fall in love with him; he mistakes the dead rabbits for puppies) exemplify his obtuseness. His perceptions are always to be questioned. Occasionally, however, even a denizen of the conventional world may gain a glimpse of the forces at work beneath the surface of reality. Lockwood's dream of the dead Cathy, which sets off his curiosity and Heathcliff's final plans, is a reminder that even the placid, normal world may be disrupted by the psychic violence of a willful personality.

The presentation of two family units and parallel brother-sister, husband-wife relationships in each also emphasizes the dialectic. That two such opposing modes of behavior could arise in the same environment prevents the reader from easy condemnation of either pair. The use of flashback for the major part of the narration—it begins in medias res—reminds the reader that he or she is seeing events out of their natural order, recounted by two individuals whose reliability must be questioned. The working out of the plot over three generations further suggests that no one group, much less one individual, can perceive the complexity of the human personality.

Taken together, the setting, plot, characters, and structure combine into a whole when they are seen as parts of the dialectic nature of existence. In a world where opposing forces are continually arrayed against each other in the environment, in society, in families, and in relationships, as well as within the individual, there can be no easy route to perception of another human soul. *Wuthering Heights* convincingly demonstrates the complexity of this dialectic and portrays the limitations of human perception.

Lawrence F. Laban

OTHER MAJOR WORKS

POETRY: *Poems by Currer, Ellis, and Acton Bell*, 1846 (with Charlotte Brontë and Anne Brontë); *The Complete Poems of Emily Jane Brontë*, 1941 (C. W. Hatfield, editor); *Gondal's Queen: A Novel in Verse by Emily Jane Brontë*, 1955 (Fannie E. Ratchford, editor).

NONFICTION: *Five Essays Written in French*, 1948 (Lorine White Nagel, translator); *The Brontë Letters*, 1954 (Muriel Spark, editor).

BIBLIOGRAPHY

Barnard, Robert. *Emily Brontë*. New York: Oxford University Press, 2000. Barnard, chairman of the Brontë Society, provides an incisive overview of Brontë's life and work. Includes bibliography, maps, illustrations (some in color), index, and chronology.

Benvenuto, Richard. *Emily Brontë*. Boston: Twayne, 1982. Brief biography of the Brontë sister whose life remains relatively obscure. Although only three of her letters survive, Benvenuto stays within the documentary record to provide a convincing portrait of her life and personality.

Berg, Maggie. "*Wuthering Heights*": *The Writing in the Margin*. New York: Twayne, 1996. Provides a good introduction to Emily Brontë's masterpiece. A chronology of her life and works is followed by a section devoted to the literary and social context of the novel and a reading emphasizing the importance of the novel's "marginal spaces," such as the diary that Catherine keeps in the blank spaces of books.

Davies, Stevie. *Emily Brontë: Heretic*. London: Women's Press, 1994. Feminist interpretation of Brontë's life and work contradicts the legends of Brontë's sexual innocence and unworldliness, showing how *Wuthering Heights* and the author's poetry offer evidence of her sophistication and sexuality.

Frank, Katherine. *A Chainless Soul: A Life of Emily Brontë*. Boston: Houghton Mifflin, 1990. Biographical study demonstrates the complex relationships between Emily Brontë and her family members.

Glen, Heather, ed. *The Cambridge Companion to the Brontës*. New York: Cambridge University Press, 2002. Essays examining the lives and work of the three sisters include analysis of *Wuthering Heights* and Emily's poetry, a feminist perspective on the sisters' work, and a discussion of the Brontës and religion.

Liddell, Robert. *Twin Spirits: The Novels of Emily and Anne Brontë*. London: Peter Owen, 1990. Presents analysis of *Wuthering Heights* and includes a companion essay on Anne Brontë's 1848 novel *The Tenant of Wildfell Hall*, showing that the latter is Anne's answer to Emily's novel.

Miller, Lucasta. *The Brontë Myth*. London: Jonathan Cape, 2001. Biography of the Brontës emphasizes how previous biographers have shaped readers' understanding of the three sisters' lives and work. Corrects misinformation contained in nineteenth century biographies, which exaggerated the authors' miserable childhoods, as well as in later books that interpreted their work from Freudian, feminist, and poststructural perspectives.

Pykett, Lyn. *Emily Brontë*. Savage, Md.: Barnes & Noble, 1989. Feminist assessment of Brontë's work suggests that *Wuthering Heights* is a distinctive novel because of the particular way it combines the female gothic genre and the realistic domestic novel that was becoming popular in Brontë's lifetime.

Rollyson, Carl, and Lisa Paddock. *The Brontës A to Z: The Essential Reference to Their Lives and Work*. New York: Facts On File, 2003. Covers every aspect of the three sisters' lives and work in more than five hundred alphabetically arranged essays. Includes seventeen pages of plot summary and analysis for *Wuthering Heights*.

Vine, Steve. *Emily Brontë*. New York: Twayne, 1998. Presents biographical information as well as critical analysis of *Wuthering Heights* and Brontë's poetry. Intended as an introduction for general readers.

Winnifrith, Tom, ed. *Critical Essays on Emily Brontë*. New York: G. K. Hall, 1997. Collection of two dozen essays by distinguished critics focuses on a range of topics, including Brontë's religion, her reading and education, *Wuthering Heights*, and her poetry. In one essay, Virginia Woolf compares *Wuthering Heights* to Charlotte Brontë's *Jane Eyre*.

SAMUEL BUTLER

Born: Langar Rectory, Nottinghamshire, England; December 4, 1835
Died: London, England; June 18, 1902

PRINCIPAL LONG FICTION

Erewhon, 1872
The Fair Haven, 1873
Erewhon Revisited, 1901
The Way of All Flesh, 1903

OTHER LITERARY FORMS

The Shrewsbury editions of Samuel Butler's works, published between 1923 and 1926, reveal the breadth of his interests. Butler's fiction was perhaps less important to him than his work in other fields, notably his theorizing on religion and evolution. He was also an art critic (*Ex Voto*, 1888; *Alps and Sanctuaries of Piedmont and the Ticino*, 1881), a literary critic (*The Authoress of the "Odyssey,"* 1897; *Shakespeare's Sonnets Reconsidered*, 1899), a letter writer, a poet, and the biographer of his famous grandfather, Dr. Samuel Butler. An age that produces "specialists" may find Butler to be a talented dabbler or dilettante, but his unifying philosophy gives a center to all his work.

ACHIEVEMENTS

Samuel Butler was a figure of controversy during his lifetime, and perhaps his greatest achievement resides in his ability to challenge: He contended with Charles Darwin and Darwinism; he took on the established scholars of William Shakespeare, classical literature, and art; and he was part of the nineteenth century revolt against traditional religion. He approached all of these areas in such a way that his opponents could not ignore him; whether he was right or wrong, any subject benefited by his treatment, which opened it up to new and candid thought.

Of his four works that may be labeled as fiction, by far the greatest is *The Way of All Flesh*. Virginia Woolf described this novel as a seed from which many others developed—a biological image that would have pleased Butler. In earlier novels, indifferent or cruel families had been portrayed as agents of the heroes' youthful unhappiness—witness Charles Dickens's *David Copperfield* (1849-1850, serial; 1850, book)—but in *The Way of All Flesh*, an oppressive, cruel family life becomes a theme in itself, worthy of generation-by-generation treatment.

BIOGRAPHY

Samuel Butler was born in 1835, the son of a clergyman who wished him to go into the church. After a successful career at Cambridge University, Butler prepared for a career in the clergy but found himself unable to face the prospect of that life. Letters between Butler and his father show the young man to be considering a half dozen plans at once—art, the army, cotton growing, and bookselling among them. Finally, father and son agreed that the young man should emigrate to New Zealand and try his fortune there, with Butler's father providing capital. Both father and son hoped that the experience would "settle" Butler and build his character.

Butler arrived in New Zealand in January of 1860 and remained there for four years. It was a useful time: He made money, which freed him of his family, at least financially, and he saw an unusual country that gave him a subject and setting for his later writings. New Zealand, however, was too rough a land to be his permanent home. His "hut" there was an island of comfort and civilization, where Butler devoted himself to music and study. His optimistic letters home became the basis of *A First Year in Canterbury Settlement* (1863), a book assembled and published by Butler's father.

Returning to England in 1864, Butler settled at Clifford's Inn in London, which would be his home for the rest of his life. He began to study art; his paintings had some success. He wished to do something greater, however—something that would express his developing ideas. Out of this desire grew *Erewhon*, a satire that was published anonymously in 1872 at the author's own expense. By that time, Butler was already at work on *The Fair Haven*. This book may or may not be considered fiction; it is a dispute over the validity of Christianity, but the dispute is conducted in a fictional frame.

The following year, 1873, was an important one for Butler. *The Fair Haven* was published, his mother died, he made a risky financial investment, and he began *The Way of All Flesh*. All of these events shaped his later years. *The Fair Haven*, following on the heels of *Erewhon*, marked him as a belligerent enemy of traditional religion. His mother's death caused him some grief, but it spurred him to begin *The Way of All Flesh*, the work for which he is most remembered. That work was slowed, however, by financial troubles. Butler invested his New Zealand fortune in a Canadian venture that soon failed. He salvaged less than a quarter of his investment and had to seek help from his father. Not until 1886, when his father died, was Butler wholly free of financial pressures.

The next several years were occupied by work on evolution and religion. In 1882, Butler returned to *The Way of All Flesh*, completing it the following year. He felt, however, that the book should not be published while anyone who could be hurt by it was still alive; therefore it did not appear until a year after his own death.

In 1883, Butler began to write music. Music and music criticism were to occupy him intermittently for several years, interspersed with art criticism. The last decade of his life was filled with the study of literature, culminating in his publications on Shakespeare's sonnets and his translations of Homer's *Iliad* (1898) and *Odyssey* (1900). These works were characterized by the combativeness that to some degree sums up Butler's life. He was always the rebellious, contradictory son.

Butler's life was shaped by a number of intense relationships. His relationship with his family was unresolved; the work (*The Way of All Flesh*) that might have laid the ghosts to rest was haunted by another ghost, Butler's lifelong friend Eliza Mary Ann Savage. A fellow art student, she gave the writer friendship, friendly criticism, advice, and approval. Her own understanding of the relationship can never be known, but Butler feared she wished to marry him. His implicit rejection disturbed him deeply after her death. Other friendships were equally ambiguous. Charles Paine Pauli consumed much of Butler's attentions and resources from their first meeting in New Zealand until Pauli's death in 1897, when Butler discovered that Pauli had been supported by two other men. The perhaps sexual ambiguities of this relationship were repeated in Butler's affection for a young Swiss, Hans Faesch, and to a lesser degree in his long-lasting bonds with Henry Festing Jones and Alfred Emery Cathie. Butler's emotional makeup seems similar to that of Henry James. Both men formed passionate attachments to other men; both appreciated women more as memories than as living beings.

Analysis

On his deathbed, Samuel Butler spoke of the "pretty roundness" of his career, beginning with *Erewhon* and ending, thirty years later, with *Erewhon Revisited.*

Erewhon

Erewhon must be understood first of all as a satire rather than as a novel. It is in the tradition of Jonathan Swift's *Gulliver's Travels* (1726) and Samuel Johnson's *Rasselas, Prince of Abyssinia* (1759), works that sacrifice unity and development to a vision of the writer's society in the guise of an imaginary foreign land. Like Rasselas and Gulliver, Higgs of *Erewhon* is a young man ready for adventure, out to learn about the world. He quickly reveals his image of himself as sharp, cunning, and bold. Before he tells his story, he lets the reader know the things he will hold back, so that no one reading the tale will be able to find Erewhon and thus profit financially from Higgs's exploration.

His story begins as he is working on a sheep farm in a colony, the name of which he will not reveal. Intending to find precious metals or at least good sheep-grazing land, he journeys alone inland, over a mountain range. On the other side, he finds a kingdom called Erewhon (Nowhere), which looks very much like England. Higgs's point of reference is England; all aspects of Erewhonian life he measures by that standard.

Many such satires work through the narrators' quick judgments that the new lands they encounter are either much better or much worse than their native countries: In each case, the narrator's rather simple view plays against the author's more complex perspective. In *Erewhon*, however, the narrator is not quite so naïve. His own failings, rather than his naïveté, become part of the satire, which thus has a dual focus, much like book 4 of *Gulliver's Travels*. Higgs, like many good Victorian heroes, is out to make money. It is this prospect that motivates him most strongly. Coexisting with his desire for fortune is his religiosity. Here, Butler's satire on his character is most pronounced and simplistic. Higgs observes the Sabbath, but he seduces Yram (Mary) with no regret. He plans to make his fortune by selling the Erewhonians into slavery, arguing that they would be converted to Christianity in the process; the slaveholders would be lining their pockets and doing good simultaneously. Butler thus exposes, to no one's great surprise, the mingled piety and avarice of British colonialists.

Butler satirizes European culture through the Erewhonians more often than through his hero, Higgs, gradually unfolding their lives for the reader to observe. Their lives are, on the surface, peaceful and pleasant; they are a strikingly attractive race. Only through personal experience does Higgs learn the underpinnings of the society: When he is ill, he learns that illness is a crime in Erewhon, while moral lapses are regarded in the same way as illnesses are in England. When his pocket watch is discovered, he learns that all "machines" have been banned from Erewhon. Erewhonian morality is based on reversals: The morally corrupt receive sympathy, while the ill are imprisoned; a child duped by his guardian is punished for having been ignorant, while the guardian is rewarded; children are responsible for their own birth, while their parents are consoled for having been "wronged" by the unborn. This pattern of reversals is of necessity incomplete, a problem noted by reviewers of *Erewhon* in 1872.

"The Book of the Machines" is the section of the satire that has drawn the most attention, because of its relationship to Darwinian thought. It may well be, as it has often been considered, a *reductio ad absurdum* of Darwinism, but the chapter also takes on reasoning by analogy as a less complex target of satire. "The Book of the Machines" is Higgs's translation of the Erewhonian book that led to the banning of all mechanical devices. Its author claimed that machines had developed—evolved—more rapidly than humankind and thus would soon dominate, leaving humans mere slaves or parasites. He argued that machines were capable of reproduction, using humans in the process as flowers use bees. The arguments proved so convincing that all machines in Erewhon were soon destroyed, leaving the country in the rather primitive state in which Higgs found it.

The purpose of "The Book of the Machines" becomes clearer in the following two chapters, which detail Erewhonian debates on the rights of animals and the rights of vegetables. At one point in the past, insistence on the rights of animals had turned Erewhon into a land of vegetarians, but the philosophers went a step further and decreed that vegetables, too, had rights, based on their evolving consciousness. Again, Butler plays with argument by analogy, as the philosophers compare the vegetables' intelligence to that of a human embryo.

The Erewhonians who believed in the rights of vegetables were led nearly to starvation by their extremism, and it is this same extremism that causes Higgs to leave Erewhon. Fearful that disfavor is growing against his foreign presence, he plans to escape by balloon, taking with him his beloved Arowhena. The perilous escape takes place, and the hero, married to Arowhena and restored to England, becomes a fairly successful hack writer. His account of Erewhon, he says at the end, constitutes an appeal for subscriptions to finance his scheme to return to Erewhon.

EREWHON REVISITED

The broad, traditional satire of *Erewhon* is abandoned in its sequel. Written years later, *Erewhon Revisited* reflects the maturity of its author, then in his sixties. In the later work, Butler treats Erewhon as a habitation of human beings, not satiric simplifications. *Erewhon Revisited* is thus a novel, not a satire; its focus is on human relationships. Butler had already written (though not published) *The Way of All Flesh*, and the preoccupations of that work are also evident in *Erewhon Revisited*. Both works grew out of Butler's fascination with family relationships, especially those between father and son.

The narrator of *Erewhon Revisited* is John Higgs, the son of George Higgs and Arowhena. He tells of his mother's early death and of his father's desire to return to Erewhon. This time, however, Higgs's desire is sentimental; he has grown past his earlier wish to profit from the Erewhonians. He goes to Erewhon, returns in ill health, tells the story of his adventure to John, and dies. The book in this way becomes John's tribute to his father.

Although *Erewhon Revisited* may be identified as a novel rather than as a satire, it does have a satiric subject as part of its plot. Upon reentering Erewhon, Higgs discovers that his ascent by balloon has become the source of a new religion. The Erewhonians revere his memory and worship him as the "Sun Child." Higgs is horrified to find that there are theologians of Sunchildism fighting heretics. Sadly, Sunchildism has not made the Erewhonians a better or kinder people. Here is the heart of Butler's satire: that a religion based on a supernatural event will divide people, place power in the wrong hands, and humiliate reason.

In *Erewhon*, Higgs was a pious and hypocritical prig, a target of satire himself. In the sequel, he is a genial, loving humanist, appalled by the "evolution" of his frantic escape into the ascent of a god. Much of *Erewhon Revisited* develops his plans to deflate Sunchildism, to reveal himself as the "Sun Child" and tell the truth about his "ascent."

Higgs has a special motive that transcends his disgust with Sunchildism. Upon arriving in Erewhon, he meets a young man whom he soon recognizes as his own son, a son he did not know he had. The young man is the product of Higgs's brief romance with Yram, the jailer's daughter. Higgs keeps his identity from his son (also named George) for a while, but eventually the two are revealed to each other in a touching and intense scene. To earn his newfound son's respect, Higgs determines to deflate Sunchildism. Thus, the process of satire in *Erewhon Revisited* is rooted in its human relationships.

Higgs's son John, the narrator of the novel, feels no jealousy toward his half brother. Instead, he shares the elder Higgs's enthusiasm for young George. Following his father's death, John goes to Erewhon himself to meet George and to deliver a large gift of gold to him. This legacy exemplified one of Butler's tenets about parent-child relations: that the best parents are kind, mostly absent, and very free with money. This theme is repeated throughout *The Way of All Flesh*. In *Erewhon Revisited*, however, it has a simpler expression. The relationship of Higgs and his two sons forms the emotional center of the novel and creates the impetus for some of its plot, but it is distinct from the satire on religion that makes up much of the book.

THE FAIR HAVEN

It is fitting that Butler's last work, *Erewhon Revisited*, should have presented a genial hero determined to strip away what he saw as ridiculous supernatural beliefs. Much of "Sunchildism" is a response to the religious foment of the nineteenth century with which Butler had begun contending early in his career. *The Fair Haven* was his first satire concerned with Christian belief. This work is "fiction" only in a very limited sense: Butler creates a persona, John Pickard Owen, whose arguments in favor of Christianity are in fact the vehicle for Butler's satire against it. *The Fair Haven* begins with a fictional memoir of John Pickard Owen by his brother. The memoir reveals that Owen moved from faith to disbelief to faith, and that his efforts to prove the validity of his religion pushed him to mental exhaustion and, eventually, death.

THE WAY OF ALL FLESH

The characters of *The Fair Haven* are forerunners of the Pontifex family in *The Way of All Flesh*, Butler's fullest and most characteristic work. *The Way of All Flesh* encompasses all of Butler's concerns: family life, money, sexual attitudes, class structure, religion, and art. This novel too is a satire, but in it Butler does not portray an Erewhon; much more disturbingly, he keeps the reader at home.

The Way of All Flesh is Ernest Pontifex's story, but it does not begin with Ernest. Butler the evolutionist shows Ernest as the product of several generations of social changes and personal tensions. The genealogical background, as well as the title and biblical epigraph, "We know that all things work together for good to them that love God," helps to create the ironic treatment of religion that will permeate the novel. What is the way of all flesh? The biblical echo suggests sin and decay; Butler's fiction, however, reminds the reader that the way of all flesh is change, for better or worse.

Ernest is the product of three generations of upward mobility. His great-grandfather is a simple, kind craftsman who sends his only son into the city. The son, George Pontifex, becomes successful as a publisher and even more successful as a bully. He chooses the Church as a career for his second son, Theobald, who revolts briefly, then acquiesces and evolves into the image of his father. Butler is careful to show personalities as products of environment. George's bullying is only that of an egotistical, self-made man; Theobald's is more harsh, the product of his own fear and suppressed anger. The unfortunate object of this anger is Theobald's firstborn son, Ernest Pontifex.

Ernest's childhood is dominated by fear of his father. His mother, Christina, is of little help; Butler portrays her as the product of her own family life and the larger social system, both of which make marriage a necessity for her. Like Theobald, Christina becomes a hypocrite pressed into the service of "what is done." Much later in life, Ernest reflects that the family is a painful anachronism, confined in nature to the lower species. His opinion is shared by Overton, the narrator of the novel, an old family friend who takes an interest in young Ernest and becomes his lifelong friend and adviser. The two of them, in fact, eventually come to constitute a kind of family—an evolved, freely chosen family, not one formed by mere biological ties.

This outcome occurs only after long agony on Ernest's part. As a child, he believes all that is told: that he is, for example, a wicked, ungrateful boy who deserves Theobald's frequent beatings. His young life is lightened, however, by the interest taken in him by his aunt Alethea and by Overton, who has known all of the Pontifexes well and who tells their story with compassion.

Ernest is still an innocent and unformed young man when he goes to Cambridge to prepare for a career in the Church. Near the end of his peaceful, happy years there, he comes under the influence of an Evangelical group that alters his perceptions of what his life as a clergyman ought to be. Instead of stepping into a pleasant rural parish, Ernest becomes a missionary in the slums of London. He falls under the spell of the oily clergyman Nicholas Pryor, who "invests" Ernest's money and eventually absconds with it. Pryor, the Cambridge enthusiasts, and Theobald Pontifex all represent the clerical life; they are radically different kinds of people, and they are all portrayed negatively. Butler took no prisoners in his war on the clergy; his use of the genial Overton as a narrator partially masks this characteristic.

Sexual ignorance, imposed (and shared) by Theobald and his kind, provides Butler with his next target for satire. In despair over his religious life, Ernest seeks a prostitute and approaches the wrong woman, the eponymous Miss Snow. Ernest's ignorance lands him in prison and cuts him off forever from mere gentility. It redeems him, however, from a life circumscribed by his father: Ironically, Theobald's strict control over Ernest liberates Ernest at last. In prison, stripped of all his former identity, Ernest begins to come to terms with what his life has been and may be. A long illness serves to clarify his mind; he rejects traditional religion, society, and his family's condescending offers of help. Overton alone stands by Ernest, and it is at this point in Ernest's development that they become fast friends. Overton takes on the role of the ideal father—fond, genteel, and moneyed.

It is in this last area that Overton's role is most important to the events of the book: He keeps Alethea's substantial bequest in trust for Ernest, allowing him knowledge of it and access to it, according to Alethea's wish, only when he judges that Ernest is prepared to use it wisely. Ernest's ill-advised marriage and his decision to work as a tailor cause Overton to hold the money back. Eventually, Ernest's maturity evolves to a level acceptable to Overton, and the two of them lead a pleasant life of wealth and, on Ernest's side at least, accomplishment: He has become a writer who, like Butler, writes thoughtful, theoretical books.

In his role as a father, Ernest also has evolved. The children of his marriage to Ellen are reared by simple country people and grow up free of the pressures of Ernest's childhood. After four generations, the Pontifexes have returned to the peaceful and happy life of Ernest's great-grandfather.

Liberal amounts of money, however, keep Ernest's son and daughter from any want that ordinary country folk might experience. Ernest's son wants to be a riverboat captain: Ernest buys him riverboats. This scenario is nearly as idealized a version of country life as was Marie Antoinette's. What makes this vision disconcerting is that Ernest's attitudes are clearly shared by Butler. Early in the novel, Ernest the bullied child is the object of the reader's pity. As a student and young cleric, he has experiences that create a sense of pity but also create humor. The more fully Ernest evolves, however, the less appealing the reader is likely to find him. The Ernest who finally comes into his aunt's fortune is a rather dull prig, who, upon learning of his wealth, considers how his emotion might be rendered in music. He tells Overton that he regrets nothing—not his parents' brutality, not prison—because everything has contributed to his evolution away from the "swindle" of middle-class expectations. Unfortunately, this self-satisfied view makes his character seem shallow, consisting only of words and affectations.

In spite of this problem, Butler's achievement is considerable. *The Way of All Flesh* is an immensely ambitious book, and much of it succeeds. Butler articulates fully and convincingly the varied stresses of family life, and that aspect alone makes the novel worthwhile. *Erewhon* and *Erewhon Revisited* share some of that evocative power. They also express Butler's optimism. For all his satiric vision and contentiousness, Butler does offer happy endings: Higgs's successful escape from Erewhon with his beloved, the reunion of the brothers in *Erewhon Revisited*, and the pleasant life of Ernest and Overton in *The Way of All Flesh*. Though societies may often be in the wrong, Butler seems to tell the reader, there is hope in freely chosen human relationships.

Deborah Core

OTHER MAJOR WORKS

NONFICTION: *A First Year in Canterbury Settlement*, 1863; *Life and Habit*, 1877; *Evolution, Old and New*, 1879; *God the Known and God the Unknown*, 1879; *Unconscious Memory*, 1880; *Alps and Sanctuaries of Piedmont and the Ticino*, 1881; *A Psalm of Montreal*, 1884; *Luck or Cunning*, 1887; *Ex Voto*, 1888; *The Life and Letters of Dr. Samuel Butler*, 1896; *The Authoress of the "Odyssey,"* 1897; *Shakespeare's Sonnets Reconsidered*, 1899; *The Note-books*, 1912 (H. Festing Jones, editor).

TRANSLATIONS: *Iliad*, 1898 (of Homer's epic poem); *Odyssey*, 1900 (of Homer's epic poem).

BIBLIOGRAPHY

Bekker, Willem Gerard. *An Historical and Critical Review of Samuel Butler's Literary Works*. 1925. Reprint. New York: Russell & Russell, 1964. Full-length study of Butler written by a native of Holland, where *Erewhon* found popularity and immediate acceptance. Bekker argues for the unity in Butler's works.

Daniels, Anthony. "Butler's Unhappy Youth." *New Criterion* 23, no. 5 (January, 2005): 11-17. Discusses *The Way of All Flesh*, Butler's autobiographical novel, arguing that it may be the most devastating literary assault on a father ever written by a son. Describes how Butler's father, Thomas, and the father in the novel, Theobald Pontifex, stand accused of committing odious acts.

Henderson, Philip. *Samuel Butler: The Incarnate Bachelor.* 1954. Reprint. New York: Barnes & Noble Books, 1968. Readable and illuminating work is one of the best biographies of Butler available. Focuses on his personality rather than his work, and argues against the prevailing view that Butler hated his father. Includes a detailed chronology.

Holt, Lee E. *Samuel Butler.* Rev. ed. Boston: Twayne, 1989. Provides a good introduction to Butler and his writings. Includes chapters on Butler's major fiction, a chronology, and an annotated bibliography.

Jeffers, Thomas L. *Samuel Butler Revalued.* University Park: Pennsylvania State University Press, 1981. An appreciation rather than a panegyric, this critical study focuses on *The Way of All Flesh* because it was composed during the period when Butler thought most creatively about evolution, his religion, and his family. Contains lengthy notes, a selected bibliography, and an index.

Jones, H. F. *Samuel Butler, Author of "Erewhon" (1835-1902): A Memoir.* 2 vols. 1919. Reprint. New York: Octagon Books, 1968. Remains the standard biography, presenting a wealth of detail about the events of Butler's life, his personal characteristics, and the creation and reception of his literary works.

Paradis, James G., ed. *Samuel Butler, Victorian Against the Grain: A Critical Overview.* Toronto, Ont.: University of Toronto Press, 2007. Collection of essays includes discussions of Butler's views on evolution, the relationship between evolutionary psychology and *The Way of All Flesh*, Butler's bachelorhood, his travel writing, and his photography.

Parrinder, Patrick. "Entering Dystopia, Entering Erewhon." *Critical Survey* 17, no.1 (2005): 6-21. Describes the characteristics of dystopian romances written in the late Victorian era, focusing on the representations of dystopia in *Erewhon* and W. H. Hudson's *A Crystal Age* (1887).

Raby, Peter. *Samuel Butler: A Biography.* Iowa City: University of Iowa Press, 1991. Comprehensive, scholarly biography intelligently recounts the details of Butler's personal life and career. Includes detailed notes, bibliography, photographs, and drawings.

LEWIS CARROLL
Charles Lutwidge Dodgson

Born: Daresbury, Cheshire, England; January 27, 1832
Died: Guildford, Surrey, England; January 14, 1898
Also known as: Charles Lutwidge Dodgson

PRINCIPAL LONG FICTION
Alice's Adventures in Wonderland, 1865
Through the Looking-Glass and What Alice Found There, 1871
Sylvie and Bruno, 1889
Sylvie and Bruno Concluded, 1893
The Wasp in a Wig: The "Suppressed" Episode of "Through the Looking-Glass and What Alice Found There," 1977

OTHER LITERARY FORMS

Before and after writing his novels for children, Lewis Carroll published volumes in his primary vocation, mathematics: *A Syllabus of Plane Algebraical Geometry* (1860), *An Elementary Treatise on Determinants* (1867), *Curiosa Mathematica, Part I: A New Theory of Parallels* (1888), *Curiosa Mathematica, Part II: Pillow Problems Thought During Wakeful Hours* (1893), and *Symbolic Logic, Part I: Elementary* (1896). His gift for light verse, demonstrated in his novels, also led to four books of poems, with some duplication of content: *Phantasmagoria, and Other Poems* (1869), *The Hunting of the Snark: An Agony in Eight Fits* (1876), *Rhyme? and Reason?* (1883), and the posthumous *Three Sunsets and Other Poems* (1898). His literary and mathematical sides were fused in *A Tangled Tale* (1885), a series of mathematical word problems in the form of short stories, and *Euclid and His Modern Rivals* (1879), a closet drama in which Euclid is defended by various scholars and spirits.

ACHIEVEMENTS

In 1898, a few months after Lewis Carroll's death, the *Pall Mall Gazette* published a survey of the popularity of children's books, and the overwhelming front-runner was *Alice's Adventures in Wonderland*. Queen Victoria enjoyed *Alice's Adventures in Wonderland* so much that she asked Carroll to dedicate his next book to her (ironically, his next book, *An Elementary Treatise on Determinants*, proved to be nothing like the whimsical adventure the queen had admired).

Carroll encouraged the stage versions of the Alice books that appeared in his lifetime, though he was dismayed at his lack of legal control over adaptations. The Alice books have been translated into dozens of languages and are quoted more often than any English work, after that of William Shakespeare. *Alice's Adventures in Wonderland* is noteworthy for more than its popularity, however; it was the first work of literature for children that did

Lewis Carroll
(Library of Congress)

not have an overtly didactic or moralistic nature. In fact, Carroll parodied didactic children's works in verse, such as "You Are Old, Father William" in *Through the Looking-Glass and What Alice Found There*, and through characters such as the Duchess in *Alice's Adventures in Wonderland*. Writers as abstruse and complex as British philosopher Ludwig Wittgenstein and Irish novelist James Joyce were drawn to the deeper implications of Carroll's work, especially the lighthearted sense of play and the role of nonsense in human thought. The absurdist writers of the twentieth century saw Carroll as their prophet, and a few of his nonsense words, such as "Boojum," "Jabberwocky," and "chortle," have become seemingly permanent parts of the English language. His term for a particular method of coining compound words, "portmanteau," has since become a standard linguistic name for the process.

BIOGRAPHY

Charles Lutwidge Dodgson was the third of eleven children and the eldest son of the Reverend Charles Dodgson and Frances Jane Lutwidge. The younger Charles Dodgson was left-handed and spoke with a stutter, an affliction from which he would suffer his whole life. With eight younger siblings, he very early developed the knack of amusing children, an ability he would keep as an adult. For their amusement, he wrote and drew little magazines that demonstrated the whimsy later seen in his Alice books. Some of the verses in the Alice books received their first auditions in these family magazines.

At age twelve, Dodgson attended Richmond Grammar School, and the following year, the famous public school at Rugby. Nearly four years at Rugby, which he later recalled with displeasure, prepared him for Oxford University: He entered Christ Church College there on January 24, 1851. He distinguished himself in mathematics and classics, though difficulty with philosophy and history kept him in the lower third of his class. On December 18, 1854, he received his A.B. with first-class honors in mathematics. He stayed on at Christ Church as a tutor and lecturer. At this time his earliest stories and poems appeared in periodicals at Oxford and Whitby.

Early in 1856 Dodgson acquired his first camera, then a relatively rare and complicated device restricted to use by specialists. A large number of his photographs, mostly of young girls, survive, and one historian of photography has declared Dodgson the most outstanding child photographer of the nineteenth century. A month after he had purchased the camera, one young model, the four-year-old daughter of an Oxford dean, caught Dodgson's eye. Her name was Alice Liddell. Six years later he would extemporize, on a boating expedition, a story about Alice that was to become the famous Alice stories. However, until then, Dodgson's energies went into his vocations of mathematics and the clergy: He published his first book on mathematics in 1860, and he was ordained a deacon just before Christmas of 1861.

By February of 1863, Dodgson had committed to paper the story from the 1862 excursion with the Liddell sisters. He published it in 1865 (though it did not appear until 1866) as *Alice's Adventures in Wonderland*. Dodgson used the pseudonym Lewis Carroll for his publications, a name seemingly derived from the names Lutwidge and Charles. In 1867, Dodgson made the only voyage of his lifetime away from England, touring the Continent (mostly Russia). He had already begun his sequel to *Alice's Adventures in Wonderland*, which appeared near Christmas, 1871, as *Through the Looking-Glass and What Alice Found There*. When his father died in 1868, Dodgson moved his siblings to Guildford, and he moved into rooms at Tom Quad, Oxford, where he remained the rest of his life. In 1881 his income from writing was sufficient for him to resign his lectureship in mathematics, although he remained at Oxford. The following year he was elected curator of the Senior Common room, a post he held for ten years. He continued writing until his death in 1898, though he never equaled the success of the Alice books.

Analysis

Lewis Carroll's first great contribution to children's literature is that he freed it from the heavy didacticism of previous children's books. The second is his legitimating of nonsense in children's literature, though in this claim he is preceded by fellow Victorian Edward Lear, whose *A Book of Nonsense* (1846) preceded the Alice books by two decades. It is perhaps in his nonsense that one can see the connection between Reverend Dodgson, the mathematician, and Lewis Carroll, the writer. Nonsense is self-referential; that is, it lacks "sense," if sense means a relationship to the world outside the work of nonsense. It is thus like certain mathematical systems or logic games. Carroll's works are in fact games, which is one of the reasons for their appeal to children.

ALICE'S ADVENTURES IN WONDERLAND

Lewis Carroll's first novel, *Alice's Adventures in Wonderland*, successfully creates and maintains a dream consciousness. Its dreamlike quality is revealed not merely in its conventional ending, with Alice waking up to discover her adventures in Wonderland were "all a dream"; its episodic movements are dreamlike in that one episode melts into the other and has no necessarily logical connection to the previous. Identities constantly shift: A baby turns into a pig; the Cheshire Cat fades away into a grin. Because the logic of dreams, like the logic of Wonderland, is closed, internal, and self-referential, *Alice's Adventures in Wonderland* resists interpretations that attempt to "explain" the novel by connecting its elements to structures outside it, such as biographical, historical, psychoanalytic, or political interpretations.

The story begins with Alice drowsing while her sister reads a boring book. Alice's attention is arrested by a white rabbit, which she follows, only to fall down a rabbit hole, where she finds a world where nothing is like the world she left. When she eats and drinks the Wonderland foods, she changes drastically in size, becoming small as a mouse, then large as a house. When small, she finds her way into a garden, where she meets a caterpillar, rescues a baby from a mean duchess, attends a mad tea party, plays croquet with the Queen of Hearts, listens to a mock turtle's life story, and attends the trial of the Knave of Hearts. When the angry subjects of the Queen rush at Alice, she awakens to find them to be only, in the real world, falling leaves.

The novel is narrated in the third person, but with limited omniscience, allowing the reader to view Wonderland from Alice's perspective. The creation of the Alice character (though it must be remembered that she is modeled on a real girl of the author's acquaintance) is one of Carroll's most stunning achievements. It is seen immediately in the opening paragraph, which presents her thoughts as she peers into a book her sister is reading; the book bores her because it has no pictures or conversations. This is clearly a child's perspective. Even Alice's precipitous changes in size reflect the point of view of children who are given contradictory messages: that they are too big for some things and too little for others. Alice is the most fully realized of the characters in the book, all others being functionally flat. The flatness of the characters is essential to the humor of the book, particularly the slapstick elements, for the whimsy of the Mad Hatter and the March Hare dunking the Dormouse in a teapot is lost if we sympathize with the Dormouse as a real character with feelings.

Through the Looking-Glass and What Alice Found There

Carroll's second novel is a sequel to the first, with the same main character. This time the "wonderland" is the looking-glass world, the world one sees when one looks in a mirror, a reverse image of the real world. As a photographer who needed to visualize finished photographs from their negative images, Carroll had an intuitive understanding of the implications of a "reverse" world. The consciousness of his "abnormality" of being a left-handed boy may also have played into the creation of *Through the Looking-Glass and What Alice Found There.*

In the novel's opening chapter, Alice passes through a mirror to find a house precisely the reverse of her own. She goes out into the garden, where she meets the Red Queen, then to the surrounding country, where she encounters strange insects, Tweedledee and Tweedledum, the White Queen, Humpty Dumpty, the lion and the unicorn, and the White Knight. In chapter 9, Alice becomes queen, and she upsets the board of chess pieces in a transition from dream to waking precisely like that of the first *Alice* book. The transition is handled in two truncated chapters, one of fifty-nine words, in which Alice shakes the Red Queen, and one of only six words, in which the Red Queen turns out to be Alice's kitten, and she is awake. The final chapter is an epilogue, in which Alice poses an unanswered question on the relation of dream to reality.

Sylvie and Bruno

Carroll's last two novels were not as successful commercially as the Alice books, and, according to their earliest critics, they were unsuccessful artistically as well. Carroll continues to play with dreams and reality in the Sylvie and Bruno books, but this time waking and dream realities are interlaced in alternating chapters. In place of Wonderland or the looking-glass world, *Sylvie and Bruno* puts forth "the eerie state," in which one becomes aware of fairies. Thus, *Sylvie and Bruno* has two parallel plots: In the waking world, which Carroll's introduction calls "the ordinary state," there is a love triangle. The noble and selfless Dr. Arthur Forester loves Lady Muriel Orme but believes that she loves her cousin, Captain Eric Linden. The cousins, in fact, become engaged, but there is a grave religious impediment: Eric is not a Christian. The novel ends with Arthur accepting a medical post in India so as not to stand in Eric's way. Simultaneously in the fairy or "eerie" realm parallel to the human one of Arthur, Eric, and Muriel, Sylvie and Bruno are innocent fairy children of the Warden of Outland. This plot is a version of the ancient myth and fairy-tale motif of the disguised god or king. The Warden temporarily abandons his rule in order to travel the kingdom disguised as a beggar. In his absence, his wicked brother Sibimet conspires with his wife and selfish son Uggug to take over Outland.

Sylvie and Bruno Concluded

In the sequel to *Sylvie and Bruno*, the interactions between the fairy realm of Outland and the human realm of Arthur and Muriel are more causally connected, as Sylvie and

Bruno work "behind the scenes" to bring the true lovers together. Sylvie, in fact, appears to be the fairyland identity of Muriel. Through the invisible ministry of Sylvie and Bruno, Arthur and Muriel are married, but shortly after the wedding Arthur must go off to combat a plague in a nearby town. Muriel reads a false account of the death of Arthur from the plague, and Arthur, ironically, is rescued by Eric, who has come to accept the Christian faith and sees his assistance to a would-be rival as divinely directed. Meanwhile, the Warden (Arthur's counterpart) returns to Outland, thwarts Sibimet (Eric's counterpart), who repents, and regains his kingdom.

Perhaps it is no surprise that the human characters in both Sylvie and Bruno books are the least believable. They are the hackneyed stock characters of sentimental romance, though no worse than others of the same genre. As in the Alice books, the title characters, Sylvie and Bruno, are the more remarkable creations, though readers may have difficulty with the cloying baby talk of the fairies and the effusive affection they lavish on one another. Sylvie and Bruno are emblems of childlike innocence, which Carroll also tried to capture in the Alice books and in his photography.

John R. Holmes

OTHER MAJOR WORKS

SHORT FICTION: "Bruno's Revenge," 1867.

POETRY: *Phantasmagoria, and Other Poems*, 1869; *The Hunting of the Snark: An Agony in Eight Fits*, 1876; *Rhyme? and Reason?*, 1883; *Three Sunsets, and Other Poems*, 1898; *For "The Train": Five Poems and a Tale*, 1932; *The Collected Verse of Lewis Carroll*, 1932 (also known as *The Humorous Verse of Lewis Carroll*, 1960).

NONFICTION: *A Syllabus of Plane Algebraical Geometry*, 1860; *An Elementary Treatise on Determinants*, 1867; *Euclid and His Modern Rivals*, 1879; *Twelve Months in a Curatorship*, 1884; *Three Months in a Curatorship*, 1886; *The Game of Logic*, 1887; *Curiosa Mathematica, Part I: A New Theory of Parallels*, 1888; *Curiosa Mathematica, Part II: Pillow Problems Thought During Wakeful Hours*, 1893; *Symbolic Logic, Part I: Elementary*, 1896; *Feeding the Mind*, 1907; *The Diaries of Lewis Carroll*, 1954; *The Unknown Lewis Carroll*, 1961; *The Magic of Lewis Carroll*, 1973; *The Letters of Lewis Carroll*, 1979 (Morton N. Cohen, editor); *The Oxford Pamphlets, Leaflets, and Circulars of Charles Lutwidge Dodgson*, Vol. 1, 1993; *The Mathematical Pamphlets of Charles Lutwidge Dodgson and Related Pieces*, 1994.

CHILDREN'S LITERATURE: *A Tangled Tale*, 1885; *"The Rectory Umbrella" and "Mischmasch,"* 1932; *The Pig-Tale*, 1975.

BIBLIOGRAPHY

Blake, Kathleen. *Play, Games, and Sport: The Literary Works of Lewis Carroll.* Ithaca, N.Y.: Cornell University Press, 1974. Very insightful study of Carroll's work focuses primarily on the Alice books, *Sylvie and Bruno*, and *The Hunting of the Snark*. Emphasis is placed on systems of logic and language constructions. Supplemented by an index.

Bloom, Harold, ed. *Lewis Carroll's Alice's Adventures in Wonderland*. New York: Chelsea House, 2006. Collection of essays about the novel includes analysis of Alice's identity, elements of folklore and fairy tales in the work, and its treatment of love and death. Includes bibliography and index.

Carroll, Lewis. *The Annotated Alice*. Introduction and notes by Martin Gardner. 1960. Definitive ed. New York: W. W. Norton, 2000. Features abundant marginal notes that explain references in the Alice tales and *The Hunting of the Snark*, linking them to Carroll's life, events and controversies in Victorian England, and mathematics. Also includes reproductions of the works' original illustrations.

Cohen, Morton N. *Lewis Carroll: A Biography*. New York: Random House, 1995. Detailed work by an author who devoted more than three decades to Carroll scholarship. Using Carroll's letters and diaries, Cohen has provided what many regard as a definitive biography. Illustrated with more than one hundred of Carroll's photographs and drawings.

Collingwood, Stuart Dodgson. *The Life and Letters of Lewis Carroll*. New York: Century, 1899. As Carroll's nephew, Collingwood had firsthand knowledge of his uncle's life, and this biographical work is accordingly full of anecdotes. The letters quoted in the text often exemplify Carroll's dexterity with humor.

De la Mare, Walter. *Lewis Carroll*. London: Faber & Faber, 1932. Well-written volume places Carroll in historical context and analyzes the different genres he utilized. Contains a detailed discussion of the two Alice books and a brief treatment of other works. Supplemented by an index and a bibliography.

Gray, Donald J., ed. *Alice in Wonderland*. New York: W. W. Norton, 1992. Provides an ideal starting point for those interested in examining Carroll's novel. In addition to extensive background and critical essays, includes helpful annotations on the two Alice novels. Many of the best essays from other collections are reprinted here, making this a reference work of first resort.

Jones, Jo Elwyn, and J. Francis Gladstone. *The Alice Companion: A Guide to Lewis Carroll's Alice Books*. New York: New York University Press, 1998. Full of information and commentary on the people and places that make up Carroll's and Alice Liddell's world in mid-nineteenth century Oxford. Also an excellent source of information regarding the extensive literature on this period in Carroll's life.

_______. *The Red King's Dream: Or, Lewis Carroll in Wonderland*. London: Jonathan Cape, 1995. Places Carroll within his life and times through the discussion of his literary milieu, friends, and influences. Includes bibliographical references and index.

Leach, Karoline. *In the Shadow of the Dreamchild: A New Understanding of Lewis Carroll*. Chester Springs, Pa.: Peter Owen, 1999. Uses findings from new research to argue that many of the long-standing assumptions about Carroll—concerning his exclusively child-centered and unworldly life, his legendary obsession with Alice Liddell, and his supposedly unnatural sexuality—are nothing more than myths.

Pudney, John. *Lewis Carroll and His World*. London: Thames and Hudson, 1976. Historical study of Carroll and his culture is both insightful and broad in scope. Features more than one hundred illustrations as well as a chronology, a select bibliography, and an index.

Thomas, Donald. *Lewis Carroll: A Portrait with Background*. London: John Murray, 1996. Thomas surmises the formative influences on Carroll's personality and intellect as he describes Victorian England. An invaluable guide for readers who want to understand how manners and ideas changed during Carroll's lifetime.

G. K. CHESTERTON

Born: London, England; May 29, 1874
Died: Beaconsfield, Buckinghamshire, England; June 14, 1936
Also known as: Gilbert Keith Chesterton

PRINCIPAL LONG FICTION

The Napoleon of Notting Hill, 1904
The Man Who Was Thursday: A Nightmare, 1908
The Ball and the Cross, 1909
The Innocence of Father Brown, 1911
Manalive, 1912
The Flying Inn, 1914
The Wisdom of Father Brown, 1914
The Incredulity of Father Brown, 1926
The Return of Don Quixote, 1926
The Secret of Father Brown, 1927
The Floating Admiral, 1931 (with others)
The Scandal of Father Brown, 1935
Basil Howe: A Story of Young Love, 2001 (wr. 1894)

OTHER LITERARY FORMS

G. K. Chesterton was a prolific writer, and in addition to novels he produced works in numerous other genres. Throughout his life he wrote poetry; his first two published books were poetical works. He also produced short fiction, especially detective stories. In addition, he wrote plays, but he was not always comfortable in the medium of drama, as he was at heart an essayist. He published a large number of nonfiction works in such areas as autobiography, biography, essays, history, and literary criticism.

ACHIEVEMENTS

Among the primary achievements of G. K. Chesterton's long writing career are the wide range of subjects he wrote about, the large number of genres he employed, and the sheer volume of publications he produced. Chesterton was primarily a journalist and essayist who wrote articles, book reviews, and essays for newspapers and periodicals. In addition to these pieces, however, he also wrote poetry, biographies, plays, history, and literary criticism as well as novels and short stories.

In his approach to fiction Chesterton rejected the "modern realistic short story" and the realistic novel. Instead, in the first instance, he turned to the detective short story and wrote extensively on its legitimacy as a literary art form. Chesterton himself helped to develop the definition of the detective story; he contended that it was the sole popular literary struc-

G. K. Chesterton
(Library of Congress)

ture expressing "some sense of the poetry of modern life," and he helped to popularize detective fiction with his fifty-one Father Brown stories and short novels.

As a novelist, Chesterton argued that "sensational novels are the most moral part of modern fiction." He liked tales about death, secret groups, theft, adventure, and fantasy. There was no genre in his day that embraced his ideas, and so he crafted his own literary structure, the "fantastic novel." In his novels Chesterton stressed such themes and issues as family, science versus religion, moral and political integrity, and local patriotism versus empire building. He also introduced such subthemes as the common man, nature, and womanhood. Above all, Chesterton's novels illustrate his "love of ideas."

BIOGRAPHY

Gilbert Keith Chesterton was born in London on May 29, 1874, to a middle-class family. His father, Edward, was an estate agent who liked literature and art, and his mother, Marie, was the daughter of a Wesleyan lay preacher. Both parents were Unitarians, but they baptized their son in the Anglican Church. Chesterton attended the Colet Court preparatory school and then, in 1887, went to St. Paul's School. His academic record was not good, but he finally began to demonstrate literary capability as a member of the Junior Debating Club, which he and some of his fellow students established during the summer of 1890. Two years later he won the Milton Prize for his poem "St. Francis Xavier."

From 1892 to 1895, Chesterton attended the Slade School to study art and took some courses in French, English, and Latin at University College, London. He did not do well, however, except in his English courses, and he left the Slade School in 1895 without taking a degree. For the next six years he worked in publishing houses, reading authors' manuscripts, and at night he did his own writing. In 1900 his first two books appeared, *Greybeards at Play: Literature and Art for Old Gentlemen—Rhymes and Sketches* and *The Wild Knight, and Other Poems*, both works of poetry. The next year he began to submit articles regularly to the *Speaker* and the *Daily News* and thus started a career as a journalist that was to last until his death. He became known for his opposition to the Boer War and his support of small nations.

In 1901 Chesterton married Frances Blogg after a courtship of five years. The couple lived first in London, and then in 1909 they moved to Beaconsfield, forty miles outside London. They had no offspring, but they enjoyed the company of the children of their friends, relatives, and neighbors.

In 1904 Chesterton's first novel, *The Napoleon of Notting Hill*, was published, and by 1914 he had written five more novels and numerous other works, including biographies (*Robert Browning*, 1903; *Charles Dickens: A Critical Study*, 1906), as well as *Heretics* (1905), which criticized what he saw as the mistakes of some contemporary writers, *Orthodoxy* (1908), a defense and support of Christianity, and a study of his friend and disputant, *George Bernard Shaw* (1909). In 1911 the first of his volumes of detective stories appeared, featuring a Catholic priest, Father Brown, as the sleuth.

Chesterton wrote his best work prior to 1914; in November of that year he became gravely ill with a form of dropsy, and it was not until June of the following year that he recovered. During the years after World War I, he traveled, visiting Palestine, the United States, Poland, and Italy. In 1922 he became a Roman Catholic, a faith that had attracted him for some time, as is reflected in his writing. The most notable nonfiction works of his later years are *The Everlasting Man* (1925) and another biography, *St. Thomas Aquinas* (1933). Chesterton's health declined during the first half of 1936, and on June 14 he died in Beaconsfield.

Analysis

Between 1904 and 1927, G. K. Chesterton wrote six full-length novels, not including the long Father Brown mysteries. All of them stressed the sensational, and they illustrated life as a fight and a battle. Chesterton thought that literature should portray life as perilous rather than as something listless. Tales of death, robbery, and secret groups interested him, and he did not think that what he called the "tea table twaddle" type of novels approached the status of significant art. The sensational story "was the moral part of fiction."

Fantasy was an important part of Chesterton's novels, and the methodology used in his long fiction emphasized adventure, suspense, fantasy, characterization, satire, narrative technique, and humor. He needed a medium to employ these techniques, so he produced the "fantastic novel." Fanstasy also involves ideas, and in all Chesterton's novels ideas are a central, indispensable feature.

Chesterton's novels served as vehicles for the dissemination of whatever his political and social ideas were at the time, and to this extent they were propagandistic. His critics have had difficulty in deciding the merits of his various writings in terms of separating propaganda from literary art. Often Chesterton used allegory as a device for conveying his controversial ideas. Critic Ian Boyd has called Chesterton's works of long fiction "political fables, parables, and allegories or more simply and conveniently . . . novels."

In Chesterton's novels, the state of bachelorhood predominates; this situation is appropriate, since this status is a fundamental element of adventure. Moreover, women rarely appear in any significant roles in his long fiction. There is no female character in his first novel, *The Napoleon of Notting Hill*, and the woman in *The Man Who Was Thursday* is a passing character. In *The Ball and the Cross* and *The Flying Inn*, women are minor figures, but they do play significant roles in *Manalive* and *The Return of Don Quixote*, works that are more involved with the family and society.

The weakest of Chesterton's nondetective novels are perhaps *Manalive*, published in 1912, and *The Return of Don Quixote*, which appeared in 1927. In *The Return of Don Quixote*, Chesterton concludes that the only good future for England involves "a remarriage" of the country with the Catholic Church, as was the case in the Middle Ages. The first three of Chesterton's novels, published from 1904 to 1909, are widely considered his best.

The Napoleon of Notting Hill

The Napoleon of Notting Hill is Chesterton's first novel. The first two chapters are distinct from the main plot, the first being an essay on prophecy showing the author working in a genre that was always congenial to him. The next chapter concerns a luncheon discussion among three government clerks and the former president of Nicaragua, Juan del Fuego. The content of their talk brings out one of the main themes of the novel, "the sanctity of small nations," a concept dear to Chesterton that stemmed from his opposition to the Boer War.

The subsequent death of del Fuego eliminates him from the work, but one of the three clerks, Auberon Quin, a zany individual and joker, is subsequently selected king in the futuristic utopian England of 1984, where a mild political despotism exists. The monarch is chosen by lot. Once crowned as king, Quin reorganizes the sections of London into separate municipalities and thus re-creates the smallness of medieval cities, complete with costumes and heraldry. Quin then encounters Adam Wayne, first as a youth and then as the serious-minded provost of Notting Hill, one of the municipalities; Wayne has embraced the king's "Charter of Cities" wholeheartedly.

Wayne, however, much to the dismay of the provosts of other London municipalities, refuses to give up a street in his domain, Pump Street, which contains several shops, so that a thoroughfare connecting three boroughs can be built. The result is a war, which Wayne wins by encouraging the patriotism of Pump Street residents and by following excellent strategy, despite being outnumbered by the opposing forces. Quin with his "Charter of Cities" and Wayne in his defense of Notting Hill both illustrate Chesterton's small-nation theme. The concluding chapters of the novel concern London twenty years later, when the powerful and dominant Notting Hill has become corrupt; the corruption causes a revolt of subject municipalities. Wayne fights in the second war but realizes that there is no longer a noble cause involved. Conflict in the novel lies in the confrontation between Wayne and Quin, the fanatic and the joker. Wayne's opponents had accused him of being mad, but Quin asserts that the only sane individuals are himself and Wayne. The last chapter is a discussion between the two men, now dead and in the afterlife, in which Wayne argues that in order to be complete both men needed each other, because the joker was without seriousness and the fanatic lacked laughter.

THE MAN WHO WAS THURSDAY

Chesterton's second novel, *The Man Who Was Thursday*, has been described by some critics as his best. Ronald Knox called it "an extraordinary book written as if the publisher had commissioned him to write something rather like the *Pilgrim's Progress* in the style of the *Pickwick Papers*." Chesterton himself called it a protest against the pessimism of the 1880's, and this protest gives rise to one of two allegories in the novel, a personal one. The other is a public or political allegory concerning an individual's clash with a world conspiracy that does not really exist. The story concerns a young poet, Gabriel Syme, who, wishing to fight a gigantic conspiracy supposedly being plotted by anarchists, joins the police and becomes a member of an undercover squad of detectives.

As a result of a bit of trickery and luck, he becomes a member of the top anarchist council, called the Council of Seven Days because each member has the name of a day of the week. Syme's name is Thursday. The council's leader, named Sunday, is an ambiguous figure. While working to stop a bombing planned for Paris, Thursday discovers that, except for Sunday, all his fellow council members are undercover police detectives. Each had been interviewed by a figure whom nobody saw in a dark room at Scotland Yard. By the conclusion of the novel, it is revealed that Sunday is both the head of the detectives and the leader of the anarchists. Some critics have seemed to think that Chesterton is condoning evil in the novel, but he himself asserted that he is questioning in the novel whether everything is evil and whether one can find good in the pessimism of the age.

THE BALL AND THE CROSS

A review published a year after the publication of *The Ball and the Cross* stated that the novel is about two individuals dueling over "the most vital problem in the world, the truth of Christianity." This work definitely deals with religion and the nature of good and evil, subjects either ignored or addressed ambiguously in Chesterton's first two novels. The book opens with Professor Lucifer depositing a captured Bulgarian monk, Michael, from a flying machine atop the cross and ball of St. Paul's Cathedral in London.

The plot continues with a confrontation between a Catholic highland Scot, Evan McIan, and another Scot, John Turnbull, an atheist and publisher of works on atheism. The two fight a duel over what McIan perceives as an insult to the Virgin Mary. The duelists are constantly interrupted, however; they go through a series of adventures and ultimately become friends. The book ends with the two men in an insane asylum, which is set on fire by a satanic figure. The inmates are led out by a monk, Michael, who had been a prisoner there. Ultimately Turnbull becomes a Christian. The novel contains much symbolism and many allegories. The ball on St. Paul's dome, for example, is the rational and independent world, while the cross represents religion. Martin Gardner views the work as reflecting the clash between St. Augustine's City of God, which in Chesterton's view is the Catholic Church, and the City of Man, which is dominated by Satan. The novel also attacks modern science and accuses modern culture of being "lukewarm."

Allan Nelson

OTHER MAJOR WORKS

SHORT FICTION: *The Tremendous Adventures of Major Brown*, 1903; *The Club of Queer Trades*, 1905; *The Perishing of the Pendragons*, 1914; *The Man Who Knew Too Much, and Other Stories*, 1922; *Tales of the Long Bow*, 1925; *Stories*, 1928; *The Sword of Wood*, 1928; *The Moderate Murder and the Honest Quack*, 1929; *The Poet and the Lunatics: Episodes in the Life of Gabriel Gale*, 1929; *The Ecstatic Thief*, 1930; *Four Faultless Felons*, 1930; *The Paradoxes of Mr. Pond*, 1936; *The Vampire of the Village*, 1947.

PLAYS: *Magic: A Fantastic Comedy*, pr. 1913; *The Judgment of Dr. Johnson*, pb. 1927; *The Surprise*, pb. 1953.

POETRY: *Greybeards at Play: Literature and Art for Old Gentlemen—Rhymes and Sketches*, 1900; *The Wild Knight, and Other Poems*, 1900 (revised 1914); *The Ballad of the White Horse*, 1911; *A Poem*, 1915; *Poems*, 1915; *Wine, Water, and Song*, 1915; *Old King Cole*, 1920; *The Ballad of St. Barbara, and Other Verses*, 1922; *Poems*, 1925; *The Queen of Seven Swords*, 1926; *Gloria in Profundis*, 1927; *Ubi Ecclesia*, 1929; *The Grave of Arthur*, 1930.

NONFICTION: *The Defendant*, 1901; *Robert Louis Stevenson*, 1902 (with W. Robertson Nicoll); *Thomas Carlyle*, 1902; *Twelve Types*, 1902 (revised as *Varied Types*; 1903; also known as *Simplicity and Tolstoy*); *Charles Dickens*, 1903 (with F. G. Kitton); *Leo Tolstoy*, 1903 (with G. H. Perris and Edward Garnett); *Robert Browning*, 1903; *Tennyson*, 1903 (with Richard Garnett); *Thackeray*, 1903 (with Lewis Melville); *G. F. Watts*, 1904; *Heretics*, 1905; *Charles Dickens: A Critical Study*, 1906; *All Things Considered*, 1908; *Orthodoxy*, 1908; *George Bernard Shaw*, 1909 (revised 1935); *Tremendous Trifles*, 1909; *Alarms and*

Discursions, 1910; *The Ultimate Lie*, 1910; *What's Wrong with the World*, 1910; *William Blake*, 1910; *Appreciations and Criticisms of the Works of Charles Dickens*, 1911; *A Defence of Nonsense, and Other Essays*, 1911; *The Future of Religion: Mr. G. K. Chesterton's Reply to Mr. Bernard Shaw*, 1911; *The Conversion of an Anarchist*, 1912; *A Miscellany of Men*, 1912; *Thoughts from Chesterton*, 1913; *The Victorian Age in Literature*, 1913; *The Barbarism of Berlin*, 1914; *London*, 1914 (with Alvin Langdon Coburn); *Prussian Versus Belgian Culture*, 1914; *The Crimes of England*, 1915; *Letters to an Old Garibaldian*, 1915; *The So-Called Belgian Bargain*, 1915; *Divorce Versus Democracy*, 1916; *A Shilling for My Thoughts*, 1916; *Temperance and the Great Alliance*, 1916; *Lord Kitchener*, 1917; *A Short History of England*, 1917; *Utopia of Usurers, and Other Essays*, 1917; *How to Help Annexation*, 1918; *Charles Dickens Fifty Years After*, 1920; *Irish Impressions*, 1920; *The New Jerusalem*, 1920; *The Superstition of Divorce*, 1920; *The Uses of Diversity*, 1920; *Eugenics and Other Evils*, 1922; *What I Saw in America*, 1922; *Fancies Versus Fads*, 1923; *St. Francis of Assisi*, 1923; *The End of the Roman Road: A Pageant of Wayfarers*, 1924; *The Superstitions of the Sceptic*, 1924; *The Everlasting Man*, 1925; *William Cobbett*, 1925; *The Catholic Church and Conversion*, 1926; *A Gleaming Cohort, Being from the Words of G. K. Chesterton*, 1926; *The Outline of Sanity*, 1926; *Culture and the Coming Peril*, 1927; *Robert Louis Stevenson*, 1927; *Social Reform Versus Birth Control*, 1927; *Do We Agree? A Debate*, 1928 (with George Bernard Shaw); *Generally Speaking*, 1928 (essays); *G. K. C. as M. C., Being a Collection of Thirty-seven Introductions*, 1929; *The Thing*, 1929; *At the Sign of the World's End*, 1930; *Come to Think of It*, 1930; *The Resurrection of Rome*, 1930; *The Turkey and the Turk*, 1930; *All Is Grist*, 1931; *Is There a Return to Religion?*, 1931 (with E. Haldeman-Julius); *Chaucer*, 1932; *Christendom in Dublin*, 1932; *Sidelights on New London and Newer York, and Other Essays*, 1932; *All I Survey*, 1933; *G. K. Chesterton*, 1933 (also known as *Running After One's Hat, and Other Whimsies*); *St. Thomas Aquinas*, 1933; *Avowals and Denials*, 1934; *Explaining the English*, 1935; *The Well and the Shallows*, 1935; *As I Was Saying*, 1936; *Autobiography*, 1936; *The Man Who Was Chesterton*, 1937; *The End of the Armistice*, 1940; *The Common Man*, 1950; *The Glass Walking-Stick, and Other Essays from the "Illustrated London News," 1905-1936*, 1955; *Lunacy and Letters*, 1958; *Where All Roads Lead*, 1961; *The Man Who Was Orthodox: A Selection from the Uncollected Writings of G. K. Chesterton*, 1963; *The Spice of Life, and Other Essays*, 1964; *Chesterton on Shakespeare*, 1971.

EDITED TEXTS: *Thackeray*, 1909; *Samuel Johnson*, 1911 (with Alice Meynell); *Essays by Divers Hands*, 1926.

MISCELLANEOUS: *Stories, Essays, and Poems*, 1935; *The Coloured Lands*, 1938; *The Collected Works of G. K. Chesterton*, 1986-1999 (35 volumes).

BIBLIOGRAPHY

Ahlquist, Dale. *G. K. Chesterton: The Apostle of Common Sense*. San Francisco, Calif.: Ignatius Press, 2003. Provides an introductory overview of Chesterton's life and work designed for general readers, with analyses of some of Chesterton's novels, including books in the Father Brown series. Designed to complement a television series of the same title created by Ahlquist, president of the American Chesterton Society.

Bloom, Harold, ed. *G. K. Chesterton*. New York: Chelsea House, 2006. Collection of essays analyzes various aspects of Chesterton's work, including the author's view of the grotesque and "terror and play" in his imagination. Editor's introduction provides an overview to Chesterton's life and work.

Boyd, Ian. *The Novels of G. K. Chesterton: A Study in Art and Propaganda*. New York: Barnes & Noble Books, 1975. Good study examines Chesterton's major novels as well as his collections of short stories. Discusses the novels chronologically, with a chapter each about novels in his early years, pre-World War I, postwar, and later years.

Clipper, Lawrence J. *G. K. Chesterton*. New York: Twayne, 1974. Useful introduction to the works of Chesterton does a fine job of describing the recurring themes in his fictional and nonfictional writings. Includes informative analysis also of Chesterton's poetry and literary criticism. Contains an excellent annotated bibliography.

Coates, John D. *G. K. Chesterton as Controversialist, Essayist, Novelist, and Critic*. Lewiston, N.Y.: Edwin Mellen Press, 2002. Refutes Chesterton's reputation as a minor writer, maintaining that his detective novels remain important and relevant works. Places Chesterton's fiction within the context of modernism and the Edwardian novel of ideas.

Conlon, D. J., ed. *Chesterton: A Half Century of Views*. New York: Oxford University Press, 1987. Contains numerous short essays on Chesterton published during the first fifty years after his death. The wide diversity of positive critical reactions shows that not only his popular fiction but also his writings on literature and religion continue to fascinate readers.

Hollis, Christopher. *The Mind of Chesterton*. Coral Gables, Fla.: University of Miami Press, 1970. Especially thoughtful study explores above all Chesterton's evolution as a writer before his conversion to Catholicism in 1922. Final chapter, titled "Chesterton and His Survival," explains why Chesterton's work continues to fascinate readers who do not share his religious beliefs.

Lauer, Quentin. *G. K. Chesterton: Philosopher Without Portfolio*. New York: Fordham University Press, 1988. Thought-provoking study addresses Chesterton's philosophical reflections on the uses and limitations of reason, Christian humanism, religious tolerance, and moral values.

Pearce, Joseph. *Wisdom and Innocence: A Life of G. K. Chesterton*. San Francisco, Calif.: Ignatius Press, 1996. Scholarly, well-written biography examines Chesterton's life and provides interesting analysis of many quotations from his works.

Ward, Maisie. *Gilbert Keith Chesterton*. New York: Sheed & Ward, 1943. Well-researched biography remains the essential resource concerning Chesterton. Ward had full access to Chesterton's manuscripts and spoke with many people who had known him personally. Reveals much about his evolution as a writer and the importance of friendship in his life.

Wills, Garry. *Chesterton*. New York: Doubleday, 2001. Biography is an updated edition of Wills's *Chesterton, Man and Mask* (1961), with a new introduction. Wills is a Catholic intellectual and best-selling author who has written several books about religion in the United States.

JOSEPH CONRAD

Jósef Teodor Konrad Nałęcz Korzeniowski

Born: Near Berdyczów, Podolia, Poland (now Berdychiv, Ukraine); December 3, 1857

Died: Oswalds, Bishopsbourne, England; August 3, 1924

Also known as: Jósef Teodor Konrad Nałęcz Korzeniowski

PRINCIPAL LONG FICTION

Almayer's Folly: A Story of an Eastern River, 1895
An Outcast of the Islands, 1896
The Children of the Sea: A Tale of the Forecastle, 1897 (republished as *The Nigger of the Narcissus: A Tale of the Sea*, 1898)
Heart of Darkness, 1899 (serial), 1902 (book)
Lord Jim, 1900
The Inheritors, 1901 (with Ford Madox Ford)
Romance, 1903 (with Ford)
Nostromo: A Tale of the Seaboard, 1904
The Secret Agent, 1907
The Nature of a Crime, 1909 (serial), 1924 (book; with Ford)
Under Western Eyes, 1911
Chance, 1913
Victory: An Island Tale, 1915
The Shadow-Line, 1917
The Arrow of Gold, 1919
The Rescue, 1920
The Rover, 1923
Suspense, 1925 (incomplete)

OTHER LITERARY FORMS

Joseph Conrad's many short stories were published in seven collected editions. The majority of the stories appeared earlier in magazine form, especially in *Blackwood's Magazine*, a periodical that Conrad referred to as "Maga." Of the short stories, three—"Youth," "The Secret Sharer," and "An Outpost of Progress"—have been widely anthologized and are generally recognized as classics of the genre. Two memoirs of Conrad's years at sea, *The Mirror of the Sea* (1906) and *Some Reminiscences* (1912), which is also known as *A Personal Record*, are prime sources of background information on Conrad's sea tales. Conrad wrote three plays: *The Secret Agent* (pb. 1921), a four-act adaptation of his novel that enjoyed a brief success on the London stage; and two short plays, *Laughing Anne* (pb. 1923) and *One Day More* (pr. 1905), which had no success. His oeuvre is rounded out by

Joseph Conrad
(Library of Congress)

two books of essays on widely ranging topics, *Notes on Life and Letters* (1921) and *Last Essays* (1926); a travel book, *Joseph Conrad's Diary of His Journey Up the Valley of the Congo in 1890* (1926); and the aborted novel *The Sisters*, left incomplete at his death in 1924 but published in fragment form in 1928.

ACHIEVEMENTS

In the late twentieth century, Joseph Conrad enjoyed an extraordinary renaissance in readership and in critical attention. Readers and critics alike have come to recognize that although one of Conrad's last novels, *The Rover*, was published in the early 1920's, he is the most modern of writers in both theme and technique.

Conrad is, in fact, the architect of the modern psychological novel, with its emphasis on character and character analysis. For Conrad, people in plot situations, rather than plot situations themselves, are the primary concern. Indeed, Conrad once professed that he was incapable of creating "an effective lie," meaning a plot "that would sell and be admirable." This is something of an exaggeration, but the fact remains that Conrad's novels center on the solitary hero who, either by chance or by choice, is somehow alienated and set apart from his fellow human beings. This theme of isolation and alienation dominates Conrad's novels and spans his work from the early sea tales to the political novels to what Conrad called his "romances."

Conrad's "loners" are manifest everywhere in his work—Jim in *Lord Jim*, Kurtz in *Heart of Darkness*, Razumov in *Under Western Eyes*. This emphasis on the alienated and isolated figure had a considerable impact on the direction of the novel in the twentieth century, and Conrad's influence may be discerned in such disparate writers as Stephen Crane, F. Scott Fitzgerald, and T. S. Eliot.

Conrad made another contribution in shaping the modern novel: He was the forerunner (although not the originator) of two techniques that have found much favor and wide employment in the novel. Conrad was among the first of the modern novelists to employ multiple narrators, or shifting points of view, as he does in *Heart of Darkness* and *Lord Jim*. This technique enabled Conrad to make the probing analyses of characters and their motivations that are the hallmarks both of his work and of the work of so many others to follow. The reader sees both Kurtz and Jim, for example, through several pairs of eyes, some sympathetic, some not, before both tales are turned over to Charlie Marlow, who does his best to sort out the conflicting testimonies and to give the reader objective and rounded views of both men.

The extensive use of the flashback in the modern novel and, indeed, in film, is another technique that Conrad pioneered. In Conrad's case, as is the case with all writers who employ the technique, the flashback creates suspense, but it also serves another and more important function in his work, enabling him to examine more thoroughly the minds and the motivations of his characters. Having presented the crisis or the moment of action or the point of decision, Conrad then goes back in time, in an almost leisurely fashion, and retraces step-by-step the psychological pattern that led to the crisis, to the action, or to the decision.

Finally, Conrad finds a place and a role among the moderns in still another way: He is one of the great Symbolists in English literature. Conrad's use of thoroughly unconventional symbols, related in some way to the metaphysical metaphors to be found in much modern poetry, has had an inestimable influence on the modern novel.

BIOGRAPHY

Joseph Conrad was born Jósef Teodor Konrad Nałęcz Korzeniowski on December 3, 1857, near the rural village of Berdyczów in Poland, under Russian domination. Conrad's mother, Ewa Bobrowski, came from an affluent and influential family of landowners who had made their peace, as best they could, with their Russian overlords. Conrad's father, Apollo Korzeniowski, was a would-be poet, a dedicated patriot, and a translator of William Shakespeare into Polish who found no peace in Russian Poland. The marriage of

Apollo and Ewa was frowned upon by the Bobrowskis, who felt that Ewa had married beneath herself, and Ewa's brother, Tadeusz, a prominent lawyer and member of the landed gentry, seldom missed an opportunity to remind his nephew, Jósef, that he bore the tainted Nałęcz blood.

Apollo Korzeniowski devoted all his energies and, ultimately, his life to the Polish freedom movement. As a result of his political activities, he was labeled an enemy of the state and exiled to Vologda in northern Russia. The five-year-old Jósef and his mother followed Apollo into exile. Three years later, her health ruined by the fierce Russian winters, Ewa Korzeniowski died, and Apollo, equally weakened by the ordeal, succumbed four years after his wife. There is little doubt that Conrad's own lifelong precarious physical state had its genesis in these years in exile.

From these blighted early years, two convictions were impressed in Conrad's consciousness that surfaced in his work: a continuing hatred for all things Russian and for autocratic regimes, and a strong sense of man as victim, instilled by his father's fate, and of man's essential loneliness and isolation, instilled by his own orphanage at the age of twelve. The victimization of the innocent lies at the heart of Conrad's political novels, especially *Under Western Eyes* and *The Secret Agent*, and is a major theme in *Heart of Darkness*. The alienated figure, forced to cope as best he can alone, is the essential Conrad.

With the deaths of Apollo and Ewa Korzeniowski, Conrad came under the tutelage of his concerned but somewhat demanding maternal uncle, Tadeusz Bobrowski. Bobrowski, a man of many affairs and very positive ideas and ideals, sent his young ward to St. Anne's School in Kraków for a brief term and later provided Conrad with a tutor and companion in the hope of creating a proper Polish gentleman. These few years constituted the extent of Conrad's formal education. An avid reader from his early childhood, Conrad was largely self-educated, and the wide knowledge of English, French, and Russian literature apparent in his works (especially in his critical essays) was acquired through his own efforts.

Bobrowski's hopes and plans for Conrad's becoming an accepted member of the right circles in Polish society were not to be realized. Chafing under the regimen of his oversolicitous uncle and, perhaps, convinced that there was no place for Apollo Korzienowski's son in Russian Poland, Conrad finally persuaded his reluctant uncle that his future lay elsewhere: at sea, a dream with which Conrad had been obsessed since seeing the Adriatic during a walking tour of northern Italy in 1873.

In 1874, Conrad left Poland for the port city of Marseilles, France, and the seaman's life to which he would devote the next twenty years. He carried with him his uncle's begrudging blessing and, more important, considerable financial support. The break with his native land was to be more complete than Conrad may have realized at the time, since he returned to Poland on only three occasions during the remainder of his life.

Conrad's adventures and misadventures during his four years in and about Marseilles provided the material, many years later, for the almost lyrical memoir *The Mirror of the Sea* and the novel *The Arrow of Gold*, the latter of which has been the subject of much critical dispute. With his uncle's backing, Conrad acquired, during that time, part ownership of the bark *Tremolino*, which was then employed in smuggling arms for the Spanish Pretender, Don Carlos. It was a period of much intrigue, and Conrad appears to have been at the center, enjoying it hugely.

What is not clear about the Marseilles years, unless one accepts Conrad's highly fictionalized version of the events in *The Arrow of Gold*, is how his ventures at that time all came to a disastrous end. Conrad apparently invested a considerable sum of money in a quixotic mining venture. Moreover, if the Doña Rita of *The Arrow of Gold* did, in fact, exist as Conrad describes her in the novel, then a particularly painful and hopeless love affair complicated Conrad's desperate financial straits. In any event, in February, 1878, Conrad attempted suicide and almost succeeded by placing a bullet in his chest, very near the heart.

Uncle Tadeusz made a hasty trip to Marseilles and restored some kind of order to Conrad's tangled affairs, and, on April 24, 1878, Conrad signed on to the British ship *Mavis*, bound from Marseilles to England. Conrad's career as a seaman—more particularly, as a British seaman—had begun. In the next twenty years, sailing on a variety of ships on passages that encompassed half the globe, Conrad accomplished an incredible feat. An alien from a landlocked country, bearing an unpronounceable foreign name and speaking English with a strong Slavic-French accent, Conrad rose from able seaman to master mariner in the British Merchant Service. He took great pride in being addressed as Captain Korzeniowski, just as he took great pride in his British citizenship, acquired in 1885.

Many of the ships on which Conrad sailed make appearances in his works. For example, there actually was a *Narcissus* on which Conrad sailed from Bombay to Dunkirk and a *Palestine* that became the *Judea* of "Youth"; the SS *Roi des Belges* was the counterpart of Marlow's "tinpot" steamboat in *Heart of Darkness*. In similar fashion, many of Conrad's characters are based on real-life prototypes, men whom Conrad had encountered or of whom he had heard while at sea. These include the characters Jim, MacWhirr, Almayer, Axel Heyst, and Tom Lingard; the real-life Charlie Marlow was born Jósef Korzeniowski.

In 1889, while between ships in London, Conrad began work on the strange tale of Kaspar Almayer. The work continued sporadically during Conrad's six-month tour in the Belgian Congo in 1890, a sojourn that later provided the material for his first major work, *Heart of Darkness*, and also succeeded in further undermining his already unstable health. In 1893, Conrad, then first mate of the ship *Torrens*, showed the nine completed chapters of *Almayer's Folly* to an English passenger and was encouraged to finish the book. *Almayer's Folly* was published in 1895, to be followed by *An Outcast of the Islands* in 1896, *The Nigger of the Narcissus* in 1897, *Heart of Darkness* (in serial form) in 1899, and *Lord Jim* in 1900.

Conrad enjoyed almost immediate critical acclaim, but despite the string of critical successes, he had only a modest public following. In fact, Conrad did not have a best seller until 1913, with *Chance.* Ironically, the reading public did not find Conrad until after he had written his best work. Given this limited popular success, Conrad did not feel secure enough to devote himself entirely to a writing career, and, for a six-year period, 1889 to 1895, he vacillated between the safety of a master's berth aboard ship and the uncertainty of his writing table. Even as late as 1898, when he was well established with a publisher and several reputable magazines were eager for his work, Conrad seriously considered returning to the sea.

With his marriage to Jessie George in 1894, Conrad had, in effect, returned from the sea and settled down to a life of hectic domesticity and long, agonizing hours of writing. Jessie, an unassuming, maternal woman, was the perfect mate for the often unpredictable, volatile, and ailing Conrad, and she cheerfully nursed him through his frequent attacks of malaria, gout, and deep depression. The marriage produced two sons, Borys and John, and lasted until Conrad's death.

Except for a brief trip to his native Poland in 1914, a few holidays on the Continent, and an even briefer trip to the United States in 1923, Conrad was resigned to the endless hours at his desk and content to live the life of an English gentleman in his adopted land. The Conrads were something of a nomadic family, however, moving frequently whenever Conrad tired of one of their rented dwellings. His last five years were spent at Oswalds, Bishopsbourne, near Canterbury.

After World War I, the acclaim and the recognition that he had so richly earned finally came to Conrad—an offer of knighthood (which he declined) and the friendship and the respect of many of the literary greats of the time. Essentially a very private man, Conrad, while never denying his Polish origins or renouncing his Roman Catholic faith, tried to live the quiet life of the quintessential English country squire. There was always, however, something of the foreigner about him—the monocle, the Continental-style greatcoat, the slightly Asian eyes, the click of the heels and the formal bow from the waist—which did not go unnoticed among his English friends and neighbors. Like so many of the characters in his novels, Conrad remained somehow apart and alienated from the mainstream of the life about him.

On August 3, 1924, Conrad succumbed to a massive heart attack at his home near Bishopsbourne. He is buried in the cemetery at Canterbury, in—according to the parish register of St. Thomas's Church—"that part reserved for Catholics." Even in death, Conrad, like so many of his fictional creations, found himself alone and apart.

ANALYSIS

Three themes are dominant among Joseph Conrad's sea tales, considered by most critics as his best work. The first of these themes is an unremitting sense of loyalty and duty to the ship; this quality is exemplified by Conrad's seamen who are successful in practicing their craft. In *The Mirror of the Sea*, Conrad summarizes this necessity for keeping faith, as he also does through Singleton, the exemplar of the faithful seaman in *The Nigger of the Narcissus*, in observing, "Ships are all right. It's the men in them." The note of fidelity is struck again in *A Personal Record*, when Conrad says of his years at sea, "I do not know whether I have been a good seaman, but I know I have been a very faithful one." Conversely, it is the men who break faith—Jim is the prime example—who fail and who are doomed to be set apart.

A second major theme in the sea tales, noted by virtually all of Conrad's critics, is the therapeutic value of work. To Conrad, the ancient adage "Idle hands are the devil's workshop" was not a cliché but a valid principle. The two most damning words in Conrad's lexicon are "undisciplined" and "lazy," and, again, it is the men whose hands and minds are without meaningful employment who get into difficulties, who fail, and who suffer the Conradian penalty for failure, alienation and isolation. Kurtz, in *Heart of Darkness*, is Conrad's chief exemplar here, but Jim's failure, too, partially results from the fact that he has very little to do in the way of work during the crucial passage aboard the *Patna*.

Finally, a sense of tradition, of one's place in the long continuum of men who have gone to sea, is a recurring theme in Conrad's sea tales. Marlow expresses this sense of tradition best when he speaks of the faithful seamen who band together and are bonded together in what he calls "the fellowship of the craft." The Jims, on the other hand, the captains who display cowardice, the seamen who panic under stress, all those who bring disgrace on the men who have kept faith and do keep faith, are dismissed from the fellowship and are set apart, isolated and alienated. Conrad, then, played a central role in setting the stage for the alienated, solitary figures and, ultimately, the rebels-at-arms who people the pages of the modern novel.

HEART OF DARKNESS

In *Heart of Darkness*, the first of Conrad's recognized masterpieces and one of the greatest novellas in the English language, a number of familiar Conradian themes and techniques coalesce: the author's detestation of autocratic regimes and their special manifestation, colonialism; the characteristic Conradian alien figure, isolated and apart; the therapeutic value of work; and the use of multiple points of view and of strikingly unconventional symbols.

Charlie Marlow, the ostensible narrator of the story, finds himself (as Conrad did on occasion during his sea career) without a ship and with few prospects. As a last resort, he signs on to command a river steamboat for a Belgian trading company, then seeking ivory in the Congo. In a curious way, Marlow's venture into the Congo represents a wish fulfillment, since, Marlow recalls, as a child he had placed his finger on a map of Africa and said, "Someday, I will go there," "there" being the Congo. (This is "autobiography as fiction" again in that Conrad himself had once expressed such a desire and in exactly the terms Marlow employs.)

The mature Marlow, however, has few illusions about what he is undertaking. He characterizes his "command" as "a two-penny-half-penny river-steamboat with a penny whistle attached," and he is quite aware that he will be working for a company whose chief concern is turning a profit, and a large one at that. Moreover, the Company's success will come only at the expense of the innocent and helpless natives who have the misfortune of living in an area that has immense possibilities as a colony.

Marlow, like Conrad, abhors the concept of one people dominating another unless, as he says, the colonizing power is faithful to the "idea" that provides the sole rationale for colonialism—that is, the "idea" of actually bringing the benefits of civilization to the colonized. He believes that only in the British Crown Colonies is the "idea" being adhered to, and he has grave reservations about what he will find in the Congo. Despite these reservations, Marlow is hardly prepared for what awaits him.

Marlow finds in the Congo disorder bordering on lunacy, waste, intrigue, inefficiency, and the cruelest kind of exploitation. The "pilgrims of progress," as Marlow calls them, go about their aimless and pointless tasks while the steamboat he is to command sits idle in the river with a hole in its bottom. Mountains are leveled to no purpose, while equipment and supplies rust or rot in the African sun or never reach their destination. As long as the ivory flows from the heart of darkness, however, no one is overly concerned. Marlow is appalled by the hypocrisy of the situation. An entire continent is being ruthlessly ravaged and pillaged in the name of progress, when, in fact, the real motivation is sheer greed. Nor is there the slightest concern for the plight of the natives in the Company's employ. Marlow sees once proud and strong tribesmen, divorced from their natural surroundings and from all that is familiar to them, sickened and weakened, sitting passively in the shade waiting to die.

Herein is Marlow/Conrad's chief objection to colonialism. By taking people from their normal mode of life and thrusting upon them a culture that they neither want nor understand, colonialism places people in isolation and makes them aliens in their own land. The cannibals who serve as woodcutters for Marlow's steamboat have lost their muscle tone and belong back in the jungle practicing the peculiar rites that, however revolting by other standards, are natural for them. The native fireman on the steamboat—"an improved specimen," Marlow calls him—watches the water gauge on the boiler, lest the god inside become angry. He sits, his teeth filed, his head shaved in strange patterns, a voodoo charm tied to his arm, a piece of polished bone inserted through his lower lip. He represents the perfect victim of the white man's progress, and "he ought to have been clapping his hands and stamping his feet on the bank."

The evil that colonialism has wrought is not, however, confined to the natives. The whites who seek adventure or fortune in the Congo are equally uprooted from all that is natural for them, equally isolated and alienated. The doctor who gives Marlow a perfunctory examination in the Company's headquarters in Brussels asks apologetically for permission to measure Marlow's head while, at the same time, noting that the significant changes will occur "inside." To some degree or other, such changes have come to the whites whom Marlow encounters in Africa. The ship on which Marlow sails to the Congo passes a French gunboat firing aimlessly into the jungle as an object lesson to the natives. The accountant at the Central Station makes perfectly correct entries in his impeccable ledgers while just outside his window, in the grove of death, the mass of displaced natives is dying of fever and malnutrition. The Company's brick maker makes no bricks because there has been no straw for more than a year, but he remains placid and unconcerned.

Marlow's summation of what he has seen in the Congo is acerbic, withering in its emotional intensity, but it is also an accurate statement of Conrad's feelings toward this, the cruelest exercise of autocratic power. Marlow says, "It was just robbery with violence, aggravated murder on a great scale . . . and with no more moral purpose at the back of it than there is in burglars breaking into a safe." The voice is Charlie Marlow's, but the sentiments are Joseph Conrad's.

One man alone among the Company's disreputable, if not depraved, white traders appears to be an exception, a man who is faithful to the "idea" and is bringing progress and betterment to the natives in exchange for the ivory he gathers. Kurtz is by far the Company's most productive trader, and his future in Brussels seems assured. At the same time, Kurtz is both hated and feared by all the Europeans in the Company's employ. He is hated because of the unconventional (an ironic adjective) methods he has adopted, and he is feared because these methods are apparently working.

With the introduction of Kurtz into the tale, Conrad works by indirection. Neither Marlow nor the reader is allowed to see Kurtz immediately. Rather, one is exposed to Kurtz through many different viewpoints, and, in an effort to allow the reader to see Kurtz from all perspectives, Conrad brings forth other narrators to take over the story briefly: the accountant, the brick maker, the manager of the Central Station, the Russian. Penultimately, Marlow himself serves as narrator, and ultimately, Kurtz's fiancé, the Intended. In addition to the many shifting points of view that Conrad employs, it should be noted that the story, from beginning to end, is told by a dual narrator. Charlie Marlow speaks, but Marlow's unnamed crony, the fifth member of the group gathered on the fantail of the *Nellie*, is the actual narrator of the story, retelling the tale as he has heard it from Marlow. In some sense, then, it is difficult to say whether *Heart of Darkness* is Kurtz's story or Marlow's story or the anonymous narrator's story, since Marlow's tale has obviously had a significant impact on the silent listener.

Marlow is fascinated by Kurtz and what his informants tell him of Kurtz, and throughout the long journey upriver to the Inner Station, he is obsessed with meeting this remarkable man, but he is destined for a shocking disappointment. Kurtz is perhaps the extreme example among all the isolated and alienated figures to be found in Conrad's works. Philosophically and spiritually alienated from the "pilgrims of progress," he is also physically isolated. He is the only white man at the Inner Station, and, given the steamboat debacle, nothing has been heard from or of him for months. He has been alone too long, and the jungle has found him out. He is, in Marlow's words, "a hollow man" with great plans and hopes but totally lacking in the inner resources vital for survival in an alien environment. As a result, he has regressed completely to the primitive state; he has become a god to the natives, who worship him in the course of "unspeakable rites." He has taken a native woman as a consort, and the Russian trader who tried to befriend him has been relegated to fool and jester in Kurtz's jungle court. Kurtz exercises absolute power of life and death over the natives, and he punishes his enemies by placing their severed heads on poles about his hut as ornaments. The doctor in Brussels, Marlow recalls, was fearful of what physical and spiritual isolation might do to people's minds, and on Kurtz, the effect has been devastating. Kurtz is mentally unbalanced, but even worse, as Marlow says, "His soul was mad."

Marlow has confessed that he, too, has heard the appeal of "the fascination of the abomination," the strange sounds and voices emanating from the banks of the river as the steamboat makes its way to Kurtz. Meaningless and unintelligible as the sounds and voices are, they are also somehow familiar to Marlow and strike deep at some primordial instinct within him. Yet, while Kurtz is destroyed, Marlow survives, "luckily, luckily," as he observes. The difference between the two men is restraint, a recurrent term in the novel: With restraint, a man can survive in isolation. The cannibals on the steamboat have it, and Marlow is at a loss to explain the phenomenon. The manager at the Central Station also has it, largely the result of his unfailing good health, which permits him to serve, virtually unscathed, term after term in the darkness. The accountant has restraint by virtue of concentrating on his correct entries in his meticulous ledgers and, at the same time, by forfeiting his humanity and closing his mind to the chaos around him.

Chiefly, however, restraint (in Conrad's worldview) is a function of work, and Conrad's major statement of the redeeming nature of work comes in *Heart of Darkness*. Marlow confesses that, like most human beings, he does not like work per se. He does, however, respond to "what is in the work," and he recognizes its salutary effect, "the chance to find yourself." Indeed, the fact that Marlow has work to do in the Congo is his salvation. The steamboat must be salvaged; it must be raised from the bottom of the river. No supplies are available, and the boiler is in disrepair. Marlow needs rivets and sheeting to patch the gaping hole in the boat. The task seems hopeless, but Marlow attacks it enthusiastically, almost joyously, because his preoccupation with rescuing his "two-penny, half-penny" command effectively shields him from "the fascination of the abomination." Later, during the trip upriver to the Inner Station, it is again the work of piloting the vulnerable steamboat around and through the myriad rocks and snags of the convoluted river and the intense concentration required for the work that shut Marlow's eyes and, more important, his mind to the dangers to psyche and spirit surrounding him. Marlow does not leave the Congo completely untouched; he has paid a price, both physically and mentally, for venturing into the darkness, but he does escape with his life and his sanity. As he later recognizes, he owes his escape to the steamboat, his "influential friend," as he calls it, and to the work it provided.

Symbols abound in *Heart of Darkness*, many of them conventional: the interplay of light and darkness throughout the novel, for example, carrying essentially the traditional symbolic meanings of the two terms, or the rusting and decaying equipment Marlow comes across at the Central Station, symbolizing the callous inefficiency of the Company's management. More striking, however, is Conrad's use of thoroughly unconventional symbols; dissimilar images are yoked together in a startling fashion, unique in Conrad's time. Kurtz's totally bald head, for example, is compared to a ball of ivory, and the comparison moves beyond metaphor to the realm of symbol, adumbrating the manner in which the lust for and preoccupation with ivory have turned flesh-and-blood human beings into cold, lifeless ivory figures. There are also the shrunken heads fixed as ornaments on the fence posts surrounding Kurtz's hut. These are Kurtz's "rebels," and, notably, all but one are facing inward, so that, even in death, they are compelled to worship their god. The one facing outward, however, is irretrievably damned and without hope of salvation.

Lord Jim

Similar in many ways to *Heart of Darkness*, *Lord Jim* is considered by many critics to be not only Conrad's greatest sea tale but also his greatest novel. *Lord Jim* is not a sea tale, however, in the purest sense, since most of the action of the novel takes place on land. *Lord Jim* is one of Conrad's psychological studies; Jim's mind and his motivations are searched and probed in meticulous detail in an effort to "see Jim clearly." In making this effort, Conrad employs two characteristic techniques: shifting, multiple points of view and the extensive use of flashbacks.

The narrative begins conventionally with an unnamed third-person narrator who brings the reader to the point of Marlow's first encounter with Jim at the Board of Inquiry investigating the strange case of the pilgrim ship *Patna*. At this point, Marlow takes over the tale, recounting his meeting with Jim. Marlow's account, however, is filtered through the consciousness of the anonymous narrator, much as is the case in *Heart of Darkness*. The manipulation of the narrative voices in *Lord Jim* is much more complex, however, since Jim speaks through Marlow and Marlow through the ultimate narrator.

Again, as in *Heart of Darkness*, other narrators enter the scene briefly, and Marlow gives way to a series of speakers, each of whom is qualified to tell the reader something more about Jim. Montague Brierly, captain of the crack ship *Ossa*, is troubled by Jim's failure to meet the demands of "the fellowship of the craft" and is also troubled by his doubts about his own ability to meet those demands. The French lieutenant who boarded the abandoned *Patna* and brought it safely to port is a bit more sympathetic toward Jim's moment of cowardice but is also more rigid in his condemnation of Jim's loss of honor. At the opposite end of the scale, Chester, the preposterous seaman-at-large, dismisses Jim's canceled mate's certificate as nothing more than "a bit of ass's skin" and solicits Marlow's aid in involving Jim in Chester's lunatic scheme of extracting guano from an island that is totally inaccessible. In Chester's view, Jim is the right man for the job, since he is now good for nothing else. Through Chester as interim narrator, Marlow recognizes how desperate Jim's plight is and how equally desperate Jim is for his help.

Marlow does help by putting Jim in touch with Mr. Denver, the owner of a rice mill, and Jim thrives for a time, becoming, in essence, a surrogate son to his employer. The specter of the *Patna* affair overtakes Jim, however, in the form of the fated ship's second engineer, who comes to work at the rice mill. Through Denver, through Egström, who employs Jim briefly as a water clerk, and, finally, through the seedy Schomberg, proprietor of an equally seedy hotel in Bangkok, Marlow learns of Jim's gradual decline and his erratic flight from the *Patna* or, as Marlow puts it, his flight "from himself."

In an attempt to help Jim, Marlow turns to Stein, an extraordinary trader and shrewd judge of both butterflies and people. Stein's eminently "practical" solution is to send Jim to Patusan, virtually the ends of the earth, where the *Patna* has never been heard of and from where Jim need run no more. Marlow's visit to Patusan and to Jim is relayed, as is the bulk of the novel, through the unnamed listener among Marlow's small circle of friends gathered over their evening cigars, to whom Marlow has been addressing his tale. In the final chapters, Conrad's tour de force of narrative technique takes yet another twist. The disaster in Patusan is recounted through the medium of a lengthy letter that Marlow writes to the ultimate narrator, the narration thus coming full circle from third-person narrator, to Marlow, to a series of intermediate narrators, and finally returning to the speaking voice that began the tale.

Adding to the difficulties that Conrad's dizzying shift of narrators presents for the reader is his frequent use of time shifts in the narrative. Jim's long colloquy with Marlow in Marlow's room at the Malabar House, for example, takes the reader back in time to the events aboard the *Patna*, which occurred several months earlier. While observing the seemingly bored Brierly in the courtroom at the Board of Inquiry, Marlow abruptly moves ahead in time to Brierly's suicide, which follows a week after the end of the trial, and then ahead again some two years for the mate's detailed account of Brierly's methodical leap over the side of the *Ossa*. Marlow's letter, which Conrad employs to bring the novel to its close, represents yet another flashback. Examples of this movement back and forth in time in the novel could be multiplied.

Conrad's complex manipulation of his narrators and of the disjointed time sequence of the events of the novel have a single purpose: to give the reader a complete view of a psychologically complex figure. It is an effort, as Marlow insists several times, to "see Jim clearly." Yet, for all Conrad's (and Marlow's) efforts, Jim remains an enigma. Marlow, in fact, confesses at the end of his letter that Jim continues to be "inscrutable."

Two particular problems have plagued critics in coming to grips with Jim. Stein, on whom Marlow relies for enlightenment, pronounces Jim "a romantic," which Stein says is "very bad . . . and very good too." In attempting to resolve the problem of how a romantic may cope with reality, Stein uses the metaphor of a man falling into the sea (the overtones of Jim's leap from the *Patna* are obvious here). Stein continues, "The way is to the destructive element submit yourself, and with the exertions of your hands and feet in the water make the deep, deep sea keep you up." The trouble here is that Stein does not make clear whether it is Jim's dream of heroes and heroics that is the "destructive element" or whether it is the practical and mundane world in which he must endeavor to carry out this dream that is destructive. Does Jim immerse himself in the dream yet keep his head above "water" in the world of reality, or immerse himself in the world of reality and yet keep the dream alive directly above the surface? The critical controversy that Stein's cryptic advice has provoked continues.

Critics are also divided on the meaning of the end of the novel. When Jim presents himself to the old nakhoda, Doramin, and suffers the pistol shot that ends his life, is this the act of a man who has finally accepted that he is capable of failure and who "has mastered his destiny," or is it merely the desperate act of a man who has simply run out of options? The distinction may seem fine, since, in any case, Jim's gesture is a positive act, but it governs the reader's final judgment on whether Marlow is correct in accepting Jim as "one of us."

If Jim is not "one of us," he is clearly one of "them," them being the familiar Conradian figures, the isolated and alienated solitaries, and he is so both spiritually and physically. In abandoning the *Patna*, Jim has violated a cardinal principle of the seaman's code, placing his own safety above that of the pilgrims who have entrusted themselves to him. As Brierly puts it, "We are trusted," and he is unforgiving of Jim's dereliction, as is Marlow, although Marlow is willing to admit mitigating circumstances. To the seamen whom Jim encounters, who raise the specter of the *Patna*, Jim is a pariah who has broken the bond of "the fellowship of the craft." Jim himself is quite conscious of his alienation. When he sails aboard Marlow's ship from Bangkok, he takes no interest in the passage as a seaman would, but instead, in Marlow's words, skulks below deck, "as though he had become a stowaway."

Jim is also isolated physically. In a moving passage, Marlow speaks with great feeling of the seaman's ties with and affection for his native land, for home. Jim, however, can never go home; he has, in effect, no home, and his destiny lies everywhere and anywhere but in the village in Essex where he came into being.

On Patusan, Jim's physical isolation is complete. Except for the unspeakable Cornelius, he is the only white man for hundreds of miles. With the *Patna* safely behind him, as he supposes, Jim thrives in isolation, bringing order and security to the troubled land, and is called by the natives "Tuan Jim," "which is to say, Lord Jim." The years of unparalleled success take their toll. Jim is convinced that "nothing can touch me," and his egotism proves fatal when Gentleman Brown finds him out. Jim spends his last hours isolated, and he dies alone.

In addition to the alienated hero, another familiar Conradian motif may be observed in *Lord Jim*: Conrad's continuing insistence on the redeeming nature of work. Earlier in the novel, the unnamed narrator makes an attempt to sum up Jim, and it comes in the form of Jim's failure to accept or to appreciate the nature of the demands of life at sea. The narrator says that "the only reward [one may expect in the seafaring life] is in the perfect love of the work. This reward eluded him." Notably, throughout the novel, Jim is most vulnerable when he is without work. During his long stay in the hospital at Singapore, he is infected by the malaise of the seamen ashore who have been in the East too long and who have given up all thought of returning to the more demanding Home Service. Under this debilitating influence, Jim takes the fateful step of signing aboard the *Patna*. The ship's passage is deceptively uneventful and undemanding, and Jim has so little to do as mate that his "faculty of swift and forestalling vision," as Marlow calls it, is given free reign. Thus, in the emergency, Jim sees with his imagination rather than with his eyes. In like fashion, after the initial heroics on Patusan, the demands on Jim are minimal. In the absence of anything practical for Jim to do, except carry out his role as Tuan Jim, he is again vulnerable. Gentleman Brown is enabled, as a result, to catch Jim off guard, to find the "weak spot," "the place of decay," and Jim's idyllic but precarious world comes crashing down.

Conrad the Symbolist may also be observed in *Lord Jim*. Again, as in *Heart of Darkness*, some of the symbols are conventional. Jim's retreat from the *Patna*, for example, is always eastward toward the rising sun, and Jim has bright blue eyes—the eyes, one assumes, of the romantic that darken in moments of stress—and wears immaculate white attire during his climactic confrontation with Gentleman Brown across the creek in Patusan.

As in *Heart of Darkness*, however, some of the symbols in *Lord Jim* are thoroughly original. In pronouncing Jim a "romantic," Stein is, in part, also pronouncing judgment on himself. Stein's romanticism, however, is mixed with a strong alloy of the practical, and he is prepared, as Jim is not, to act or to react immediately when action is called for, as is evident when he is ambushed and defends himself with skill and daring. Thus, Stein the romantic collects butterflies, while Stein the practical man collects beetles. The ring that Doramin gives his old "war-comrade" Stein as a talisman of the bond between white and native ultimately assumes symbolic import. Stein, in turn, gives the ring to Jim as his entrée to Patusan, and Jim wears it proudly during his brief days of glory. In the midst of the Gentleman Brown affair, Jim sends the ring to Doramin's son, Dain Waris, as a token of the white man's faith. In the closing scene of the novel, the ring, taken from the finger of the dead Dain Waris and placed in Doramin's lap, falls to the ground at Jim's feet. Jim glances down at it, and, as he raises his head, Doramin shoots Jim. The ring, then, paradoxically, is both a symbol of faith and of a breach of faith.

VICTORY

Victory, one of Conrad's later novels, was published in 1915. As such, it represents in one sense a Conrad who had mastered the techniques of the genre he had made his own, the novel, and in another sense a Conrad in decline as a creative artist. The early experimentation in narrative technique—the multiplicity of narrators and the complex, and sometimes confusing, manipulation of chronology—is behind Conrad. *Victory* is a linear narrative told by a single, first-person speaking voice without interruption of the forward chronological thrust of the tale. For the noncritical reader, this straightforward handling of his material on Conrad's part was a boon and may very well account for the fact that not until *Chance*, in 1913, and *Victory*, two years later, did Conrad enjoy genuine popular success.

At the same time, Conrad made forward strides in narrative technique and in command of the language in the fifteen years between *Lord Jim* and *Victory*. These steps took him past clarity to simplicity. *Victory* is, perhaps, too straightforward a tale, freed of occasional confusion and of the varied and variable speaking voices but also lacking the richness and the range contributed by those same voices. Confined as Conrad is to one point of view, the extensive searching and probing of his characters, seen in Kurtz and Jim, are denied him. Axel Heyst is an interesting character, but he is only that. He is not, like Kurtz and Jim, a provocative, puzzling, and ultimately enigmatic figure.

The other characters in the novel are similarly unimpressive. Heyst finds the heroine, Alma, or Lena, a thoroughly intriguing young woman, but the reader is at a loss to understand the fascination, even the appeal, she seems to have for Heyst. Other than the commitment Heyst has made to Lena in rescuing her from the odious Schomberg, the tie between the two is tenuous. Many critics have noted that Conrad's women are generally lifeless, and it is true that, with the possible exception of Doña Rita in *The Arrow of Gold* (and here Conrad may have been writing from direct emotional involvement), women generally remained mysteries to him. As his greatest work attests, he was essentially a man's writer.

The three other principal characters in *Victory* are male, yet they, too, are wooden and artificial. Much has been made of "plain Mr. Jones," Ricardo, and Pedro's representing Conrad's most searching study of evil. In this construct, Jones stands for intellectual evil, Ricardo for moral (or amoral) evil, and Pedro for the evil of force. On the whole, however, they emerge as a singularly unimpressive trio of thugs. The lanky, emaciated Jones, called the "spectre," is indeed a ghostlike figure whose presence is observed but scarcely felt. Ricardo, with his bluster and swagger, is almost a comic character, and some of his lines are worthy of a nineteenth century melodrama. Pedro's chief function in the novel appears to be his availability to be bashed on the head and suffer multiple contusions. Compared to Gentleman Brown, "the show ruffian of the Australian coast" in *Lord Jim*, they are theatrical, and while they may do harm, the evil they represent pales beside that ascribed by Conrad to Brown, "akin to madness, derived from intense egoism, inflamed by resistance, tearing the soul to pieces and giving factitious vigor to the body."

Victory is a talky novel, with long passages devoted to inconclusive conversations between Heyst and Lena. It is relevant here to contrast the lengthy exchange between Jim and Marlow in the Malabar House and the "getting to know one another" colloquies in which Heyst and Lena engage. In the former, every line is relevant and every word tells; in the latter, the emotional fencing between the two ultimately becomes tedious.

Gone, indeed, in *Victory* are the overblown passages of the earlier works, which can make even the most devout Conradian wince. Gone too, however, are the great passages, the moments of magic in which by the sheer power of words, Conrad moves, stirs, and thrills the reader. On the whole, the style in *Victory*, like the format of the novel itself, is straightforward; the prose is clear, but the interludes of splendor are sadly missing, and missed.

Whatever differences are to be found in the later works in Conrad's technical handling of the narrative and in his style, one constant remains. Heyst—like Kurtz, Jim, and so many of the figures who fill Conrad's pages—is an alien, isolated and apart, both spiritually and physically. He does differ somewhat from his counterparts, however, in that he stands alone by choice. Heyst, following the dying precept of his gifted but idealistic father—"Look-on—make no sound"—proposes to spend his life aloof and divorced from humankind; in this way, he believes, nothing can ever touch him. In general, except for his brief involvement with the unfortunate Morrison, Heyst manages to maintain his role of the amused and detached skeptic, living, as Conrad puts it, an "unattached, floating existence." He accommodates himself to all people but makes no commitments to anyone. Thus, chameleonlike, he is known under many guises; he is called, for example, "Enchanted Heyst" because of his expressed enchantment with the East and, on other occasions by would-be interpreters, "Hard Facts Heyst," "the Utopist," "the Baron," "the Spider," and "the Enemy." A final sobriquet, "the Hermit," is attached to Heyst when, with the collapse of the Tropical Belt Coal Company, he chooses to remain alone on the deserted island of Samburan. Heyst's physical isolation is now of a piece with his spiritual isolation.

The encounter with Lena changes this attitude. With his commitment to Lena, Heyst is no longer the detached observer of the world, and with the flight to Samburan, his wanderings come to an end. Paradoxically, this commitment brings about both his spiritual salvation and his physical destruction. It is a redeemed Heyst, freed at last from the other enchantment of his life (the living presence of his dead father), who, at Lena's death, is able to assert, "Woe to the man whose heart has not learned while young to hope, to love—and to put its trust in life!" Thus, Heyst differs from Conrad's other alien spirits in that he "masters his destiny," as Jim could not and Kurtz, perhaps, would not.

In still another way, Heyst "masters his destiny" as Jim and Kurtz do not. Kurtz dies the victim of his own excesses and of the debilitating effect of the jungle; Jim places his life in the hands of Doramin. Heyst, however, governs his own fate and chooses to die with Lena, immolating himself in the purgative fire that he sets to destroy all traces of their brief idyll on Samburan, a fire that, ironically, blazes over the ruins of a defunct coal company.

Other echoes of the earlier Conrad may be seen in *Victory*. For example, albeit to a lesser degree than in *Lord Jim*, *Heart of Darkness*, *The Arrow of Gold*, and *Almayer's Folly*, *Victory* is another instance of Conrad's writing "autobiography as fiction." In the Author's Note to the novel, Conrad speaks of a real-life Heyst whom he remembers with affection but also with a sense of mystery. So too, Mr. Jones, Ricardo, and Pedro come from Conrad's store of memories, although he encountered each individually and not as the trio they compose in the book. The character of Lena is drawn from a brief encounter in a café in the south of France with a group of entertainers and with one girl in the company who particularly caught Conrad's eye. The settings of *Victory*, exotic names such as Malacca, Timor, and Sourabaya, were, of course, as familiar to the seagoing Conrad as the streets of London, and there is no reason to doubt that somewhere in the tropics, the fictional Samburan has its counterpart.

Finally, in *Victory*, Conrad the Symbolist may again be seen. Noticeably, however, in this later novel, just as Conrad's narrative technique and his style have become simplified and his ability to create vivid characters has declined, the symbols employed lack the freshness and the depth of those of the earlier novels. Conrad makes much of the portrait of the elder Heyst that dominates the sparse living room on Samburan, just as the subject of the portrait has dominated Heyst's existence. In fact, Conrad makes too much of the portrait as a symbol, calling attention to it again and again until the reader can virtually predict that each time Heyst enters the room, the portrait will be brought to his and to the reader's attention. As a symbol, then, the portrait is overdone, overt, and obvious. Similarly, the darkening storm that threatens Samburan as the events of the novel reach their climax is a bit heavy-handed and hardly worthy of Conrad at his best.

Even so, there is a brief moment of the true Conrad shortly before the climactic violence that brings about both Heyst's redemption and destruction. Conrad writes: "The thunder growled distantly with angry modulations of its tremendous voice, while the world outside shuddered incessantly around the dead stillness of the room where the framed profile of Heyst's father looked severely into space." Here the two symbols coalesce in a telling and effective manner. Regrettably, telling and effective instances such as this are rare in *Victory*. Conrad's work as a whole, however, with its stylistic and narrative innovations, testifies to the quality of his contribution to twentieth century literature.

C. F. Burgess

Other major works

short fiction: *Tales of Unrest*, 1898; *Youth: A Narrative, and Two Other Stories*, 1902; *Typhoon, and Other Stories*, 1903; *A Set of Six*, 1908; *'Twixt Land and Sea, Tales*, 1912; *Within the Tides*, 1915; *Tales of Hearsay*, 1925; *The Sisters*, 1928; *The Complete Short Stories of Joseph Conrad*, 1933.

plays: *One Day More: A Play in One Act*, pr. 1905; *The Secret Agent: A Drama in Four Acts*, pb. 1921; *Laughing Anne: A Play*, pb. 1923.

nonfiction: *The Mirror of the Sea*, 1906; *Some Reminiscences*, 1912 (also known as *A Personal Record*); *Notes on Life and Letters*, 1921; *Joseph Conrad's Diary of His Journey Up the Valley of the Congo in 1890*, 1926; *Last Essays*, 1926; *Joseph Conrad: Life and Letters*, 1927 (Gérard Jean-Aubry, editor); *Joseph Conrad's Letters to His Wife*, 1927; *Conrad to a Friend*, 1928 (Richard Curle, editor); *Letters from Joseph Conrad, 1895-1924*, 1928 (Edward Garnett, editor); *Lettres françaises de Joseph Conrad*, 1929 (Jean-

Aubry, editor); *Letters of Joseph Conrad to Marguerite Doradowska*, 1940 (John A. Gee and Paul J. Sturm, editors); *The Collected Letters of Joseph Conrad*, 1983-2005 (7 volumes; Frederick R. Karl and Laurence Davies, editors).

BIBLIOGRAPHY

Davis, Laura L., ed. *Conrad's Century: The Past and Future Splendour.* New York: Columbia University Press, 1998. Collection of essays provides context for Conrad's work as it examines the author's life and his times. Includes bibliographical references and index.

Gordon, John Dozier. *Joseph Conrad: The Making of a Novelist.* Cambridge, Mass.: Harvard University Press, 1940. Classic work of Conrad scholarship presents excellent discussion of the author's early novels. This volume was especially important in the revival of interest in Conrad's work in the 1940's and 1950's.

Hawthorn, Jeremy. *Sexuality and the Erotic in the Fiction of Joseph Conrad.* New York: Continuum, 2007. Although Conrad's works are usually thought to be lacking in sexuality, this book opens his writing up to new interpretations by citing passages that support erotic interpretations.

Jordan, Elaine, ed. *Joseph Conrad.* New York: St. Martin's Press, 1996. Excellent introductory study of Conrad focuses on three novels: *Heart of Darkness*, *Nostromo*, and *The Secret Agent.* Discusses the works from postcolonial feminist, Marxist, and other perspectives.

Kaplan, Carola M., Peter Mallios, and Andrea White, eds. *Conrad in the Twenty-first Century: Contemporary Approaches and Perspectives.* New York: Routledge, 2005. Collection of essays examines Conrad's depictions of postcolonialism, empire, imperialism, and modernism. Section 1 contains four essays that discuss *Heart of Darkness*, while other essays focus on *The Secret Agent*, *Nostromo*, *Under Western Eyes*, and other novels.

Karl, Frederick R. *Joseph Conrad: The Three Lives.* New York: Farrar, Straus and Giroux, 1979. This book is, and will likely remain, the definitive Conrad biography, elucidating as it does Conrad's life in Poland, on the seas, and in England. The well-documented study is also replete with generously thorough analyses of Conrad's major works as well as of his artistic development and political orientation.

_______. *A Reader's Guide to Joseph Conrad.* Rev. ed. Syracuse, N.Y.: Syracuse University Press, 1997. Useful handbook for students provides in-depth analysis of Conrad's work. Includes bibliographical references and an index.

Lothe, Jakob, Jeremy Hawthorn, and James Phelan, eds. *Joseph Conrad: Voice, Sequence, History, Genre.* Columbus: Ohio State University Press, 2008. Collection of essays examines Conrad's use of narrative in his fiction and nonfiction, focusing on the four issues listed in the subtitle. Provides several perspectives on *Heart of Darkness* and *Lord Jim.*

Meyers, Jeffrey. *Joseph Conrad: A Biography.* New York: Charles Scribner's Sons, 1991. Briskly moving, no-nonsense biography surveys the key points and themes of Conrad's major works. Very good at placing Conrad within the social and intellectual milieu of his day and offering good insights from other literary figures, such as Ford Madox Ford, who significantly influenced Conrad's literary career.

Najder, Zdzislaw. *Joseph Conrad: A Chronicle.* Translated by Halina Carroll-Najder. Rev. ed. New York: Cambridge University Press, 2007. Thorough and sympathetic biography stresses the influence of Conrad's Polish heritage on his personality and art. Draws many telling and intriguing parallels between Conrad's life and his writing.

Peters, John G. *Conrad and Impressionism.* New York: Cambridge University Press, 2001. Examines the influence of impressionism on Conrad's narrative style and other literary techniques as well as on his philosophy and political opinions. Includes a valuable bibliography.

Stape, J. H., ed. *The Cambridge Companion to Joseph Conrad.* New York: Cambridge University Press, 1996. Collection of essays addresses most of Conrad's major works, including analysis of *Lord Jim*, *Nostromo*, and *Under Western Eyes*. Other topics covered include the Conradian narrative, Conrad and imperialism, Conrad and modernism, and Conrad's literary influence.

Swisher, Clarice, ed. *Readings on Joseph Conrad.* San Diego, Calif.: Greenhaven Press, 1998. Collection features essays on Conrad's works by notable authors such as J. B. Priestley, Robert Penn Warren, and Richard Adams.

DANIEL DEFOE

Born: London, England; 1660
Died: London, England; April 26, 1731
Also known as: Daniel Foe

PRINCIPAL LONG FICTION

The Life and Strange Surprizing Adventures of Robinson Crusoe, of York, Mariner, Written by Himself, 1719 (commonly known as *Robinson Crusoe*)
The Farther Adventures of Robinson Crusoe: Being the Second and Last Part of His Life, 1719
The History of the Life and Adventures of Mr. Duncan Campbell, a Gentleman Who, Tho' Deaf and Dumb, Writes Down Any Stranger's Name at First Sight, with Their Future Contingencies of Fortune, 1720
The Life, Adventures and Pyracies of the Famous Captain Singleton, 1720
Memoirs of a Cavalier: Or, A Military Journal of the Wars in Germany, and the Wars in England, from the Year 1632 to the Year 1648, 1720
Serious Reflections During the Life and Surprising Adventures of Robinson Crusoe with His Vision of the Angelick World, 1720
The Fortunes and Misfortunes of the Famous Moll Flanders, Written from Her Own Memorandums, 1722 (commonly known as *Moll Flanders*)
The History and Remarkable Life of the Truly Honourable Col Jacque, Commonly Call'd Col Jack, 1722 (commonly known as *Colonel Jack*)
A Journal of the Plague Year, 1722 (also known as *The History of the Great Plague in London*)
The Fortunate Mistress, 1724 (also known as *Roxana*)
The Memoirs of an English Officer Who Serv'd in the Dutch War in 1672, to the Peace of Utrecht in 1713, by Capt George Carleton, 1728 (also known as *A True and Genuine History of the Last Two Wars* and *The Memoirs of Cap George Carleton*)

OTHER LITERARY FORMS

Although Daniel Defoe (dih-FOH) is mainly remembered as the author of *The Life and Strange Surprizing Adventures of Robinson Crusoe, of York, Mariner, Written by Himself*, more commonly known as *Robinson Crusoe*, he did not begin to write fiction until he was fifty-nine years old. He spent the earlier part of his writing career primarily in producing essays and political pamphlets and working for strongly partisan newspapers. He also wrote travel books, poetry (usually on political or topical issues), and biographies of rogues and criminals.

Daniel Defoe
(Library of Congress)

ACHIEVEMENTS

Daniel Defoe's principal contribution to English literature is in the novel, and he has been called the first English novelist. The extent of his contribution, however, has been debated. A contemporary of Defoe, Charles Gildon, wrote an attack on *Robinson Crusoe*, criticizing, in part, inconsistencies in the narrative. Such problems are not infrequent in Defoe's long and episodic plots. Nevertheless, readers of almost any of Defoe's works find themselves in real and solid worlds, and Defoe's constant enumeration of *things*—such as, in *Moll Flanders*, the layettes for Moll's illegitimate children, the objects she steals, even her escape routes through London—has earned for the author a reputation as a realist and for his style the label "circumstantial realism." To see Defoe as a photographic realist, however, is also to see his limitations, and some of his critics argue that the formlessness of his novels shows his lack of the very shaping power that belongs to great art. Further, even his circumstantial realism is not of the visual sort: Once Moll has named an object, for example, she rarely goes on to describe it in such detail that the reader may visualize it.

In the late twentieth century, Defoe's novels underwent a reassessment, and critics started to see him as more than a mere assembler of objects. Although these critics diverge widely in their interpretation of his techniques, they do agree that Defoe consciously developed themes and used his narratives to shape these themes, all of which center on the conflict between spiritual and earthly values. Instead of viewing Defoe as a plodding literalist, some critics see a keen irony in his work: Moll's actions and her commentary on those actions, they argue, do not always agree. The reader is thus allowed to cultivate a certain ironic detachment about Moll. While few readers would judge Defoe to be a deeply psychological novelist, this double perspective does contribute to a rudimentary analysis of character. Others see a religious vision in his works, one that underwrites an almost allegorical interpretation of his novels: The ending of *Robinson Crusoe*, the killing of the wolves, is seen as Crusoe slaying his earthly passions. While such a reading may seem forced, one should perhaps remember that John Bunyan was a near contemporary of Defoe—he even preached at Morton's Academy at Stoke Newington while Defoe was a student there—and that readers in his time were accustomed to reading allegorically.

Part of the fascination—and achievement—of Defoe may well lie in the tension between realism and allegory that informs his work. Using natural dialogue and a kind of realistic detail, Defoe can yet go beyond these to create events and characters that are, finally, mythic.

BIOGRAPHY

Daniel Defoe was born Daniel Foe in the parish of St. Giles, London, the son of James Foe, a Dissenter and a tallow chandler. (Only after the age of forty did Defoe change his last name, perhaps to seem more aristocratic.) The date of his birth is conjectural: In 1683, he listed his age on his marriage license as twenty-four, but since his sister, Elizabeth, was born in 1659, it is probable that Defoe was born the next year. Not much is known of his early childhood, but his education was certainly important in molding his interests. Being a Dissenter, Defoe was not allowed to attend Oxford or Cambridge; instead, he went to a dissenting academy presided over by the Reverend Charles Morton. While offering a study of the classics, the academy also stressed modern languages, geography, and mathematics, practical subjects neglected at the universities. This interest in the practical seems to have stayed with Defoe all his life: When his library was sold after his death, the advertisements listed "several hundred Curious, Scarce Tracts on . . . Husbandry, Trade, Voyages, Natural History, Mines, Minerals, etc." Defoe's appreciation of the objects and processes by which one is enabled to live in the world is obvious: After making a table and chair, Crusoe reflects that "by stating and squaring everything by reason and by making the most rational judgment of things, every man may be in time master of every mechanic art."

Although his father intended him for the ministry, Defoe became a merchant after leaving school and probably traveled on the Continent as part of his business. In 1684, he married the daughter of another dissenting merchant, and she brought him a considerable dowry. Defoe's fortunes seemed to be rising, but in 1685, he was briefly involved in the duke of Monmouth's rebellion, a Protestant uprising. Although he escaped the king's soldiers, this event illustrates Defoe's willingness to espouse dangerous political causes: Three former schoolmates who joined the rebellion were caught and hanged. While his affairs seemed to prosper during this time, there were disquieting lawsuits—eight between 1688 and 1694, one by his mother-in-law, whom he seems to have swindled—that cast doubt on both Defoe's economic stability and his moral character. In fact, by 1692 he was bankrupt, a victim of losses at sea and his own speculations. Defoe's character is always difficult to label; while the lawsuits show his unsavory side, he did make arrangements after his ruin to repay his creditors, which he seems to have done with surprising thoroughness.

Defoe then began building a brick factory on some land that he owned in Tilbury. This enterprise went well and, with William and Mary on the throne, Defoe could praise the government with a clear conscience. He admired William's religious toleration, foreign policy, and encouragement of English trade. He wrote several pamphlets supporting William's policy of containing Louis XIV's political aspirations, a policy not always popular in England. When William's followers from Holland were harassed by the English, Defoe wrote *The True-Born Englishman: A Satyr* (1701), a long poem arguing that the English are themselves a mixed race who cannot afford to deride other nationalities.

With the accession of Queen Anne of England in 1702, the Dissenters—and Defoe—suffered serious political grievances. Fiercely loyal to the Church of England, Anne looked with disfavor on other religious groups, and bills were introduced to limit the freedom of Dissenters. While both houses of Parliament debated the Occasional Conformity Bill in 1702—a bill that would have effectually prevented Dissenters from holding political office—Defoe published "The Shortest Way with the Dissenters," an ironic pamphlet urging the government to annihilate this group entirely. At first it was taken at face value and applauded by the High Church party, but when its irony was perceived, a warrant was issued for Defoe's arrest, and he went into hiding.

Fearful of imprisonment and the pillory, Defoe sent letters to Daniel Finch, second earl of Nottingham, the secretary of state, trying to negotiate a pardon: He would raise a troop of horses for the government at his own expense; he would volunteer to fight—and possibly die—in the Netherlands. Nottingham was inflexible, however, and when Defoe was found, he was imprisoned in Newgate, the scene of Moll's incarceration. Two months later, he was fined two hundred marks, forced to stand in the pillory three times, imprisoned at the queen's discretion, and forced to provide sureties for his good behavior for the next seven years. This experience helps, perhaps, to explain Defoe's later political views, which seemed to his contemporaries based on expediency rather than conviction: In a letter to a friend, he said that, after Newgate, he would never feel himself maligned if called a coward. When Defoe describes Moll's stay in prison, he knows whereof he speaks.

How long Defoe might have remained in Newgate at the queen's discretion cannot, of course, be known; certainly the government showed no sign of releasing him during the summer or in the fall. He appealed to Robert Harley, a man destined to take Nottingham's place when the latter had been dismissed by the queen. After leisurely negotiations—perhaps to render Defoe more grateful when his pardon finally did come—Harley obtained Defoe's release in November, 1703, the queen even going so far as to send money to Mrs. Defoe and another sum to Defoe to settle his debt.

Harley continued to be influential in Defoe's life; indeed, popular opinion seems to have been that Defoe prostituted himself, abandoning all political ideals for Harley. Still, it is hard to imagine how a forty-three-year-old ruined businessman, with a wife and seven children to support, could begin life over if not with the help of a powerful ally. Defoe's letters to Harley also suggest that Harley sometimes kept him short of funds on purpose, perhaps to make him more compliant. In any case, Defoe's career was definitely the writing of political pamphlets—usually in favor of Harley's policies—and he also edited and wrote most of *A Weekly Review*, which ran from 1704 to 1713. Perhaps Defoe's most significant work for Harley was the establishment of a spy system in England to determine what the national sentiment was for the government. This project—which was Defoe's own idea—began in 1704 when Harley sent Defoe on a preliminary reconnaissance trip through the country. This was the first of several such trips, including one to Edinburgh, Scotland, in 1706 to determine local opinion about the proposed union of the English and Scottish parliaments. On all these trips, Defoe had to assume fictitious identities, and he seems to have relished this subterfuge; it is perhaps significant that Defoe's characters usually are forced to assume many varied disguises in the course of their eventual lives. Even Defoe's tracts and pamphlets bear witness to his fascination with assuming various roles: One critic has estimated that Defoe created eighty-seven personae in these works.

After Harley's political decline and Queen Anne's death, Defoe continued to work for the government, characteristically, in a role requiring deception. Pretending to be a Tory out of favor with the government, he obtained a job on *Mist's Weekly Journal*, one of the most influential Tory papers. In this way, he was able to temper the writing so that the paper's attacks on the government became less virulent. Defoe's shadowy activities are difficult to follow, but it seems that he was also performing the same service to the government on other papers: *Dyer's News-Letter*, *Dormer's News-Letter*, and *Mercurius Politicus*. Defoe's easy transition from Harley's Tory government to the succeeding Whig regime angered many people, who claimed that he had no principles. Defoe's reply, difficult to counter, was always that he was working for moderation, no matter on which side.

Only toward the end of his life did Defoe begin to write prose fiction: *Robinson Crusoe* and its sequels, *The Life, Adventures and Pyracies of the Famous Captain Singleton*, *The Fortunes and Misfortunes of the Famous Moll Flanders, Written from Her Own Memorandums* (commonly known as *Moll Flanders*), *A Journal of the Plague Year*, *The History and Remarkable Life of the Truly Honourable Col Jacque, Commonly Call'd Col Jack*, and *The Fortunate Mistress* (also known as *Roxana*). Even after completing this enormous output, he continued to produce biographies of criminals and imaginary biographies of soldiers and sailors.

To all appearances, Defoe seemed to embark on a comfortable old age; Henry Baker, his son-in-law, reported that Defoe had retired from London to a handsome house in Stoke Newington, where he lived a leisurely life, growing a garden, pursuing his studies, and writing. In 1730, however, Defoe vanished from his home and, in a rather cryptic letter to Baker, wrote about his "Load of insupportable Sorrows," a "wicked, perjur'd, and contemptible Enemy," and the "inhuman dealing of my own son," who reduced his "dying Mother to beg . . . Bread at his Door." The enemy seems to have been Mary Brooke, the wife of one of Defoe's former creditors. Although Defoe appears to have paid Brooke—at least Brooke's executor accepted Defoe's story—Brooke died before destroying his record of the debt, and his wife was determined to collect it. Once again, Defoe was being hounded by a creditor. His reference to his unnatural son is a bit more puzzling but may show that he had transferred most of his money and property to his son to keep it out of Mary Brooke's hands; if so, his son seems to have abused the trust placed in him. Defoe died in April, 1731, while hiding in a lodging house in Ropemaker's Alley.

Although Defoe's colorful life almost calls too much attention to itself—some critics have tried to deduce his exact birth date through events in his characters' lives—it is hard not to see a link between the elements of disguise and trickery in so many of his novels and his own eventful life, spent, in large part, in fabricating identities for himself in his government work. Like his character Moll Flanders, Defoe had personal experience with Newgate, and his biographies of criminals and rogues show a fascination with the inventive powers that allow one to thrive in a treacherous world. In this respect, Defoe and his characters seem to have a great deal in common: They are all survivors in an often hostile environment. This sense of alienation may also have a link with Defoe's religion, a creed that was sometimes tolerated but rarely encouraged by the Crown.

ANALYSIS

Although *A Journal of the Plague Year* is not Daniel Defoe's first work of fiction, it offers an interesting perspective from which to examine all of the author's novels. Purporting to be a journal, one man's view of a period in a city's history, this work shows especially well the nexus between realistic reporting and imaginative invention that is the hallmark of Defoe's novels.

A JOURNAL OF THE PLAGUE YEAR

Defoe himself lived through one siege of the plague, and although he was only five years old when the disease swept through London, he presumably would have retained some recollections of this catastrophic event, even if only through conversations he would have heard among family members. In *A Journal of the Plague Year*, he also refers frequently to the mortality list, drawing on actual documents of the time to give his narrative a sense of reality. In spite of the realistic foundations of the work, however, its imaginative—not to say fantastic—elements outweigh its realism. Defoe, in fact, often shows a surprising interest in the occult or grotesque for one who is supposedly forging the realistic novel in English. Dreams and premonitions often assail his characters—Crusoe's dream of the angel, Moll's telepathic contact with her Lancashire husband, Roxana's precognitive vision of the dead jeweler—and the utter incomprehensibility of the plague takes this work far beyond cause-and-effect realism.

Perhaps the main thing to consider in *A Journal of the Plague Year* is the narrator, H. L., who, like many of Defoe's characters, is divided spiritually: He must decide whether to flee London or stay and trust God's divine Providence. Like Crusoe, H. L. in times of stress opens the Bible randomly and applies its words to his immediate situation. A problem with theme—often Defoe's weakness—immediately arises, for while the passage that he finds in the Bible convinces him to stay, by the end of the novel he has decided that flight is the only sensible option. His stay in the city is not developed as a moral flaw, however, although, given the religious concerns of the novel, it seems as though it should be: Some critics even see him as guilty of overstraining God's Providence. This view seems inconsistent with the overall sympathetic character of H. L., and one feels that Defoe is not, perhaps, completely in control of his theme.

Even more significant for theme is the origin of the plague. H. L., a sensible, levelheaded man, insists that the plague's cause is natural; he is just as insistent, however, that God has used natural means to bring about the plague. In fact, he makes frequent biblical references that, if not providing specific emblematic types for the plague, do give it a resonance beyond that of a mere disease. Thus, the narrator's insistence on seeing all the horrors of the plague for himself—even though he admits he would be safer at home—has led some critics to see his curiosity as a desire to understand God's workings directly. Again, one encounters an awkward thematic problem. Is H. L. really curious about God's wisdom, or is his seeming inability to stay home simply a narrative necessity? There would, after all, be no journal without an eyewitness. Like many thematic problems in Defoe's works, this becomes one only in retrospect; H. L.'s emphasis on the particulars he describes can be so interesting—even if gruesome—that it is not until the reader has finished the book that these problems surface.

Two episodes from this work show how effective Defoe can be with detail. The first involves H. L.'s journey to the post office. Walking through silent and deserted streets, he arrives at his destination, where he sees "in the middle of the yard . . . a small leather purse with two keys hanging at it, with money in it, but nobody would meddle with it." There are three men around the courtyard who tell H. L. that they are leaving it there in case the owner returns. As H. L. is about to leave, one of the men finally offers to take it "so that if the right owner came for it he should be sure to have it," and he proceeds to carry out an elaborate process of disinfection. This episode, on the surface merely straightforward description, is fraught with drama and ambiguity.

While it is realistic for the streets to be deserted as people take to the safety of their houses, the silence lends an eerie backdrop to this scene. Furthermore, the men's motivations are hardly straightforward. Are they leaving the purse there out of honesty or are they fearful of contamination? Are they simply playing a waiting game with one another to see who leaves first? Does one man finally take the purse to keep it for the owner or for himself? Finally, why does he have all the disinfecting materials—including red-hot tongs—immediately available? Was he about to take the purse before H. L. arrived? H. L.'s remarks about the money found in the purse—"as I remember . . . about thirteen shillings and some smooth groats and brass farthings"—complete this episode: The particularity of the amount is typical of Defoe's realism, and H. L.'s hesitant "as I remember" also persuades the reader that he or she is witnessing the mental processes of a scrupulously honest narrator. In fact, this whole passage is so effective that one tends to overlook an internal inconsistency: Early in the paragraph H. L. says that the sum of money was not so large "that I had any inclination to meddle with it," yet he only discovers the sum at the end of this episode. Defoe is prone to narrative slips of this kind, but, like this one, they are usually unimportant and inconspicuous.

Another vivid episode concerns H. L. going to check on his brother's house while he is away. Next to the house is a warehouse, and as H. L. approaches it, he finds that it has been broken into and is full of women trying on hats. Thievery is by no means uncommon during the plague, although the women's interest in fashion does seem bizarre. What is remarkable about this description, however, is its ambience: Instead of grabbing the hats and fleeing, the women are behaving as if they are at a milliner's, trying on hats until they find those that are most becoming. This scene shows Defoe ostensibly writing realistically when, in fact, he is creating a picture that borders on the surreal.

A Journal of the Plague Year does not always achieve the degree of success that these two episodes display; much of the book is filled with descriptions of the cries and lamentations the narrator hears as he walks the streets. Even horror, if undifferentiated, can become monotonous, and Defoe does not always know how to be selective about details. One device that he employs to better effect here than in his other works is the keeping of lists. Defoe's characters often keep balance sheets of their profits and expenditures, and while this may indicate, as Ian Watt contends, Defoe's essentially materialistic bias, these lists often seem examples of the crudest form of realism. In *A Journal of the Plague Year*, however, the mortality lists scattered throughout are rather more successful and provide almost a thudding rhythm to what is being described: God's terrible visitation.

Robinson Crusoe

Robinson Crusoe, like *A Journal of the Plague Year* and much of Defoe's fiction, is based on a factual event: Alexander Selkirk, a Scottish sailor, lived for four years on the island of Juan Fernandez until he was rescued in 1709. Defoe supplemented accounts of Selkirk's adventures with information from travel books: Richard Hakluyt's *The Principall Navigations, Voiages, and Discoveries of the English Nation* (1589, 1598-1600), William Dampier's *New Voyage Round the World* (1697), and Robert Knox's *An Histori-*

cal Relation of Ceylon (1681). Nevertheless, it is as fiction—not a pastiche of other people's books—that *Robinson Crusoe* engrosses the reader.

Because the story centers on one character, it depends on that character for much of its success, and critics have tended to divide into two groups: those who see Crusoe as the new middle-class economic man with only perfunctory religious feelings and those who see him as a deeply spiritual person whose narrative is essentially that of a conversion experience. The answer, perhaps, is that both views of Crusoe coexist in this novel, that Defoe was not sure in this early work exactly where his story was taking him. This ambiguity is not surprising given that the same problem surfaces in *Moll Flanders*; it was not until *Roxana* that Defoe seems to have worked out his themes fully.

The opening frame to Crusoe's island adventure provides a logical starting point for examining his character. Writing in retrospect, Crusoe blames his shipwreck and subsequent sufferings on his "propension of nature," which made him reject his father's counsel of moderation and prompted him to go to sea. His father's speech seems to echo the idea of a great chain of being: Crusoe's life belongs to the "middle state," and he should not endanger himself by reckless acts. If Crusoe's filial disobedience seems trivial to modern readers, it was not to Defoe: His *The Family Instructor, in Three Parts* (1715) and *A New Family Instructor* (1727) make clear how important the mutual obligations of parents and children are. Crusoe himself, recounting his exile from the perspective of old age, talks about his father in biblical terms: After Crusoe's first shipwreck, his father is "an emblem of our blessed Saviour's parable, [and] had even killed the fatted calf for me." When Crusoe reflects, then, on his sinful and vicious life, the reader has to accept Defoe's given: that Crusoe's early giddy nature is a serious moral flaw.

Even with this assumption, however, the reader may have problems understanding Crusoe's character. Throughout the novel, for example, images of prison and capture recur. This makes sense, for the island is both a prison and, if the reader believes in Crusoe's conversion, a means of attaining spiritual freedom. Crusoe himself is imprisoned early in the novel by some Moors and escapes only after two years (the events of which, like the events that take place over many long stretches of time in Defoe's novels, are only briefly summarized) with a boy named Xury, a captive who soon becomes Crusoe's helpmate and friend. Once Crusoe is free, however, he sells Xury willingly and misses him only when his plantation grows so large that he needs extra labor. Indeed, it is indicative of his relations with other people that when Crusoe meets Friday, Friday abases himself to Crusoe, and Crusoe gives his own name as "Master." Perhaps one should not expect enlightened social attitudes about slavery or race in an eighteenth century author. Even so, there seems pointed irony—presumably unintended by Defoe—in Crusoe gaining his freedom only to imprison others; Crusoe's attitude does not seem sufficient for the themes and imagery that Defoe himself has woven into this work.

Crusoe does not behave appreciably better with Europeans. When he rescues Friday and his father, he also rescues a Spaniard who, with a group of Spaniards and Portuguese, has been living peaceably with Friday's tribe. Crusoe begins to think about trying to return to civilization with the Europeans and sends the Spaniard back to Friday's tribe to consult with the others. Before he returns, however, a ship with a mutinous crew arrives on the island. Crusoe rescues the captain and regains control of most of the mutineers. They leave the worst mutineers on the island and sail off for civilization; Crusoe apparently gives no thought to the Spaniard, who will return to the island only to find a motley collection of renegades. Defoe may, of course, simply have forgotten momentarily about the Spaniard as his narrative progressed to new adventures, but if so, this is an unfortunate lapse because it confuses the reader about character and, therefore, about Crusoe's humanity.

Another problem—this time having to do with theme—occurs at the end of the novel. After being delivered to Spain, Crusoe and another group of travelers set out to cross the Pyrenees, where they are beset by fierce wolves. They manage to escape, and Crusoe returns to England, marries, has three children, travels back to his island, and continues having adventures, which, he says, "I may perhaps give a farther account of hereafter." One might argue that the adventures after he leaves the island are anticlimactic, although some critics try to justify them on thematic grounds, the killing of the wolves thus being the extermination of Crusoe's earthly passions. The question remains whether the narrative can bear the weight of such a symbolic—indeed, allegorical—reading. The fact that the sequels to *Robinson Crusoe* are merely about external journeys—not internal spiritual states—shows, perhaps, that Defoe was not as conscious an allegorist as some critics imagine.

Given these thematic problems, it may seem odd that the novel has enjoyed the popularity it has over the centuries. In part, this may simply be due to the element of suspense involved in Crusoe's plight. On one level, the reader wonders how Crusoe is going to survive, although the minute rendering of the day-to-day activities involved in survival can become tedious. Of more interest are Crusoe's mental states: His fluctuating moods after he finds the footprint, for example, have a psychological reality about them. Further, the very traits that make Crusoe unappealing in certain situations lend the novel interest; Crusoe is a survivor, and, while one sometimes wishes he were more compassionate or humane, his will to endure is a universal one with which the reader can empathize.

Aside from the basic appeal of allowing the reader to experience vicariously Crusoe's struggles to survive, the novel also offers the reader a glimpse of Crusoe's soul. While some of Crusoe's pieties seem perfunctory, Defoe is capable of portraying the character's internal states in sophisticated ways. For example, early in his stay on the island Crusoe discovers twelve ears of barley growing, which convinces him "that God had miraculously caused this grain to grow without any help of seed sown and that it was so directed purely for my sustenance on that wild miserable place." Two paragraphs later, however, "it occurred to my thoughts that I had shook a bag of chicken's meal out in that place, and then the wonder began to cease; and I must confess, my religious thankfulness to God's Providence began to abate too." The mature Crusoe who is narrating this story can see in retrospect that "I ought to have been as thankful for so strange and unforeseen Providence as if it had been miraculous; for it was really the work of Providence as to me" that God allowed the seed to take hold and grow. Here the reader finds Defoe using a sophisticated narrative situation as the older Crusoe recounts—and comments on—the spiritual states of the young Crusoe. Indeed, one problem in the novel is determining when Crusoe's egocentric outlook simply reflects this early unregenerate state of which his mature self would presumably disapprove and when it reflects a healthy individualism in which Defoe acquiesces. Perhaps Crusoe is most appealing when he is aware of his own foibles—for example, when he prides himself on building a gigantic canoe only to find that he cannot possibly transport it to water.

COLONEL JACK

If *Robinson Crusoe* shows an uneasy balance between egocentricity and spiritual humility, materialism and religion, *The Life, Adventures and Pyracies of the Famous Captain Singleton*, more commonly known as *Captain Singleton*, displays what Everett Zimmerman calls a "soggy amalgam of the picaresque and Puritan." This problem reappears in *The History and Remarkable Life of the Truly Honourable Col Jacque, Commonly Call'd Col Jack*, known to readers simply as *Colonel Jack*. Jack's motives are often suspect. When he becomes an overseer in Virginia, for example, he finds that he cannot whip his slaves because the action hurts his arms. Instead, he tells the slaves they will be severely punished by an absentee master and then pretends to have solicited their pardon. Grateful for this mercy, the slaves then work for Jack willingly and cheerfully. While Jack describes this whole episode in words denoting charity and mercy, the reader is uneasily aware that Jack is simply playing on the slaves' ignorance. It is method rather than mercy that triumphs here.

MOLL FLANDERS *and* ROXANA

The confusion in *Captain Singleton* and *Colonel Jack* between expediency and morality can also be found in *Moll Flanders* and, to a lesser extent, in *Roxana*. What makes these latter novels enduring is the power of their central characters. Both Moll and Roxana bear many children, and although they manage to dispose of their offspring conveniently so that they are not hampered in any way, their physical fertility sets them apart from Defoe's more sterile male heroes. This fertility may, of course, be ironic—Dorothy Van Ghent calls Moll an earth mother, but only insofar as she is a "progenitrix of the wasteland"—but it adds a dimension to the characters that both Jack and Singleton lack. One also feels that Defoe allows his female characters greater depth of feeling: Each one takes husbands and lovers for whom she has no regard, but Moll's telepathic communication with her Lancashire husband and Roxana's precognitive vision of her jeweler lover's death imply that both women are involved deeply in these relationships—even though Roxana manages to use the jeweler's death as a way of rising in the world by becoming the Prince's mistress. Defoe's heroines may mourn their losses yet also use them to their advantage.

Another difference between the female and male protagonists in Defoe's novels is that neither Moll nor Roxana descends to murder, whereas Defoe's male picaros often do. Although Moll can occasionally rejoice when a criminal cohort capable of exposing her is hanged, she feels only horror when she contemplates murdering a child from whom she steals a necklace. Similarly, while Roxana may share an emotional complicity in Amy's murder of her importunate daughter, she explicitly tells Amy that she will tolerate no such crime. *Roxana* also seems to have more thematic unity than Defoe's other novels: Instead of advocating an uneasy balance between spiritual and material values, *Roxana* shows a tragic awareness that these are finally irreconcilable opposites. Roxana, although recognizing her weaknesses, cannot stop herself from indulging in them, and her keen awareness of what she calls her "secret Hell within" aligns her more with John Milton's Satan than with Defoe's earlier protagonists.

If Defoe begins to solve the thematic problems of his earlier novels in *Moll Flanders* and *Roxana*, he does so through fairly dissimilar characters. Moll equivocates and justifies her actions much more than does Roxana; when she steals the child's necklace, she reflects that "as I did the poor child no harm, I only thought I had given the parents a just reproof for their negligence in leaving the poor lamb to come home by itself, and it would teach them to take more care another time." She also shows a tendency to solve moral dilemmas by the simple expedient of maintaining two opposing moral stances simultaneously. When she meets a man at Bartholomew Fair who is intoxicated, she has sex with him and then robs him. She later reflects on his "honest, virtuous wife and innocent children" who are probably worrying about him, and she and the woman who disposes of her stolen goods both cry at the pitiable domestic scene Moll has painted. Within a few pages, however, she has found the man again and taken him as her lover, a relationship that lasts for several years.

Moll seems to see no conflicts in her attitudes. Her speech also shows her ability to rationalize moral problems, and she often uses a type of equivocation that allows her to justify her own actions. When a thief is pursued through a crowd of people, he throws his bundle of stolen goods to Moll. She feels herself free to keep them "for these things I did not steal, but they were stolen to my hand."

Contrary to the character of Moll, Roxana recognizes her failings. After her first husband leaves her in poverty, her landlord offers to become her lover. Although he has a wife from whom he is separated, he argues that he will treat Roxana in every way as his legal wife. Throughout their life together, Roxana distinguishes between their degrees of guilt: The landlord, she says, has convinced himself that their relationship is moral; she, however, knows that it is not and is thus the greater sinner.

Indeed, Roxana is portrayed in much greater psychological depth than is Moll; one measure of this is the relationship between Roxana and her maid, Amy. While Defoe's characters often have close friends or confidants—Friday in *Robinson Crusoe*, the midwife in *Moll Flanders*, Dr. Heath in *A Journal of the Plague Year*—it is only in *Roxana* that the friend appears in the novel from the beginning to the end and provides an alter ego for the main character. When Roxana is deciding whether to take the landlord as her lover, for example, Amy volunteers several times to sleep with him if Roxana refuses. Once the landlord and Roxana are living together, Roxana decides to put Amy into bed with the landlord, which she does—literally tearing off Amy's clothes and watching their sexual performance. By the next day, the landlord's lust for Amy has turned to hatred and Amy is suitably penitent. The logical question is why Roxana does this destructive deed, and the answer seems to be that, since she herself feels intense guilt at sleeping with the landlord, she wants to degrade Amy and the landlord as well.

Amy, similarly manipulative, is less passive than Roxana. At the end of the novel, Susan, one of Roxana's daughters, appears, guesses her mother's identity, and begs Roxana to acknowledge her. Amy's suggestion is that she kill Susan, who alone can reveal Roxana's past, having been, unknowingly, a maid in her mother's household when Roxana had many lovers. Roxana recoils from this idea although she admits that Amy "effected all afterwards, without my knowledge, for which I gave her my hearty Curse, tho' I could do little more; for to have fall'n upon Amy, had been to have murther'd myself." Some critics argue that Roxana actually acquiesces in Susan's murder, even though she forbids Amy to do it; her statement that to fall upon Amy would be to destroy herself does lend credence to this view. Amy, perhaps, acts out the desires that Roxana will not admit, even to herself.

In fact, both *Moll Flanders* and *Roxana* seem to hint at an irrational perverseness in their characters that explains, in part, their crimes. At one point after beginning her life as a thief, Moll actually tries to earn her living with her needle and admits that she can do so, but temptation makes her return to crime. She appears to enjoy living outside the law, no matter how much she may talk of her fears of Newgate Prison. Similarly, she once steals a horse simply because it is there; she has no way to dispose of it, but the irrational impulse in her that leads her to crime causes her to commit the theft anyway. Defoe is not given to high comedy, but the picture of Moll leading the horse through the streets, wondering how she is ever going to rid herself of it, is a memorably comic scene.

The frequent irrationality of Moll's behavior seems reiterated in the actions of Roxana; without Moll's self-justifying rationalizations, however, Roxana becomes a tragic figure who knows that her behavior is wrong but cannot stop it. About halfway through the novel, for example, she meets a Dutch merchant who helps her out of some difficulties; she has sex with him, but when he proposes marriage she refuses him on the grounds that marriage is a kind of slavery for women. Actually, she fears that he is trying to take over her fortune. When he answers this unspoken objection, promising not to touch her wealth, she is left in the uncomfortable position of having to admit that her initial reluctance was based solely on financial considerations or else continue her spirited defense of female freedom. She chooses the latter option, arguing until the merchant admits defeat. After she is left alone, Roxana regrets her decision and wishes the merchant back, arguing that no "Woman in her Senses" would ever behave as she did.

In these two novels, Defoe seems to be exploring the nature of evil, and it is seen repeatedly as an irrational drive that can deprive its victims of free choice. In fact, *Roxana* is noteworthy for the ambiguously dark atmosphere that pervades the novel, even apart from Roxana's actions. Although *Moll Flanders* touches on incest, madness, and murder, these seem to be the understandable results of understandable causes: If you do not know your mother, you may marry your brother; if your brother-husband discovers your identity, he may go mad with grief; if you steal from a child, you may contemplate murder to cover up your crime. In *Roxana*, however, many of the characters seem motivelessly malignant, obscurely evil. The midwife whom the Prince hires for Roxana seems so murderous that Roxana has him dismiss her, yet there has been no suggestion in the novel that the Prince intends Roxana harm. On the contrary, he seems delighted with her pregnancy and even spends some time with her during labor. The sexual promiscuity found in *Moll Flanders* turns to sexual perversion in *Roxana*: Roxana's final lover before she goes to live with the Quaker disgusts her "on some Accounts, which, if I cou'd suffer myself to publish them, wou'd fully justifie my Conduct; but that Part of the Story will not bear telling."

Even the Quaker is an ambiguous figure. Although strictly truthful—Roxana states several times that the woman will not tell a lie—she hardly seems above reproach: She shows a surprising adeptness at bringing together Roxana and her former lover; she knows how to disguise the smell of alcohol on one's breath; she says at one point that she is almost tempted to abandon her sober Quaker attire and wear Roxana's Turkish costume, although the costume by this time has come to be an emblem of Roxana's sinful life.

Perhaps Defoe's darkening vision is best seen through a comparison of the conclusions of *Moll Flanders* and *Roxana*. After a life of crime—through which she becomes quite wealthy—Moll is finally caught and sent to Newgate. Sentenced to die, she is instead transported, but not before she meets Jemmy, her Lancashire husband, who has been a highwayman and who also ends up in Newgate. They leave for America together, and since they have enough money to pay the captain of the ship handsomely, they are treated like gentry on their voyage. Once in America, they prosper, only returning to England at the end of the novel, presumably repentant but certainly wealthy from their life of crime.

The uneasy balance of religion and roguery in *Moll Flanders*—Moll's pieties interspersed throughout the work sometimes sound as perfunctory as Crusoe's—shifts in *Roxana*, where Defoe's character finally realizes that one cannot reconcile sin and prosperity in the easygoing synthesis that Moll seems to achieve. The novel ends with Susan's death and Amy's desertion; the final paragraph tells the reader that Roxana and her husband prospered for a while but that a "Blast from Heaven" finally destroyed Roxana's tranquillity and she ended her days miserably. The abruptness of this conclusion makes for an unsatisfactory ending, but at least it does show Defoe solving the thematic problems inherent in all his earlier novels: Roxana recognizes a higher power but is unable to obey it. Instead of having the best of two worlds—prosperity and religion—she is doomed by a just Providence that punishes her unrepentance.

If, like Defoe's heroes and heroines, one is given to keeping balance sheets, one might summarize Defoe's weaknesses and strengths easily. On a basic level, Defoe is often slipshod in his handling of narrative: At one point Moll tells the reader how many lovers she has had in her life, but Moll's list of lovers falls far short of the number she mentions in her own narrative. More serious are the thematic problems that Defoe seems to solve only in his final novel. Finally, his realism is quite crude in some places; descriptions of objects assail the reader without having any sensuous reality to them. To Defoe's credit, he is able to establish a convincing conversational tone for most of his characters, and they often have an energy that far exceeds their function as counters through whom Defoe can manipulate his episodic plots. When reading Defoe, however, one does not tend to think in terms of balance sheets. In his best works, the problems in Defoe's writings are so well masked by the vitality of his fiction as to be unnoticeable. Like all artists, Defoe has the ability to make his readers suspend disbelief.

Carole Moses

OTHER MAJOR WORKS

SHORT FICTION: *A True Relation of the Apparition of One Mrs. Veal*, 1706.

POETRY: *The True-Born Englishman: A Satyr*, 1701.

NONFICTION: *An Essay upon Projects*, 1697; *The Shortest Way with the Dissenters*, 1702; *The History of the Union of Great Britain*, 1709; *An Appeal to Honour and Justice*, 1715; *The Family Instructor, in Three Parts*, 1715; *A New Voyage Round the World by a Course Never Sailed*, 1724; *A Tour Thro' the Whole Island of Great Britain*, 1724-1727 (3 volumes); *A General History of the Robberies and Murders of the Most Notorious Pyrates*, 1724-1728 (2 volumes); *The Complete English Tradesman*, 1725-1727 (2 volumes); *The Four Years Voyages of Capt George Roberts*, 1726; *A New Family Instructor*, 1727; *Augusta Triumphans: Or, The Way to Make London the Most Flourishing City in the Universe*, 1728; *A Plan of the English Commerce*, 1728.

MISCELLANEOUS: *The Novels and Miscellaneous Works of Daniel Defoe*, 1840-1841 (20 volumes; Walter Scott, editor); *Romances and Narratives by Daniel Defoe*, 1895 (16 volumes; George Aitken, editor); *The Shakespeare Head Edition of the Novels and Selected Writings of Daniel Defoe*, 1927-1928 (14 volumes).

BIBLIOGRAPHY

Blewett, David. *Defoe's Art of Fiction: "Robinson Crusoe," "Moll Flanders," "Colonel Jack," and "Roxana."* Toronto, Ont.: University of Toronto Press, 1979. In an examination of Defoe's letters and nonfiction, Blewett finds a worldview that sees the individual as isolated in an indifferent or hostile universe. Shows how four of Defoe's novels artfully voice this outlook. An epilogue considers Defoe's contribution to the development of prose fiction.

Bloom, Harold, ed. *Daniel Defoe*. New York: Chelsea House, 1987. Contains thirteen essays representing three decades of criticism. Subjects include point of view, theme, style, and characterization. Bloom's introduction, Leo Braudy's "Daniel Defoe and the Anxieties of Autobiography," and John J. Burke, Jr.'s "Observing the Observer in Historical Fictions by Defoe" are of particular interest. Includes chronology, brief bibliography, and index.

Lund, Roger D., ed. *Critical Essays on Daniel Defoe*. New York: G. K. Hall, 1997. Collection of essays discusses Defoe's domestic conduct manuals, his travel books, his treatment of slavery, his novels, and his treatment of the city. Includes an informative introduction and an index.

Novak, Maximillian E. *Daniel Defoe: Master of Fictions—His Life and Ideas*. New York: Oxford University Press, 2001. Biographical study by a leading Defoe scholar focuses on Defoe's writings. Includes analysis of *Robinson Crusoe*, *Moll Flanders*, and other novels as well as discussion of the author's works in other genres.

_______. *Realism, Myth, and History in Defoe's Fiction*. Lincoln: University of Nebraska Press, 1983. Treats various aspects of Defoe's artistry, such as the psychological realism of *Roxana*, the use of history in *A Journal of the Plague Year* and *Memoirs of a Cavalier*, and mythmaking in *Robinson Crusoe*.

Richetti, John J. *Daniel Defoe*. Boston: Twayne, 1987. Argues that examination of Defoe's fiction should be balanced by a careful study of his nonfiction. This valuable work looks at both, noting both similarities and inconsistencies. Includes chronology, biographical overview, notes, and bibliography with secondary sources briefly annotated.

_______. *Life of Daniel Defoe: A Critical Biography*. Malden, Mass.: Blackwell, 2005. Provides a thorough look at Defoe's writing within the context of his life and opinions, including analysis of his fiction and political and religious journalism. Focuses on Defoe's distinctive literary style.

_______, ed. *The Cambridge Companion to Daniel Defoe*. New York: Cambridge University Press, 2008. Collection of essays designed to introduce students to Defoe includes discussions of Defoe and criminal fiction, money and character in Defoe's fiction, Defoe as a narrative innovator, and gender issues in *Moll Flanders* and *Roxana*.

Rogers, Pat, ed. *Daniel Defoe: The Critical Heritage*. 1972. Reprint. New York: Routledge, 1995. Comprehensive collection of critical commentary on Defoe's work is essential for an understanding of such a complex figure. The editor's introduction provides an excellent overview. Includes appendixes, bibliography, and index.

Spaas, Lieve, and Brian Stimpson, eds. *"Robinson Crusoe": Myths and Metamorphoses*. New York: St. Martin's Press, 1996. Collection of essays explores many aspects of the seminal novel. Includes examinations of Crusoe's women and of the novel within the context of eighteenth century history; several essays focus on how other writers and filmmakers have adapted Defoe's novel for their own works.

Watt, Ian. *The Rise of the Novel: Studies in Defoe, Richardson, and Fielding*. 2d ed. Berkeley: University of California Press, 2001. Discusses *Robinson Crusoe*, *Moll Flanders*, and Defoe's contribution to the realistic novel. Relates Defoe's fiction to the social and economic conditions of his age.

West, Richard. *Daniel Defoe: The Life and Strange, Surprising Adventures*. New York: Carroll & Graf, 1998. Covers all aspects of Defoe's careers as journalist, novelist, satirist, newsman, and pamphleteer as well as tradesman, soldier, and spy. Written with considerable flair by a journalist and historian of wide-ranging experience.

GEORGE ELIOT

Mary Ann Evans

Born: Chilvers Coton, Warwickshire, England; November 22, 1819
Died: London, England; December 22, 1880
Also known as: Mary Ann Evans; Marian Lewes; Marian Evans

PRINCIPAL LONG FICTION

Adam Bede, 1859
The Mill on the Floss, 1860
Silas Marner: The Weaver Raveloe, 1861
Romola, 1862-1863
Felix Holt, the Radical, 1866
Middlemarch, 1871-1872
Daniel Deronda, 1876

OTHER LITERARY FORMS

Three of George Eliot's early stories, "The Sad Fortunes of the Reverend Amos Barton," "Mr. Gilfil's Love Story," and "Janet's Repentance," originally published in *Blackwood's Magazine*, were collected as *Scenes of Clerical Life* in 1858. She wrote two other stories, "The Lifted Veil," also published in *Blackwood's Magazine* in 1859, and "Brother Jacob," published in the *Cornhill Magazine* in 1864. *The Impressions of Theophrastus Such*, a miscellany of sketches and essays, was published in 1879. Eliot's poetry does not achieve the high quality of her prose; the most notable examples are *The Spanish Gypsy* (1868), a verse drama, and *The Legend of Jubal, and Other Poems* (1874). Eliot wrote more than seventy periodical essays and reviews; a comprehensive collection of these is found in *Essays of George Eliot* (1963), edited by Thomas Pinney. Eliot also translated David Friedrich Strauss's *Das Leben Jesu* as *The Life of Jesus Critically Examined* (1846) and Ludwig Feuerbach's *Das Wesen des Christentums* as *The Essence of Christianity* (1854). Her translation of Baruch Spinoza's *Ethica* (1677; *Ethics*, 1870) has never been published.

ACHIEVEMENTS

George Eliot's pivotal position in the history of the novel is attested to by some of the most distinguished English novelists. Reviewing *Middlemarch* in 1873, Henry James concluded, "It sets a limit, we think, to the development of the old-fashioned English novel." *Middlemarch* does, indeed, take what James calls the panoramic novel—"vast, swarming, deep-colored, crowded with episodes, with vivid images, with lurking master-strokes, with brilliant passages of expression," seeking to "reproduce the total sum of life in an English village"—to an unsurpassed level of achievement. Eliot was also an innova-

George Eliot
(Library of Congress)

tor. In the words of D. H. Lawrence, "It all started with George Eliot; it was she who put the action on the inside," thus giving impetus to the rise of the psychological novel, where the most significant actions derive from the motives of the characters rather than from external events. Eliot's work is, then, both the culmination of the panoramic Victorian novel as practiced by Charles Dickens and William Makepeace Thackeray and the beginning of the modern psychological novel as practiced by James, Lawrence, and many others.

More than anyone else, Eliot was responsible for making the novel, a genre that had traditionally been read primarily for entertainment, into a vehicle for the serious expression of ideas. Few novelists can equal Eliot's depth of intellect or breadth of learning. Deeply involved in the religious and philosophical ferment of her time, Eliot was probably the first major English novelist who did not subscribe, at least nominally, to the tenets of Christian theology. Nevertheless, her strong moral commitment, derived from her Evangelical Christian heritage, led her to conceive of the novel as an instrument for preaching a gospel of duty and self-renunciation.

Moral commitment alone, however, does not make a great novelist. In addition, Eliot's extraordinary psychological insight enabled her to create characters who rival in depth and complexity any in English or American fiction. Few novelists can equal her talents for chronicling tangled motives, intricate self-deceptions, and anguished struggles toward noble acts. She creates a fictional world that combines, in a way unsurpassed in English fiction, a broad panorama of society and psychological insight into each character.

Biography

The woman known to countless readers as George Eliot—a name she did not use until she was nearly forty—was born on November 22, 1819, and christened Mary Ann Evans, the third child of Robert Evans and his second wife Christina Pearson. Evans, a man of extraordinary competence and unimpeachable integrity, worked as a general overseer of Arbury Hall, the seven-thousand-acre estate of the Newdigate family in Warwickshire. A shy and homely girl, Eliot excelled as a student in nearby boarding schools. Under the influence of a favorite teacher, Maria Lewis, the strict and conventional adherence to the Church of England that Eliot learned from her parents acquired an overlay of pious Evangelicalism.

After her mother's death and her father's retirement, Eliot and her father moved to a new home outside Coventry. She soon established a close and lasting friendship with Charles and Cara Bray and Cara's sister Sara Hennell. Her conversations with the Brays, who were Unitarians and whose views of religion were more intellectual than those with which Eliot had been acquainted, accelerated the process of religious questioning that she had already experienced. At Bray's suggestion, she began to translate *Das Leben Jesu*, a key work of the German theologian David Friedrich Strauss. Strauss, by applying the methods of scientific research and criticism to the Bible, questioned the divinity of Christ. Eliot's work on this translation, published anonymously in 1846, completed the destruction of her religious orthodoxy.

Following the death of her father in 1849 and a brief stay in Switzerland, Eliot moved to London, where she began to write for the *Westminster Review*. The fact that, while in Switzerland, she began to spell her name Marian suggests her awareness of a new and different life ahead of her.

Although the *Westminster Review* was nominally edited by John Chapman—a man with whom Eliot may have been romantically involved—Eliot assumed most of the responsibilities of editorship and was, especially after Chapman bought the periodical in January, 1852, virtual editor. Her work with the *Westminster Review* placed her near the center of the intellectual life of Victorian England and brought her into contact with many of the prominent thinkers of the time. One of the persons whom Eliot met at this time was George Henry Lewes, who later became her common-law husband. A man of unusual versatility, Lewes had written novels, a blank-verse tragedy, a history of philosophy, and many periodical articles on a variety of subjects. He was, with Thornton Leigh Hunt, coeditor of a weekly newspaper called *The Leader*.

Lewes, Hunt, and Lewes's wife Agnes subscribed to the notion that passions could not be restricted by social conventions; thus, when Agnes, after bearing Lewes four sons, delivered a fifth son who had been fathered by Hunt, Lewes quietly registered the child as his own. By the time Agnes bore a second child fathered by Hunt, however, Lewes no longer considered her his wife, although he continued to support her and to be on friendly terms with her and Hunt, with whom he continued to work on *The Leader*. Victorian laws made divorce virtually impossible and prohibitively expensive; the fact that Lewes had accepted Hunt's child as his own precluded his citing adultery as possible grounds.

Under the circumstances, Eliot and Lewes had the choice of living together in a common-law marriage or not living together at all. They chose the former, and on July 20, 1854, traveled to Germany as husband and wife. Eliot wrote to her friends to explain her new status and to ask that henceforth they address her as Marian Lewes.

Although the couple had no children, their relationship was in many respects a model Victorian marriage. They lived happily together until Lewes's death in 1878; with their writing, they supported not only themselves but also Lewes's four sons and Agnes and her children by Hunt. Lewes's sons appeared to regard Eliot with great affection. In other respects, however, the irregularity of their relationship cut Eliot off from much of the social life of the time, since only the most courageous Victorian women dared risk their own respectability by calling on her. Eliot's family, especially her brother Isaac, also cut her off, condemning her relationship with Lewes as adulterous.

Encouraged by Lewes, Eliot published her first work of fiction, "The Sad Fortunes of the Reverend Amos Barton," in *Blackwood's Magazine* in January, 1857. Because Eliot wished to protect her standing as an editor and reviewer and because she feared that her unconventional marriage to Lewes would prejudice the reception of her fiction, she published under the pseudonym George Eliot. Encouraged by the favorable reception of these stories and protected by Lewes from adverse criticism, Eliot published her first full-length novel, *Adam Bede*, in 1859.

For the next two decades the chief events in Eliot's life were the publications of her novels—*The Mill on the Floss*, *Silas Marner*, *Romola*, *Felix Holt, the Radical*, *Middlemarch*, and *Daniel Deronda*. Of these novels, only *Romola*, a meticulously researched historical novel set in fifteenth century Florence, was less than successful; the others won Eliot both an enthusiastic popular audience and critical recognition as the major English novelist of her time.

As the success of Eliot's novels and the continuing acceptance of Lewes's articles and books also brought considerable prosperity, the Leweses' life together was punctuated by trips to various parts of England and the Continent and by a series of moves to houses in more attractive parts of London. In November, 1878, only a few months after they moved to a long-sought-after house in the country, Lewes died.

Devastated by the loss of the emotional support that Lewes provided, on May 6, 1880, Eliot married John Cross, who, although twenty years younger than she, had long been a close friend and frequent visitor to the Lewes household. In the eyes of her sternly conventional brother Isaac, this marriage conferred respectability; he wrote to his sister for the first time since 1854 to offer his "sincere congratulations." Their marriage, though happy, was brief: Eliot died in December, 1880.

ANALYSIS

Discussions of George Eliot's fiction often begin by quoting chapter 17 of *Adam Bede*, in which she makes one of the most persuasive statements of the creed of the realistic novelist to be found in nineteenth century literature. Indicating that she is seeking that "rare, precious quality of truthfulness that I delight in [in] many Dutch paintings," she goes on to state the need for "men ready to give the loving pains of a life to the faithful representing of commonplace things—men who see beauty in these commonplace things, and delight in showing how kindly the light of heaven falls on them." Through the truthful and sympathetic rendering of a fictional world no better than the actual one "in which we get up in the morning to do our daily work," novelists should win the reader's sympathy for "the real breathing men and women, who can be chilled by your indifference or injured by your prejudice, who can be cheered and helped onward by your fellow-feeling, your forbearance, your outspoken, brave justice." These statements suggest that Eliot conceived of fiction as a moral force, not because it is didactic in any narrow sense but because it inculcates in the reader an attitude of sympathy for his or her fellow people, which in turn leads to everyday acts of justice and compassion that lighten the burden of the human lot.

Fiction, then, performs one of the functions that is commonly associated with the church as a Christian community by reminding readers of Christ's second commandment, that they love their neighbors as themselves. Indeed, although Eliot's belief in Christian theology waned when she was in her twenties, her devotion to the major elements of Christian morality as she understood them remained steadfast throughout her life and provided the moral framework for her fiction. Her practice as a novelist eventually goes beyond her statement in *Adam Bede* in both complexity and subtlety, but this statement remains as the foundation of her creed as a novelist.

As her career developed, Eliot's characters became complex moral paradigms that could serve her readers as both examples and warnings. The highest moral achievement of her characters is renunciation of their own claims to happiness in order to minister to the needs of others, sometimes less deserving, whose lives impinge on theirs. The act of renunciation involves acknowledgment of the claims of community and often provides a sense of continuity with the character's past or traditions. Conversely, the characters whom Eliot condemns most severely are those who evade their responsibilities by a process of self-delusion or self-indulgence, avoiding hard choices and hoping that chance will deliver them from the consequences of selfish actions. Characters are often moved toward renunciation by others who act as "messengers"—almost secularized angels—to guide them; their acts of renunciation and sense of community are often associated with the sacraments of baptism or communion. The process of egotistical self-indulgence, on the other hand, is often associated with a sexual relationship that is clearly inappropriate, although not necessarily illicit. Later in her career, Eliot treated the difficulty of finding an arena for purposeful life in the England of her time, but she never abandoned her intense commitment to individual moral responsibility.

ADAM BEDE

Eliot's first full-length novel, *Adam Bede*, is built on two pairs of contrasting characters, one male and one female. Adam, a carpenter of consummate skill, is a model of rectitude and self-discipline whose only flaw is his intolerance of any weakness in others. Contrasting with Adam is Arthur Donnithorne, a well-intentioned young landowner whose moral weakness causes the principal catastrophe of the novel. There is a similar contrast between the two major female characters: Dinah Morris, a self-effacing Methodist preacher whose primary concern is doing what she can for others, and Hetty Sorrel, a young farm girl whose kittenish appeal conceals a hard core of egotism. The fact that both Adam and Arthur love Hetty intensifies the contrast between them. Adam, captivated by her charms, admires her as a paragon of femininity without ever perceiving her indifference to him. Arthur, without really intending to, takes advantage of Hetty's self-deluding dreams of being a wealthy landowner's wife to indulge in an affair with her. Frightened when she discovers that she is pregnant, Hetty runs away from home in a vain attempt to find Arthur, who has gone to rejoin his regiment. After her baby is born, she abandons it in a forest, where it dies of exposure. When she is arraigned for child murder, she appears hard and indifferent until Dinah moves her to repentance. Although Arthur succeeds in obtaining a pardon that saves Hetty from hanging, the young woman disappears from the story and, like the overwhelming majority of fallen women in Victorian fiction, dies. The somewhat improbable marriage of Adam and Dinah provides the happy ending that the contemporary audience expected.

The melodramatic aspects of *Adam Bede* tend to obscure, especially in summary, Eliot's primary concerns in the novel. Most conspicuously, the relationship between Arthur and Hetty is not simply a trite story of a sexual encounter between a wealthy young man and a simple farm girl; the sexual aspect of their relationship is less important than their self-delusion, self-indulgence, and egotism. Both characters embody moral issues that Eliot returned to again and again in her career: Arthur is attractive, likable, and well-intentioned, but he lacks both strength of purpose and self-knowledge. Intending to break off his relationship with Hetty, he finds himself contriving meetings with her; dreaming of being a model landowner, he comes near to destroying the happiness of his best tenants. Hetty's flaw is even more damaging: Although she appears to be a creature of simple charm with the "beauty of young frisking things, round-limbed, gambolling, circumventing you by a false air of innocence," her egotism makes her indifferent to almost everything except her own beauty and her self-deluding dreams.

Similarly, Dinah's success in leading Hetty to repentance is a prototype of much more complex processes that occur in later novels, when characters who have greater potential for moral growth than Hetty are enabled to develop that potential. Dinah's willingness to take on responsibility for sympathetically ministering to the needs of people around her—a moral virtue Eliot lauds above all others—has to be learned by Adam, whose own stalwart rectitude causes him to scorn weakness in others. His success in learning sympathy is symbolized by his acceptance of a meal of bread and wine in an "upper room" the morning of Hetty's trial—one of several instances in Eliot's fiction where objects associated with a Christian sacrament are used to suggest the establishment of a sense of community.

Although it is a major achievement for a first novel, *Adam Bede* pales in comparison to Eliot's later fiction. Eliot's depiction of the self-deception and egotism of Arthur and Hetty looks ahead to the fuller development of this theme in later novels, but neither the characters nor their situation provides the opportunity for the depth of psychological insight Eliot shows later. Similarly, Arthur's last-minute rescue of Hetty from the very foot of the gallows is reminiscent of the clichés of nineteenth century melodrama and seems almost pointless in the light of Hetty's immediate disappearance from the story and her early death. The marriage of Adam and Dinah caters too obviously to the Victorian taste for this kind of conventional "happy ending" and seems inconsistent with the earlier description of Dinah. Adam himself is too idealized a character to be convincing.

Many minor characters, however, demonstrate Eliot's impressive gift for characterization. Mr. Irwine is the first of several Eliot clergymen who are virtuous but hardly spiritual; Mrs. Poyser's pungent sayings indicate Eliot's humor; and Adam's mother Lisbeth combines maternal love with grating querulousness and self-pity.

THE MILL ON THE FLOSS

More than any of Eliot's other novels, *The Mill on the Floss*, her second novel, focuses on a single character—Maggie Tulliver. Considered one of Eliot's most complex creations, Maggie embodies both the tendency toward self-indulgence that Eliot condemns elsewhere and the earnest desire for moral achievement by renunciation of one's own happiness that is the hallmark of the characters of whom Eliot appears to approve most highly.

These conflicting tendencies in Maggie, although evident in the long childhood section of the novel, assume their full significance when Maggie begins a series of secret meetings with Philip Wakem, the crippled son of a lawyer whom Maggie's father regards as a mortal enemy. In some respects, these meetings are innocent enough: Philip and Maggie are both lonely, as Philip is set apart by his physical handicap and Maggie is isolated by her family's financial distresses, and their conversations provide them with companionship they find nowhere else. More significant, however, is that Maggie's meetings with Philip are wrong because they require her to deceive her family and because they would, if discovered, add to her father's already overflowing cup of grief and bitterness. Although the standard of conduct that Maggie is being asked to meet seems almost pointlessly rigid, Eliot makes it clear that Maggie errs by not meeting it. When Maggie's narrowly righteous brother Tom discovers the meetings and harshly puts a stop to them, even Maggie feels that the "sense of a deliverance from concealment was welcome at any cost."

Maggie's failure to meet the standards of conduct required of her has much more serious consequences when she allows herself to go away with Stephen Guest, a young man who is virtually engaged to her cousin Lucy. Although Maggie rejects Stephen's offer of marriage, their apparent elopement causes a scandal that prostrates Lucy and bitterly divides Maggie's family. Tom is especially adamant in condemning her.

Maggie is a character who is sometimes almost painful to read about, for she has too little self-discipline to avoid slipping into actions that she knows to be wrong and too sensitive a conscience not to feel acutely the consequences of her errors. The ideal of conduct that she longs for and ultimately achieves when she decides to reject Stephen's second proposal of marriage is expressed by passages marked in an old volume of Saint Thomas à Kempis that is in a package of books given to Maggie in the depths of the Tullivers' poverty. Reading the words "Forsake thyself, resign thyself, and thou shall enjoy much inward peace," Maggie seems to see "a sudden vision" and feels this "direct communication of the human soul's belief and experience . . . as an unquestioned message."

Maggie is spared further conflict by the melodramatic conclusion of the novel. A flood gives her the opportunity to demonstrate her love for Tom by rescuing him from the mill. Maggie and Tom are briefly reconciled; then a floating mass of machinery bears down on their boat, drowning them both. Their epitaph—"In death they were not divided"—suggests a harmony that Maggie hungered for but seldom achieved in life.

The collision that results in the drowning of Maggie and Tom is, in fact, a kind of deus ex machina employed to achieve a resolution for Maggie that would be hard to envision otherwise. More intelligent and gifted than any of the other women in the novel, Maggie would hardly have found the fulfillment in marriage that appears to be the only resource for the women of the village, especially since marriage to Philip would have brought her into irreconcilable conflict with Tom and marriage to Stephen could have been achieved only at the cost of Lucy's happiness. Finally, since Maggie's sensitive compassion has conflicted with Tom's narrow dogmatism throughout the novel, it seems unlikely that their reconciliation could have been permanent. Even the renunciation she learns about in Thomas à Kempis seems to offer more a model of resignation than a pattern for a fruitful and fulfilling life. In the melodramatic ending, therefore, the issues raised by the novel finally remain unresolved.

As in *Adam Bede*, Eliot's brilliant creation of minor characters is one of the finest achievements of *The Mill on the Floss*. Especially noteworthy are the Dodson sisters, Maggie's aunts, who embody the common qualities of a proud and clannish family and yet have traits that clearly distinguish them according to their ages, degrees of prosperity, and individual temperaments.

SILAS MARNER

Eliot's third and most perfectly constructed novel, *Silas Marner*, embodies her complex moral vision with the precision of a diagram. Like *Adam Bede*, the novel is built on morally contrasting characters, but Silas Marner and Godfrey Cass reveal with much greater clarity than any of the characters in the earlier novel Eliot's concern with the moral patterns of renunciation and self-indulgence.

In a sort of prologue to the main action of the novel, Silas, a linen weaver who is a member of a pious religious sect in a large industrial city, is accused of stealing church funds by a close friend who actually stole the money. When a trial by lots sponsored by the sect declares Silas guilty, he loses faith in God and humanity and flees to a distant country village, where he isolates himself from the community and finds solace in constant weaving, like a "spinning insect."

Through years of weaving, Silas accumulates a hoard of gold coins that become the only object of his affections. When his gold is stolen by Godfrey Cass's irresponsible brother Dunstan, Silas is utterly devastated, until Godfrey's daughter by a secret marriage toddles into his house after her mother dies of exposure and an overdose of laudanum. The presence of this child, whom Silas takes in and rears as his own, restores the contact with his fellow men and women that Silas had lost; Eliot compares the girl to the "white-winged angels" that "in old days . . . took men by the hand and led them away from the city of destruction."

Almost every act that Silas performs in relation to the loss of his gold and the rearing of the child takes on near-symbolic significance. His spontaneous turning to the men assembled at the village tavern when his gold is stolen and to the New Year's assemblage at the Cass house when he finds the child suggest an instinctive searching for community. His heeding of the parish clerk's admonition not to accuse the innocent after his gold is stolen and his choice of his younger sister's "Bible name" of Hepzibah (shortened to Eppie) for the child suggest the reestablishment of ties to his past. In particular, his acceptance of lard cakes with "I.H.S." (a Christogram derived from the first three letters of the Greek name for Jesus) pricked on them from his kindly neighbor Dolly Winthrop provides a secularized communion that suggests that ties between human beings and God may be replaced in importance by ties between individuals, as Eppie has replaced the white-winged angels of older days. It may also be significant that Silas spends Christmas in lonely isolation, while Eppie comes to his house on New Year's Eve.

Similarly, Godfrey embodies the consequences of a self-indulgent avoidance of one's responsibilities. Prevented by his secret marriage to the dissolute mother of Eppie from marrying Nancy Lammeter, he weakly trusts to chance, "the god of all men who follow their own devices instead of obeying a law they believe in," to relieve him somehow of the consequences of his actions. Godfrey has none of the malice of his younger brother Dunstan; nevertheless, his anxiety is so great that his "one terror" when Silas comes to his house with Eppie is that his wife might *not* be dead. He sees that the child is his but fails to acknowledge her, salving his conscience by giving Silas a half-guinea when he finds that Silas has determined to keep her.

The chance that has relieved Godfrey of the consequences of his secret marriage eventually brings retribution. His marriage to Nancy is childless, and when Dunstan's body is discovered with Silas's long-lost gold, Godfrey finally tells Nancy that Eppie is his child. Their plan of relieving their childlessness by adopting Eppie comes to nothing when Eppie tells them that she can only think of Silas as her father. With poetic justice that even Godfrey recognizes, the man who admits that he "wanted to pass for childless once" will now "pass for childless against my wish."

MIDDLEMARCH

Middlemarch is unquestionably Eliot's finest achievement as a novelist. Whereas *Silas Marner* presents the moral patterns of renunciation and self-indulgence with unparalleled clarity, *Middlemarch* explores them with profound subtlety and psychological insight. The vast scope of *Middlemarch*—the novel is more than twice the length of *Adam Bede* or *The Mill on the Floss*—gives Eliot room for a panoramic view of provincial life, and her focus on the upper middle class and gentry gives her an opportunity to deal with characters whose experience is wider and whose motives are more sophisticated and complex than those of many of the characters in the early novels. In this "study of provincial life," as the novel's subtitle describes it, Eliot explores the familiar moral territory of renunciation and self-indulgence by developing four more or less distinct plot lines. The most important of these concern Dorothea Brooke and Tertius Lydgate, but Fred Vincy and Nicholas Bulstrode also claim a substantial amount of Eliot's attention.

This vast novel is unified not only by Eliot's moral concerns and by various cross-connections among the plot lines but also by a pervasive theme of reform. The implied contrast between the climate for "far-resonant" action that existed when a "coherent social faith" allowed Saint Theresa to find "her epos in the reform of a religious order" and the time of the novel, which ends "just after the Lords had thrown out the Reform Bill [of 1832]," suggests the difficulty of achieving meaningful action in the fragmented world of contemporary England. More than any previous novel, *Middlemarch* explores the moral achievements and failures of individuals against the background of an entire society, a society that does not provide many opportunities for people to put their best talents to use.

These issues are perhaps most fully embodied in Dorothea Brooke, a young heiress with "a nature altogether ardent, theoretic and intellectually consequent" who is "struggling in the bands of a narrow teaching, hemmed in by a social life which seemed nothing but a labyrinth of petty courses, a walled-in maze of small paths that led no whither." Seeking a way to give her life consequence and purpose, she marries Edward Casaubon, a desiccated pseudoscholar, whom she naïvely thinks of as a John Locke or a John Milton, a "winged messenger" who can guide her along the "grandest path." She soon discovers that Casaubon is not a great man; rather, he is pathetic egotist who is morbidly sensitive to real or imagined criticism of his work, pettishly jealous of Dorothea's friendship with his nephew Will Ladislaw, and incapable of offering her any real affection. She also learns that his projected work, grandly titled "Key to All Mythologies," is nothing but a monumental collection of trivia already rendered obsolete by superior German scholarship. Nevertheless, Dorothea prepares to promise her husband, who is suffering from a "fatty degeneration of the heart," that she will continue his work after his death, a sacrifice from which she is saved by his timely demise.

Like Dorothea, Tertius Lydgate finds his ambitions for significant achievement frustrated by social pressures, but unlike Dorothea he adds to his difficulties by a tendency toward heedless self-indulgence. His well-intentioned plans for medical reform are jeopardized by his lack of sensitivity to the feelings of both patients and other practitioners and by his regrettable involvement with Nicholas Bulstrode, an unpopular but powerful leader in community affairs. More important, he shackles himself by marriage to Rosamond Vincy, the beautiful and self-centered daughter of the mayor of Middlemarch. This marriage, which Lydgate slips into more or less intentionally, blights his hopes of success. He gets heavily into debt as both he and Rosamond carelessly incur expenses on the unconsidered assumption that they ought to live well. Rosamond, utterly unwilling to make any sacrifices, simply blames him for their problems.

These two plot lines come together when Dorothea, deeply moved by Lydgate's marital and financial problems and eager to clear him from blame in a scandal involving Bulstrode, offers to call on Rosamond. She finds Rosamond in what appears to be a compromising tête-à-tête with Will, whom she had come to love since Casaubon's death. Deeply distressed by what she assumes about Will's conduct, she nevertheless forces herself to "clutch [her] own pain" and think only of the "three lives whose contact with hers laid an obligation on her." Feeling "the largeness of the world and the manifold wakings of men to labour and endurance," she compels herself to make a second visit. She has some success in reconciling Rosamond to Lydgate and finds that Will's conduct was indeed blameless.

Although Dorothea's renunciation of herself has the unexpected result of opening the way for her marriage to Will, she never achieves her potential as a latter-day Saint Theresa, "for the medium in which [her] ardent deeds took shape is forever gone." Her "full nature" spends itself "in channels which had no great name on earth" but that nonetheless bring benefits to her fellow men and women. Lydgate, who allowed himself to slip into marriage with the paralyzingly egotistical Rosamond, achieves financial success as a society doctor but "always regarded himself as a failure; he had not done what he once meant to do."

The other two plot lines, although less important than those centering on Dorothea and Lydgate, afford Eliot opportunity to round out her study of provincial life. Fred Vincy, who is Rosamond's brother, overcomes his tendency to fritter away his money in casual pleasures when he realizes the distresses that his failure to pay a debt will cause the Garth family, who represented security for him, and recognizes that Mary Garth will not marry him unless he undertakes a worthwhile career. The plot line centering on Nicholas Bulstrode, although the least extensive of the four, contains some of Eliot's most perceptive explorations of self-delusion. Bulstrode, who had gathered a fortune dealing in stolen goods before coming to Middlemarch, aspires to leadership in the community as a banker and as an Evangelical Christian. Although he assiduously conceals his former life, he is no simple hypocrite; rather, he is an ambitious man who aims at "being an eminent Christian," capable of deluding himself even in his prayers. His lifetime habit of confusing his own desires with God's will comes to a climax when he allows his housekeeper to administer brandy to an alcoholic former associate who has been blackmailing him—a treatment that, although common at the time, has been forbidden by Lydgate. Only after the man dies does Bulstrode discover that the former associate has already revealed Bulstrode's long-guarded secrets in his drunken ramblings.

Although the principal themes of *Middlemarch* are developed primarily in the four major plot lines, the novel's extraordinary richness of minor characters is surely one of its outstanding features. Mr. Brooke, Dorothea's uncle, is one of Eliot's supreme comic creations, a man "of acquiescent temper, miscellaneous opinions, and uncertain vote." Caleb Garth, "one of those rare men who are rigid with themselves and indulgent to others," is a model of sturdy rectitude. The description of Mrs. Bulstrode's loyal support of her guilty husband and her acceptance of "a new life in which she embraced humiliation" is one of Eliot's finest passages. The list could be continued almost at will, amply justifying the claim of the novel's subtitle to be a "study of provincial life."

The subtitle is also appropriate in that it calls attention to Eliot's recognition, more fully expressed in this novel than in any of her earlier ones, of the ways in which the circumstances of society limit her characters' options. Dorothea achieves the ideal of self-renunciation that characters in the earlier novels strive for, but the conditions of her life prevent her from achieving her potential; Lydgate fails not only because of his ill-advised marriage but also because the community views his eagerness to advance medical practice with suspicion and prejudice. Conditions of society, as well as moral flaws, frustrate the ambitions of even the worthiest characters.

DANIEL DERONDA

Daniel Deronda, Eliot's final novel, emphasizes the search for purpose more than the ideal of renunciation. Eliot continues her examination of egotism and self-indulgence, but these themes are muted with pathos in the portrayal of Gwendolen Harleth. In subject matter, Eliot also takes another step or two up the social ladder, dealing in this novel with the wealthy upper middle class and aristocracy.

The protagonist, Daniel Deronda, is such a paragon at the beginning of the novel that he has little need of the lessons in renunciation that Eliot's other protagonists must learn. Handsome, well-educated, and generously supported by Sir Hugo Mallinger, Deronda is concerned only with finding something purposeful to do with his life. His only burden is the assumption that he is Sir Hugo's illegitimate son. His discovery of a cause to which he can dedicate himself proceeds by easy stages. His rescue of Mirah, a Jewish singer who is preparing to drown herself, prompts his interest in Judaism. He succeeds in reuniting Mirah with her terminally ill brother, Mordecai, a visionary Jewish mystic. When Mordecai sees Deronda from a bridge, which he describes as "a meeting place for spiritual messengers," he assumes that Deronda has been sent to bring him "my new life—my new self—who will live when this breath is all breathed out." Finally, Deronda discovers that he is actually the son of a distinguished Jewish singer who had asked Sir Hugo to bring him up as an Englishman. The discovery that he is Jewish enables him to marry Mirah, take up the torch from the dying Mordecai, and dedicate himself to the "restoration of a political existence to my people, giving them a national center, such as the English have." (In assigning this cause to Deronda, Eliot anticipated the Zionist movement by some twenty years and, indeed, gave powerful stimulus to the movement for the development of a Jewish national state.)

In Gwendolen Harleth, Eliot examines again the anatomy of egotism. Concerned only with her own comforts, Gwendolen rules imperiously over the household of her twice-widowed mother, Mrs. Davilow. Gwendolen's manifest dislike of men and her habit of sleeping in her mother's bedroom suggest sexual frigidity. Nevertheless, she is on the verge of marrying Henleigh Grandcourt, Sir Hugo's nephew and heir, when she discovers that Grandcourt has had four children by a mistress who deserted her own husband and whom Grandcourt still supports. An invitation to visit Germany with some family friends allows Gwendolen to evade a decision, but when her family loses its fortune, she decides on marriage rather than having her mother live in painfully reduced circumstances while she is forced to take the ignominious position of governess.

Gwendolen's motives in marriage are intriguingly mixed. To be sure, she is essentially egotistical and assumes that she will be able to control her husband. The family's dismal prospects after their catastrophic financial losses inevitably influence her. She is especially concerned for her mother, the one person for whom she feels genuine affection. Nevertheless, she also suffers an agony of guilt in her sense that her marriage has deprived Grandcourt's illegitimate children of any claim to his wealth.

Once they are married, the ruling hand is entirely Grandcourt's. Gwendolen bears his elegantly polite sadism with proud reserve, but is inwardly tormented by dread that her fear and hatred of her husband may drive her to some desperate act. When he drowns, perhaps because she fails to throw him a rope, she is overwhelmed with guilt. Desolated by the marriage of Deronda, whom she has turned to as a moral guide and mentor, she takes solace in Deronda's admonition that she "may live to be one of the best of women," although, as she adds in a final letter to Deronda, "I do not yet see how that can be."

Although Gwendolen's willingness to accept suffering scourges her egotism and brings her to a prospect of redemption that Rosamond Vincy glimpses only briefly, *Daniel Deronda* is in most ways Eliot's bleakest novel. An air of futility hangs like a pall over most of the characters; without a tradition of commitment to some place or purpose, they lack a future also. Mrs. Davilow moves from one rented house to another, and the estates passed down to Sir Hugo from the time of William the Conqueror will finally be inherited by Grandcourt's illegitimate son. Jewish characters such as Mirah's father and Deronda's mother wander over Europe, rejecting even an obligation to their own children. Only the dedication to art of Herr Kelsmer, a German musician, and the acceptance of Mordecai's dream of a national Jewish homeland by Deronda provide a sense of purpose or direction, and these vocations are ones from which most of the characters are inevitably excluded. Except in unusual cases, it appears that even the desire to renounce oneself may not be efficacious. The very circumstances of modern life work against moral achievement.

Erwin Hester

Other major works

SHORT FICTION: *Scenes of Clerical Life*, 1858.

POETRY: *The Spanish Gypsy*, 1868; *The Legend of Jubal, and Other Poems*, 1874.

NONFICTION: *The Impressions of Theophrastus Such*, 1879; *Essays of George Eliot*, 1963 (Thomas Pinney, editor); *The Journals of George Eliot*, 1998 (Margaret Harris and Judith Johnston, editors).

TRANSLATIONS: *The Life of Jesus Critically Examined*, 1846 (with Mrs. Charles Hennell; of David Friedrich Strauss's philosophical history); *The Essence of Christianity*, 1854 (of Ludwig Feuerbach's philosophical history).

Bibliography

Ashton, Rosemary. *George Eliot: A Life*. New York: Penguin Books, 1997. Introduction to Eliot's life and work by an admirer of her fiction. Interlaces discussions of Eliot's life with analysis of her fiction and the context of her work within Victorian society and social thought. Argues that Eliot's novels most often focus on characters out of step with their culture.

Dodd, Valerie A. *George Eliot: An Intellectual Life*. New York: St. Martin's Press, 1990. Part 1 gives the intellectual background of Victorian England, discussing writers such as John Stuart Mill and Thomas Carlyle; part 2 discusses Eliot's work in relation to that intellectual background. Includes a useful bibliography.

Ermarth, Elizabeth Deeds. *George Eliot*. Boston: Twayne, 1985. Excellent short reference work on Eliot provides a biographical sketch and outlines Eliot's career, including analyses of *Middlemarch*, *Silas Marner*, *Romola*, and other novels. The select bibliography is helpful, as is the chronology.

Hardy, Barbara. *George Eliot: A Critic's Biography*. London: Continuum, 2006. Presents an examination of Eliot's life combined with an analysis of her works; intended for readers with some prior knowledge of her writings. Includes an outline of Eliot's works in the context of the events in her life.

Harvey, W. J. *The Art of George Eliot.* New York: Oxford University Press, 1962. Addresses the structure of Eliot's work—the omniscient narrator, the treatment of time, and characterization. A helpful source for a close study of Eliot's work. Supplemented by a short bibliography.

Hughes, Kathryn. *George Eliot: The Last Victorian.* London: Fourth Estate, 1998. Good standard biography suitable for the general reader. Includes bibliographical references and index.

Hutchinson, Stuart, ed. *George Eliot: Critical Assessments.* 4 vols. East Sussex: Helm Information, 1996. Volume 1 consists of biography, nineteenth century reviews, and responses; volume 2 contains perspectives from 1900-1970 on Eliot's work; volume 3 provides critical essays on individual works; volume 4 includes perspectives from the 1970's to the mid-1990's.

Karl, Fred. *George Eliot: Voice of a Century.* New York: W. W. Norton, 1995. Biography draws on previously unavailable archival material and on feminist criticism, depicting Eliot as an author whose work symbolized "the ambiguities, the anguish, and divisiveness of the Victorian era."

Levine, George, ed. *The Cambridge Companion to George Eliot.* New York: Cambridge University Press, 2001. Collection of essays analyzes Eliot's works, including her early and late novels, from various perspectives. Addresses Eliot's realism and her approaches to philosophy, science, politics, religion, and gender.

Menon, Patricia. *Austen, Eliot, Charlotte Brontë, and the Mentor-Lover.* New York: Palgrave Macmillan, 2003. Examines and compares how Jane Austen, Eliot, and Brontë handled matters of gender, sexuality, family, behavior, and freedom in their work.

Rignall, John, ed. *Oxford Reader's Companion to George Eliot.* New York: Oxford University Press, 2000. Encyclopedic volume contains entries that cover everything about the novelist, including her pets and homes as well as the themes in her fiction and the various contexts in which to place her works.

Taylor, Ina. *A Woman of Contradictions: The Life of George Eliot.* New York: William Morrow, 1989. Interesting and provocative book focuses on Eliot's personal life. Taylor claims to work from sources different from those on which all previous biographies drew—all of which, she says, come from one beginning: Eliot's husband, John Cross. Includes photographs of Eliot, her family, and friends.

HENRY FIELDING

Born: Sharpham Park, Somersetshire, England; April 22, 1707
Died: Lisbon, Portugal; October 8, 1754

PRINCIPAL LONG FICTION

An Apology for the Life of Mrs. Shamela Andrews, 1741 (commonly known as *Shamela*)
The History of the Adventures of Joseph Andrews, and of His Friend Mr. Abraham Adams, 1742 (commonly known as *Joseph Andrews*)
The History of the Life of the Late Mr. Jonathan Wild the Great, 1743 (revised 1754; commonly known as *Jonathan Wild*)
The History of Tom Jones, a Foundling, 1749 (commonly known as *Tom Jones*)
Amelia, 1751

OTHER LITERARY FORMS

Henry Fielding's literary output, aside from his novels, can be categorized into three groups: plays, pamphlets and miscellaneous items, and journals. In addition, the publication of his three-volume *Miscellanies* (1743) by subscription brought together a number of previously published items as well as new works, including the first version of *Jonathan Wild*, and an unfinished prose work, "A Journey from This World to the Next."

Fielding's dramatic works, many presented with great success at either London's Little Theatre in the Haymarket or the Drury Lane Theatre, include ballad opera, farce, full-length comedy, and adaptations of classical and French drama. Most are overtly political in theme. Because of their contemporary subject matter, few have survived as viable stage presentations, although *The Covent Garden Tragedy* (pr., pb. 1732) was presented by the Old Vic in London in 1968. Fielding also wrote a number of prologues, epilogues, and monologues that were performed in conjunction with other dramatic pieces.

The pamphlets and miscellaneous items that are currently attributed to Fielding, excluding those for which he merely wrote introductions or epilogues, are "The Masquerade" (1728), a poem; *The Military History of Charles XII King of Sweden* (1740), a translation; "Of True Greatness" (1741), a poem; "The Opposition: A Vision" (1741), a poem; "The Vernoniad" (1741), a poem; "The Female Husband" (1746); "Ovid's Art of Love Paraphrased" (1747); "A True State of the Case of Bosavern Penlez" (1749); "An Enquiry into the Causes of the Late Increase in Robbers" (1751); "Examples of the Interposition of Providence in the Detection and Punishment of Murder" (1752); "A Proposal for Making an Effectual Provision for the Poor" (1753); "A Clear State of the Case of Elizabeth Canning" (1753); and *The Journal of a Voyage to Lisbon*, which was published posthumously (1755).

Fielding edited and made major contributions to four journals: *The Champion* (No-

Henry Fielding
(Library of Congress)

vember 15, 1739-June, 1741; the journal continued publication without Fielding until 1742); *The True Patriot* (November 5, 1745-June 17, 1746); *Jacobite's Journal* (December 5, 1747-November 5, 1748); and *The Covent-Garden Journal* (January 4-November 25, 1752).

ACHIEVEMENTS

Fielding's lasting achievements in prose fiction—in contrast to his passing fame as an essayist, dramatist, and judge—result from his development of critical theory and from his aesthetic success in the novels themselves. In the preface to *Joseph Andrews*, Fielding establishes a serious critical basis for the novel as a genre and describes in detail the elements of comic realism; in *Joseph Andrews* and *Tom Jones*, he provides full realizations of this theory. These novels define the ground rules of form that would be followed, to varying degrees, by Jane Austen, William Makepeace Thackeray, George Eliot, Thomas Hardy, James Joyce, and D. H. Lawrence, and they also speak to countless readers across many generations. Both novels, in fact, have been translated into successful films (*Tom Jones* was released in 1963; *Joseph Andrews*, in 1977).

The historical importance of the preface to *Joseph Andrews* results from both the seriousness with which it treats the formal qualities of the novel (at the time a fledgling and barely respectable genre) and the precision with which it defines the characteristics of the genre, the "comic epic-poem in prose." Fielding places *Joseph Andrews* in particular and the comic novel in general squarely in the tradition of classical literature and coherently argues its differences from the romance and the burlesque. He also provides analogies between the comic novel and the visual arts. Fielding thus leads the reader to share his conception that the comic novel is an aesthetically valid form with its roots in classical tradition and a form peculiarly suited to the attitudes and values of its own age.

With his background in theater and journalism, Fielding could move easily through a wide range of forms and rhetorical techniques in his fiction, from direct parody of Samuel Richardson in *An Apology for the Life of Mrs. Shamela Andrews* to ironic inversion of the great man's biography in *Jonathan Wild* to adaptation of classical structure (Vergil's *Aeneid*, c. 29-19 B.C.E.; English translation, 1553) in *Amelia*. The two major constants in these works are the attempt to define a good, moral life, built on benevolence and honor, and a concern for finding the best way to present that definition to the reader. Thus the moral and the technique can never be separated in Fielding's works.

Joseph Andrews and *Tom Jones* bring together these two impulses in Fielding's most organically structured, brilliantly characterized, and masterfully narrated works. These novels vividly capture the diversity of experience in the physical world and the underlying benevolence of the natural order, embodying them in a rich array of the ridiculous in human behavior. Fielding combines a positive assertion of the strength of goodness and benevolence (demonstrated by the structure and plot of the novels) with the sharp thrusts of the satirist's attack on the hypocrisy and vanity of individual characters. These elements are held together by the voice of the narrator—witty, urbane, charming—who serves as moral guide through the novels and the world. Thus beyond the comic merits of each of the individual novels lies a collective sense of universal moral good. The voice of the narrator conveys to the reader the truth of that goodness.

Although the novels were popular in his own day, Fielding's contemporaries thought of him more as playwright-turned-judge than as novelist. This may have been the result of the low esteem in which the novel as a form was held as well as of Fielding's brilliant successes in these other fields. These varied successes have in common a zest for the exploration of the breadth and variety of life—a joy in living—that finds its most articulate and permanent expression in the major novels.

Today Fielding is universally acknowledged as a major figure in the development of the novel, although there is still some debate about whether he or Richardson is the "father" of the British novel. Ian Watt, for example, has asserted that Richardson's development of "formal realism" is more significant than Fielding's comic realism. Other critics, notably Martin Battestin, have demonstrated that Fielding's broader, more humane moral vision, embodied in classical structure and expressed through a self-conscious narrator, is the germ from which the richness and variety of the British novel grows. This disagreement ultimately comes down to personal taste, and there will always be Richardson and Fielding partisans to keep the controversy alive. There is no argument, however, that of their type—the novel of comic realism—no fiction has yet surpassed *Joseph Andrews* or *Tom Jones*.

BIOGRAPHY

Henry Fielding was born April 22, 1707, in Sharpham Park, Somersetshire, to Edmund and Sarah Fielding. His father, an adventurer, gambler, and swaggerer, was a sharp contrast to the quiet, conservative, traditional gentry of his mother's family, the Goulds. In 1710, the family moved to Dorset, where Fielding and his younger brother and three sisters (including the future novelist Sarah Fielding) would spend most of their childhood on a small estate and farm given to Mrs. Fielding by her father, Sir Henry Gould.

The death of Fielding's mother in April, 1718, ended this idyllic life. Litigation over the estate created a series of family battles that raged for several decades. In 1719, Fielding was sent to Eton College, partly because the Goulds wanted him influenced as little as possible by his father, who had resumed his "wild" life in London, and partly because Fielding disliked his father's new Catholic wife. Remaining at Eton until 1724 or 1725, Fielding made many friends, including George Lyttleton and William Pitt. At Eton he began his study of classical literature, which became a profound influence on his literary career.

Few details are known of Fielding's life during the several years after Eton. He spent a good deal of time with the Goulds in Salisbury, but he also led a hectic, boisterous life in London, spending much time at the theater, where the popular masquerades and burlesques influenced him greatly. His visits to the theater stimulated him to try his own hand at comedy, and in February, 1728, *Love in Several Masques*, based on his own romantic adventures of the previous year, was performed at Drury Lane. In March, 1728, Fielding enrolled in the Faculty of Letters at the University of Leyden (Netherlands), where he pursued his interest in the classics. In August, 1729, at the age of twenty-two, he returned to London without completing his degree.

It is clear from his literary output in the 1730's that Fielding was intensely involved in theatrical life. From 1730 through 1737 he authored at least nineteen different dramatic works (as well as presenting revivals and new productions of revised works), most with political themes, at both the Little Theatre in the Haymarket and the Drury Lane. In addition to writing ballad opera, full-length comedies, translations, and parodies, Fielding was also producing, revising the plays of other writers, and managing theater business. He also formed a new, important friendship with the artist William Hogarth.

His theatrical career came to an abrupt halt (although a few more plays appeared in the 1740's) with the passage of the Licensing Act of 1737 which resulted in the closing of many theaters. Fielding's political satire offended Prime Minister Sir Robert Walpole and had been part of the motivation for the government's desire to control and censor the theaters.

In addition to this theatrical activity with its political commentary, Fielding found time in the years 1733-1734 to court and marry Charlotte Cradock of Salisbury. Charlotte's mother died in 1735, leaving the entire estate to the Fieldings and alleviating many of the financial problems caused by the legal disputes over the estate in Dorset. The couple moved from London to East Stour the same year, although Fielding regularly visited London, because he was manager, artistic director, and controller in chief of the Little Theatre. The first of their three children, Charlotte, was born April 17, 1736.

Fielding's relentless energy (and desire to add to his income) compelled him to begin a new career in late 1737, whereupon he began to study law at the Middle Temple. He became a barrister on June 20, 1740, and spent the next several years in the Western Circuit. During this service he became friends with Ralph Allen of Bath. He remained active in the practice of justice, as attorney and magistrate, until he left England in 1754.

Fielding continued to involve himself in political controversy, even while studying law. He edited, under pseudonyms, *The Champion*, an opposition newspaper issued three times a week, directed against Prime Minister Walpole (a favorite subject of Fielding's satire). Later he would edit *The True Patriot* in support of the government during the threat of the Jacobite Rising, *Jacobite's Journal*, and *The Covent-Garden Journal.*

From theater to law to journalism—Fielding had already charged through three careers when the first installment of Richardson's *Pamela: Or, Virtue Rewarded* appeared on November 6, 1740. Deeply disturbed by the artificiality of the novel's epistolary technique, and appalled by its perversion of moral values, Fielding quickly responded with *An Apology for the Life of Mrs. Shamela Andrews*, often referred to as *Shamela*, an "antidote" to *Pamela.* Although published anonymously, Fielding's authorship was apparent and created ill feelings between the two authors that would last most of their lives.

The success of *Shamela* encouraged Fielding to try his hand at a more sustained satire, which eventually grew into *Joseph Andrews*. In 1743 he published, by subscription, the *Miscellanies*, a collection of previously published works, and two new ones: an unfinished story, "A Journey from This World to the Next," and the first version of *Jonathan Wild.*

Although the mid-1740's brought Fielding fame, success, and money, his personal life was beset with pain. He suffered continually from gout, and his wife died in November, 1744. In the following year he became involved in the propaganda battles over the Jacobite Rising. On November 27, 1747, he married his wife's former maid, Mary Daniel, and some sense of peace and order was restored to his private life. They would have five children.

While forming new personal ties and continuing strong involvement in political issues, Fielding was preparing his masterwork, *Tom Jones*. He also took oath as justice of the peace for Westminster and Middlesex, London, in 1748, and he opened an employment agency and estate brokerage with his brother in 1749. His last novel, *Amelia*, was not well received, disappointing those readers who were expecting another *Tom Jones*.

The early 1750's saw Fielding's health continue to decline, although he remained active in his judgeship, producing a number of pamphlets on various legal questions. In June of 1754, his friends convinced him to sail to Lisbon, Portugal, where the climate might improve his health. He died there on October 8, 1754, and is buried in the British Cemetery outside Lisbon. *The Journal of a Voyage to Lisbon*, his last work, was published one year after his death.

ANALYSIS

Analysis and criticism of Henry Fielding's fiction have traditionally centered on the moral values in the novels, the aesthetic structure in which they are placed, and the relationship between the two. In this view, Fielding as moralist takes precedence over Fielding as artist, since the aesthetic structure is determined by the moral. Each of the novels is judged by the extent to which it finds the appropriate form for its moral vision. The relative failure of *Amelia*, for example, may be Fielding's lack of faith in his own moral vision. The happy ending, promulgated by the deus ex machina of the good magistrate, is hardly consistent with the dire effects of urban moral decay that have been at work upon the Booths throughout the novel. Fielding's own moral development and changes in outlook also need to be considered in this view. The reader must examine the sources of Fielding's moral vision in the latitudinarian sermons of the day, as well as the changes in his attitudes as he examined eighteenth century urban life in greater detail, and as he moved in literature from *Joseph Andrews* to *Amelia*, and in life from the theater to the bench of justice.

As is clear from the preface to *Joseph Andrews*, however, Fielding was equally interested in the aesthetics of his fiction. Indeed, each of the novels, even from the first parody, *Shamela*, conveys not only a moral message but a literary experiment to find the strongest method for expressing that message to the largest reading public. This concern is evident in the basic plot structure, characterization, language, and role of the narrator. Each novel attempts to reach the widest audience possible with its moral thesis. Although each differs in the way in which Fielding attempts this, they all have in common the sense that the *how* of the story is as important as the *what*. The novels are experiments in the methods of moral education—for the reader as well as for the characters.

This concern for the best artistic way to teach a moral lesson was hardly new with Fielding. His classical education and interests, as well as the immediate human response gained from theater audiences during his playwriting days, surely led him to see that fiction must delight as well as instruct. Fielding's novels are both exemplars of this goal (in their emphasis on incidents of plot and broad range of characterization) and serious discussions of the method by which to achieve it (primarily through structure and through narrative commentary).

The direct stimulation for Fielding's career as novelist was the publication of Samuel

Richardson's *Pamela*, a novel that disturbed Fielding both by its artistic ineptitude and by its moral vacuousness. Fielding was as concerned with the public reaction to *Pamela* as he was with its author's methods. That the reading public could be so easily misled by *Pamela*'s morals disturbed Fielding deeply, and the success of that novel led him to ponder what better ways were available for reaching the public with his own moral thesis. His response to *Pamela* was both moral (he revealed the true state of Pamela/Shamela's values) and aesthetic (he exposed the artificiality of "writing to the moment").

Sermons and homilies, while effective in church (and certainly sources of Fielding's moral philosophy), were not the stuff of prose fiction; neither was the epistolary presentation of "virtue rewarded" of *Pamela* (or the "objectively" amoral tone of Daniel Defoe's *The Fortunes and Misfortunes of the Famous Moll Flanders, Written from Her Own Memorandums*, 1722). Fielding sought a literary method for combining moral vision and literary pleasure that would be appropriate to the rapidly urbanizing and secular society of the mid-eighteenth century. To find that method he ranged through direct parody, irony, satire, author-narrator intrusion, and moral exemplum. Even those works, such as *Jonathan Wild* and *Amelia*, which are not entirely successful, live because of the vitality of Fielding's experimental methods. In *Joseph Andrews* and *Tom Jones*, he found the way to reach his audience most effectively.

Fielding's informing moral values, embodied in the central characters of the novels (Joseph Andrews, Parson Adams, Tom Jones, Squire Allworthy, Mr. Harrison) can be summarized, as Martin Battestin has ably done, as Charity, Prudence, and Providence. Fielding held an optimistic faith in the perfectability of humanity and the potential for the betterment of society, based on the essential goodness of human nature. These three values must work together. In the novels, the hero's worth is determined by the way in which he interacts with other people (charity), within the limits of social institutions designed to provide order (prudence). His reward is a life full of God's provision (Providence). God's Providence has created a world of abundance and plenitude; man's prudence and charity can guarantee its survival and growth. Both Joseph Andrews and Tom Jones learn the proper combination of prudence and charity. They learn to use their innate inclination toward goodness within a social system that ensures order. To succeed, however, they must overcome obstacles provided by the characters who, through vanity and hypocrisy, distort God's Providence. Thus Fielding's moral vision, while optimistic, is hardly blind to the realities of the world. *Jonathan Wild*, with its basic rhetorical distinction between "good" and "great," and *Amelia*, with its narrative structured around the ill effects of doing good, most strongly reflect Fielding's doubts about the practicality of his beliefs.

These ideas can be easily schematized, but the scheme belies the human complexity through which they are expressed in the novels. Tom Jones is no paragon of virtue, but he must learn, at great physical pain and spiritual risk, how to combine charity and prudence. Even Squire Allworthy is, as Sheldon Sacks has observed, a "fallible" paragon. These ideas do not come from a single source, but are derived from a combination of sources, rooted in Fielding's classical education; the political, religious, and literary movements of his own time; and his own experience as dramatist, journalist, and magistrate.

Fielding's familiarity with the classics, begun at Eton and continued at the University of Leyden, is revealed in many ways: through language (the use of epic simile and epic conventions in *Joseph Andrews*), through plot (the symmetry of design in *Tom Jones*), through theme (the importance of moderation in all the novels), and through structure (the relationship of *Amelia* to Vergil's *Aeneid*). The preface to *Joseph Andrews* makes explicit how much Fielding saw in common between his own work and classical literature. His belief in the benevolent order of the world, especially illustrated by country living, such as at Squire Allworthy's estate (Paradise Hall), is deeply rooted in the pastoral tradition of classical literature. These classical elements are combined with the beliefs of the latitudinarian homilists of the seventeenth and eighteenth centuries, who stressed the perfectibility of humankind in the world through good deeds (charity) and good heart (benevolence).

While Fielding's thematic concerns may be rooted in classical and Christian thought, his literary technique has sources that are more complex, deriving from his education, his own experience in the theater, and the influence of Richardson's *Pamela*. It is difficult to separate each of these sources, for the novels work them into unified and original statements. Indeed, *Joseph Andrews*, the novel most closely related to classical sources, is also deeply imbued with the sense of latitudinarian thought in its criticism of the clergy, and satire of Richardson in its plot and moral vision.

The London in which Fielding spent most of his life was a world of literary and political ferment, an age of factionalism in the arts, with the Tory wits (Jonathan Swift, Alexander Pope, John Gay, John Arbuthnot) allied against Colley Cibber, the poet laureate and self-proclaimed literary spokesman for the British Isles. Swift's *Gulliver's Travels* (1726) and Gay's *The Beggar's Opera* (1728) had recently appeared; both were influential in forming Fielding's literary methods—the first with its emphasis on sharp political satire, the second with the creation of a new literary form, the ballad opera. The ballad opera set new lyrics, expressing contemporary political and social satire, to well-known music. Fielding was to find his greatest theatrical success in this genre and was to carry it over to his fiction, especially *Jonathan Wild*, with its emphasis on London low life and its excesses of language.

It was a time, also, of great political controversy, with the ongoing conflicts between the Tories and Jacobites about the questions of religion and succession. Prime Minister Walpole's politics of expediency were a ripe subject for satire. Fielding's career as journalist began as a direct response to political issues, and significant portions of *Joseph Andrews* and *Tom Jones*, as well as *Jonathan Wild*, deal with political issues.

These various sources, influences, and beliefs are molded into coherent works of art through Fielding's narrative technique. It is through the role of the narrator that he most clearly and successfully experiments in the methods of teaching a moral lesson. Starting with the voice of direct literary parody in *Shamela* and moving through the varied structures and voices of the other novels, Fielding's art leads in many directions, but it always leads to his ultimate concern for finding the best way to teach the clearest moral lesson. In *Tom Jones* he finds the most appropriate method to demonstrate that the world is a beautiful place if people practice charity and prudence.

SHAMELA

The key to understanding how *Shamela* expresses Fielding's concern with both the moral thesis and the aesthetic form of fiction is contained in the introductory letters between Parsons Tickletext and Oliver. Oliver is dismayed at Tickletext's exuberant praise of *Pamela* and at the novel's public reception and popularity. The clergy, in particular, have been citing it as a work worthy to be read with the Scriptures. He contends that the text of *Shamela*, which he encloses, reveals the "true" story of Pamela's adventures and puts them in their proper moral perspective. By reading Oliver's version, Tickletext will correct his own misconceptions; by reading *Shamela* (under the guidance of the prefatory letters), the public will laugh at *Pamela* and perceive the perversity of its moral thesis.

Shamela began, of course, simply as a parody of Richardson's novel, and, in abbreviated form, carries through the narrative of the attempted seduction of the young serving girl by the squire, and her attempts to assert her virtue through chastity or marriage. Fielding makes direct hits at Richardson's weakest points: His two main targets are the epistolary technique of "writing to the moment" and the moral thesis of "virtue rewarded" by pounds and pence (and marriage).

Fielding parodies the epistolary technique by carrying it to its most illogical extreme: Richardson's technical failure is not the choice of epistolary form, but his insistence on its adherence to external reality. Shamela writes her letters at the very same moment she is being attacked in bed by Squire Booby. While feigning sleep she writes: "You see I write in the present tense." The inconsistency of Pamela's shift from letters to journal form when she is abducted is shown through Fielding's retention of the letter form throughout the story, no matter what the obstacles for sending and receiving them. He also compounds the criticism of Richardson by including a number of correspondents in addition to Shamela (her mother, Henrietta Maria Honora Andrews, Mrs. Jewkes, Parson Williams) and including various complications, such as letters within letters within letters.

Fielding retains the essential characters and key scenes from *Pamela*, such as Mr. B's hiding in the closet before the attempted seduction, Pamela's attempted suicide at the pond, and Parson Williams's interference. For each character and scene Fielding adopts Richardson's penchant for minute descriptive detail and intense character response to the event; he also parodies the method and seriousness of the original by revealing the motives of the characters.

The revealing of motives is also Fielding's primary way of attacking the prurience of Richardson's presentation as well as the moral thesis behind it. He debunks the punctilio (decorum) of the central character. Shamela's false modesty ("I thought once of making a little fortune by my person. I now intend to make a great one by my virtue") mocks Pamela's pride in her chastity; the main difference between them is Shamela's recognition and acceptance of the mercenary motives behind her behavior and Pamela's blindness to her own motivation. Richardson never examines the reliability of Pamela's motivations, although he describes her thoughts in detail. Fielding allows Shamela to glory in both her ability to dupe the eager Squire Booby and her mercenary motives for doing so. The reader may, as Parson Oliver wants Tickletext to do, easily condemn Shamela for a villain but never for a hypocrite.

Fielding also attacks Richardson's refusal to describe the sexual attributes of his characters or to admit the intensity of their sexual desires, particularly in the case of Pamela herself. Pamela always hints and suggests—and, Fielding claims, wallows in her suggestiveness. Fielding not only describes the sexual aspects directly, but exaggerates and reduces them to a comic level, hardly to be taken sensually or seriously. *Shamela* quickly, fully, and ruthlessly annihilates the moral thesis of "virtue rewarded" through this direct exaggeration. Fielding does not, however, in his role as parodist, suggest an alternative to *Pamela*'s moral thesis; he is content, for the time, with exposing its flaws.

This first foray into fiction served for Fielding as a testing ground for some of the rhetorical techniques he used in later works, especially the emphasis on satiric inversion. These inversions appear in his reversal of sexual roles in *Joseph Andrews*, the reversal of rhetoric in the "good" and "great" in *Jonathan Wild*, and the reversal of goodness of motive and evil of effect in *Amelia*. Fielding's concern to find a rhetorical method for presenting a moral thesis was confined in *Shamela* to the limited aims and goals of parody. He had such success with the method (after all, he had his apprenticeship in the satiric comedy of the theater), that he began his next novel on the same model.

JOSEPH ANDREWS

Like *Shamela*, *Joseph Andrews* began as a parody of *Pamela*. In his second novel, Fielding reverses the gender of the central character and traces Joseph's attempts to retain his chastity and virtue while being pursued by Lady Booby. This method of inversion creates new possibilities, not only for satirizing Richardson's work but for commenting on the sexual morality of the time in a more positive way than in *Shamela*. The most cursory reading reveals how quickly Fielding grew tired of parody and how *Joseph Andrews* moved beyond its inspiration and its forerunner. Even the choice of direct narration rather than epistolary form indicates Fielding's unwillingness to tie himself to his model.

Most readers agree that the entrance of Parson Adams, Joseph's guide, companion, and partner in misery, turns the novel from simple parody into complex fiction. Adams takes center stage as both comic butt, preserving Joseph's role as hero, and moral guide, preserving Joseph's role as innocent.

Adams's contribution is also part of Fielding's conscious search for the best way to convey his moral thesis. The narrative refers continually to sermons, given in the pulpit or being carried by Adams to be published in London. These sermons are generally ineffectual or contradicted by the behavior of the clergy who pronounce them. Just as experience and the moral example of Adams's life are better teachers for Joseph than sermons—what could be a more effective lesson than the way he is treated by the coach passengers after he is robbed, beaten, and stripped?—so literary example has more power for Fielding and the reader. Adams's constant companion, his copy of Aeschylus, is further testament to Fielding's growing faith in his exemplary power of literature as moral guide. In *Joseph Andrews*, narrative art takes precedence over both parody and sermon.

Fielding's concern for method as well as meaning is given its most formal discussion in the preface. The historical importance of this document results from both the seriousness with which it treats the formal qualities of the novel and the precision with which it defines the characteristics of the genre, the "comic epic-poem in prose." The seriousness is established through the careful logic and organization of the argument and through the parallels drawn between the new genre and classical literature (the lost comic epic supposedly written by Homer) and modern painting (Michelangelo da Caravaggio and William Hogarth).

Fielding differentiates the "comic epic-poem in prose" from contemporary romances such as *Pamela*. The new form is more extended and comprehensive in action, contains a much larger variety of incidents, and treats a greater variety of characters. Unlike the serious romance, the new form is less solemn in subject matter, treats characters of lower rank, and presents the ludicrous rather than the sublime. The comic, opposed to the burlesque, arises solely from the observation of nature, and has its source in the discovery of the "ridiculous" in human nature. The ridiculous always springs from the affectations of vanity and hypocrisy.

Within the novel itself, the narrator will continue the discussion of literary issues in the introductory chapters to each of the first three of four books: "of writing lives in general," "of divisions in authors," and "in praise of biography." These discussions, although sometimes more facetious than serious, do carry through the direction of the opening sentence of the novel: "Examples work more forcibly on the mind than precepts." Additionally, this narrative commentary allows Fielding to assume the role of reader's companion and guide that he develops more fully in *Tom Jones*.

While the preface takes its cue from classical tradition, it is misleading to assume that *Joseph Andrews* is merely an updating of classical technique and ideas. Even more than *Shamela*, this novel brings together Fielding's dissatisfaction with Richardson's moral thesis and his support of latitudinarian attitudes toward benevolence and charity. Here, too, Fielding begins his definition of the "good" man in modern Christian terms. Joseph redefines the place of chastity and honor in male sexuality; Parson Adams exemplifies the benevolence all people should display; Mrs. Tow-wowse, Trulliber, and Peter Pounce, among others, illustrate the vanity and hypocrisy of the world.

The structure of the novel is episodic, combining the earthly journey and escapades of the hero with suggestions of the Christian pilgrimage in John Bunyan's *The Pilgrim's Progress* (1678, 1684). Fielding was still experimenting with form and felt at liberty to digress from his structure with interpolated tales or to depend on coincidence to bring the novel to its conclusion. The immediate moral effect sometimes seems more important than the consistency of rhetorical structure. These are, however, minor lapses in Fielding's progression toward unifying moral thesis and aesthetic structure.

JONATHAN WILD

In *Jonathan Wild*, Fielding seems to have abandoned temporarily the progression from the moral statement of parody and sermon to the aesthetic statement of literary example. *Jonathan Wild* was first published in the year immediately following *Joseph Andrews* (revised in 1754), and there is evidence to indicate that the work was actually written before *Joseph Andrews*. This is a reasonable assumption, since *Jonathan Wild* is more didactic in its method and more negative in its moral vision. It looks back toward *Shamela* rather than ahead to *Tom Jones*.

Jonathan Wild is less a novel, even as Fielding discusses the form in the preface to *Joseph Andrews*, than a polemic. Critic Northrop Frye's term "anatomy" may be the most appropriate label for the work. Like other anatomies—Sir Thomas More's *De Optimo Reipublicae Statu, deque Nova Insula Utopia* (*Utopia*, 1551), Swift's *Gulliver's Travels*, and Samuel Johnson's *Rasselas, Prince of Abyssinia* (1759)—it emphasizes ideas over narrative. It is more moral fable than novel, and more fiction than historical biography, altering history to fit the moral vision.

More important, it was Fielding's experiment in moving the moral lesson of the tale away from the narrative (with its emphasis on incident and character) and into the rhetoric of the narrator (with its emphasis on language). Fielding attempted to use language as the primary carrier of his moral thesis. Although this experiment failed—manipulation of language, alone, would not do—it gave him the confidence to develop the role of the narrative voice in its proper perspective in *Tom Jones*.

Fielding freely adapted the facts of Wild's life, which were well known to the general public. He chose those incidents from Wild's criminal career and punishment that would serve his moral purpose, and he added his own fictional characters, the victims of Wild's "greatness," especially the Heartfrees. Within the structure of the inverted biography of the "great" man, Fielding satirizes the basic concepts of middle-class society. He differentiates between "greatness" and "goodness," terms often used synonymously in the eighteenth century. The success of the novel depends on the reader's acceptance and understanding of this rhetorical inversion.

"Goodness," characterized by the Heartfrees, reiterates the ideals of behavior emphasized in *Joseph Andrews:* benevolence, honor, honesty, and charity, felt through the heart. "Greatness," personified in Wild, results in cunning and courage, characteristics of the will. The action of the novel revolves around the ironic reversal of these terms. Although

Wild's actions speak for themselves, the ironic voice of the narrator constantly directs the reader's response.

Parts of *Jonathan Wild* are brilliantly satiric, but the work as a whole does not speak to modern readers. Fielding abandoned the anatomy form after this experiment, recognizing that the voice of the narrator alone cannot carry the moral thesis of a novel in a convincing way. In *Jonathan Wild*, he carried to an extreme the role of the narrator as moral guide that he experimented with in *Joseph Andrews*. In *Tom Jones*, he found the precise balance: the moral voice of the narrator controlling the reader's reaction through language and the literary examples of plot and character.

TOM JONES

In *Tom Jones*, Fielding moved beyond the limited aims of each of his previous works into a more comprehensive moral and aesthetic vision. No longer bound by the need to attack Richardson or by the attempt to define a specific fictional form, such as the moral fable or the "comic epic-poem in prose," Fielding dramatized the positive values of the good man in a carefully structured narrative held together by the guiding voice of the narrator. This narrator unifies, in a consistent pattern, Fielding's concern for both the truthfulness of his moral vision and the best way to reach the widest audience.

The structure of *Tom Jones*, like that of *Joseph Andrews*, is based on the secularization of the spiritual pilgrimage. Tom must journey from his equivocal position as foundling on the country estate of Squire Allworthy (Paradise Hall) to moral independence in the hellish city of London. He must learn to understand and control his life. When he learns this lesson, he will return to the country to enjoy the plenitude of paradise regained that Providence allows him. He must temper his natural, impetuous charity with the prudence that comes from recognition of his own role in the larger social structure. In precise terms, he must learn to control his animal appetites in order to win the love of Sophia Western and the approval of Allworthy. This lesson is rewarded not only by his gaining these two goals, but by his gaining the knowledge of his parentage and his rightful place in society. He is no longer a "foundling."

Unlike the episodic journey of *Joseph Andrews*, *Tom Jones* adapts the classical symmetry of the epic in a more conscious and precise way. The novel is divided into eighteen books. Some of the books, such as 1 and 4, cover long periods of time and are presented in summary form, with the narrator clearly present; others cover only a few days or hours, with the narrator conspicuously absent and the presentation primarily scenic. The length of each book is determined by the importance of the subject, not the length of time covered.

The books are arranged in a symmetrical pattern. The first half of the novel takes Tom from his mysterious birth to his adventures in the Inn at Upton; the second half takes him from Upton to London and the discovery of his parentage. Books 1 through 6 are set in Somerset at Squire Allworthy's estate and culminate with Tom's affair with Molly. Books

7 through 12 are set on the road to Upton, at the Inn, and on the road from Upton to London; the two central books detail the adventures at the Inn and Tom's affair with Mrs. Waters. Books 13 through 18 take Tom to London and begin with his affair with Lady Bellaston.

Within this pattern, Fielding demonstrates his moral thesis, the education of a "good man," in a number of ways: through the narrative (Tom's behavior continually lowers his moral worth in society); through characters (the contrasting pairs of Tom and Blifil, Allworthy and Western, Square and Thwackum, Molly and Lady Bellaston); and through the voice of the narrator.

Fielding extends the role of the narrator in *Tom Jones*, as teller of the tale, as moral guide, and as literary commentator and critic. Each of these voices was heard in *Joseph Andrews*, but here they come together in a unique narrative persona. Adopting the role of the stagecoach traveler, the narrator speaks directly to his fellow passengers, the readers. He is free to digress and comment whenever he feels appropriate, and there is, therefore, no need for the long interpolated tales such as appeared in *Joseph Andrews*.

To remind his readers that the purpose of fiction is aesthetic as well as moral, the narrator often comments on literary topics: "Of the Serious in Writing, and for What Purpose it is introduced"; "A wonderful long chapter concerning the Marvelous"; "Containing Instructions very necessary to be perused by modern Critics." Taken together, these passages provide a guide to Fielding's literary theory as complete as the preface to *Joseph Andrews*.

Although in *Tom Jones* Fielding still schematically associates characters with particular moral values, the range of characters is wider than in his previous novels. Even a minor character, such as Black George, has a life beyond his moral purpose as representative of hypocrisy and self-servingness.

Most important, *Tom Jones* demonstrates Fielding's skill in combining his moral vision with aesthetic form in a way that is most pleasurable to the reader. The reader learns how to live the good Christian life because Tom learns that lesson. Far more effective than parody, sermon, or moral exemplum, the combination of narrative voice and literary example of plot and character is Fielding's greatest legacy to the novel.

Lawrence F. Laban

OTHER MAJOR WORKS

PLAYS: *Love in Several Masques*, pr., pb. 1728; *The Author's Farce, and the Pleasures of the Town*, pr., pb. 1730; *Rape upon Rape: Or, Justice Caught in His Own Trap*, pr., pb. 1730 (also known as *The Coffee-House Politician*); *The Temple Beau*, pr., pb. 1730; *Tom Thumb: A Tragedy*, pr., pb. 1730 (revised as *The Tragedy of Tragedies: Or, The Life and Death of Tom Thumb the Great*, pr., pb. 1731); *The Letter-Writers: Or, A New Way to Keep a Wife at Home*, pr., pb. 1731; *The Welsh Opera: Or, The Grey Mare the Better Horse*, pr., pb. 1731 (revised as *The Grub-Street Opera*, pb. 1731); *The Covent Garden Tragedy*, pr., pb. 1732; *The Lottery*, pr., pb. 1732; *The Mock Doctor: Or, The Dumb Lady Cur'd*, pr., pb. 1732 (adaptation of Molière's *Le Medecin malgré lui*); *The Modern Husband*, pr., pb. 1732 (five acts); *The Old Debauchees*, pr., pb. 1732; *The Miser*, pr., pb. 1733 (adaptation of Molière's *L'Avare*); *Don Quixote in England*, pr., pb. 1734; *The Intriguing Chambermaid*, pr., pb. 1734 (adaptation of Jean-François Regnard's *Le Retour imprévu*); *An Old Man Taught Wisdom: Or, The Virgin Unmask'd*, pr., pb. 1735; *The Universal Gallant: Or, The Different Husbands*, pr., pb. 1735 (five acts); *Pasquin: Or, A Dramatic Satire on the Times*, pr., pb. 1736; *Tumble-Down Dick: Or, Phaeton in the Suds*, pr., pb. 1736; *Eurydice Hiss'd: Or, A Word to the Wise*, pr., pb. 1737; *Eurydice: Or, The Devil's Henpeck'd*, pr. 1737 (one act); *The Historical Register for the Year 1736*, pr., pb. 1737 (three acts); *Miss Lucy in Town*, pr., pb. 1742 (one act); *The Wedding-Day*, pr., pb. 1743 (five acts; also known as *The Virgin Unmask'd*); *The Fathers: Or, The Good-Natured Man*, pr., pb. 1778 (revised for posthumous production by David Garrick).

NONFICTION: *The Journal of a Voyage to Lisbon*, 1755.

TRANSLATION: *The Military History of Charles XII King of Sweden*, 1740.

MISCELLANEOUS: *Miscellanies*, 1743 (3 volumes).

BIBLIOGRAPHY

Battestin, Martin C. *A Henry Fielding Companion*. Westport, Conn.: Greenwood Press, 2000. Comprehensive reference work covers the life and writings of Fielding in a thorough fashion. Includes sections on where Fielding lived, his family, and significant historical figures and literary influences, in addition to material on Fielding's works, themes, and characters. Includes bibliography and index.

Battestin, Martin C., with Ruthe R. Battestin. *Henry Fielding: A Life*. New York: Routledge, 1989. The *Sunday Times* of London voted this work one of the four best biographies of the year. Based on fourteen years' research, this detailed biography provides a definitive story of Fielding. Includes a useful bibliography of Fielding's writings.

Bertelsen, Lance. *Henry Fielding at Work: Magistrate, Businessman, Writer*. New York: Palgrave, 2000. Presents analysis of Fielding in his roles as writer, magistrate, and businessman, discussing how his various work experiences affected the form and content of his writing. Includes bibliography and index.

Dircks, Richard J. *Henry Fielding*. Boston: Twayne, 1983. Provides a useful introduction to Fielding, integrating his central ideas and vision of life as they are experienced in his works as a novelist, dramatist, journalist, and pamphleteer. Focuses on Fielding's major works. Includes an excellent bibliography and a chronology.

Mace, Nancy A. *Henry Fielding's Novels and the Classical Tradition*. Newark: University of Delaware Press, 1996. Examines the classical influence on Fielding's novels and other writings, discussing his knowledge of classical literature and his use of classical allusions and quotations.

Pagliaro, Harold E. *Henry Fielding: A Literary Life*. New York: St. Martin's Press, 1998. Excellent work presents an interesting account of Fielding's life and writings, with one chapter devoted to his novels and other prose fiction. Includes bibliographical references and index.

Paulson, Ronald. *The Life of Henry Fielding: A Critical Biography*. Malden, Mass.: Blackwell, 2000. Examines how Fielding's literary works—novels, plays, and essays—all contained autobiographical elements. Each chapter begins with an annotated chronology of the events of Fielding's life in the period covered within the chapter. Includes bibliography and index.

Rawson, Claude, ed. *The Cambridge Companion to Henry Fielding*. New York: Cambridge University Press, 2007. Collection of essays, commissioned for this volume, includes an examination of Fielding's life and discussion of his major novels, his style, his theatrical career, and his journalism work.

Rivero, Albert J., ed. *Critical Essays on Henry Fielding*. New York: G. K. Hall, 1998. Interesting collection of essays about Fielding that were published originally in the 1980's and 1990's, including discussions of the novels *Joseph Andrews*, *Tom Jones*, *Amelia*, and *Jonathan Wild*. Includes bibliographical references and index.

Watt, Ian. *The Rise of the Novel: Studies in Defoe, Richardson, and Fielding*. 2d American ed. Berkeley: University of California Press, 2001. Focuses on three novelists—Fielding, Daniel Defoe, and Samuel Richardson—in tracing the social conditions, public attitudes, and literary practices in eighteenth century England that contributed to the emergence of the novel as an important literary genre. Includes a chapter titled "Fielding and the Epic Theory of the Novel" as well as a chapter analyzing *Tom Jones*.

E. M. FORSTER

Born: London, England; January 1, 1879
Died: Coventry, Warwickshire, England; June 7, 1970
Also known as: Edward Morgan Forster

PRINCIPAL LONG FICTION

Where Angels Fear to Tread, 1905
The Longest Journey, 1907
A Room with a View, 1908
Howards End, 1910
A Passage to India, 1924
Maurice, 1971 (wr. 1913)

OTHER LITERARY FORMS

In addition to his novels, E. M. Forster wrote short stories, travel books, biographies, essays, and criticism. A number of these works, as well as his novels, appear in the seventeen-volume standard Abinger Edition (1972-1998). *The Celestial Omnibus, and Other Stories* (1911) includes his frequently anthologized story "The Road from Colonus" and five other stories written in a fantastic vein that is found much less frequently in his novels. Forster's *Aspects of the Novel* (1927) remains one of the most widely read discussions of that genre, and the essays of *Abinger Harvest* (1936) and *Two Cheers for Democracy* (1951) have also found many receptive readers. In *Marianne Thornton: A Domestic Biography, 1797-1887* (1956), Forster recalls his great-aunt, a woman whose long life plunged him into the social history of a milieu going back to the closing years of the eighteenth century. A useful description of Forster's uncollected writings by George H. Thomson may be found in *Aspects of E. M. Forster* (1969), a Festschrift honoring the author on his ninetieth birthday. In the same volume, Benjamin Britten recounts one more achievement: the libretto Forster coauthored with Eric Crozier for Britten's opera *Billy Budd* (1951).

ACHIEVEMENTS

E. M. Forster will continue to stand a little apart from other major novelists of the twentieth century. Because he made it difficult to decide by which standards his work should be judged, assessing it fairly presents problems. Unlike many of his Bloomsbury friends, he did not rebel against the Victorians or their literary habits; neither did he embrace the literary trends of his own time with any great enthusiasm. He lamented the encroachment of a commercial culture, but he did not declare war on the modern world. Although he composed a set of lectures on the novel, its plural title, *Aspects of the Novel*, anticipates his refusal to develop therein any single theory of the form in which he distinguished himself. On one hand, his work is impossible to pigeonhole; on the other hand, his six novels do not entitle him to a lonely eminence overshadowing his most able contemporaries.

Readers of the novel will not lose sight of Forster, however, because the very ambiguities and inconsistencies that frustrate efforts to find a niche for him continue to intrigue critics. Forster lived long enough to see his reputation fade and then rebound strongly. He had gained critical acclaim while still in his twenties, written a masterpiece in midlife, and published no fiction for nearly two decades before Lionel Trilling's *E. M. Forster* (1943) swung critical attention back to him. Since that time, a formidable body of books and articles dealing with Forster has formed, and many aspects of his work have been studied in great detail. While incapable of putting Forster in a specific place, his critics agree overwhelmingly that he deserves a place of honor among English novelists.

Forster's critics, fortunately, do not hold his unusually protracted silence against him. The author's failure to write a novel in the final forty-six years of his life has been explained in various ways—for example, it has been noted that instead of exercising his talents in succession, husbanding his resources, exhausting one mode before moving to another, Forster put all of himself into the first six novels and then ceased at an age when many novelists are just reaching their prime. Whatever the reason for his early retirement from a literary form successfully practiced by so many older writers, Forster furnished his critics no occasion to regret the decline of his powers.

Those powers yielded fiction marked by a blend of qualities—intelligence, wit, sensitivity, compassion, and ever-alert moral imagination—that few other writers can match. No doubt, many readers begin *A Passage to India* in the line of duty—for it has attained the rank of "classic"—but they are likely to complete it, and then begin the earlier novels, out of a desire to know better a man who could write so movingly and yet so tough-mindedly about the climate created by racial and religious prejudice. Few such readers are disappointed, for while the earlier novels are less fine, the distance between *Where Angels Fear to Tread* and *A Passage to India* is not nearly so great as that between the apprentice efforts and the masterworks of most writers. Even if his final novel is, as one critic has put it, "Forster's sole claim upon posterity," those who delve into his other works will continue to reap rewards in proportion to the attention they bestow on them, for neither wit nor wisdom is ever far away.

The critical consensus is that Forster's most successful mode is comic irony, and his name is often coupled with those of Jane Austen and George Meredith, whose test for comedy—"that it shall awaken thoughtful laughter"—Forster passes with flying colors. Critics invariably hasten to point out that Forster refused to confine himself to this mode; in the midst of deploring these deviations from high comedy, they find in Forster's odd blends of comedy, melodrama, fantasy, lyricism, and tragedy a distinctiveness they would not willingly relinquish.

BIOGRAPHY

Edward Morgan Forster lived a long but rather uneventful life. Born on New Year's Day, 1879, he was reared by his possessive mother and worshipful great-aunt (whose biography he later wrote) after the death of his father from tuberculosis before Forster turned two. Happy, protected, and dominated by women in his early years, he suffered painfully the transition to the masculine, athletically oriented Tonbridge School—later the model for Sawston School in *The Longest Journey.* After a more congenial four years, 1897 to 1901, at King's College, Cambridge, he took a second-class degree. In the next few years, he wrote seriously, traveled in Italy and Greece, tutored the children of a German countess, and indulged in walking tours of his native land.

His first novel, *Where Angels Fear to Tread*, much of which is set in Italy, received favorable reviews in 1905, and Forster produced three more novels in the next five years, of which *A Room with a View* drew also on his Italian experience, while *The Longest Journey* and *Howards End* both reflect his keen delight in the English countryside. Thereafter, having attained a considerable reputation as a novelist, he slowed his pace. He began, but could not finish, a novel called *Arctic Summer*; completed a novel about homosexuality, his own orientation, which he knew to be unpublishable; and brought out a volume of short stories. Among his many friends he numbered Virginia Woolf as well as others of the Bloomsbury group, of which, however, he was never more than a fringe member. World War I found him in Egypt as a Red Cross worker. Although he disliked Egypt, his life there led to the writing of two nonfiction books.

Forster had first visited India in 1912, but his second sojourn there as personal secretary to the maharaja of Dewas gave him the opportunity to observe the political and social life closely enough to inspire him to write another novel. *A Passage to India*, which appeared in 1924, increased his fame and led to an invitation to deliver the Clark Lectures at Trinity College, Cambridge, in 1927; the lectures were published later that year as *Aspects of the Novel.* Although he continued to write for several more decades, he published no more novels. Forster received a number of honors, culminating in the Order of Merit, presented to him on his ninetieth birthday. He died in June of 1970.

ANALYSIS

E. M. Forster's most systematic exposition of the novelist's art, *Aspects of the Novel*, is no key to his own practice. Written three years after the publication of *A Passage to India*, the work surveys neither his achievement nor his intentions. While full of the insights, charm, and homely but colorful metaphors that also distinguish Virginia Woolf's *Common Reader* volumes (1925, 1932), the book is an enthusiast's, rather than a working writer's, view of the novel, as if Forster were already distancing himself from the form that earned him his fame as a writer.

A lecture given twenty years later by Lionel Trilling, who had already published his book on Forster, gives a better sense of Forster's achievement. In "Manners, Morals, and the Novel," later published in *The Liberal Imagination* (1950), Trilling explains the novel as the writer's response to the modern world's besetting sin of snobbery, which he defines as "pride in status without pride in function." Europeans, and perhaps especially the English, familiar with snobbery as a manifestation of class structure, require less explanation than do Americans of the novel's relation to snobbery. The central tradition of the English novel from Henry Fielding through Jane Austen, Charles Dickens, William Makepeace Thackeray, and George Meredith—and indeed English comedy as far back as Geoffrey Chaucer's *The Canterbury Tales* (1387-1400)—stands as evidence.

In Forster's time, however, that tradition was being modified. For one thing, the greatest English novelists at work during Forster's formative years were a wealthy American expatriate and a retired Polish mariner. No one as sensitive as Forster could escape the influence of Henry James and Joseph Conrad, but these men made curious heirs to Dickens and Thackeray and George Eliot. James, while intensely interested in the textures of society, focused his attention on the relations between the English (and Continental) leisure class and those American travelers whom Mark Twain had christened "innocents abroad," thus limiting his social scrutiny, in Forster's opinion, to the narrow perceptions of a few wealthy idlers. Conrad diverged even more sharply from the path of previous English novelists, for he neither understood nor cared to understand any level of English society. A man of his temperament and interest might be imagined as a literary force in the midcentury United States of Nathaniel Hawthorne's *The Scarlet Letter* (1850) and Herman Melville's *Moby Dick* (1851), but not in the England of Thackeray's *Vanity Fair* (1847-1848, serial; 1848, book) and Dickens's *Bleak House* (1852-1853, serial; 1853, book). Nevertheless, Conrad was more in tune with his own literary milieu than was Meredith, who at the end of the century reigned as the grand old man of English letters, and Conrad's work, like that of James, diverted the creative energy of many of the new century's novelists into new channels.

Of native English novelists still regarded as substantial, the most active at the time of Forster's entry into the field were Arnold Bennett, H. G. Wells, and John Galsworthy—all men born in the 1860's and all inheritors of the native tradition of the novel, albeit on a somewhat reduced scale. The next generation of novelists, born slightly after Forster in the 1880's, included Woolf, James Joyce, and D. H. Lawrence, all of whom published their initial works after Forster had already written five of his six novels. This latter group obviously belongs to a new literary dispensation. Society and its network of snobbery, though still significant, have receded into the background, and the conflicts of the protagonists are waged at a more personal, intimate, sometimes semiconscious level. Clearly the work of psychologists such as Sigmund Freud and Henry James's brother William James influenced these later writers and drove them to develop literary techniques adequate to the task of a more truly psychological novel.

Forster, as has been suggested, stands in the middle. A friend of Virginia Woolf and in her mind, certainly, no part of the decaying tradition she trounced so severely in her essay "Mr. Bennett and Mrs. Brown," Forster nevertheless anticipated few of the technical innovations of the novelists who reached their maturity after World War I. His last novel stands with the post-Freudian achievements. *Howards End*, his most ambitious novel, is in most respects a novel of the old school. It is denser, symbolically richer, than the characteristic work of Bennett, Wells, and Galsworthy, but the same might be said of *Bleak House*, written more than half a century earlier.

Only around the time of Forster's birth did novelists begin to insist on the novel as an art form and write theoretical defenses of it. Meredith delivered a lecture on "The Idea of Comedy and the Uses of the Comic Spirit" (1877), which, though mentioning Miguel de Cervantes and Fielding, has more to say of Aristophanes and Molière; Henry James's essay "The Art of Fiction" appeared in 1884. By the century's end, novelists had achieved respectability, and Conrad could soberly echo Longinus: "Art is long and life is short, and success is very far off."

Such new expressions of the novelist's kinship with poet and playwright did not end the nineteenth century habit of producing loose, baggy narratives in a diversity of modes, punctuated by their author's abrupt changes of direction, interpolated moral essays, and episodes introduced for no better reason than a hunch that readers, who cared nothing for artistic integrity, would enjoy them. Stock literary devices that storytellers had accumulated over the centuries—bizarre coincidences, thoroughly improbable recognition scenes thrust into "realistic" contexts, the bundling forth of long-lost (often supposedly deceased) personages in the interests of a happy or surprising denouement, all devices that twentieth century novels would shun—still flourished in Forster's youth, and he used many of them unashamedly.

If Forster's moment in literary history partly explains his wavering between Victorian and modern canons, his skeptical, eclectic temperament must also be cited. His astute analyses of the morals and manners of society involved him in comedy, tragedy, romance, and fantasy—the sort of "God's plenty" that the supposedly neoclassical John Dryden admired in Chaucer and Ben Jonson in William Shakespeare. Such men would write any sort of work and take up with any sort of character. Forster was similarly indiscriminate. His veneration for Leo Tolstoy's *Voyna i mir* (1865-1869; *War and Peace*, 1886), though "such an untidy book," betrays his Englishman's weakness in believing that God's plenty would overcome the artist's scruples.

Of course, Forster's novels are not as long as *War and Peace* or the Victorian ones that readers worked their way through in installments spread over many months. Compared to the seamless garments of Woolf or even the longer works of Joyce and William Faulkner (both of whom exhibit an un-English type of variety but also an astonishing coherence), Forster's juxtapositions of sharply contrasting modes invite criticism by readers who take in his works in two or three successive evenings. Thus, while Forster does not belong with Wells and Galsworthy, neither does he quite keep company with the greatest of his slightly younger contemporaries, for he loved too much the variety and freedom that most earlier English novelists permitted themselves.

Nevertheless, his motto for *Howards End*—"Only connect"—applies to his work generally. If he does not always make the artistic connections, his consistent theme is the necessity of making moral connections with fellow humans, of struggling against the class divisions that so many Englishmen, including a number of his fellow novelists, took for granted. In his novels, prudence is invariably on the side of those who, like Henry Wilcox in *Howards End* and Ronnie Heaslop in *A Passage to India*, resist the breakdown of social barriers; but courage, generosity, friendship, and sympathy are found among Forster's liberal opponents of snobbery. In the world of Forster's novels, the closed class is always sterile and corrupt.

Forster's eclecticism, his versatility, his refusal to ignore the claims either of heart or head make the reading of his novels an ambiguous but rich experience. Never does he seem like a mere exhibitionist, however. Rather, his openness to life's variety amounts to a perpetual invitation to the participation of alert and open-minded readers. He is far less afraid of a gaucherie than of a missed opportunity to "connect."

WHERE ANGELS FEAR TO TREAD

Forster's shortest and most tightly focused novel is *Where Angels Fear to Tread.* A young man named Philip Herriton is commissioned by his mother and sister Harriet to bring back from Italy the infant son of Lilia Carella, the widow of another of Mrs. Herriton's sons. Within a year after marrying Gino Carella, the aimless son of a small-town dentist, Lilia died giving birth to a son. Aided by Harriet and by Caroline Abbott, who as Lilia's traveling companion had been able to do nothing to ward off the offensive marriage, Philip finds Gino resistant to Mrs. Herriton's pocketbook and ultimately becomes involved in a shabby kidnapping venture engineered by Harriet—a venture that ends with the accidental death of the child. On the way home, Philip finds himself drawn emotionally to Caroline, who reveals that she too has fallen in love with Gino. In the common effort to minister to the pitifully unregenerate Harriet, however, Philip and Caroline become friends.

Thus summarized, the novel bears some resemblance to one by Henry James. Forster enjoys contrasting Anglo-Saxon and Italian mores, and he shares James's fascinated horror over the machinations and intrigues of sophisticated schemers. He may have owed the idea of centering the story on a somewhat detached emissary to James, whose novel *The Ambassadors* (1903) appeared shortly before Forster began work on his own book.

Forster's handling of his material, however, differs substantially from James's. He cannot resist scathing treatment of the characters whose company he expects his readers to keep and with whom they are to sympathize. Harriet, appalled by Italy's uncleanliness, carries a bottle of ammonia in her trunk, but Forster has it "burst over her prayer-book, so that purple patches appeared on all her clothes." Prayer brings out the worst in many of Forster's characters, an exception being Caroline, who is able to pray in the church in Gino's hometown, "where a prayer to God is thought none the worse of because it comes next to a pleasant word to a neighbor." For Philip to develop neighborliness is a struggle. Not only is he much less experienced and resourceful than Strether or any other Jamesian ambassador, he is also decidedly unattractive: callow, priggish, and cowardly. Caroline's assessment of him in the final chapter, though tardily arrived at, is accurate enough: "You're without passion; you look on life as a spectacle, you don't enter it; you only find it funny or beautiful." By the time he hears this, however, Philip has learned what neither his mother nor his sister ever suspects: that the son of an Italian dentist can love his child more than wealth, that he is capable of trust and friendship, that he can be not merely angered but also hurt by a betrayal. Philip has also felt enough by this time to be hurt by Caroline's words.

Though selfish and shortsighted, Gino is without the treachery of a Jamesian Italian such as Giovanelli in *Daisy Miller* (1878). Indeed, Forster makes him morally superior to the Herriton women. Fixing on a domestic vignette of a sort impossible in any well-appointed English household (or in a James novel, for that matter)—Gino bathing his infant son—Forster draws Caroline into helping him and lets Philip come upon them so engaged, "to all intents and purposes, the Virgin and Child, with Donor." Forster's heroes tend to idealize people who are only behaving a little better than expected, but the capacity to idealize is a symptom of their regeneration.

Harriet tricks Philip into the kidnapping; he discovers the ruse only after the baby has died and his own arm has been broken in a carriage accident. He returns to confess the transgression, only to have the grief-stricken Gino cruelly twist his broken arm and then nearly choke him to death before Caroline appears to stop him. In a typically Forsterian piece of symbolism, she persuades Gino and Philip together to drink the milk that had been poured for the child. In a pattern that Forster repeats in later novels, Philip, though excessive in his estimate of Caroline's goodness, is nevertheless "saved" by it. Salvation is partly illusion, but such an illusion serves him better than the cynicism that Philip has spent his youth imbibing.

THE LONGEST JOURNEY

Like Philip, Rickie Elliot of *The Longest Journey* is frail and aesthetic. In addition, a deformed foot, a trait inherited from his father, marks him as different from his Cambridge classmates. At the beginning of the novel, both his father, whom he despised, and his beloved mother are dead; his father's sister, Mrs. Failing, is his closest relative. On her Wiltshire estate lives a young man, Stephen Wonham, an illegitimate half brother to Rickie. Rude, truculent, undiscriminating in his choice of companions, and more or less a habitual drunkard, Stephen also proves loyal and almost pathetically trusting. The relationship between the two brothers forms the core of the novel.

The title of the book, from Percy Bysshe Shelley's poem *Epipsychidion* (1821), alludes to the folly of denying the rest of the world for the sake of "a mistress or a friend," with whom, in consequence, one must "the dreariest and longest journey go." In the midst of mulling over the poem, Rickie ironically decides to take his journey with Agnes Pembroke, a girl whose first lover, a strapping athlete, has died suddenly of a football injury. Death, it may be noted, always strikes with unexpected suddenness in Forster's novels. The marriage disgusts Rickie's closest friend, Stewart Ansell, and Rickie himself comes soon enough to regret it. Discouraged by Agnes and her elder brother Herbert from pursuing a career as a writer, Rickie takes a teaching post at Sawston School, where Herbert is a master. By a strange coincidence, a maladjusted boy at the school writes a letter to Stephen Wonham, among other total strangers, asking Stephen to "pray for him." Agnes's practical mind senses trouble if Stephen appears at the school, but mercifully the boy withdraws before Stephen can carry out an offer to come visit him. Rickie, while not fond of Stephen, is willing for him to receive his aunt's property when she dies; not so Agnes. When Mrs. Failing sends the troublesome Stephen packing, he decides to visit Sawston and inform Rickie of their relationship—about which Rickie already knows.

Outside the school, Stephen meets Stewart Ansell, on hand to verify for himself the death of his friend's spirit in his loveless union with the Pembrokes, and, after receiving an insult, knocks him down. Before Stephen can see Rickie, Agnes intercepts him and offers him the money she is sure he wants in return for leaving Sawston and sparing Rickie the embarrassment of acknowledging him. Stunned and stung, the utterly unmercenary Stephen leaves, but Ansell, won over not only by Stephen's fist but also by his principles, breaks into the Sawston dining hall during Sunday dinner and, in front of masters, students, and all, rebukes Rickie for turning away his own brother in the latter's deepest distress. As the assemblage gapes, Ansell reveals what he has correctly intuited: that Stephen is not the son of Rickie's father, as Rickie had supposed, but of his beloved mother. At this news Rickie faints.

Although wildly improbable, the scene has an electric intensity about it. Ansell, with all the clumsy insistence of a true egalitarian and all the insight of a true friend, has, while mistakenly charging Rickie with complicity in Agnes's treachery, stripped away the hypocrisy behind which the couple has hidden. There is about this revelation something of the quality of the recognition scene of a tragedy such as Sophocles' *Oidipous Tyrannos* (c. 429 B.C.E.; *Oedipus Tyrannus*, 1715), with Rickie the lame protagonist faced with the consequences of his disastrous marriage and of his unjust assumption about his father as well as of his denial of his brother.

From the time Rickie listened mutely to his classmates' discussion of whether the cow in the field was "there" if no one was present to perceive her, he has searched unavailingly for reality. He has misinterpreted his love for Agnes as real, watched his son—inevitably deformed like his father and himself—die in infancy, and seen his attempt at a schoolmaster's life tumble. Now he tries, none too successfully, to effect a reconciliation with his brother. He leaves Agnes and the school and tries to rekindle the flame of his short-story writing. When Stephen disappoints him on a visit to Mrs. Failing by breaking a promise not to drink, Rickie concludes that people are not "real." Finding Stephen sprawled drunkenly across the tracks at a railroad crossing, Rickie finds the strength to move him from the path of an oncoming train—but not the strength to save himself.

Rickie's aunt and brother-in-law, incapable of seeing his rescue of Stephen as worthwhile, see him as a failure whose life is mercifully over. Stephen, who is no thinker, is not so sure. In the final chapter, he feels himself to be in some sense the future of England, for he is now the father of a girl who bears the name of his and Rickie's mother. Dimly, he acknowledges that his salvation is from Rickie.

Not only does *The Longest Journey* run to melodrama, but it also incorporates some rather tedious moralizing, both on the part of Mrs. Failing and in an interpolated essay by Forster that forms the whole twenty-eighth chapter (although the chapter is a short one). Probably the greatest burden, however, is the one Stephen Wonham is forced to carry. First of all, he is the disreputable relative who knocks people down and falls down drunk himself. He serves a contrasting and complementary purpose as a kind of spiritual extension of Rickie, particularly after Rickie, recognizing him as his mother's son, begins to invest him with her excellencies, as recollected. In the final chapter, Stephen becomes the consciousness of the novel itself.

Without Stephen, however, Forster's brilliant portrait of Rickie is not only incomplete but also depressing, for Rickie dies, sad to say, murmuring agreement with Mrs. Failing's antihumanist convictions that "we do not live for anything great" and that "people are not important at all." Stephen exists and procreates and retains the idea of greatness to prove Rickie wrong.

A Room with a View

Forster sends his principals off to Italy again in *A Room with a View.* The room in question is one that Lucy Honeychurch and her elder cousin Charlotte Bartlett do not enjoy at the beginning of their stay in a Florentine hotel but that two other travelers, the elderly Mr. Emerson and his son George, are more than willing to exchange for the one that furnishes the ladies with only a disappointing view of the courtyard. Characteristic of Forster's well-bred characters, they lose sight of Emerson's generosity in their horror at the directness and bluntness of his offer, for he has interrupted their conversation at dinner before other guests: "I have a view, I have a view." Having defied the convention that forbids hasty and undue familiarity with a stranger, Mr. Emerson must be certified by an English clergyman, after which the ladies somewhat stiffly accept the view. Mr. Emerson, of course, has throughout the novel a "view" that the cousins, who hate the darkness but blanch at openness, achieve only with difficulty.

Soon an unexpected adventure literally throws Lucy and George Emerson more closely together. While enthusiastically and uncritically buying photographs of Italian masterpieces, Lucy witnesses a stabbing in a public square. She faints; George catches her and, after throwing her blood-spattered photographs into the River Arno, conducts her away gently. Later, Lucy puzzles over the affair and comes to the conclusion that, despite his kind intentions, George Emerson is devoid of "chivalry."

When circumstances throw them together again, George impulsively kisses Lucy. Such behavior drives Lucy and Charlotte to Rome, where they meet Cecil Vyse. He is propriety itself, never once offering to kiss Lucy, and back in England Lucy and Vyse become engaged. By coincidence, Vyse has met the Emersons and introduces them to the neighborhood where Lucy and her mother live. Though well-intentioned, Vyse is one of Forster's snobs. He is also a drab lover, and when Lucy finally tastes one of his unsatisfactory kisses, she is thrown into a panic by the prospect of another meeting with George. They meet again, and George kisses her again, with the result that Lucy deems George impossible and Vyse intolerable and breaks her engagement to the latter with the resolve never to marry anyone.

Clearly Forster is on a different, more wholeheartedly comic, course in this novel, and the denouement fulfills the tradition of romantic comedy, the inevitable marriage of Lucy and George being brought about through the ministrations of a lady who casts off her role as an apparently irredeemable snob—cousin Charlotte. What Forster says of the Honeychurch house, Windy Corner, might almost be said of the novel: "One might laugh at the house, but one never shuddered." Despite the play of Forster's wit throughout the novel and the sympathy he extends to a girl as silly as Lucy, the reader does shudder occasionally. Two murders, the real one Lucy sees and a supposed one, interrupt the proceedings. The latter is a rumor, bruited about by a clergyman named Eager, that Mr. Emerson has murdered his wife. The charge is baseless and seems to have been injected to deepen Emerson's character as a man of sorrows. The real death is even more gratuitous—unless it is meant to validate George Emerson's seriousness and dependability.

Events lead Lucy into a series of lies that she supposes to be little white ones but that threaten general unhappiness until Mr. Emerson, whom she has led to believe that she still intends to marry Vyse, induces heart's truth and persuades her to marry George. The novel ends with the honeymooners back in Florence speculating on Charlotte's motive in bringing about Lucy's climactic meeting with Mr. Emerson. They conclude that "she fought us on the surface, and yet she hoped."

Mr. Emerson, in two respects at least, echoes the writer of the same name. He is convinced of the importance of discovering Nature, and he is an apostle of self-trust. A good man, he grows tedious after the initial chapter, functioning finally as his son's advocate. George himself never quite comes into focus, and the reader is forced to accept on faith Charlotte's change of heart. The lightest of Forster's novels, *A Room with a View*—had it been lighter yet and avoided the rather heavy-handed symbolism of the "view" and the dark—might not have turned out the weakest of the five novels Forster published in his lifetime.

HOWARDS END

Howards End, Forster's most ambitious novel, recounts the adventures of two sisters, Margaret and Helen Schlegel, after two encounters with people not of their quiet, cultivated London set. At the beginning, while a guest at the country home of the Wilcoxes (a family the Schlegels had met while traveling abroad), Helen has become engaged—at least in her own mind—to one of the Wilcox sons, Paul. Her visit and engagement end awkwardly when her aunt whisks her back to London. The second incident grows out of Helen's inadvertently taking home from the theater the umbrella of a bank clerk named Leonard Bast. Standing "at the extreme verge of gentility," Leonard wishes to approach closer. The idealistic Schlegels appreciate the impulse and strike up an acquaintance. Meanwhile, the Wilcox connection is reestablished when the Wilcoxes rent a flat across from the house where the Schlegels, including younger brother Tibby, live, and Margaret, the eldest Schlegel, comes to know Mrs. Wilcox.

A quiet, even dull woman, Ruth Wilcox is an utterly charitable person who conveys to Margaret "the idea of greatness." Her husband Henry, a prosperous businessman, and the three Wilcox children—young adults like Helen and Tibby—radiate energy, good humor, and physical health but lack wit, grace, and any sense of beauty. Suddenly, a quarter of the way through the novel, Ruth Wilcox dies.

In marrying Henry Wilcox, Margaret proves very nearly as improvident as Lilia Herriton or Rickie Elliot. The two have little in common, and before long a series of fortuitous events shakes their precarious union. As a result of offhand bad advice from Henry, duly passed on by the Schlegel sisters, Leonard Bast loses his job. Leonard makes a pilgrimage to Oniton, one of several Wilcox estates on which Henry and Margaret are living. Unfortunately, Leonard chooses to bring along his unbecoming common-law wife, who turns out to be a former mistress of Henry Wilcox. When Henry angrily turns the Basts away, the conscience-stricken Helen insists on trying to compensate Bast. Like Stephen Wonham, he indignantly refuses her money. The impulsive and emotionally overwrought Helen refuses to abandon him. Later Helen disappears into Germany for a time; on her return Margaret discovers that she has conceived a son by Leonard.

When Margaret relays to her husband Helen's request that she be permitted to stay at the unused Howards End for one night, he indignantly refuses, and Margaret realizes that Henry, the betrayer of his own first wife, is unrepentant in his maintenance of a moral double standard. One tragic scene remains. Leonard appears at Howards End to beg forgiveness for sinning with Helen; Charles Wilcox (Henry's other son) totally misunderstands the intruder's motive and strikes him down with the flat of a sword, and Leonard's weak heart gives way. Charles is convicted of manslaughter, and at the end, Margaret, Helen and her child, and the broken-spirited Henry are living together at Howards End.

Although *Howards End* clearly bears similarities to Forster's first two published novels—the melodrama, the improbable coincidences, the often awkward modulations between comic and tragic tone, and so on—the pattern of events in this work is both more richly and less intrusively symbolic. As many critics have observed, this is a novel about England, written in the uneasy pre-World War I years of growing antagonism between Germany and England. Forster permits himself a series of meditations on, paeans of praise to, his native isle in the manner of John of Gaunt's "This blessed plot, this earth, this realm, this England" speech in Shakespeare's *Richard II* (pr. c. 1595-1596). At the same time, Forster clearly intimates that England is also the Wilcoxes—insular in their outlook, stolid in their prejudices, merciless in their advocacy of the class structure. The Schlegel sisters spring from a German father and revere German Romantic culture. Chapter 5 of the novel celebrates their (and Forster's) extraordinary sensitivity to Ludwig van Beethoven; it is after a performance of the Fifth Symphony that Helen takes Leonard's umbrella.

Margaret also loves England, typified by Howards End, which is no ancient seat of the Wilcoxes but a property that had belonged to Mrs. Wilcox herself, even though she sometimes seems to be amid alien corn there. England, Forster seems to say, needs to unite the best in its Wilcoxes, its providers and healthy consumers of material goods, with the Schlegel principle, expressed in the love of art and civilized discussion. By themselves the Schlegels are ineffectual. They can only watch helplessly as commercial development dooms their London house. After Helen has been carried away by her feeling for Leonard's plight, she flees to her father's ancestral home but cannot live there. Only at Howards End can she live securely and watch her child grow up.

As a symbol for England and for the possibilities of a balanced life, Howards End might seem to have some deficiencies. It is lacking in beauty and tradition. It has become the seat of a philistine family, for even the saintly Ruth demonstrates no artistic interest more highly developed than a fondness for flowers and for a certain adjacent meadow in the early morning. On her first visit to Howards End, Helen Schlegel sees more of nature's beauties than any of the Wilcoxes, who are preoccupied with croquet, tennis, and "calisthenic exercises on a machine that is tacked on to a greengage-tree," ever perceive.

The agent who renders Howards End truly habitable is an uneducated farm woman who refuses to accept her "place." When Margaret first visits Howards End, where, it is thought, they will *not* make their home, she finds Miss Avery there. The old woman, who for a second mistakes Margaret for the first Mrs. Wilcox, has taken it upon herself to guard the empty house. Her presumptuousness, which in the past has taken the form of wedding gifts to both Henry's daughter and daughter-in-law—gaucheries the Wilcoxes are quick to condemn—extends shortly thereafter to unpacking the Schlegel books and other personal belongings, which have been stored there following the expiration of the lease on the London house. After arranging the Schlegel library in bookcases and arranging the Schlegel furniture to suit herself, the woman declines to accept even polite criticism: "You think that you won't come back to live here, Mrs. Wilcox, but you will."

Thus it is an intuitive country person who joins the half-foreign Schlegel culture to the native Wilcox stock. Miss Avery also sends over a country boy, Tom, after Helen and Margaret, in defiance of Henry, spend a night together at Howards End. "Please, I am the milk," says Tom, speaking more truth than he knows. As in *Where Angels Fear to Tread*, the milk is spiritual as well as physical nourishment. Peopled with such life-affirming folk, Howards End becomes a sustaining place, an embodiment of what English life might yet be if the deepening disorder of 1910 is somehow averted. Finally won over to permitting Helen to reside there—and thus at least tacitly acknowledging his own fornication—

Henry decrees that at his death the property will pass to Margaret; Ruth Wilcox herself had wanted to give it to her.

The motto of *Howards End* is "Only connect." In the house, "the prose and passion" of life, the Wilcox and Schlegel principles, are joined through the ministrations of another of Forster's characters willing to defy the class system in the interests of a nobler order.

The central symbol of *Howards End* is hay. Ruth Wilcox is first observed "smelling hay," a product that the naturally fertile estate produces in abundance. The rest of the Wilcoxes, Miss Avery at one point observes maliciously, all suffer from hay fever. Forster uses the hay very much as Walt Whitman, whom he occasionally quotes and from whom he appropriated the title of his final novel, uses the grass: to suggest life, sustenance, hope, democracy. At the end of the novel, the chastened Henry's case of hay fever seems to have subsided when Helen, her baby, and Tom burst in from the meadow, with Helen exclaiming, "It'll be such a crop of hay as never!"

MAURICE

Written a few years after *Howards End*, *Maurice* did not see print until the year following Forster's death. In a later "terminal note" to this novel of a gay man, Forster observed a change in the public's reaction to this subject from one of "ignorance and terror" at the time he wrote it to "familiarity and contempt" in his old age, so he continued to withhold the work. Maurice Hall also defies the class system, for his sexual partner is a gamekeeper on a college classmate's estate. Given the rigid penal code of the time, the novel is also about criminality.

Aside from his sexual orientation, Maurice resembles his creator very little, being rather ordinary in intellect, little drawn to the arts, and rather robust physically. Whereas Rickie Elliot had been effeminate, his deformed foot a symbolic impediment to satisfactory heterosexuality, Maurice seems quite "normal" to his friends. His college friend Clive Durham, leaning somewhat to homosexuality in college, ironically changes after an illness and a trip to Greece, and marries. The Durhams are gentlefolk, though somewhat reduced, and Maurice has gotten on well with them, but Clive's marriage drives a wedge between them. After indulging in, and apparently escaping from, a furtive but passionate affair with Alec Scudder, their gamekeeper, Maurice suffers a blackmail threat from his former lover, but in the end Alec proves true, and instead of emigrating with whatever conscience money he might have extracted, Alec returns to the Durham estate, where, in the boathouse, the two come together again. At the end, Maurice's revelation to the conventionally horrified Clive leaves the latter trying "to devise some method of concealing the truth from Anne"—his wife.

Maurice demonstrates Forster's conviction that the desire for loving human relations is proof against the snobbery of all social classes. Although it could not be printed when it was written, the novel now seems more dated than Forster's other works, perhaps because its style is plain and drab. It obviously suffers from its lack of a contemporary audience, although Forster showed it to Lytton Strachey and received some constructive advice. Significantly, when Oliver Stallybrass, the editor of the Abinger Edition of Forster's works, assembled his favorite quotations from Forster, he could find nothing in *Maurice* worth including.

A PASSAGE TO INDIA

Although Forster committed himself wholeheartedly to friendship, it cannot be called the central theme of any of his novels until *A Passage to India*. The friendship of Rickie Elliot and Stewart Ansell, while vital to the former's development and self-discovery, is subordinated to the theme of brotherhood, in its familial sense, and Rickie can find no basis for friendship with Stephen. The incipient friendship of Margaret Schlegel and Ruth Wilcox is aborted by the latter's death. *A Passage to India*, while treating of brotherhood in its largest sense, is at heart a novel of friendship and its possibilities in the context of a racially and religiously fragmented society.

Beginning with the visit to India of the mother and fiancé of Ronnie Heaslop, the young colonial magistrate, and the complications of their encounters with a few educated natives, the narrative comes to focus on the friendship that as a consequence waxes and wanes between the English schoolmaster Cyril Fielding and the young Muslim Dr. Aziz. Forster dedicated the book to another Anglo-Indian friendship: his own with Syed Ross Masood, who first knew Forster as his tutor in Latin prior to Masood's entrance to Oxford in 1906, and who provided the impetus for Forster's own initial passage to India a few years later. Since Anglo-Indian prejudice was one of the loquacious Masood's favorite subjects, Forster understood it well by the time he came to write the novel. Indeed, his friendship with Masood demonstrated the possibility of such a relationship surviving the strains imposed on it by one partner's determination to pull no punches in discussing it.

Aziz, accused by Ronnie's fiancé, Adela Quested, of assaulting or at least offending her (for she remains vague about the matter throughout) in a cave they were exploring, is a less masterful and self-confident figure than Masood, and the reader knows all along that there must be some mistake. Adela has seen how Ronnie's Indian service has exacerbated the weaker aspects of his character, and she has broken off their engagement, but she is not, as Aziz affects to believe, a love-starved female—at least not in the crude sense Aziz intends.

Forster draws an unforgettable picture of the tensions between the colonial rulers and the Indian professional class. The most idealistic Englishmen, it seems, succumb to the prevailing intolerance. It is an effort to consider the natives as human, as when Ronnie, told by his mother, Mrs. Moore, of her meeting with a young doctor, replies: "I know of no young doctor in Chandrapore," though once he learns that his mother has actually been consorting with a Muslim, he identifies him readily enough.

An exception to the rule is Fielding, already over forty when he came to India and a continuing believer in "a globe of men who are trying to reach one another." When Aziz' trial divides the community more openly and dangerously than usual, Fielding supports the young doctor—a move that assures the enmity of the English without guaranteeing the affection of the skeptical Indians. After Adela withdraws her charges against Aziz, the intimacy between the two men reaches its height; almost immediately, however, they quarrel over Aziz' determination to make his tormentor pay damages.

Fielding cannot persuade Aziz to show mercy, but Mrs. Moore can, even though she has left the country before the trial and in fact has died on her return passage. For the sake of the mother of the detested man whom Aziz still believes Adela will marry, he spares the young woman, knowing that the English will interpret this decision as an indication of guilt. With Adela finally gone, Aziz mistakenly assumes that Fielding, now contemplating a visit to England, intends to marry her himself. When the friends meet again two years later, the old frankness and intimacy has been shattered. Although Fielding has married, his bride is the daughter of Mrs. Moore.

The final chapter is a particularly excellent one. As Aziz and Fielding ride horses together, the former vowing that they can be friends but only after the Indians "drive every blasted Englishman into the sea," the horses swerve apart, as if to counter Fielding's objection. Not religion, land, people, even animals want the friendship now. It is difficult to escape the conclusion that under imperial conditions no rapprochement is possible.

Much of the interest in this novel has centered on Mrs. Moore, a rather querulous old woman with a role not much larger than Mrs. Wilcox's in *Howards End*. Although she joins the roster of Forster's admirable characters who defy the taboos that divide people, she refuses to involve herself in the Aziz trial. Nevertheless, the Indians make a legend out of her and invest her with numinous powers. Critics have tended to regard her as a more successful character than Mrs. Wilcox. Part of the explanation may lie in Forster's decision to allow the reader to see her not only at first hand but also through the eyes of the Indians. If their view of Mrs. Moore is partly illusion, the illusion itself—like the more familiar illusions of the English—becomes itself a part of the truth of the situation. It is one of Forster's virtues that he knows and communicates the often conflicting values and attitudes of native Indians.

Nor is the Indian version of Mrs. Moore completely illusory, for in addition to her openness and candor, Mrs. Moore in one respect surpasses all the Europeans, even the gentle Fielding. She loves and respects life, especially unfamiliar life. It is illuminating to contrast her attitude with that of two incidental characters—missionaries who live among the people and never come to the whites' club. They measure up to their calling very well for Forster clergymen, allowing that God has room in his mansions for all people. On the subject of animals they are not so sure; Mr. Sorley, the more liberal of the two, opts for monkeys but stumbles over wasps. Mrs. Moore, more alert to the native birds and animals than she is to many people, is even sympathetic to a wasp ("Pretty dear") that has flown into the house. It is doubtless significant that the wasp is very different from the European type. Long after she is gone, Professor Godbole, Aziz' Hindu friend, remembers her in connection with the wasp. Love of humble forms of life, which the other Westerners in the novel notice only as irritations if at all, is for the Indians of Forster's *A Passage to India* a reliable indication of spirituality.

The sensitivity of Mrs. Moore and the goodwill of Fielding seem like frail counterweights to the prevailing cynicism and prejudice that stifle the necessarily furtive social initiatives of well-intentioned victims such as Aziz. If these flawed but genuine human beings have little impact on the morally bankrupt society in which they move, they have for more than half a century heartened readers of like aspirations.

Robert P. Ellis

Other major works

SHORT FICTION: *The Celestial Omnibus, and Other Stories*, 1911; *The Eternal Moment, and Other Stories*, 1928; *The Collected Tales of E. M. Forster*, 1947; *The Life to Come, and Other Stories*, 1972; *Arctic Summer, and Other Fiction*, 1980.

PLAYS: *Billy Budd*, pb. 1951 (libretto; with Eric Crozier).

NONFICTION: *Alexandria: A History and a Guide*, 1922; *Pharos and Pharillon*, 1923; *Aspects of the Novel*, 1927; *Goldsworthy Lowes Dickinson*, 1934; *Abinger Harvest*, 1936; *Virginia Woolf*, 1942; *Development of English Prose Between 1918 and 1939*, 1945; *Two Cheers for Democracy*, 1951; *The Hill of Devi*, 1953; *Marianne Thornton: A Domestic Biography, 1797-1887*, 1956; *Commonplace Book*, 1978; *Selected Letters of E. M. Forster*, 1983-1985 (2 volumes; Mary Lago and P. N. Furbank, editors); *The Feminine Note in Literature*, 2001.

MISCELLANEOUS: *The Abinger Edition of E. M. Forster*, 1972-1998 (17 volumes; Oliver Stallybrass, editor).

Bibliography

Beauman, Nicola. *E. M. Forster: A Biography*. New York: Alfred A. Knopf, 1994. Biography devoted primarily to the first forty-five years of Forster's life, when he was developing as a fiction writer, discusses the origins of Forster's fictional themes in his family background. Argues that his most successful years as a writer were also his unhappiest as a person owing to his sexual repression and his conflicts over his homosexuality.

Bradshaw, David, ed. *The Cambridge Companion to E. M. Forster*. New York: Cambridge University Press, 2007. Collection of essays examines various aspects of Forster's life and work. Topics discussed include Forster and the novel, Forster and women, and Forsterian sexuality. Among the novels analyzed are *A Room with a View*, *Howards End*, and *A Passage to India*.

Edwards, Mike. *E. M. Forster: The Novels*. New York: Palgrave, 2002. Demonstrates how readers can analyze four of Forster's novels—*A Room with a View*, *Howards End*, *A Passage to India*, and *The Longest Journey*—to understand the author's treatment of characters, locations, relationships, and other aspects of these works. Also provides ideas to help readers engage in further analysis, information about Forster's life, and examples of how four literary critics have approached Forster's writing.

Furbank, Philip N. *E. M. Forster: A Life*. New York: Harcourt Brace Jovanovich, 1978. Authorized biography successfully creates an authentic, intimate, and illuminating portrait of the man behind the writer and controversial public figure. The wealth of previously unavailable material presented makes this an indispensable source on Forster's life, times, and work.

Gardner, Philip, ed. *E. M. Forster: The Critical Heritage*. New York: Routledge, 1997. Collection of critical reviews of Forster's works that were published in British and American newspapers and journals between 1905 and 1971, including articles by D. H. Lawrence and Virginia Woolf. Includes bibliographical references and index.

McDowell, Frederick P. W. *E. M. Forster*. Rev. ed. Boston: Twayne, 1982. Brilliant work provides a well-balanced and compendious overview of Forster's life, times, career, work, and achievements. Includes useful chronology, select bibliography, and index.

Medalie, David. *E. M. Forster's Modernism*. New York: Palgrave, 2002. Examines the relationship of Forster's writings to modernism, analyzing his works to demonstrate their modernist elements. Places Forster within the context of early twentieth century social, political, and aesthetic developments.

Rapport, Nigel. *The Prose and the Passion: Anthropology, Literature, and the Writing of E. M. Forster*. New York: St. Martin's Press, 1994. Looks at Forster's work from both anthropological and literary perspectives, providing excellent interpretation and criticism of the author's writings. Includes bibliography and references.

Stone, Wilfred. *The Cave and the Mountain: A Study of E. M. Forster*. Stanford, Calif.: Stanford University Press, 1966. Well-researched, scholarly work contains a vast amount of useful information about Forster's background, career, aesthetics, and work. Employs psychological and Jungian approaches in offering insightful and masterly critiques of Forster's fiction. Supplemented by notes and a comprehensive index.

Trilling, Lionel. *E. M. Forster: A Study*. Norfolk, Conn.: New Directions, 1943. Pioneer study by a noted American literary critic was instrumental in establishing Forster's reputation. Assesses Forster's artistic achievement in terms of his liberal humanism and moral realism.

THOMAS HARDY

Born: Higher Bockhampton, Dorset, England; June 2, 1840
Died: Dorchester, Dorset, England; January 11, 1928

PRINCIPAL LONG FICTION

Desperate Remedies, 1871
Under the Greenwood Tree, 1872
A Pair of Blue Eyes, 1872-1873 (serial), 1873 (book)
Far from the Madding Crowd, 1874
The Hand of Ethelberta, 1875-1876 (serial), 1876 (book)
An Indiscretion in the Life of an Heiress, 1878 (serial), 1934 (book)
The Return of the Native, 1878
The Trumpet-Major, 1880
A Laodicean, 1880-1881 (serial), 1881 (book)
Two on a Tower, 1882
The Mayor of Casterbridge: The Life and Death of a Man of Character, 1886
The Woodlanders, 1886-1887 (serial), 1887 (book)
Tess of the D'Urbervilles: A Pure Woman Faithfully Presented, 1891
Jude the Obscure, 1895
The Well-Beloved, 1897

OTHER LITERARY FORMS

In addition to his novels, Thomas Hardy published four collections of short stories, *Wessex Tales* (1888), *A Group of Noble Dames* (1891), *Life's Little Ironies* (1894), and *A Changed Man, The Waiting Supper, and Other Tales* (1913). In the latter part of his life, after he had stopped writing novels altogether, he published approximately one thousand poems in eight separate volumes, which have since been collected in one volume by his publisher, Macmillan and Company. In addition to this staggering body of work, Hardy also published an epic drama of the Napoleonic wars in three parts between 1903 and 1908 titled *The Dynasts*, a one-act play titled *The Famous Tragedy of the Queen of Cornwall* (pr., pb. 1923), and a series of essays on fiction and other topics that have been collected in individual volumes. All the novels and stories are available in a uniform library edition in eighteen volumes published in the early 1960's by Macmillan. *The Early Life of Thomas Hardy* (1928) and *The Later Years of Thomas Hardy* (1930), although ostensibly a two-volume biography of Hardy by his second wife, Florence Hardy, is generally recognized to be Hardy's own autobiography compiled from his notes in his last few years.

Thomas Hardy
(Library of Congress)

ACHIEVEMENTS

Thomas Hardy is second only to Charles Dickens as the most written-about and discussed writer of the Victorian era. Certainly in terms of volume and diversity alone, Hardy is a towering literary figure with two admirable careers—one as novelist and one as poet—to justify his position.

Interest in Hardy's work has followed two basic patterns. The first was philosophical, with many critics discussing metaphysical structures that supposedly underlay his fiction. In the late twentieth century, however, interest shifted to that aspect of Hardy's work most scorned before—his technical facility and generic experimentation. One hundred years after his heyday, what once was termed fictional clumsiness was reevaluated in terms of poetic technique.

Furthermore, Hardy's career as a poet, which has always been under the shadow of his fiction, has been reevaluated. Hardy was a curious blend of the old-fashioned and the modern. With a career that began in the Victorian era and did not end until after World War I, Hardy was contemporary with both Matthew Arnold and T. S. Eliot. Critics, including Babette Deutsch and Vivian de Sola Pinto, have asserted that Hardy bridged the gulf between the Victorian sensibility and the modern era. In his unflinching confrontation with meaninglessness in the universe, Hardy embodied Albert Camus's description of the absurd creator in *Le Mythe de Sisyphe* (1942; *The Myth of Sisyphus*, 1955); he rebelled against the chaos of the world by asserting his own freedom to persist in spite of that meaninglessness.

Hardy was a great existential humanist. His hope for humanity was that people would realize that creeds and conventions that presuppose a god-oriented center of value are baseless. He hoped that humans would loosen themselves from those foolish hopes and creeds and become aware of their freedom to create their own value. If human beings would only realize that all people are equally alone and without hope for divine help, then perhaps they would realize also that it is the height of absurdity for such lost and isolated creatures to fight among themselves.

BIOGRAPHY

Thomas Hardy was born in the small hamlet of Higher Bockhampton in Stinsford parish on June 2, 1840. His father was a master mason, content with his low social status and at home in his rural surroundings. His mother, however, whom Hardy once called "a born bookworm," made Hardy aware of his low social status and encouraged his education. John Hicks, a friend of Hardy's father and a Dorchester architect, took the boy on as a pupil at the age of sixteen. The well-known poet William Barnes had a school next door to Hicks's office, and Hardy developed an influential friendship with the older man that remained with him. Another early influence on the young Hardy was Horace Moule, a classical scholar with a Cambridge education who was an essayist and reviewer. Moule introduced Hardy to intellectual conversation about Greek literature as well as contemporary issues; it was at Moule's suggestion that Hardy read John Stuart Mill as well as the infamous broad-church volume of essays on religion *Essays and Reviews* (1860), both of which contributed to the undermining of Hardy's simple religious faith.

Hardy was twenty-two years old when he went to London to pursue his architectural training. By that time he also entertained literary ambitions and had begun writing poetry. The publication of Algernon Charles Swinburne's *Poems and Ballads* in 1866 so influenced Hardy that he began a two-year period of intensive study and experimentation in writing poetry; none of the many poems he sent out was accepted, however, and he returned to Bockhampton in 1867. It was at this point that Hardy decided to turn to writing fiction. In his old age, he wrote in a letter that he never wanted to write novels at all, but that circumstances compelled him to turn them out.

Hardy's first fictional effort, "The Poor Man and the Lady," based on the contrast between London and rural life, received some favorable responses from publishers, but after a discussion with George Meredith, Hardy decided not to publish it and instead, on Meredith's advice, wrote *Desperate Remedies* in imitation of the detective style of Wilkie Collins. Later, eager to publish works that would establish his career as a writer, Hardy took the advice of a reader who liked the rural scenes in his unpublished novel and wrote the pastoral idyll *Under the Greenwood Tree*. The book was well received by critics, but sales were poor. One editor advised Hardy to begin writing serials for periodical publication. With the beginning of *A Pair of Blue Eyes*, Hardy said good-bye to architecture as a profession and devoted the rest of his life to writing.

In 1874, Hardy married Emma Lavinia Gifford, a dynamic and socially ambitious young woman who shared his interest in books. In the meantime, *Far from the Madding Crowd* had appeared to many favorable reviews, and editors began asking for Hardy's work. While living with his wife in a cottage at Sturminister Newton, Hardy composed *The Return of the Native* and enjoyed what he later called the happiest years of his life. Hardy and his wife began a social life in London until he became ill and they decided to return to Dorset, where, while writing *The Mayor of Casterbridge*, he had his home, Max Gate, built. For the next several years, Hardy continued his writing, traveled with his wife, and read German philosophy.

His enthusiasm for *Tess of the D'Urbervilles* was dampened when the work was turned down by two editors before being accepted for serial publication by a third. The publication of the work brought hostile reaction and notoriety—a notoriety that increased after the publication of *Jude the Obscure*. Hardy was both puzzled and cynical about these reactions, but he was by then financially secure and decided to return to his first love: After 1897 he wrote no more fiction, instead concentrating solely on poetry. His volumes of poetry were well received, and his experiment with metaphysics in the epic drama *The Dynasts* brought him even more respect, honor, and fame.

The final years of Hardy's life appear to have been spoiled only by the death of his wife in 1912. Within four years following her death, however, he married Florence Dugdale, who had been a friend of the family and had done secretarial work for him. She cared for him for the remainder of his life. Hardy continued to write poetry regularly, and his final volume of poems, *Winter Words in Various Moods and Metres*, was ready to be published when he died on January 11, 1928. His cremated remains were placed in Westminster Abbey.

ANALYSIS

In *The Courage to Be* (1952), Paul Tillich asserts that "the decisive event which underlies the search for meaning and the despair of it in the twentieth century is the loss of God in the nineteenth century." Most critics of the literature of the nineteenth century have accepted this notion and have established a new perspective for studying the period by demonstrating that what is now referred to as the "modern situation" or the "modern artistic dilemma" actually began with the breakup of a value-ordered universe in the Romantic period. Thomas Hardy, in both philosophical attitude and artistic technique, firmly belongs in this modern tradition.

It is a critical commonplace that at the beginning of his literary career Hardy experienced a loss of belief in a divinely ordered universe. The impact of this loss on Hardy cannot be overestimated. In his childhood recollections he appears as an extremely sensitive boy who attended church so regularly that he knew the service by heart and who firmly believed in a personal and just God who ruled the universe and took cognizance of the situation of humanity. Consequently, when he moved to London in his twenties and was exposed to the concept of a demythologized religion in the *Essays and Reviews* and the valueless nonteleological world of Charles Darwin's *On the Origin of Species by Means of Natural Selection: Or, The Preservation of Favoured Races in the Struggle for Life* (1859), the loss of his childhood god was a traumatic experience.

What is often called Hardy's philosophy can be summed up by one of his earliest notebook entries in 1865: "The world does not despise us; it only neglects us." An interpretation of any of Hardy's novels must begin with this assumption. The difference between Hardy and other nineteenth century artists who experienced similar loss of belief is that while others were able to achieve a measure of faith—William Wordsworth reaffirmed an organic concept of nature and of the creative mind that can penetrate it, and Thomas Carlyle finally came to a similar affirmation of nature as alive and progressive—Hardy never made such an affirmative leap to transcendent value. Hardy was more akin to another romantic figure, Samuel Taylor Coleridge's Ancient Mariner, who, having experienced the nightmarish chaos of a world without meaning or value, can never fully get back into an ordered world again.

Hardy was constantly trying to find a way out of his isolated dilemma, constantly trying to find a value to which he could cling in a world of accident, chance, and meaningless indifference. Since he refused to give in to hope for an external value, however, he refused to submit to illusions of transcendence; the only possibility for him was to find some kind of value in the emptiness itself. Like the Ancient Mariner, all Hardy had was his story of loss and despair, chaos and meaninglessness. If value were to be found at all, it lay in the complete commitment to this story—"facing the worst," and playing it back over and over again, exploring its implications, making others aware of its truth. Consequently, Hardy's art can be seen as a series of variations in form on this one barren theme of loss and chaos—"questionings in the exploration of reality."

While Hardy could imitate popular forms and create popular novels such as *Desperate Remedies*, an imitation of Wilkie Collins's detective novel, or *The Hand of Ethelberta*, an imitation of the social comedy popular at the time, when he wished to write a serious novel, one that would truly express his vision of humanity's situation in the universe, he could find no adequate model in the novels of his contemporaries. He solved this first basic problem in his search for form by returning to the tragic drama of the Greek and Elizabethan ages—a mode with which he was familiar through extensive early reading. Another Greek and Elizabethan mode he used, although he was less conscious of its literary tradition, was the pastoral narrative—a natural choice because of its surface similarity to his own subject matter of isolated country settings and innocent country people.

Hardy's second problem in the search for form arose from the incompatibility between the classical tragic vision and his own uniquely modern view. The classical writers saw humanity within a stable and ordered religious and social context, while Hardy saw humanity isolated, alone, searching for meaning in a world that offered none. Because Hardy denied the static and ordered worldview of the past, he was in turn denied the broad context of myth, symbol, and ritual that stemmed from that view. Lost without a God-ordered mythos, Hardy had to create a modern myth that presupposed the absence of God; he needed a pattern. Hardy's use of the traditional patterns of tragedy and pastoral, combined with his rejection of the old mythos that formerly gave meaning to these patterns, resulted in a peculiar distortion as his novels transcended their original patterns.

Nature in Hardy's "pastoral" novels, *The Woodlanders* and *Far from the Madding Crowd*, is neither benevolent nor divinely ordered. Similarly, the human dilemma in his "tragic" novels, *The Return of the Native* and *The Mayor of Casterbridge*, is completely antithetical to what it was for the dramatists of the past. The Greek hero was tragic because he violated a cosmic order; Hardy's heroes are tragic precisely because there is no such order. For the Greek hero there is a final reconciliation that persuades him to submit to the world. For Hardy's hero there is only the never-ending dialectic between people's nostalgia for value and the empty, indifferent world.

In *Tess of the D'Urbervilles* and *Jude the Obscure*, Hardy rejected the traditional tragic and pastoral patterns and allowed the intrinsic problems of his two protagonists to order the chaotic elements of the works. The structure of these novels can be compared to that of the epic journey of Wordsworth in *The Prelude: Or, The Growth of a Poet's Mind* (1850) and Coleridge in *The Rime of the Ancient Mariner* (1798). As critic Morse Peckham has noted, the task of the nineteenth century artist was no longer to find an external controlling form, but to "symbolize the orientative drive itself, the power of the individual to maintain his identity by creating order which would maintain his gaze at the world as it is, at things as they are." The loss of order is reflected in the structure of *Tess of the D'Urbervilles*, as the young heroine is literally evicted from the familiarity of her world and must endure the nightmarish wandering process of trying to get back inside. The structuring drive of *Jude the Obscure* is Jude's search for an external order that will rid him of the anguish of his own gratuitousness.

FAR FROM THE MADDING CROWD

Hardy's first important novel, *Far from the Madding Crowd*, was the first in which he successfully adapted a traditional form, the pastoral, to his own purposes, greatly altering it in the process. Hallet Smith has described the pastoral as constituting the ideal of the good life: In the pastoral world, nature is the true home of humankind, and the gods take an active concern in human beings' welfare; the inhabitants of this world are content and self-sufficient. The plot complications of the pastoral usually arise through the intrusion of an aspiring mind from the outside, an antipastoral force that seeks to overthrow the idyllic established order. On the surface, *Far from the Madding Crowd* conforms perfectly to this definition of the pastoral. The story is set in an agricultural community, the main character is a shepherd, and the bulk of the inhabitants are content with their lives. The plot complications arise from the intrusion of the antipastoral Sergeant Troy and the love of three different men for the pastoral maid Bathsheba. To see the novel as a true pastoral, however, is to ignore living form in order to see a preestablished pattern. The pastoral ideal cannot be the vision of this novel because Hardy was struggling with the active tension between human hopes and the world's indifference.

Far from the Madding Crowd begins in a lighthearted mood with the comic situation of Gabriel Oak's unsuccessful attempts to woo the fickle maid Bathsheba, but Gabriel, often called the stabilizing force in the novel, is an ambiguous figure. Although he is described as both a biblical and a classical shepherd, he is unequivocally neither. Moreover, the first section of the novel hovers between tragedy and comedy. Even the "pastoral tragedy," the "murder" of all of Gabriel's sheep by a foolish young dog, is equivocal; the dog is not so much destroyed for his crime as he is executed. Gabriel's character, as well as the entire tone of the novel, shifts after this short prologue. When he next appears he is no longer the contented shepherd with modest ambitions; rather, he has developed the indifference to fate and fortune that, Hardy says, "though it often makes a villain of a man, is the basis of his sublimity when it does not."

The change that takes place in Gabriel is caused by his loss and is more significant than the change in Bathsheba because of her gain of an inheritance. Bathsheba, a typical pastoral coquette in the prologue of the novel, makes an ostensible shift when she inherits a farm of her own, but she is still coquettish and vain enough to be piqued by farmer William Boldwood's indifference to her charms and to send him a valentine saying "Marry Me." Boldwood, "the nearest approach to aristocracy that this remote quarter of the parish could boast of," is a serious, self-sufficient man who sees "no absurd side to the follies of life." The change the valentine causes in him is so extreme as to be comic.

The Bathsheba-Gabriel relationship is complicated by this new wooer. In this section of the novel, until the appearance of Sergeant Troy, there appears a series of scenes in which Gabriel, Boldwood, and Bathsheba are frozen into a tableau with the ever-present sheep in the background. The death and physical suffering of the sheep take on a sinister, grotesque imagery to make an ironic commentary on the absurdity of humanity's ephemeral passions in a world dominated by cruelty and death. The irrationality of physical passion is more evident when Bathsheba is overwhelmed by Troy. Their relationship begins with the feminine frill of her dress being caught in his masculine spur and blossoms with her submission to his dazzling sword exercises. After Boldwood's complete demoralization and the marriage of Bathsheba and Troy, the antipastoral Troy corrupts the innocent harvest festival until it becomes a wild frenzy and then a drunken stupor. The pastoral world of the "good life" is turned upside down as an approaching storm transforms the landscape into something sinister. It is significant that the rustics are asleep during the storm, for they are truly unaware of the sickness of the world and its sinister aspect. Troy, too, is unaware of the storm, as he is always unaware of any incongruity between humanity and the indifferent world. Only Gabriel, Bathsheba, and Boldwood, the involved and suffering characters of the novel, react to this symbolic storm.

Just as the death of the sheep forms the ever-present background to the first two parts of the novel, the death of Fanny Robin dominates the third section. From the time her body begins its journey in Joseph Poorgrass's wagon until the "Gurgoyle" washes Troy's flowers off her grave, death becomes the most important element in the book. By far the most important effect of Fanny Robin's death is on Bathsheba. When she opens the coffin to find out that Fanny was pregnant with Troy's child, the scene is "like an illusion raised by some fiendish incantation." Many critics have asserted that Bathsheba's then running away to seclude herself in the wood is her reconciliation with the natural world of the pastoral, but this view is wholly untenable: Her retreat is on the edge of a swamp of which the "general aspect was malignant." There is no pastoral goodness about the hollow in which she hides. It is a "nursery of pestilences. . . . From its moist and poisonous coat seemed to be exhaled the essences of evil things in the earth." This is one of those grotesque situations in which people become aware of their isolated state, when their need for solace in the natural world is met with only indifference, when they become aware of the absurdity of their demands on a barren and empty world. Bathsheba changes after her experience in this "boundary situation"; she gains the awareness that has characterized Gabriel all along.

After this climactic scene of confrontation with the indifferent world, the book loses its focus. In a diffuse and overlong denouement, Boldwood presses his advantage with Bathsheba until the night of the party, when she is on the point of giving in. Troy's return at this moment and his murder by Boldwood seem forced and melodramatic. Bathsheba's return to marry Gabriel is a concession to the reading public as much as it is to the pastoral pattern of the novel itself. *Far from the Madding Crowd*, a fable of the barrenness and death of the pastoral world and the tragic results of wrong choices through the irrationality of sexual attraction, truly ends with Bathsheba's isolation and painful new awareness in the pestilent swamp.

THE WOODLANDERS

The Woodlanders, although more explicit in its imagistic presentation of the unhealthy natural world and more complex in its conflicts of irrational sexual attraction, manifests much of the same kind of formal distortion as is found in *Far from the Madding Crowd*. The world of Little Hintock, far from being the ideal pastoral world, is even more valueless, more inimical a world than Weatherbury. Instead of the grotesque death of sheep, trees become the symbolic representation of humanity's absurd situation in an empty world. Little Hintock is a wasteland, a world of darkness, isolation, guilt, and human cross-purposes. One's nostrils are always filled with the odor of dead leaves, fermenting cider, and heavy, blossomy perfume. One cannot breathe or stretch out one's arms in this world.

The so-called natural inhabitants of the Wood are dissatisfied with the nature of the world around them. Grace's father, Mr. Melbury, cramped and crippled by his lifetime struggle to make his living from the trees, wants his daughter to be able to escape such a world by marrying an outsider. A conflict is created, however, by the guilt he feels for a wrong he did to Giles Winterborne's father; he tries to atone for it by promising Grace to Giles. John South, Marty's father, on whose life the landholdings of Giles depend, is neurotically afraid of the huge tree in his yard. The tree takes on a symbolic aura as representative of the uncontrollable force of the natural world.

Furthermore, the sophisticated outsiders in the novel are cut off from the world they inhabit and are imaged as "unnatural." Strange unnatural lights can be seen from the house of the young Dr. Fitzpiers, who is said to be in league with the devil. The bored Felice Charmond is so unnatural that she must splice on the luxuriance of natural beauty by having a wig made of Marty South's hair. The isolated and cramped Hintock environment creates a boredom and ennui in these two characters that serve to further the narrative drive of the novel.

Grace, the most equivocal character in the novel, is the active center of its animating conflicts. Her wavering back and forth between the natural world and the antinatural is the central tension that crystallizes the tentative and uncomfortable attitude of all the characters. It is her dilemma of choice that constitutes the major action, just as it is Bathsheba's choice that dominates *Far from the Madding Crowd*. The choices that the characters make to relieve themselves of tension are made through the most irrational emotion, love, in a basically irrational world. Grace marries Fitzpiers in an effort to commit herself to a solid world of value. Fitzpiers sees in Grace the answer to a Shelleyan search for a soul mate. To commit oneself to a line of action that assumes the world is ordered and full of value, to choose a course of action that hopes to lessen the tentativeness of life, to deceive oneself into thinking that solidarity exists—these are the tragic errors that Hardy's characters repeatedly make.

The marriage begins to break up when Fitzpiers, aware that Grace is not the ideal he desired, goes to the lethargic Mrs. Charmond, and when Grace, aware that her hope for solidarity was misdirected, tries to go back to the natural world through the love of Giles. Social conventions—which Hardy views as holdovers from outmoded creeds—interfere, however. Grace is unable to obtain a divorce, for the law makes her irrational first choice inflexible. Despairing of the injustice of natural law as well as of social law, she runs away to Giles, who, too self-effacing to rebel against either code, lets her have his house while he spends the night in an ill-sheltered hut.

At this point, confused and in anguish about what possibility there is left for her, uncertain of the value of any action, Grace confronts the true nature of the world and the absurdity of her past hopes for value in it. The storm that catches Grace alone in the house is a climactic representation for her of the inimical natural world, just as the pestilent swamp is for Bathsheba. "She had never before been so struck with the devilry of a gusty night in the wood, because she had never been so entirely alone in spirit as she was now. She seemed almost to be apart from herself—a vacuous duplicate only." Grace's indecision and absurd hopes have been leading to this bitter moment of realization in which she is made aware of the ephemeral nature of human existence and the absurdity of human hopes in a world without intrinsic value.

Just as in *Far from the Madding Crowd*, the tension of the action collapses after this confrontation. Giles dies, and Fitzpiers returns after having ended his affair with Mrs. Charmond. After a short period of indifference, Grace, still his wife by law, returns to him. In his customary ironic way, however, Hardy does not allow this reconciliation to be completely satisfying, for it is physical only. Grace, having narrowly missed being caught in a mantrap set for Fitzpiers, is enticingly undressed when Fitzpiers rushes to her and asks to be taken back. This physical attraction is the only reason that Fitzpiers desires a reconciliation. Grace is still indifferent to him, but it is now this very indifference that makes their reunion possible. Seeing no one reaction as more valuable than another, she takes the path of least resistance. The rural chorus ends the novel by commenting that they think the union will not last.

The Return of the Native

Although many critics have pointed out the formal framework of *The Return of the Native*—the classical five-act division; the unity of time, place, and line of action; and the character similarities to Oedipus and Prometheus—others have struggled with the book's ambiguities and the difficulties involved in seeing it as a classical tragedy. Certainly, the pattern is classical, but the distortion of the pattern becomes the more significant structuring principle. Egdon Heath is the landscape from which God has departed. People in such an empty world will naturally begin to feel an affinity with the wasteland, such as islands, moors, and dunes. Little more needs to be said here about the part the Heath plays in the action, for critics have called it the principal actor in the drama. Indeed, it does dominate the scene, for the actions of all the characters are reactions in some way to the indifference the Heath represents.

As in *Far from the Madding Crowd*, there is a chorus of rustics in *The Return of the Native*. They belong on the Heath because of their ignorance of the incongruity between human longing for meaning and the intractable indifference of the world. They still maintain a mythical, superstitious belief in a pagan animism and fatalistically accept the nature of things. The Druidical rites of the opening fires, the unimportance of Christian religion, the black mass and Voodoo doll of Susan Nonesuch—all of these characterize the pagan fatalism of the rustics.

The main characters, however, do not belong with the rustics. They make something other than a fatalistic response to the Heath and are characterized by their various reactions to its indifference. Mrs. Yeobright is described as having the very solitude exhaled from the Heath concentrated in her face. Having lived with its desolation longer than any of the others, she can no longer escape, but she is desperate to see that Clym does. Damon Wildeve does not belong to the Heath but has taken over a patch of land a former tenant died in trying to reclaim. Although he is dissatisfied, he is not heroic; he is involved in no search, no vital interaction with the indifferent world. Tomasin Yeobright is characterized in a single image, as she is in the house loft, selecting apples: "The sun shone in a bright yellow patch upon the figure of the maiden as she knelt and plunged her naked arms into the soft brown fern." She aligns herself with the natural world through her innocence and consequently perceives no incongruity. Diggory Venn, the most puzzling figure in the novel, is an outcast. The most typical image of him is by his campfire alone, the red glow reflecting off his own red skin. He simply wanders on the open Heath, minding other people's business and waiting for his chance to marry Tomasin.

These characters, regardless of their conflicts with the irrationality of human choice or the indifference of the Heath, are minor in comparison with the two antithetical attitudes of Eustacia Vye and Clym Yeobright. The most concrete image of Eustacia is of her wandering on the Heath, carrying an hourglass in her hand, gazing aimlessly out over the vast wasteland. Her search for value, her hope for escape from the oppressive indifference of the Heath, lies in being "loved to madness." Clym, however, sees friendliness and geniality written on the Heath. He is the disillusioned intellectual trying to make a return to the mythic simplicity of the natural world. Clym would prefer not to think, not to grapple with the incongruities he has seen. The very disease of thought that forces him to see the "coil of things" makes him desire to teach rather than to think. He is indeed blind, as his mother tells him, in thinking he can instill into the peasants the view that "life is a thing to be put up with," for they have always known it and fatalistically accepted it. Furthermore, he shows his blindness by marrying Eustacia, thinking she will remain with him on the Heath, while Eustacia reveals that she is as misdirected as he is by idealizing him and thinking that he will take her away from the Heath. Both characters search for a meaning and basis for value, but both are trapped by the irrationality of love and vain hopes in an irrational world.

At the beginning of book 4, Clym literally goes blind because of his studying and must actually look at the world through smoked glasses. He welcomes the opportunity to ignore the incongruities of the world by subsuming himself in the Heath and effacing himself in his furze cutting. In his selfish attempt to "not think" about it, he ignores what this means to Eustacia. She can find no meaning at all in such self-effacing indifference; it is the very thing against which she is rebelling. She returns again to her old pagan ways at the village dance and considers the possibility of Wildeve once more.

Mrs. Yeobright's journey across the Heath, a trip colored by grotesque images of the natural world—the tepid, stringy water of nearly dried pools, where "maggoty" shapes cavort; the battered, rude, and wild trees whose limbs are splintered, lopped, and distorted by the weather—is a turning point in the action of the book. In a concatenation of chance events and human misunderstanding, Eustacia turns Mrs. Yeobright away from the door, and the old woman dies as a result. At this point, Eustacia blames some "colossal Prince of the world for framing her situation and ruling her lot."

Clym, still selfish, ignores the problems of the living Eustacia and concentrates on the "riddle of death" of his mother. Had he been able to practice what he professed—human solidarity—he might have saved Eustacia and himself, but instead he bitterly blames her for his mother's death and is the immediate cause of Eustacia's flight. Eustacia's trip across the Heath to her death is similar to Mrs. Yeobright's in that the very natural world seems antagonistic to her. She stumbles over "twisted furze roots, tufts of rushes, or oozing lumps of fleshly fungi, which at this season lay scattered about the Heath like the rotten liver and lungs of some colossal animal." Her leap into the pool is a noble suicide. It is more a rebellion against the indifference of the world around her than it is a submission to its oppressiveness. It is the admission of the absurdity of human hopes by a romantic temperament that refuses to live by such absurdity.

THE MAYOR OF CASTERBRIDGE

The tragic pattern of *The Mayor of Casterbridge* has been said by most critics to be more explicit than that of *The Return of the Native*; by the late twentieth century, however, critics were quick to point out that there are serious difficulties involved in seeing *The Mayor of Casterbridge* as an archetypal tragic ritual. Although Henchard is Oedipus-like in his opposition to the rational, Creon-like Farfrae, the plot of the novel, like that of *The Return of the Native*, involves the reactions of a set of characters to the timeless indifference of the world. In this case, the mute and intractable world is imaged in the dead myths and classical legends of Casterbridge.

Secluded as much as Little Hintock, the world of *The Woodlanders*, Casterbridge is "huddled all together, shut in by a square wall of trees like a plot of garden by a box-edging." The town is saturated with the old superstitions and myths of the past. The primary image of the desolate world of the town and its dead and valueless past is the Casterbridge Ring, a relic of an ancient Roman amphitheater. The Ring is a central symbol that embodies the desolation of the old myths of human value. It formerly had been the gallows site, but now it is a place for illicit meetings of all kinds, except, Hardy notes, those of happy lovers. A place of man's inhumanity to man is no place for the celebration of love.

The inhumanity of one person to another and the human need for love play important roles in the action of the novel. While the classical Oedipus is guilty of breaking a cosmic law, Henchard is guilty of breaking a purely human one. By selling his wife, he treats her as a thing, not a human being. He rejects human relationships and violates human interdependence and solidarity. This is the sin that begins to find objectification years later when the blight of the bread agitates the townspeople and when his wife, Susan, returns.

It is not this sin alone that means tragedy for Henchard, just as it is not Oedipus's violation alone that brings his downfall. Henchard's character—his irrational behavior, his perverse clinging to the old order and methods, his rash and impulsive nature—also contributes to his defeat. Henchard is an adherent of the old ways. Though he is ostensibly the mayor, an important man, he is actually closer to the rustic, folk characters than the hero of any other Hardy novel. He is not a rebel against the indifference of the world so much as he is a simple hay stacker, trying desperately to maintain a sense of value in the worn-out codes and superstitions of the past. In the often-quoted "character is Fate" passage in the novel, Hardy makes explicit Henchard's problem. He calls him a Faust-like character, "a vehement, gloomy being who had quitted the ways of vulgar men without light to guide him on a better way." Henchard is thus caught between two worlds, one of them dead and valueless, the other not worthy enough to be a positive replacement. The levelheaded business sense of Farfrae, the social climbing and superficiality of Lucetta, the too-strict rationality of Elizabeth-Jane—all representing the new order of human attitudes—appear anemic and self-deceived in the face of Henchard's dynamic energy.

It often seems that the nature of things is against Henchard, but the nature of things is that events occur that cannot be predicted, and that they often occur just at the time when one does not want them to. Many such unpredicted and ill-timed events accumulate to cause Henchard's tragedy. For example, just when he decides to marry Lucetta, Susan returns; just at the time of Susan's death, he is once more reminded of his obligation to Lucetta; just at the time when he tells Elizabeth-Jane that she is his daughter, he discovers that she is not; and just at the time when he calls on Lucetta to discuss marriage, she has already met and found a better mate in Farfrae.

Many of the events that contribute to Henchard's own downfall are a combination of this "unholy brew" and his impulsive nature. That the weather turned bad during his planned entertainment he could not prevent, but he could have been more prepared for the rain had he not been in such a hurry to best Farfrae. The unpredictable nature of the weather at harvest time was also beyond his control, but again had he not been so intent on ruining Farfrae he might have survived. He begins to wonder if someone is roasting a waxen image of him or stirring an "unholy brew" to confound him. Moreover, the attitudes of other characters accumulate to contribute to Henchard's downfall. Farfrae, as exacting as a machine, rejects Henchard's fatherly love and makes few truly human responses at all. Lucetta, once dependent on Henchard, becomes so infatuated with her new wealth that she no longer needs him. At the beginning of the novel, Susan's simple nature makes her incapable of realizing that Newsom's purchase of her is not valid, and at the end, her daughter, Elizabeth-Jane, is so coldly rational that she can cast Henchard off without possibility of reconciliation. None of these characters faces the anguish of being human as Henchard does.

The ambiguity that arises from the combination of all these forces makes it difficult to attribute Henchard's tragedy to any one of them. His death in the end marks the inevitable disappearance of the old order, but it is also the only conclusion possible for the man who has broken the only possible existing order when a cosmic order is no longer tenable—the human order of man himself. The reader is perhaps made to feel that Henchard has suffered more than he deserved. As a representative of the old order, his fall must be lamented even as the search is carried on for a new foundation of value and order. At the death of the old values in *The Mayor of Casterbridge*, a new order is not available.

TESS OF THE D'URBERVILLES

The form and meaning of *Tess of the D'Urbervilles* springs from Tess's relation to the natural world. At the beginning of the novel she is a true child of nature who, although sensitive to painful incongruities in her experience, is confident that the natural world will provide her with a basis of value and will protect and sustain her. When nature fails her, her perplexity throws her out of the comfortable world of innocence and natural rapport. Tess then begins a journey both inward and outward in search of a stable orientation and a reintegration into a relationship with the natural world.

Tess first appears in her "natural home" in the small hamlet of Marlott, where her innocence is dramatized as she takes part in the May Day dance. There is a sensitivity in Tess that sets her apart from the other inhabitants. Shame for her father's drunken condition makes her volunteer to take the beehives to market, and despair for the laziness of her parents makes her dreamily watch the passing landscape and ignore where she is going. When, as a result, the horse Prince is killed, Tess's sense of duty to her family, now in economic difficulties, overcomes her pride, and she agrees to go to her aristocratic relatives for help. It is her first journey outside the little world of Marlott and her first real encounter with corruption. Alec, her cousin, is a stock figure of the sophisticated, antinatural world. Their first scene together is formalized into an archetypal image of innocence in the grasp of the corrupt.

Just as it is Tess's natural luxuriance and innocence that attracts Alec, it is also her innocence that leads to her fall. When he takes her into the woods, strangely enough she is not afraid of him as before. She feels that she is in her natural element. She so trusts the natural world to protect her that she innocently falls asleep and is seduced by Alec. The antinatural force that began with her father's alleged nobility works together with Tess's own innocence and sensitivity and her naïve trust in the world to make her an outcast. When her illegitimate child dies and the church refuses it a Christian burial, Tess unequivocally denies the validity of organized religion. She probes within herself to try to find some meaning in her despair. Suddenly she becomes quite consciously aware of the abstract reality of death: "Almost at a leap Tess thus changed from simple girl to complex woman." The facing of the idea of death without a firm hope for transcendence is the conclusion of Tess's inward search in this second phase of her experience, when, still maintaining a will to live and enjoy, she has hopes of submerging herself into the natural world again.

The Valley of the Great Dairies where Tess goes next is the natural world magnified, distorted, thrown out of proportion. It is so lush and fertile as to become a symbolic world. As Tess enters the valley, she feels hope for a new reintegration. For the time being, she dismisses the disturbing thought of her doubt in her childhood God and is satisfied to immerse herself within the purely physical world of the farm's lushness. She manages to ignore her moral plight until she meets the morally ambiguous Angel Clare. In contrast to Tess, Angel's moral perplexity arises from intellectual questioning rather than from natural disillusionment. Intellectually convinced that he has lost faith, Angel rebels against the conventions of society and the church and goes to the Valley of the Great Dairies, where he believes innocence and uncontaminated purity and goodness prevail. For Angel, Tess represents the idealistic goal of natural innocence, but the natural world no more affirms this relationship than it condemned the former one. On the first night of their marriage, Tess confesses to Angel her relationship with Alec. Angel, the idealist, has desired to see a natural perfection in Tess. Doubting that perfection, he rejects her as antinatural. Angel cannot accept the reality of what nature is truly like; he is tied to a conventional orientation more than he realizes.

After Angel leaves her, Tess wanders about the countryside doing farmwork at various places until one morning on the road she awakes to find dead pheasants around her. At this point, Tess becomes aware that in a Darwinistic universe, without teleological possibility and without inherent goodness, violation, injury, and even death are innate realities. Tess realizes that she is not guilty by the laws of such a world. After this realization she can go to the barren world of Chalk-Newton and not feel so much the incongruity of the place. With its "white vacuity of countenance with the lineaments gone," Chalk-Newton represents the wasteland situation of a world without order or value. Tess can remain indifferent to it because of her new realization of its indifference to her.

Cold indifference, however, offers no escape from her moral conflict. Alec D'Urberville comes back into her life, proclaiming that he has accepted Christianity and exhorting her not to "tempt" him again. Ironically, by trying to convince him of her own realization of a world without God and by propounding Angel's uncommitted humanism to him, she only succeeds in reconverting Alec back to his old demoniac nature and thus creates another threat to herself. When her father dies and the family loses its precarious freehold, Tess gives in to Alec's persistent urging once more. When Angel, in the rugged South American mountains, comes to the same realization that Tess experienced on the road, he returns to find that Tess has renounced life and self completely, allowing her body to drift, "like a corpse upon the current, in a direction dissociated from the living will." After the return of Angel, when Tess finds her last hopes dashed, she sees in Alec all the deception and meaninglessness of a world she trusted. When she kills him, she is transformed by her rebellion. Like Percy Bysshe Shelley's Beatrice Cenci, she is aware of no guilt; she transcends any kind of moral judgment. She acknowledges her absolute freedom, and in that fearful moment, she is willing to accept the human penalties for such freedom.

In the last part of the novel, when Angel and Tess wander without any real hope of escape, Tess is already condemned to die. Isolated in the awareness of her own ephemerality in a valueless world, Tess vows that she is "not going to think of anything outside of now." The final scene at Stonehenge is a triumph of symbolic realization of place; the silent, enigmatic stones, mysterious and implacable, resist any attempt at explanation. Tess, in saying that she likes to be there, accepts the indifferent universe. Lying on the altar of a heathen temple, she is the archetypal sacrifice of human rebellion against an empty world. When the carriers of the law of nature and society arrive, Tess, having rebelled against these laws and rejected them, can easily say, "I am ready."

Tess's real tragedy springs from her insistent hope throughout the novel to find external meaning and justification for her life. Only at the end of the novel, when she rebels by killing Alec, does she achieve true awareness. Unlike the classical tragic hero, she is not reconciled to the world through an acceptance of universal justice. Her very salvation, the only kind of salvation in Hardy's world, lies in her denial of such a concept.

JUDE THE OBSCURE

With some significant differences, *Jude the Obscure* is concerned with the same problem that animates *Tess of the D'Urbervilles*—the absurdity and tragedy of human hopes for value in an indifferent universe. As a literary creation, it is a "process" through which Hardy tries to structure the symbolic journey of every person who searches for a foundation, a basis for meaning and value. The problem, however, is that all the symbols that represent meaning to Jude—the colleges, the church, the ethereal freedom of Sue Bridehead, and even the physical beauty of his wife Arabella—are illusory. By contrast, those things that have real symbolic value in the world are the forbidding, sacrosanct walls of the college complex, which Jude cannot enter; the decaying materiality of the churches that he tries to restore; the neurotic irrationality of Sue, which he fails to understand; and his own body, to which he is inextricably tied. It is precisely Jude's "obscurity," his loss of "at-homeness" in the world, with which the novel is concerned. He is obscure because he is without light, because he tries in every way possible to find an illumination of his relation to the world, but without success.

It is significant that the novel opens with the departure of the schoolmaster Phillotson, for to Jude, orphaned and unwanted by his aunt, the teacher has been the center of the world. His leaving marks the necessity of Jude's finding a new center and a new hope to relieve his loneliness. The first projection of his hopes to find value is naturally toward Christminster, the destination of his teacher. In the first part of the book his dream is seen only as an indefinable glow in the distance that offers all possibilities by its very unknown nature. Although he consciously devotes himself to the Christian framework, one night after having read a classical poem, he kneels and prays to Diana, the goddess of the moon. Both of these value systems—Christian faith and Greek reason—are projected on his vision of Christminster, but both of them are temporarily forgotten when he meets Arabella, "a substantial female animal." Later, when she tells him that she is pregnant, although it destroys all his former plans, he idealizes the marriage state, calls his hopes for Christminster "dreams about books, and degrees and impossible fellowships," and dedicates himself to home, family, and the pedestrian values of Marygreen. His discovery that Arabella has deceived him is only the first reversal in his search for unity and value.

In the second phase of Jude's development, the long-planned journey to Christminster is prompted by the immediacy of seeing a picture of Sue Bridehead; she becomes a concrete symbol of his vision. His first glimpse of Sue has the quality of idealistic wish fulfillment. His growing desire for her expresses a need for an "anchorage" to his thoughts. He goes to the church she attends, and this church, associated with his vision of Sue, temporarily becomes that anchorage. Sue is not, however, representative of Christian values; rather, she is the classical pagan. This dichotomy of values creates a recurring tension in Jude's search throughout the book.

Jude's first major disillusionment at Christminster comes when he is turned down by all five colleges to which he has applied. After this disappointment, he shifts his hopes from the reason and knowledge of the schools to the faith of the church. This religious impulse dominates Jude's hopes in the third phase of his development. He practices the rituals of the church in the hope that he can find a meaning for himself, but Sue, who laughed at his idealistic notions of the intellectual life, tells him that the Church is not the way either. Sue, who changes in Jude's eyes as his goals change, is always important to him as a symbol of his aspirations and ideals. When he loses her to Phillotson, he is struck even more by the "scorn of Nature for man's finer emotions and her lack of interest in his aspirations."

Phase four of Jude's search is a transition section presenting the decay of the values of the past. Jude, studying theology and church ritual with a last weakening hope, is only vaguely aware of the decay and aridity around him. His need for Sue, an ambiguous mixture of desire for the ideal and the physical, begins to take on more importance for him until he decides that he is unfit "to fill the part of a propounder of accredited dogma" and burns all his theology books. Sue, a spiritual creature, cannot live with Phillotson any longer. She goes to Jude, who, having rejected everything else, is ready to project his desires for meaning entirely on an ambiguous union with her as both physical wife and Shelleyan soul mate.

The fifth part of the novel is a phase of movement as Jude and Sue wander from town to town, living as husband and wife in all respects except the sexual. Not until Arabella returns and Sue fears she will lose Jude does she give in to him, but with infinite regret. In the final phase of Jude's development, after the birth of his children, including the mysterious child named Father Time, the family moves back to Christminster. Instead of being optimistic, Jude is merely indifferent. He recognizes himself as an outsider, a stranger to the universe of ideals and hopes of other men. He has undergone a process that has slowly stripped him of such hopes for meaning. He sees the human desire for meaning as absurd in a world that has no concern for humanity, a universe that cannot fulfill dreams of unity or meaning.

The tragedy of Father Time causes Sue to alter her belief that she can live by instinct, abjuring the laws of society. She makes an extreme shift, accepting a supreme deity against whose laws she feels she has transgressed; her self-imposed penance for her "sin" of living with Jude is to go back to Phillotson. After Sue leaves, Jude goes to "a dreary, strange flat scene, where boughs dripped, and coughs and consumption lurked, and where he had never been before." This is a typical Hardy technique for moments of realization: The natural world becomes an inimical reflection of the character's awareness of the absurd. After this, Jude's reaction to the world around him is indifference: He allows himself to be seduced by Arabella again and marries her. Jude's final journey to see Sue is a journey to death and a final rejection of the indifferent universe of which his experiences have made him aware.

In his relentless vision of a world stripped of transcendence, Hardy is a distinctly modern novelist. As Nathan A. Scott has said of him, "not only does he lead us back to that trauma in the nineteenth century out of which the modern existentialist imagination was born, but he also brings us forward to our own time."

Charles E. May

OTHER MAJOR WORKS

SHORT FICTION: *Wessex Tales*, 1888; *A Group of Noble Dames*, 1891; *Life's Little Ironies*, 1894; *A Changed Man, The Waiting Supper, and Other Tales*, 1913; *The Complete Short Stories*, 1989 (Desmond Hawkins, editor).

PLAYS: *The Dynasts: A Drama of the Napoleonic Wars*, pb. 1903, 1906, 1908, 1910 (complete; verse drama; abridged by Harley Granville-Barker); *The Famous Tragedy of the Queen of Cornwall*, pr., pb. 1923 (one act).

POETRY: *Wessex Poems, and Other Verses*, 1898; *Poems of the Past and Present*, 1901; *Time's Laughingstocks, and Other Verses*, 1909; *Satires of Circumstance*, 1914; *Selected Poems of Thomas Hardy*, 1916; *Moments of Vision and Miscellaneous Verses*, 1917; *Late Lyrics and Earlier*, 1922; *Human Shows, Far Phantasies, Songs, and Trifles*, 1925; *Winter Words in Various Moods and Metres*, 1928; *Collected Poems of Thomas Hardy*, 1943; *The Complete Poetical Works*, 1982-1985 (3 volumes; Samuel Hynes, editor).

NONFICTION: *Life and Art*, 1925 (Ernest Brennecke, editor); *The Early Life of Thomas Hardy*, 1928; *The Later Years of Thomas Hardy*, 1930; *Personal Writings*, 1966 (Harold Orel, editor); *The Collected Letters of Thomas Hardy*, 1978-1988 (7 volumes; Richard Little Purdy and Michael Millgate, editors).

BIBLIOGRAPHY

Carpenter, Richard C. *Thomas Hardy*. Boston: Twayne, 1964. Examines the characterization, descriptions, plots, and social themes in Hardy's fiction and poetry as well as elements of symbolism, myth, impressionism, and drama in the works. Includes chronology, bibliography, and index.

Chew, Samuel C. *Thomas Hardy: Poet and Novelist.* 1928. Reprint. New York: Russell & Russell, 1964. Although it does not lack sentiment, this volume is still one of the most respected of the traditional analyses of Hardy's work. Examines Hardy's pessimism, his use of coincidence, his conflict of intellect and intuition, and the structural excellence of his Wessex novels, which Chew considers to be a clarification of Victorian technique. Includes bibliography and index.

Daleski, H. M. *Thomas Hardy and Paradoxes of Love.* Columbia: University of Missouri Press, 1997. Reevaluates the treatment of gender in Hardy's novels, defending the author from charges of sexism and maintaining that some of Hardy's female characters are depicted sympathetically.

Gatrell, Simon. *Thomas Hardy and the Proper Study of Mankind.* Charlottesville: University Press of Virginia, 1993. Analyzes Hardy's technique of presenting character in relationship to society. In addition to chapters on individual novels, devotes chapters to Hardy's use of the dance as a folk ritual and to the imperial theme in his fiction.

Guerard, Albert J. *Thomas Hardy: The Novels and Stories.* Cambridge, Mass.: Harvard University Press, 1949. One of the classic critical works on Hardy, examining his poetry and fiction in Victorian and modern contexts. Argues that in relation to Joseph Conrad and André Gide, Hardy is an old-fashioned storyteller, but he anticipates modern elements of antirealism in his conflicting impulses, his symbolic use of coincidence, and his artful technique.

Howe, Irving. *Thomas Hardy.* New York: Macmillan, 1967. One of the earliest book-length studies of Hardy's novels, poetry, and short fiction, tracing his development as a writer and the influences of his background and intellectual environment. The chapter "Let the Day Perish" focuses on Hardy's women characters, especially Tess, who illustrates the transformation and ennobling of a cultural stereotype. Complemented by a primary bibliography and an index.

Kramer, Dale, ed. *The Cambridge Companion to Thomas Hardy.* New York: Cambridge University Press, 1999. Provides an essential introduction and general overview of all Hardy's work and specific demonstrations of Hardy's ideas and literary skills. Individual essays explore Hardy's biography, his aesthetics, and the impact on his work of developments in science, religion, and philosophy in the late nineteenth century. Includes a detailed chronology of Hardy's life.

Millgate, Michael. *Thomas Hardy: A Biography Revisited.* New York: Oxford University Press, 2004. Enhances and replaces Millgate's 1982 biography, considered to be one of the best and most scholarly Hardy biographies available. Includes bibliography and index.

Page, Norman, ed. *Oxford Reader's Companion to Hardy.* New York: Oxford University Press, 2000. Encyclopedic work contains three hundred alphabetically arranged entries examining Hardy's work and discussing his family and friends, important places in his life and work, his influences, critical approaches to his writings, and the history of his works' publication. Also includes a chronology of his life, lists of places and characters in his fiction, a glossary, and a bibliography.

Ray, Martin, ed. *Thomas Hardy Remembered*. London: Ashgate, 2007. Collection of interviews with Hardy and recollections of him by his friends and acquaintances offers readers a fresh perspective on the writer. Also contains observations by Hardy on his writing and his contemporaries' opinions about his life.

Seymour-Smith, Martin. *Hardy*. New York: St. Martin's Press, 1994. Literary biography not only provides detailed information on Hardy's life but also summarizes and critiques previous criticism of Hardy and discusses in a straightforward, nontheoretical way the author's most important works. Includes analysis of the critical reception of Hardy's work and description of critical controversies that have arisen over his fiction and thought.

Tomalin, Claire. *Thomas Hardy*. New York: Penguin Books, 2007. Thorough and finely written biography by a respected Hardy scholar illuminates the novelist's drive to indict the malice, neglect, and ignorance of his fellow human beings. Includes discussion of aspects of Hardy's life that are apparent in his literary works.

HENRY JAMES

Born: New York, New York; April 15, 1843
Died: London, England; February 28, 1916
Also known as: Henry James, Jr.

PRINCIPAL LONG FICTION

Roderick Hudson, 1876
The American, 1876-1877 (serial), 1877 (book)
Daisy Miller, 1878
The Europeans, 1878
An International Episode, 1878-1879 (serial), 1879 (book)
Confidence, 1879-1880 (serial), 1880 (book)
Washington Square, 1880
The Portrait of a Lady, 1880-1881 (serial), 1881 (book)
The Bostonians, 1885-1886 (serial), 1886 (book)
The Princess Casamassima, 1885-1886 (serial), 1886 (book)
The Aspern Papers, 1888
The Reverberator, 1888
The Tragic Muse, 1889-1890 (serial), 1890 (book)
The Spoils of Poynton, 1897
What Maisie Knew, 1897
The Awkward Age, 1898-1899 (serial), 1899 (book)
In the Cage, 1898
The Turn of the Screw, 1898
The Sacred Fount, 1901
The Wings of the Dove, 1902
The Ambassadors, 1903
The Golden Bowl, 1904
The Outcry, 1911
The Ivory Tower, 1917
The Sense of the Past, 1917

OTHER LITERARY FORMS

Fiction was assuredly where Henry James's essential talent and interest lay, and it was the form to which he devoted almost all of his literary efforts. His more than twenty novels (the count is inexact because some of his middle-length pieces, such as *The Turn of the Screw* and *Daisy Miller*, can be categorized as novellas) and roughly 112 tales attest his lifetime of dedication to this genre. Despite this clear emphasis on fiction, however, James was seduced by his desire to regain his lost popularity with the general public and his wish

Henry James
(Library of Congress)

to attempt a kind of writing that he had studied for many years, writing drama.

For a five-year period, from 1890 to 1895, James concentrated on playwriting; during this time he wrote no novels but continued to publish short stories. While his failure to gain a public with his plays somewhat embittered James (an emotion that has been exaggerated by some biographers; he always had loyal and appreciative readers and friends), he never lost confidence in the legitimacy of his art, and he returned to fiction with what many scholars believe to be a stronger, more ambitious inspiration, resulting in what has been called the "major phase" of his writing. It is perhaps indicative of the primacy of fiction in James's career that his most successful play was *The American* (pr. 1891), an adaptation of his earlier novel.

Unlike many creative writers, James produced an enormous volume of critical writings, chiefly literary, in which he not only studied the works of other authors (the most noteworthy are Nathaniel Hawthorne, Walt Whitman, Ralph Waldo Emerson, Ivan Turgenev, Gustave Flaubert, George Eliot, Anthony Trollope, Robert Louis Stevenson, Honoré de Balzac, and Guy de Maupassant) but also performed a detailed analysis of his own work. This latter effort appears primarily in the form of the prefaces to the New York edition (1907-1909) of his novels and tales. Inasmuch as the New York edition occupies twenty-six volumes, these prefaces provide a considerable body of critical material that has proved to be of great value to James scholars. His often reprinted essay "The Art of Fiction" (1884) presents his general theories on the art. Aside from his literary criticism, James wrote numerous studies and critiques on other subjects, such as painting (which greatly interested him) and travel.

In the late twentieth century, James's books and travel sketches attained critical admiration for their graceful style and penetrating insight into times that have gone and places that will never be the same. As might be expected, his studies of Italy, France, and England (the countries that most intrigued him) are detailed and entertaining. More surprising is his finest work in this genre, *The American Scene* (1907), the fruit of a long visit to the United States; he toured the country extensively, in part to visit friends and places that he had not seen and others that he had not been to for a long time, and in part to deliver lectures on literary topics. His account of the United States at the beginning of the twentieth century fuses the poignance of a native's return with the distance and objectivity of a European perspective.

ACHIEVEMENTS

Henry James was the first American novelist to bring to the form a sense of artistic vocation comparable to Flaubert. Except for the wide popularity of *Daisy Miller*, which appealed to audiences both in Europe and in the United States, no work of James achieved a wide readership in his lifetime. This fact, though it caused him pain, did not impel this most discriminating of writers to lower his standards in order to appeal to a mass audience. Those who did appreciate his work tended to be the better educated, more sophisticated readers, though even some of these occasionally had blind spots concerning James's novels—his brother, William, for example, once wrote to James that his fiction was "bloodless." Except for the disastrous essay into drama, James adhered to his principles, always convinced that what he was doing would improve the quality of the novel and even raise the standards of conscientious readers. Events after his death have proved him right.

With the growth of courses of study in modern American literature, James earned the wide readership that was denied him during his lifetime, and after World War II, critical studies and biographical works devoted to him proliferated in staggering numbers. This is not to say that James is without his critics. He has frequently been criticized for a lack of scope and feeling, for concentrating his formidable talents on the psychological maneuvering of the privileged few. His later style has often been judged impenetrable, grotesquely mannered—though some critics regard his late novels as the highest achievements of the novelist's art, unsurpassed before or since.

As to James's influence on the subsequent course of the novel, however, there can be no question. He refined the novelistic art, purified it, and gave it directions never thought of before his time. Four areas of emphasis have especially attracted scholars in their attempts to isolate the essential contributions to the art of fiction with which James can be credited: point of view, psychological realism, style, and the connection of moral and aesthetic values.

Throughout his career, James experimented with the varieties of consciousness (the word can be found everywhere in his fiction and criticism) through which stories can be told. The completely objective point of view, in which the reader is presented solely with what anyone present would see and hear, and the first-person point of view, in which a character tells the story as he or she perceives it, were both traditional, and James used them frequently. As his writing became more complex and dense, however, he endeavored to relate the action more in terms of what goes on in people's minds, the most impressive example of such a "center of consciousness" being Lambert Strether in *The Ambassadors*. As Percy Lubbock noted as early as 1921 in *The Craft of Fiction*, James achieves in *The Ambassadors* a point of view remarkable for its appropriateness to the story told and astounding in its focus on Strether's consciousness, which is made possible by James's using the third-person limited point of view but relating the hero's thoughts and feelings in a way that he himself could never manage—in short, the reader sees Strether's perceptions both from the inside and from the outside, with James gently guiding attention to the more important features of Strether's cognition. This sort of advanced work in viewpoint did two important things: It helped to prepare the way for the stream-of-consciousness novel, and it deepened the psychological realism that was to be James's chief intellectual contribution to the novel form.

Realism was in the literary air when James was starting out as a writer, but he focused his attention on fidelity to the movements of consciousness in a way that no previous writer had done. In a James novel, what is most significant is not what transpires in the plot, per se, but rather the attitudes and emotions and discoveries that unfold in the consciousness of each individual character. Even in a work in the objective mode, such as *The Awkward Age*, which consists almost entirely of dialogue, what interests the attentive reader is the tides of feeling and realization that are implied by the speech. James appreciated the realistic aspects of the novels of Stendhal, Balzac, and Flaubert, but he resisted the naturalistic emphasis on the scientific and empirical—he believed Émile Zola to be misguided and unliterary. Indeed, James became a necessary counterfoil to this powerful literary movement in the later years of the nineteenth century.

As a stylist, James introduced the scrupulous craftsmanship of Flaubert to English-language readers. Like Flaubert, he weighed every phrase, every nuance of diction and rhythm, every comma. Indeed, for James, style was a moral imperative. Joseph Conrad, a great admirer of James (the feeling was reciprocated, but with less enthusiasm), once asserted that the American writer was "the historian of fine consciences." Certainly, no one who reads James closely could fail to note the delicate but constant attention paid to right and wrong in the novels. What might escape detection, however, is that James evidently believed that ethics are, in somewhat intricate ways, related to aesthetics. This does not mean that all the "good" characters are beautiful and the evil ones ugly. On the contrary, in many instances, physically attractive characters such as Christina Light (in *Roderick Hudson*) and Kate Croy (in *The Wings of the Dove*) are sources of much wickedness (such characters also are usually very charming); while less prepossessing ones, such as Madame Grandoni (in *The Princess Casamassima*) and Henrietta Stackpole (in *The Portrait of a Lady*), appear to represent the forces of virtue.

The true relationship between beauty and morality in James rests on his evident conviction that those elements of life that are positive and benevolent, such as freedom and personal development, have within them great beauty—and James takes considerable pains to express these qualities fully and with impressive aesthetic form. The appreciation of Fleda Vetch, in *The Spoils of Poynton*, for the beautiful appurtenances and objets d'art of the country house in the title constitutes, to some degree, a basis for the acts of renunciation and self-effacement that provide evidence of her virtue. Ever determined not to oversimplify, James offers such concatenations cautiously. This most subtle of moralists was equally understated in his presentation of beauty, revealing the ways in which it can conceal evil as well as the ways in which it can enrich life and give it greater meaning. After reading James, one cannot doubt the sincerity of his avowal, in his 1915 letter to H. G. Wells, that "It is art that *makes* life, makes interest, makes importance, for our consideration and application of these things, and I know of no substitute whatever for the force and beauty of its process."

BIOGRAPHY

If one wished to create for oneself a background and early life that was appropriate for preparing to be an important and dedicated American novelist during the later years of the nineteenth century and the early years of the twentieth century, one might very well choose just the sort of family and early experience that fate created for Henry James, born in 1843 in New York, New York. The family circumstances were comfortable (his grandfather, William James, had amassed one of the three largest fortunes in New York), and his father, Henry James, Sr.; his mother, Mary Robertson Walsh James; his older brother, William; and his younger siblings, Garth Wilkinson, Robertson, and Alice, were all lively, articulate, and stimulating. It has been speculated that the very effervescence of his siblings helped to develop in Henry a tendency toward observation rather than participation, a trait that may have contributed to his decision never to marry and certainly helped to lead him to the vocation to which he devoted his life.

Another important feature of James's youth was his father's belief in the merit of unsystematic but broadly based education. The future novelist thus enjoyed the benefits of instruction by tutors as well as in excellent European institutions (made possible by a four-year stay, 1855-1858, in Switzerland, England, and France). Early on, the elder Henry James, an unorthodox philosopher and writer, observed that "Harry is not so fond of study, properly so-called, as of reading. He is a devourer of libraries." That this parent was not insistent on a more traditional attitude toward education is to his credit; though James was largely self-educated (his only true conventional schooling was a brief period at Harvard Law School, in 1862-1863)—resulting in some ignorance of extended areas of knowledge, such as the sciences, and in specialized concentrations, represented by his phenomenally wide reading in nineteenth century fiction but in little literature written before that era—it is generally agreed that he was one of the best informed of the major literary persons of his time.

Apart from several later trips to Europe, which finally led him to the decision to move there in 1875 and to remain there for the rest of his life (except for a number of trips to the United States, where he never established a home), James led, for his first thirty years, a largely domestic life in the family circle. In his early twenties he had decided to become a writer; his initial publication is thought to be an unsigned story that appeared in 1864. This was the first of an endless stream of tales, reviews, essays, and novels (James became so proficient at French that he also translated a few works, which achieved publication); even during the period of his attempts to write plays he was turning out short pieces regularly. He was closely attached to his older brother, William, a relationship that endured until William's death, in 1910, and to Alice and his cousin, Mary "Minny" Temple, whom James thought to be "the very heroine of our common scene." This charming young lady may have been the only real romantic love of James's life—it has been suggested that her death at the age of twenty-four, in 1870, had much to do with James's resolution never to marry—and he immortalized her in Milly Theale, the ailing heroine of *The Wings of the Dove*, and perhaps in all the bright, appealing American girls who come to grief in his novels.

James was never very close to his younger brothers, a fact that has been attributed partly to his inability to serve in the Army during the American Civil War (because of "an obscure hurt," which was probably nothing more dramatic than a back injury—James had a painful back for all of his early adulthood), in which "Wilky" and "Bob" fought, but also to the fact that he was simply temperamentally unsuited to association with these essentially unhappy men, both of whom died before him. Alice James became disabled. The element of sadness in these three lives underlines the note of tragedy that can be found in much of James's fiction. There is no reason to doubt that, when James wrote to a friend, in 1896, "I have the imagination of disaster—and see life indeed as ferocious and sinister," he had had this grim attitude for many years, perhaps from as far back as his youth. Certainly, touches of the sinister abound in his novels.

After James's removal to Europe, the rest of his life became chiefly a matter of hard work, important friendships with literary figures (he seems to have known nearly everyone of importance in French and English belles lettres of his time, from Stevenson to George Sand, from George Eliot to Zola—and he wrote many essays about their work), and extraordinary ranges of travel.

After a year in Paris, in 1875, James decided that his art would flourish more fully in

England, where he took up residence, first in London, later in Rye, Sussex. He chose this relatively remote location because, he claimed, the vigorous social life of London was draining his energy and time from writing—typically, however, it is known that he greatly enjoyed that social contact, once boasting that during a single winter he dined out 107 times. Despite the claims of some critics and biographers—most notably Van Wyck Brooks, in *The Pilgrimage of Henry James* (1925)—that James abandoned his native land to become an uncritical lover of Europe and especially of England, a careful reading of his novels reveals that he was very clear-sighted about the weaknesses and flaws in English "high" society.

Whatever one's judgment about the validity of the reasons for James's resolve to live and work in Europe, it is plain that his art was largely determined by the European experience. Abroad, James found what he believed to be lacking in America, at least for a novelist of manners interested in cultural phenomena. In his biography of Hawthorne, James listed, perhaps with tongue partly in cheek, those items that could be studied only in Europe, since they did not exist in the United States:

> No sovereign, no court . . . no aristocracy, no church, no clergy, no army, no diplomatic service, no country gentlemen, no palaces, no castles, nor manors, nor old country-houses . . . no literature, no novels, no museums, no pictures, no political society, no sporting class.

Though this list offers some hint of James's sense of humor, the works themselves are sure evidence that he was convinced that Europe provided him with indispensable materials for his novels.

James never made a great deal of money from his writing, but he always lived comfortably (he was so confident of his financial security that he turned over his share of the estate of his father, who died in 1882, to Alice). He was a generous friend, both with money and advice, to his many acquaintances and to young writers hoping to succeed. He had what some biographers call a genius for friendship, which his enormous correspondence attests. His fondness for congenial associates, particularly literary ones, did not, however, blind him to their weaknesses nor subdue his pride in his accomplishments. He once wrote home that, as to his friend Flaubert, "I think I easily—more than easily—see all round him intellectually."

Such a boast may help to explain James's remarkable adherence to his absolute belief in his powers and in the rightness of his efforts. While public taste was going in one direction (downward, in his view), James's technique was headed precisely the opposite way. This firmness has since been justified, and even in his lifetime the admiration of such respected writers as Conrad and William Dean Howells did much to console him for his lack of popularity. On James's seventieth birthday, April 15, 1913, some 270 friends presented him with a "golden bowl" and asked him to sit for a portrait by John Singer Sargent (which is now in the National Portrait Gallery in London). More formal honors were an honorary degree from Harvard University (1911) and one from Oxford (1912); perhaps the most lofty distinction was the Order of Merit, presented to James by King George V, in 1916, the year of the author's death (from heart trouble and pneumonia). This decoration was given in recognition of James's valued service to England during the opening years of World War I; James believed that the United States was dishonorable for not becoming involved.

As death approached—James wrote of it, "So here it is at last, the distinguished thing!"—he was still engaged in writing; he left two unfinished novels, *The Ivory Tower* and *The Sense of the Past*, and a number of unpublished essays and stories, all of which have since been printed. This continuation of his labors right to the end was fitting, for never before, or since, was there a man of whom it is so appropriate to say that his work *was* his life.

Analysis

Henry James's distinctive contributions to the art of the novel were developed over a long career of some fifty years. Leon Edel, possibly the most renowned and respected James scholar, has indicated that James's mature writing can be divided into three periods (with three subdivisions in the middle phase). Through the publication of *The Portrait of a Lady*, in 1880-1881, James was chiefly interested in the now famous "international theme," the learning experiences and conflicts of Americans in Europe and Europeans in America (the former situation being by far the more frequent). This first period is represented by *Roderick Hudson*, *The American*, *Daisy Miller*, and *The Portrait of a Lady*. Of these works, *Daisy Miller* and *The Portrait of a Lady* are probably the best examples of James's early work.

The more complex second period falls into three parts. The first, roughly from 1881 through 1890, displays James's concern with social issues (not the sort of topic for which he is known), as in *The Bostonians* and *The Princess Casamassima*, the former about women's rights in the United States and the latter concerning the class struggle in England. The second of these subperiods is that during which he created plays (many of which have never been performed) and produced a variety of short stories. The final subdivision is marked by the appearance of short and midlength fictions dealing with the problems of artists in their relationships with society (he had already touched on this subject in *Roderick Hudson*) and of occasionally bizarre stories, such as *The Turn of the Screw* and "The Altar of the Dead," about men, women, and children who are obsessed, haunted, and perhaps insane. Some of these pieces were written during James's calamitous endeavor with drama.

The final period, called "the major phase," from about 1896 till the close of his career, shows James returning to the international theme. The themes of this period are most obviously exhibited in the three large novels of his later years: *The Ambassadors* (which was written before the next novel but published after it), *The Wings of the Dove*, and *The Golden Bowl*.

During this extended development and shifting of interests and enthusiasms, James was continuously trying to refine his presentation of character, theme, and event. In his critical writing he stated that he finally recognized the value of "the *indirect* presentation of his main image" (he is here speaking of Milly Theale, in *The Wings of the Dove*, who is seen largely through the eyes of other characters and about whom the reader learns, even of her death, chiefly by report). Several critics, perhaps the most famous being F. R. Leavis, in *The Great Tradition* (1948), believe this "recognition" to be a grave error; they claim that James refined his presentation beyond clear comprehension (thus the common accusation of excessive ambiguity) and eventually beyond interest. Others—perhaps the most salient is F. W. Dupee, in *Henry James* (1951)—aver that these three late novels are James's masterpieces, works in which his study of the complexities of moral decisions reaches an elevation never attained by another author.

Two aspects of James's fiction have received little attention: Not much has been written about his humor, which is usually ironic but often gentle. A fine example is his presentation of Lavinia Penniman, the foolish aunt of Catherine Sloper in *Washington Square* and a widow "without fortune—with nothing but the memory of Mr. Penniman's flowers of speech, a certain vague aroma of which hovered about her own conversation." This romantic, meddling woman is depicted by James humorously, but with a clear indication of the harm that her interference causes. The image of her "flowers of speech" suggests another neglected style: the repetition of certain key words and images throughout his canon. Readers can easily become distracted by frequently encountered "flower" images such as the foregoing one and key words such as "figured" (as in "it figured for him"), "lucid" or "lucidly" (as in "he said it lucidly"), "idea" (as in "he had his idea of"), and a phrase such as "she took it in" to signify an understanding of a remark. Also, "theory"—in a phrase such as "she had a theory that"—appears many times. It is not surprising that certain terms might emerge frequently in a canon as large as James's, but his evident affection for particular expressions such as the foregoing ones does seem odd in a writer whose repertoire of verbal expression appears to be boundless. It would, for example, be hard to think of another writer, who, in characterizing the grim conversation of Mrs. Bowerbank, in *The Princess Casamassima*, would be able to suggest it by noting, "her outlook seemed to abound in cheerless contingencies."

All in all, however, there is little of James's subject matter and technique that has escaped the close inspection of scholarship. Possibly the greatest shift of critical emphasis in James scholarship has been the increasing awareness of the moral thrust of his work. Early critics frequently charged that no consistent moral attitude was clearly expressed in his work. In later times, this concern evaporated, with a realization that James was an insightful moralist who understood that general rules are of little use in dealing with complex social and personal situations. He tended to treat each novel as a sort of special problem, to be worked out by the characters. From his total production, however, two "principles" have issued: The author was a firm believer in freedom and in personal development. To become a true hero or heroine in a James novel, a character must achieve a state of self-realization (again, an acute act of consciousness is needed), must recognize the truth and face it bravely, must act freely (without emotional dependence on others), and must renounce any personal gain in order to promote the welfare of others. In this way, the person attains true personal development and achieves as much freedom as James believed the world could offer—he did not subscribe to the doctrine that human liberty is unlimited. The basic moral conflict in his novels is essentially between powerful, often heartless or thoughtless, oppressors, such as Gilbert Osmond in *The Portrait of a Lady* and Olive Chancellor in *The Bostonians*, and their "victims," such as Isabel Archer, in the former work, and Verena Tarrant, in the latter.

James's reputation, already high, is continuing to rise and is likely to continue to do so. The adaptation of several of his works for the cinema (*Daisy Miller, The Europeans, Washington Square, The Portrait of a Lady*, and *The Wings of the Dove*) and television (*The Ambassadors, The Turn of the Screw*, "The Author of Beltraffio," *The Spoils of Poynton*, and *The Golden Bowl*) is perhaps a superficial indication of increasing acclaim, but the burgeoning of critical attention is not. There is no question that James belongs, in Leavis's phrase, squarely in the "great tradition" of the novel.

DAISY MILLER

Daisy Miller, which established James's reputation as a leading novelist both in England and the United States, announces several of his recurring themes and motifs. The story is an uncomplicated one, from the standpoint of plot. Frederick Winterbourne, a sophisticated young American who lives in Europe, meets Daisy Miller, who is visiting Europe with her mother and younger brother; Mr. Miller is back in Schenectady, New York, presumably making enough money to allow his family to travel comfortably. The essence of the novella is the relationship that develops between the young, cosmopolitan expatriate (a not uncommon type in James's fiction) and the pretty, naïve, and willful girl.

In *Daisy Miller* a central issue is whether Winterbourne could have prevented the tragedy that ends Daisy's life. As he gets to know her better and comes to like her, he becomes increasingly distressed at Daisy's refusal to heed the warnings of Mrs. Costello, his aunt, and Mrs. Walker, another Europeanized American society matron (it is significant that the people who most condemn Daisy are not native Europeans but expatriates). Daisy stubbornly continues to consort with the gigolo Giovanelli, who is seen with her all about Rome, much to the dismay of the society people, who are scandalized by such "loose" behavior—even the Romans joke about it in a subdued fashion, which only irritates Winterbourne the more. He tries to warn Daisy that she is seen too much with Giovanelli—"Everyone thinks so"—but she refuses to take his cautions seriously: "I don't believe a word of it. They're only pretending to be shocked. They don't really care a straw what I do." This perverse attitude finally leads to Daisy's death, when she goes, against Winterbourne's urging, to the Colosseum at night (a place that, after dark, was reputed to have a miasma often fatal to foreigners) and contracts a mortal fever. When Winterbourne angrily asks Giovanelli why he took Daisy to such a dangerous place, the Italian answers, "*she*—she did what she liked."

The complexity of the moral nuances of the story is revealed when one remembers that Winterbourne, who is regarded as quite the perfect young gentleman and is welcomed in the best society, has a mistress back in Geneva. Clearly, in that "best" society what matters is not virtue (Daisy is quite guiltless of any actual wrongdoing) but the appearance of it—Winterbourne may not be virtuous, but he is discreet. The old theme of appearance versus reality thus emerges in this story, but with social implications not found in the work of other authors. To James, one of the most difficult problems for Americans trying to come to terms with Europe is that the appearance of virtue often counts for more than the reality. This problem is seen quite plainly in *The Reverberator*, written ten years later, in which an American businessman is puzzled that a French family is upset over some scandalous things said about them in a newspaper; so far as he is concerned, such things do not matter so long as they are not true.

James's realism is most evident in the close of the story. Winterbourne is remorseful over Daisy's death. He regrets that he did not try harder to understand her and correct her misconceptions. He tells his aunt, "She would have appreciated one's esteem." Then, he applies the lesson to himself: "I've lived too long in foreign parts." So far, the story has seemed to advance a moral thesis about the corruption of innocence and the valuable truths that can be learned. James closes the novella, however, on a note that proves how realistic his vision of human nature was:

> Nevertheless he soon went back to live at Geneva, whence there continue to come the most contradictory accounts of his motives of sojourn: a report that he's "studying" hard—an intimation that he's much interested in a very clever foreign lady.

James had no illusions about people.

THE PORTRAIT OF A LADY

While *Daisy Miller* is told in the first person, from Winterbourne's consciousness, *The Portrait of a Lady*, a much longer and more complicated fiction, is related through the minds of a number of characters. This book is probably the most generally admired of all James's full-length novels. It carries the international theme to what some consider its highest level of expression, and it offers the reader one of the most impressive characters in James's work, the delightful Isabel Archer, the "lady" of the title. Again, James is psychologically realistic: While Isabel is honest, intelligent, and sensitive, she is not without fault; she does have "an unquenchable desire to think well of herself." She is an "innocent abroad" who is "affronting her destiny." This fate is to be given, first, the chance to visit Europe (offered by Lydia Touchett, her wealthy aunt who lives in Europe) and, then, a great deal of money (provided by the will of Daniel Touchett, at the suggestion of his son,

Ralph, who becomes very fond of Isabel). This combination of high connections—Mr. Touchett associates with a number of prominent English families, most significantly that of Lord Warburton—opportunities for travel, and comfortable circumstances is common in James's novels.

In *The Portrait of a Lady*, James studies the relationships of the characters in great detail. When Lord Warburton proposes to Isabel, the situation is examined closely, and her rejection of him prepares for later plot developments and revelations of character. As is often the case with James, the money that Isabel inherits is both a blessing and a curse. It permits her to travel and to live almost lavishly, but it also attracts to her one of the few outright villains in James's fiction.

Gilbert Osmond appears to be charming, modest, intelligent, and sensitive. He proves to be proud, arrogant, idle, and cruel. In a powerful enunciation of the international theme, Osmond courts Isabel cleverly, appealing to her sense of the artistic wonders of Europe, of which he seems to be a fine judge. He wins her hand, partly through the efforts of Madame Serena Merle, an American expatriate (as is Osmond) who, Isabel later discovers, was once Osmond's mistress (they could not marry, since neither was wealthy—the topic of marrying for money is one that James explored as thoroughly as any writer ever had and with greater insight). Mme Merle is eager for Osmond to marry well, since they have a daughter, Pansy, whom she wishes to see well placed in the world. With James's usual subtlety and with his use of a device that again proves effective in *The Golden Bowl*, Isabel first suspects the unacknowledged intimacy between Mme Merle and Osmond when she sees them through a window, in a room in which she is standing and he is seated—such social touches mark James's fiction repeatedly; to him, the social graces were a great deal more than simply pleasant decorations on the fringes of human intercourse.

Of course, the marriage is a failure. Osmond comes to resent Isabel, and eventually she despises him. In the famous chapter 42, Isabel examines the grim condition of her life. In an extended passage of what is clearly a precursor of the stream-of-consciousness technique, James causes Isabel to review the terrible errors she has made—"It was her deep distrust of her husband—this was what darkened her world"—and to consider how foolish her pride has made her: Ralph Touchett, among others, warned her against Osmond. Isabel's stubbornness and refusal to heed wise advice reminds one of Daisy Miller's similar folly. The plot becomes more complex when Lord Warburton directs his affections to Pansy. Naturally, Osmond is highly in favor of such a marriage, since Warburton is very rich. Isabel incurs her husband's even more intense hatred by discouraging the English peer with the simple argument that he and Pansy do not really love each other. Here, European corruption (expressed in an American expatriate, as is often the case in James's fiction) is opposed to American innocence and emotional integrity.

The conclusion of this novel is among James's most subtle and ambiguous. Isabel returns to England to visit the deathbed of Ralph Touchett. His death has been prepared for by the announcement in the first chapter that he is in poor health. In fact, Ralph is one of

James's truly virtuous characters, as is shown by his renunciation of any thought of marrying Isabel, whom he loves, because of his failing physical condition. Isabel admits to Ralph that he was right and that she committed a monumental error in marrying Osmond. Ralph, typically, blames himself for having provided her with the money that tempted Osmond; Isabel refuses this excuse, recognizing that the mistake was her own.

The puzzling aspect of the last pages of the novel is that Isabel determines to go back to Osmond as his wife. Several explanations have been offered, all of them proving the profound depth of James's penetration of human motives. The most dramatic is that Isabel's confrontation with her old lover from America, Casper Goodwood, is so violent—he seizes her and kisses her passionately—that it frightens her (perhaps arousing an unsettling sexuality in her nature) into returning to a life that may be despicable but is safe. Another, more likely reason for the decision is that Isabel has become fond of Pansy and has promised to come back and help her to advance in life along sound and honorable lines. The most subtle reason may be that Isabel is simply too proud to admit her blunder openly to the world, which a separation would do, and prefers to live in misery rather than escape to what she would regard as shame. Whatever the true cause of her resolution (and they might all be operative), she starts back to Rome immediately. In the last passage of the book, however, Isabel's old friend and confidant, Henrietta Stackpole, suggests to Caspar that he must have patience—evidently a hint that this loyal friend of Isabel believes that she will not stay with Osmond forever.

Scholars who believe that James attained the peak of his treatment of the international theme in this novel point to the delicate illumination of Isabel's growing awareness of the sinister undertones of life and to the gallery of superb portraits of ineffectual innocence (as in Ralph, who is all goodwill and yet helps to ruin Isabel's life), black evil (in Mme Merle and Osmond), and admixtures of positive and negative traits, as in Mrs. Touchett, who is essentially well-intentioned but supremely intransigent (she does not live with the mild-mannered Mr. Touchett, and "the edges of her conduct were so very clear-cut" that they "had a knife-like effect"). Even if the reader is not quite ready to agree with the judgment of Leavis that this novel, along with *The Bostonians*, is one of "the two most brilliant novels in the language," it seems difficult to deny that *The Portrait of a Lady* is the articulate treatment of the international theme in American literature.

THE BOSTONIANS

James omitted *The Bostonians* from the New York edition because it deals with purely American subjects, Americans in the United States; it has no trace of the international theme. *The Bostonians* was undervalued by critics as well as by its author, and it has taken many years for readers to recognize the novel as, in Leavis's words, "a wonderfully rich, intelligent and brilliant book." Aside from focusing on a social topic, a rare instance of this emphasis in James, *The Bostonians* also treats skillfully another subject much on his mind during this era: the problems and aberrations of obsessed, disturbed people. The conflict between the old-fashioned conservative southerner, Basil Ransom, and his New England cousin, Olive Chancellor, makes for a novel full of tension and animation. Some of the modern interest in the book results from what has been judged a "nearly lesbian" relationship between Olive and Verena Tarrant, the attractive girl who is the source of the antagonism. As Irving Howe suggests in his introduction to the Modern Library edition of *The Bostonians* (1956), the fact that people of James's era did not have modern terms of reference such as "lesbian" does not mean that they knew less about these kinds of relationships.

The social problem underlined by the novel is that of women's rights, the difficulty being, of course, that women had few of them. Today, the victories that have been won for the right of women to vote, hold office, and the like are taken for granted, but a reading of *The Bostonians* makes clear how much painful and dreary effort went into creating these advances. As usual, however, James treats the issue specifically, in terms of individual people. In discussing the book later, James said that he took too long to get the story going and provided too much background for the characters. Many current readers, however, judge the background both necessary and interesting. It is, for example, important that Ransom be presented in both a positive and negative light, in order to prepare adequately for the somewhat ambiguous resolution of the plot. As a southerner who has come North to practice the law in a location that will provide him with opportunities not available in the war-ravaged South (it is a clever touch that James causes him to be a Civil War veteran, now living in the region populated by his recent enemies; in this way James emphasizes Basil's sense of alienation and loneliness), Ransom is both appealing—he has "a fine head and such magnificent eyes"—and repelling: "He was very long . . . and he looked a little hard and discouraging, like a column of figures."

Ransom proves very hard and discouraging. Once he meets Verena Tarrant, the daughter of a "mesmeric healer" of dubious integrity (James's depiction of this character is further evidence of his rich fund of humor), who has become, by some natural inspiration, an eloquent platform speaker on behalf of the movement to extend the rights of women, the stage is set for the great contention. Olive Chancellor reluctantly allows Basil to become acquainted with Verena—by this time, the well-to-do Boston spinster has already been overwhelmed by the innocent charm of the naïve girl. Thus, the battle lines are drawn early. Ransom soon realizes that Verena should be married, preferably to him, instead of wasting her life on a fruitless and, in his opinion, misguided cause. Ransom believes that the highest destiny to which a woman can aspire is "to make some honest man happy." He finds a formidable opponent in Olive, whose zeal for reform inspires her widowed sister, Mrs. Luna, who believes the whole movement to be ridiculous (since she is very interested in romantic relationships with men, particularly Ransom, for a time), to remark that "she would reform the solar system if she could get hold of it." The wit that James displays at the expense of the movement may seem to indicate that he, too, thinks it ridiculous. As usual, however, the author is fair, offering a warm and sensitive picture of Miss Birdseye (a character who caused James to be much criticized in his own time, since many readers believed her to be based closely on a highly respected member of the Peabody family of Boston—James always denied the charge), an old reformer who has been pursuing the cause for decades.

Verena and Basil meet but a handful of times before the climax of the novel, but their dialogues are artfully designed by the author to reveal that Verena, who has been welcomed into Olive's home as a permanent guest (the Boston spinster, while having no gift for oratory herself, is fully committed to Verena's promulgation of the cause—she is also deeply and possessively committed to Verena personally, having once cried passionately, "Promise me not to marry!"), is slowly becoming interested in Ransom. Finally, when he believes that he can afford to marry, a conviction that seems somewhat optimistic, since his career has advanced very slowly, and since his belief is based on the publication of only one essay on political and social philosophy, he proposes to Verena. James has not been widely accused of depending on coincidences in his plots, as have, for example, Charles Dickens and Thomas Hardy, but a number of them do appear. In this case, Verena turns to Olive and away from Basil chiefly because Miss Birdseye, of whom she is very fond, dies shortly after the proposal.

These circumstances lead to the highly dramatic scene at the Boston Music Hall, where Verena is scheduled to address a large crowd. Ransom, learning of the planned address, arrives, manages to get backstage (to the door of the dressing room, which is guarded by a large Boston police officer, provided by the fearful and distraught Olive), and forcefully urges Verena to go away with him. She ultimately accedes to his coercion (he seizes her and almost pushes her out the door), leaving Olive weeping and desolate. James, in his customary evenhanded dealing with themes and characters, makes it clear that the marriage of Basil and Verena will certainly be anything but "happy ever after." Verena is in tears when she is ushered from the theater by her lover, and in the last sentence of the book, James provides a typically ominous forecast of their future: "It is to be feared that with the union, so far from brilliant, into which she is about to enter, these were not the last she was destined to shed." Many readers find it astonishing that James could have so underrated this penetrating study of social movements and human beings torn between personal loyalties and abstract ideals. The climactic final scene is the most dramatic and lively that James ever wrote. This is, however, clearly not the end of the story. As Conrad has said, "One is never set at rest by Mr. Henry James's novels. His books end as an episode in life ends. You remain with the sense of the life still going on."

THE AMBASSADORS

The Ambassadors, which James considered "frankly, quite the best, 'all round,' of my productions," is now generally rated as one of his masterpieces (some critics believe it to be far and away the most accomplished work of the major phase). Like many of his novels, it was based on an incident in real life. In his notebooks, James recalls being told of a visit that his old friend Howells made to Paris in his later years. According to the anecdote, told to James by Jonathan Sturges, Howells, overcome by the beauty of Paris, remarked to his youthful friend, "Oh, you are young, you are young—be glad of it: be glad of it and *live*. Live all you can: it's a mistake not to." This passage, and the rest of the speech, is almost word for word that made by the middle-aged Lambert Strether, the hero of *The Ambassadors*, to Little Bilham (a character thought to have been based on Sturges) in the beautiful Parisian garden of the artist Gloriani (a character carried over from *Roderick Hudson*; James sometimes became so interested in a character that he revived him for a later novel).

Strether is indeed an "ambassador." He has been given the unenviable assignment (by his formidable patron, Mrs. Abel Newsome) of persuading her son, Chadwick Newsome, to return to his family and commercial responsibilities in Woollett, Massachusetts (probably representing Worcester, Massachusetts). The primary subject of this novel is joie de vivre; this quality is just what Strether finds when he arrives in Paris, where he has not been since he was a young man. It has been observed that one of the salient aspects of James's fiction is irony. Nowhere is this quality more in evidence than in *The Ambassadors*. Chad Newsome, Strether discovers, has been made a gracious gentleman by his life in Paris; Strether, charmed by the beauty and enchantment of the city, cannot in good conscience urge Chad to leave delightful Paris for dull Woollett. The irony lies in the fact that Chad is quite willing and, finally, eager to return home to make a great deal of money (the family business is very successful; it manufactures some useful article, which is, typically, unidentified by James), while Strether longs to remain in Paris. Indeed, his delay in dispatching Chad home impels Mrs. Newsome to send her intimidating daughter, Mrs. Sarah Pocock, and her husband to take up the commission, since Strether has evidently failed. Thus the forces of philistinism are present, enlivening the conflict.

This conflict is chiefly in the mind of Strether, since, in this novel, James undertook to employ the third-person limited point of view to its fullest effect. As usual, the situation is not as simple as it appears. It is not merely residence in Paris that has "civilized" Chad; it has also been his mistress, Mme Marie de Vionnet. Strether, before he knows of the intimacy between his young friend and this sophisticated and charming lady, develops an intense admiration and affection for her. Even after he learns of the liaison, accidentally seeing the two rowing on a river near an inn where they are staying, Strether is still entranced by Marie de Vionnet. When Chad decides to return home and abandon his mistress (who has been reviled, to Strether's dismay, by Mrs. Pocock, who refers to Chad's relationship with her as "hideous"), Strether recognizes her tragedy ("You are fighting for your life!") and is extremely sympathetic. He has, however, his own problems. Thanks to Mrs. Newsome's already aroused suspicions and Sarah Pocock's expected damning report, Strether sees that his comfortable position in Woollett (and possibly eventual marriage to his widowed employer) is very likely gone: "It probably *was* all at an end."

The renunciation theme, so prominent in James's novels, is perhaps more powerfully formulated at the close of this novel than in any other of his books. Despite the appeal of

Paris, and the hinted offer of an agreeable marriage to Maria Gostrey, an American expatriate who had befriended Strether when he first landed in Europe, this highly moral and responsible man resolves to return to Woollett, where he believes his duty to lie. He cannot help Mme de Vionnet. He cannot help himself. This sort of ethical resolution may seem foolish to modern readers, but it is believable in the novel, and the circumstances suggest James's belief that, in current terms, there is a price tag on everything, even happiness. The novel, then, is not only a tribute to Paris and the life of cultural elevation that it can provide but also the necessity of responsible and considerate action. James admitted that he learned a great deal from George Eliot; he shared her conviction that duty is absolute in the ethical universe. The temptation of Strether is almost overwhelming, but his New England sense of duty compels him to conquer it. It is difficult to think of another novelist, or, indeed, another novel, that illuminates so brightly the significance of conscientious moral choices.

Henry James's contributions to the evolution of the modern novel are of staggering magnitude and diversity. Perhaps his greatest contribution was best summed up by Ezra Pound shortly after James's death: "Peace comes of communication. No man of our time has so labored to create means of communication as did the late Henry James. The whole of great art is a struggle for communication."

Fred B. McEwen

OTHER MAJOR WORKS

SHORT FICTION: *A Passionate Pilgrim*, 1875; *The Madonna of the Future*, 1879; *The Siege of London*, 1883; *Tales of Three Cities*, 1884; *The Author of Beltraffio*, 1885; *The Lesson of the Master*, 1892; *The Private Life, Lord Beaupre, The Visits*, 1893; *The Real Thing*, 1893; *Terminations*, 1895; *Embarrassments*, 1896; *The Two Magics: The Turn of the Screw and Covering End*, 1898; *The Soft Side*, 1900; *The Better Sort*, 1903; *The Novels and Tales of Henry James*, 1907-1909 (24 volumes); *The Finer Grain*, 1910; *A Landscape Painter*, 1919; *Travelling Companions*, 1919; *Master Eustace*, 1920; *Stories of Writers and Other Artists*, 1944; *Henry James: Selected Short Stories*, 1950 (Quentin Anderson, editor); *Henry James: Eight Tales from the Major Phase*, 1958; *The Complete Tales of Henry James*, 1962-1965 (12 volumes; Leon Edel, editor); *The Figure in the Carpet, and Other Stories*, 1986 (Frank Kermode, editor); *The Jolly Corner, and Other Tales*, 1990 (Roger Gard, editor); *The Uncollected Henry James: Newly Discovered Stories*, 2004 (Floyd R. Horowitz, editor).

PLAYS: *Daisy Miller*, pb. 1883 (adaptation of his novel); *The American*, pr. 1891 (adaptation of his novel); *Guy Domville*, pb. 1894; *The Reprobate*, pb. 1894; *Theatricals: Tenants and Disengaged*, pb. 1894; *Theatricals, Second Series: "The Album" and "The Reprobate,"* 1895; *The High Bid*, pr. 1908; *The Saloon*, pr. 1911; *The Outcry*, pr. 1917 (wr. 1909); *The Complete Plays of Henry James*, 1949 (Leon Edel, editor); *The Other House*, pb. 1949 (wr. 1909).

NONFICTION: *Transatlantic Sketches*, 1875; *French Poets and Novelists*, 1878; *Hawthorne*, 1879; *Portraits of Places*, 1883; *The Art of Fiction*, 1884; *A Little Tour in France*, 1884; *Partial Portraits*, 1888; *Essays in London*, 1893; *William Wetmore Story and His Friends*, 1903; *English Hours*, 1905; *The American Scene*, 1907; *Views and Reviews*, 1908; *Italian Hours*, 1909; *A Small Boy and Others*, 1913 (memoirs); *Notes of a Son and Brother*, 1914 (memoirs); *Notes on Novelists*, 1914; *The Middle Years*, 1917; *The Art of the Novel: Critical Prefaces*, 1934 (R. P. Blackmur, editor); *The Notebooks of Henry James*, 1947 (F. O. Matthiessen and Kenneth B. Murdock, editors); *The Scenic Art*, 1948 (Allan Wade, editor); *Henry James Letters*, 1974-1984 (5 volumes; Edel, editor); *Henry James: Literary Criticism*, 1984; *The Art of Criticism: Henry James on the Theory and the Practice of Fiction*, 1986 (William Veeder and Susan M. Griffin, editors); *The Complete Notebooks of Henry James*, 1987 (Edel, editor); *Dear Munificent Friends: Henry James's Letters to Four Women*, 1999 (Susan E. Gunter, editor); *Henry James on Culture: Collected Essays on Politics and the American Social Scene*, 1999 (Pierre A. Walker, editor); *Dearly Beloved Friends: Henry James's Letters to Younger Men*, 2001 (Gunter and Steven H. Jobe, editors); *The Complete Letters of Henry James, 1855-1872*, 2006 (Pierre A. Walker and Greg W. Zacharias, editors).

BIBLIOGRAPHY

Bailie, Ronnie. *The Fantastic Anatomist: A Psychoanalytic Study of Henry James*. Atlanta: Rodopi, 2000. A look at James and his works from a psychological perspective, focusing on his unconscious fantasies concerning the human body, mostly the damaged or incomplete human body, and how these fantasies contributed to his creativity. Includes a bibliography and an index.

Bloom, Harold, ed. *Henry James*. New York: Chelsea House, 1987. Bloom has compiled what he considers the best in criticism available on James, presented in order of their original publication, including essays on the novels *The Bostonians*, *The Ambassadors*, *Washington Square*, and *The American*.

Coulson, Victoria. *Henry James, Women, and Realism*. New York: Cambridge University Press, 2007. Examines James's important friendships with three women: his sister Alice James and the novelists Constance Fenimore Woolson and Edith Wharton. These three women writers and James shared what Coulson describes as an "ambivalent realism," or a cultural ambivalence about gender identity, and she examines how this idea is manifest in James's works.

Freedman, Jonathan, ed. *The Cambridge Companion to Henry James*. New York: Cambridge University Press, 1998. A collection of essays that provides extensive information on James's life and literary influences and details his works and the characters contained in them. Includes a bibliography and an index.

Graham, Kenneth. *Henry James, a Literary Life*. New York: St. Martin's Press, 1996. A critical overview of James's most important writings, set within the context of his career as a novelist in the United States, England, and continental Europe. Places James within the literary and intellectual climate of his time.

Kaplan, Fred. *Henry James: The Imagination of Genius*. New York: William R. Morrow, 1992. Literary biographer Kaplan traces James's development as a writer, recounting the major events of his life and placing James within the historical context of his times.

Kventsel, Anna. *Decadence in the Late Novels of Henry James*. New York: Palgrave Macmillan, 2007. Kventsel interprets three novels—*The Ambassadors*, *The Wings of the Dove*, and *The Golden Bowl*—from the perspective of fin de siècle decadence. Includes a bibliography and an index.

Lewis, R. W. B. *The Jameses*. New York: Farrar, Straus and Giroux, 1991. Lewis recounts the family's history, beginning with grandfather William James, who emigrated from Ireland to the Untied States, and concluding with the death of novelist Henry James in 1916. The book focuses on Henry, Sr., and his three children—William, who became a leading philosopher and psychologist; Alice; and Henry, Jr., the novelist.

Pippin, Robert B. *Henry James and Modern Moral Life*. New York: Cambridge University Press, 2000. A look at the moral message James tried to convey through his writings. Pippin interprets several of James's works, including *The Portrait of a Lady*, *The Wings of the Dove*, *The Ambassadors*, and *The Golden Bowl*.

Pollak, Vivian R., ed. *New Essays on "Daisy Miller" and "The Turn of the Screw."* New York: Cambridge University Press, 1993. Aimed at undergraduate students, this book contains feminist and psychological interpretations of the two novels as well as a study of the books within the context of the Victorian period. Includes an introduction and a bibliography.

Rowe, John Carlos. *The Other Henry James*. Durham, N.C.: Duke University Press, 1998. A biography of James that examines his political and social views and his portrayal of gender and sex roles.

Stevens, Hugh. *Henry James and Sexuality*. New York: Cambridge University Press, 1998. A study of sexuality in James's work, including homosexuality and sex roles. Includes discussions of gender and representation in *The Wings of the Dove*, sexuality and the aesthetic in *The Golden Bowl*, and the eroticism of *Roderick Hudson*.

RUDYARD KIPLING

Born: Bombay (now Mumbai), India; December 30, 1865
Died: Hampstead, London, England; January 18, 1936
Also known as: Joseph Rudyard Kipling

PRINCIPAL LONG FICTION

The Light That Failed, 1890
The Naulahka: A Story of East and West, 1892 (with Wolcott Balestier)
Captains Courageous: A Story of the Grand Banks, 1897
Kim, 1901

OTHER LITERARY FORMS

Best known for his short fiction, Rudyard Kipling wrote more than 250 stories. His style of leaving a story open-ended with the tantalizing phrase "But that's another story" established his reputation for unlimited storytelling. Although the stories are uneven in quality, W. Somerset Maugham considered Kipling to be the only British writer to equal France's Guy de Maupassant and Russia's Anton Chekhov in the art of short fiction.

Kipling's early stories both satisfied and glorified the Englishman in India. The empire builder, the man who devotes his life to "civilize the sullen race," comes off in glowing colors, as in the story "The Bridge Builders." Some of his best stories skillfully blend the exotic and the bizarre; the early "The Man Who Would Be King" (1888), which is about two drifters and their fantastic dream to carve out a kingdom for themselves in Central Asia, is an excellent example of such a story. Some stories reflect the pain, suffering, and dark melancholy of Kipling's later life: "A Madonna of the Trenches," with its strange, occult atmosphere; "The Children of the Zodiac," about a young poet who dreads death by cancer of the throat; and "The Gardener," with its unrelieved sadness and autobiographical reflections on the death of a son.

The stories that make up *The Jungle Book* (1894) and *The Second Jungle Book* (1895) were written in Brattleboro, Vermont, when Kipling's mind "worked at the height of its wonderful creative power." They are in the class of animal stories and folktales that make up such world literary creations as the ancient folktales of *Aesop's Fables* (fourth century B.C.E.) and the Buddha birth stories known as the Jataka Tales. Into the Jungle Book stories, Kipling incorporated not only the clear and clean discipline of the British public school but also his favorite doctrine of the natural law. This law had a great impact on the Boy Scout movement and the origins of the Wolf Cub organization, found in the Mowgli tales.

Kipling was a prolific writer, and, as a journalist, he wrote a considerable number of articles, stories, and poems not only for his own newspapers but also for a variety of literary journals in England and the United States. In addition, he was a prolific letter writer and

Rudyard Kipling
(The Nobel Foundation)

carried on lengthy literary and political correspondence with such men as President Theodore Roosevelt, financier Cecil Rhodes, and writer H. Rider Haggard. His correspondence with Haggard has been collected in *Rudyard Kipling to Rider Haggard: The Record of a Friendship*, edited by Morton N. Cohen (1965). Two volumes of his previously uncollected works were published in 1938 under the title *Uncollected Prose*, and even some of his desultory writings, such as *American Notes*, concerned with his travels in the United States in 1891, was reissued in the late twentieth century with editorial notes.

Kipling personally supervised the publication of the Sussex edition of his work in thirty-five volumes (1937-1939). The Kipling Society, founded in 1927, publishes the quarterly *Kipling Journal*, which keeps Kipling enthusiasts informed of publications about Kipling. A great deal of biographical material on Kipling—including his autobiography, *Something of Myself: For My Friends Known and Unknown*, published posthumously in 1937—has been published, and the record of his literary achievement is now complete.

ACHIEVEMENTS

Rudyard Kipling's first book of fiction appeared in 1888. Since then, his works have undergone several editions, and several of his short stories and poems have found a permanent place in anthologies. Although England and India have both changed enormously since the beginning of the twentieth century, Kipling's stories continue to attract and fascinate new readers. He was a best-selling author during his lifetime—one of his animal stories, *Thy Servant a Dog* (1930), sold 100,000 copies in six months in 1932—and his works continue to be extremely popular in the English-speaking countries of the world. Several of his works, notably *Captains Courageous, Kim, The Jungle Book*, and some short stories, have been made into motion pictures.

Throughout his lifetime, and soon after his death, Kipling was associated with the British Empire. He had become the laureate of England's vast imperial power, his first book was praised by the viceroy in 1888, and the king used Kipling's own words to address the Empire on Christmas Day in 1932. The day Kipling's ashes were interred at Westminster Abbey—January 23, 1936—King George V's body lay in state in Westminster Hall, and the comment that "the King has gone and taken his trumpeteer with him" appropriately described the image Kipling had projected.

Kipling wanted to serve the Empire through the army or the civil service. Because he had neither family connections with which to obtain a civil service job nor strong eyesight—required for military service—Kipling turned to writing. He wrote with a passionate intensity coupled with admiration for the soldiers, bridge builders, missionaries, and civil servants in remote places who served the Empire under "an alien sky." Many of the phrases he used to narrate their tales—such as "What do they know of England who only England know?"; "East is East and West is West"; "the white man's burden"; "somewhere east of Suez"—have become part of the English language and are often repeated by those who are unfamiliar with his writings. To have used the pen in place of a gun to serve the imperial vision and have such lasting impact on British thinking constitutes a major achievement.

In 1890, Kipling published or republished more than eighty stories, including the novelette *The Light That Failed*. At twenty-five, he had become a famous literary figure. At forty-two, he became the first Englishman to win the Nobel Prize in Literature, for "the great power of observation, the original conception and also the virile comprehension and art of narrative that distinguish his literary creations." He had also become a controversial personality, as critics and readers saw in his work the effort to mix the roles of the artist and the propagandist. Kipling's writings would continue to be controversial and generate extremes of admiration or condemnation. His works tend to generate a love-hate response, and Kipling scholars frequently evaluate and interpret his writings from new perspectives. His works are neither neglected nor ignored, which is a true testimony to his importance as a writer.

BIOGRAPHY

Joseph Rudyard Kipling was born in Bombay (now Mumbai), India, on December 30, 1865. His father, John Lockwood Kipling of Yorkshire, England, was a scholar and an artist. The elder Kipling went to India as a professor of architectural sculpture in the Bombay School of Fine Arts and later became curator of the Lahore Museum, which Kipling was to describe meticulously in *Kim*. He also served as the Bombay correspondent of *The Pioneer* of Allahabad. In 1891, he published *Beast and Man in India* with the help of A. P. Watt, his son's literary agent. The book contains excerpts from Rudyard Kipling's newspaper reports to the *Civil and Military Gazette*. The book provided inspiration for Kipling's Jungle Book stories and several others: "The Mark of the Beast," "The Finances of the Gods," and "Moti Guj, Mutineer" are some examples.

Kipling's mother, Alice Macdonald, was one of five Macdonald sisters, three of whom married into prominent families. Georgina Macdonald married the distinguished Pre-Raphaelite painter Sir Edward Burne-Jones; Agnes Macdonald married another painter, Sir Edward Poynter, who was influential in helping John Kipling obtain a position in India; and a third sister married Alfred Baldwin, the railroad owner, whose son Stanley Baldwin became prime minister of England. Kipling was therefore connected with creative and intellectually stimulating families through his mother, while from his father he inherited a strong Wesleyan tradition.

Rudyard and his sister, Trix, spent the first six years of their lives in India. Surrounded by Indian servants who told them Indian folktales, Kipling absorbed the Indian vocabulary and unconsciously cultivated the habit of thinking in that vocabulary, as illustrated in his short story "Tod's Amendment." Kipling recalls these early years in his posthumously published autobiography, *Something of Myself*, noting how he and his sister had to be reminded constantly to speak English to their parents and that he spoke English "haltingly translated out of the vernacular idiom that one thought and dreamed in." This contributed to the great facility with which he uses Indian words as part of his writing style. Edmund Wilson, in his essay "The Kipling That Nobody Read," writes that Kipling even looked like an Indian as a young boy.

Like other Anglo-Indian children who were sent home to England for their education, Kipling and his sister were shipped to London to live with a relative of their father in Southsea. The pain and agony of those six years under the supervision of this sadistic woman in what Kipling calls "the house of desolation" is unflinchingly re-created in the early part of *The Light That Failed* and in the short story "Baa, Baa, Black Sheep." According to Wilson, the traumatic experiences of those six years filled Kipling with hatred for the rest of his life.

Kipling studied at the United Services College, a public school for children from families with a military background or with the government civil service. Kipling served as editor of the school newspaper, the *United Services College Chronicle*, to which he contributed several youthful parodies of poets Robert Browning and Algernon Charles Swinburne. One poem, "Ave Imperatrix," however, with its note of patriotism and references to England's destiny to civilize the world, foreshadowed Kipling's later imperial themes. Although Kipling makes fun of flag-waving in "The Flag of Their Country" (in *Stalky and Co.*, 1899), he did imbibe some of his imperial tendencies at the school, as there was an almost universal desire among the boys to join either the army or the civil service for the glory of the Empire.

In 1882, when Kipling was sixteen, he returned to India, and his "English years fell away" and never "came back in full strength." Through his father's connections, Kipling had no difficulty in becoming assistant editor on the *Civil and Military Gazette* of Lahore at the age of eighteen. Two horror stories written during this period, "The Phantom Rickshaw" and "The Strange Ride of Morrowbie Jukes, C.E.," have found their places among his best-known stories.

After four years on the *Civil and Military Gazette*, Kipling moved to Allahabad as assistant editor to *The Pioneer*, and his writings began to appear in four major newspapers of British India. Young, unattached, with servants and horses at his disposal, enfolded in the warmth of his family, Kipling found these years to be his happiest and most productive. He wrote to a friend, "I'm in love with the country and would sooner write about her than anything else." His poetry collection *Departmental Ditties* was published in 1886, and the story collection *Plain Tales from the Hills* appeared in 1888. Soon Kipling was known all over India, and a favorable review in the *Saturday Review* also created a demand for his writings in London.

In March, 1889, he left Lahore on a leisurely sea journey to London by way of Rangoon (now Yangon), Singapore, Hong Kong, Japan, and San Francisco. After making several stops across the United States, the twenty-four-year-old Kipling arrived in London in October, 1889. (He describes this journey in *From Sea to Sea*, which was published in 1899.) In London, Kipling came into contact with the American Wolcott Balestier, whom he met in the drawing room of the home of the writer Mrs. Humphry Ward. The two men subsequently collaborated on the writing of the novel *The Naulahka*. Balestier's sister Caroline was later to become Kipling's wife. Befriended by the poet W. E. Henley, Kipling published *Barrack-Room Ballads, and Other Verses* in 1892. It was a completely new poetic voice in style, language, and content. Kipling won an audience, as many readers were startled and shocked but also fascinated by his style.

Kipling left England for the United States in June, 1891, and the short visit brought him into conflict with certain members of the American press. He then returned to England and went on a long sea voyage with a sentimental stopover in India, his last visit to the subcontinent. He returned to London hurriedly because of Wolcott Balestier's death, and a few weeks later, on January 18, 1892, he married Caroline Balestier. The American author Henry James gave away the bride.

The newly married couple returned to the Balestier home in Brattleboro, Vermont, where Kipling wrote the Jungle Book stories and other works. He also became a friend of

Mark Twain. His desire for privacy, his recurrent conflicts with the press, the death of his eldest daughter, Josephine, his own illness, and the notorious publicity he received as a result of a quarrel with his brother-in-law all contributed to Kipling's decision to leave the United States in 1897, never to return.

Kipling went to South Africa during the Boer War (1899-1902) and became a good friend of another empire builder, Cecil Rhodes. It was during the war that Kipling completed his most important novel, *Kim*. Published in 1901, it was Kipling's farewell to India. In 1907, Kipling received the Nobel Prize. During World War I, Kipling lost his only son, John, and his melancholy deepened. The poem "My Boy Jack" (1916) articulates the grief and pain of that loss. In writing other works, he turned to the strange and the macabre, as in "A Madonna of the Trenches," "The Wish House," and "The Eyes of Allah."

Plagued by ill health during the last years of his life, Kipling relied on his wife for support, but she also lost her health to the crippling effects of diabetes and rheumatism. He published collections of stories in 1932 and 1934 and continued to show interest in British and world affairs, angry at the complacency of his countrymen toward the growing fascism in Europe. He died January 18, 1936, and his ashes were buried in Westminster Abbey.

ANALYSIS

Rudyard Kipling wrote four novels, one of them, *The Naulahka*, in collaboration with Wolcott Balestier. Kipling was essentially a miniaturist, and his genius was for the short story, a single event dramatized within a specific time frame. His novels reflect an episodic quality, and although Kipling brings to them a considerable amount of technical information—about cod fishing in *Captains Courageous*, army and artistic life in *The Light That Failed*, authentic topography and local color in *The Naulahka*—he fails in the development of character and in evoking an emotional response from his readers. *Kim*, however, is an exception.

THE LIGHT THAT FAILED

The Light That Failed, dedicated to Kipling's mother, has often been described by critics as "the book that failed." Kipling acknowledged a debt to the French novel *Histoire du chevalier des Grieux et de Manon Lescaut* (1731, 1733, 1753; *Manon Lescaut*, 1734, 1786) by Abbé Prévost in writing the novel. It was first published in the January, 1891, issue of *Lippincott's Monthly Magazine* and was later dramatized and filmed. When Macmillan and Company published it two months later, there were four new chapters, and the story concluded with a tragic ending and the note, "This is the story of *The Light That Failed* as it was originally conceived by the writer." The difference between the magazine version, with its more conventional ending, and the book version, with the sad ending, caused some consternation among readers and critics.

The Light That Failed has many autobiographical elements. The novel opens with two children brought up by a sadistic housekeeper; Kipling drew on his own early life in "the house of desolation" for some of the harrowing experiences of Dick and Maisie in the novel. Dick and Maisie are not related, and each has an adolescent crush on the other. They are separated, and while Dick goes to the Far East to serve on the frontiers of the Empire, Maisie pursues her dream of becoming an artist. Dick wants Maisie to travel with him, but Maisie, committed to her art, remains in England. Dick later moves to Egypt as a war artist. He returns to London, and after a period of frustration, he enjoys fame and success. Kipling draws on his familiarity with the art world to describe the life of Dick in London. He had never been to Africa, however, and for the realism of his African scenes, Kipling relied on information he obtained from his friends. When Dick expresses fury and anger at unscrupulous art dealers, Kipling is lashing out at the publishers in the United States who boldly pirated his works.

In Dick and Maisie's doomed love and its impact on Dick, readers see echoes of Kipling's own unrequited love for Violet Flo Garrard. Flo was a painter, like Maisie, and in the words of Kipling's sister, Flo was cold and obsessed with "her very ineffective little pictures." Writer Angus Wilson, in his study of Kipling, asserts that Kipling found in Flo the quintessential femme fatale, "the vampire that sucks man's life away." Kipling has transferred some of the intensity of this feeling to Dick Heldar, almost his alter ego at certain times in the novel. Dick Heldar's obsession with the single life and his desire for military life also express Kipling's own passions. When Dick goes blind after being spurned by Maisie, Kipling is again drawing on his own anxiety about the possible loss of his own vision.

The Light That Failed ends very melodramatically with Dick's death in the Sudanese battlefield amid bloody carnage. Apart from the autobiographical elements in the novel, *The Light That Failed* has little interest for the contemporary student of Kipling.

THE NAULAHKA

Subtitled *A Story of East and West* and written in collaboration with Wolcott Balestier, *The Naulahka* compares the ways of the East, represented by the princely state of Rhatore in Central India, to those of the West, represented by the village of Topaz, Colorado. Balestier supplied the Western elements of the novel, and Kipling wrote the Eastern chapters. The result is a poorly written, melodramatic, and lackluster novel.

Naulahka is a priceless necklace owned by the maharaja of Rhatore. Tarvin, an aggressive American entrepreneur, wants to bring the railroad to feudalistic Rhatore; he enlists the services of Mutrie, the wife of the president of the railroad company, to influence her husband. He promises to get her the Naulahka as a gift. Tarvin's fiancé, Kate, is also in India to help the Indian women. With her help, Tarvin tries to influence the maharaja's son. Kate wants a hospital; Tarvin wants the railroad. Kate then breaks off her relationship with Tarvin; he secures the necklace but returns it in order to save Kate's life, which is threatened by a mad priest. Finally, Kate and Tarvin return to the United States.

The characters in *The Naulahka* are one-dimensional, and the narrative style is very episodic. In writing his part of the novel, Kipling drew heavily from his earlier book *Letters of Marque* (1891), lifting entire passages and incidents.

CAPTAINS COURAGEOUS

A better novel than *The Light That Failed, Captains Courageous* is Kipling's only book that is completely American in character and atmosphere. Kipling made several visits to Gloucester, Massachusetts, with his friend Dr. John Conland to saturate himself with considerable technical information about cod fishing. He uses this information extravagantly in telling the story of *Captains Courageous*. The novel was published serially in *McClure's Magazine*, and Kipling was not pleased with its publication. In a letter to a friend, he wrote that the novel was really a series of sketches and that he had "crept out of the possible holes by labelling it a boy's story."

Captains Courageous is the story of Harvey Cheyne, the spoiled only son of a millionaire. On a voyage to Europe, Harvey falls overboard and is picked up by a fishing boat. He bellows out orders and insults the skipper, Disko. Disko decides to teach the boy a lesson and puts Harvey under a strict program of work and discipline. The plan succeeds, and Harvey emerges stronger and humanized. When the boat reaches Gloucester, laden with salted cod, a telegram is sent to Harvey's father, who rushes from San Francisco to retrieve his son. Harvey returns with his father to resume his studies and prepare himself for taking over his father's business empire.

"Licking a raw cub into shape," the central theme of *Captains Courageous*, is a favorite subject of Kipling. The technical knowledge displayed about cod fishing in the novel is impressive, but the characters themselves have no individuality. Harvey Cheyne's transformation from a stubborn, spoiled young man into a mature, responsible individual is achieved too speedily. Kipling uses the story merely to illustrate what Lord Frederick Birkenhead describes in his biography of Kipling as "the virtue of the disciplined life upon a spoiled immature mind."

KIM

T. S. Eliot considered *Kim* Kipling's greatest work. Nirad C. Chaudhury, an Indian scholar, called *Kim* "not only the finest novel in English with an Indian theme but also one of the greatest of English novels in spite of the theme." Kipling wanted to write a major book about India, and he started the project in 1885, in "Mother Maturin: An Anglo-Indian Episode." That work concerned itself with the "unutterable horrors of lower class Eurasian and native life as they exist outside reports and reports and reports." It was the story of an old Irishwoman who kept an opium den in Lahore but sent her daughter to study in London, where she marries, then returns to Lahore. Kipling's father did not like it, however, and Kipling dutifully abandoned the project. *Kim* emerged instead.

Published in 1901, *Kim* is Kipling's last book set in India. In *Something of Myself*, he notes that he had long thought of writing about "an Irish boy born in India and mixed up with native life." Written under the influence of his demon—Kipling's word to describe his guardian muse—*Kim* takes in all of India, its rich diversity and intensity of life.

In growing old and evaluating the past, Kipling turned to the best years of his life, his years in India. In *Kim*, Kipling relives his Indian years, when everything was secure and his family intact. Kim's yearning for the open road, for its smells, sights, and sounds, is part of the longing of Kipling himself for the land that quickened his creative impulse and provided his literary success.

Kim is the story of an Irish orphan boy in India, a child of the streets. He grows up among Indian children and is aware of all the subtle nuances of Indian life. At the same time, however, he has the spirit of adventure and energy of his Irish ancestry. His joining the Red Lama from Tibet on his quest for the River of Healing, and Kim's fascination for the British Indian secret service, "the Great Game," results in his own self-discovery.

Kim has the characteristic features of a boy's story, the lovable boy involved in a quest filled with adventure and intrigue. One is reminded of Robert Louis Stevenson's *Treasure Island* (1881-1882) and *Kidnapped* (1886) and Mark Twain's *The Adventures of Tom Sawyer* (1876). *Kim*, however, rises above the usual boy's story in that it has a spiritual dimension. By coming into contact with the Lama, Kim emerges a sadder and wiser being at the end of the novel. Kim's racial superiority is emphasized throughout the novel, but after his association with the Lama, Kim is able to say, "Thou hast said there is neither black nor white, why plague me with this talk, Holy One? Let me rub the other foot. It vexes me, I am *not* a Sahib. I am thy chela, and my head is heavy on my shoulders." This is an unusual admission for Kim and Kipling.

Many of Kipling's earlier themes are elaborated and incorporated into *Kim*. There is the vivid picture of the Indian army; the tale of "Lispeth," from *Plain Tales from the Hills*, repeated in the story of the Lady of Shamlegh; and the Anglo-Indian, the native, and the official worlds providing backgrounds as they do in the short stories. Administering medicine in the guise of a charm to soothe and satisfy the Indian native, Jat is an echo from the earlier story "The Tomb of His Ancestors." Buddhism, the scriptural tales of which—the Jataka Tales—supplied Kipling with a wealth of source material for his two Jungle Book collections and *Just So Stories* (1902), supplies the religious atmosphere in *Kim*. Even Kim's yearning for the open road had been expressed previously in the character of Strickland, who, incidentally, makes a brief appearance in *Kim*.

Both the Venerable Teshoo Lama and Kim, the two main characters in *Kim*, emerge as distinctive individual characters and not mere types of the Asian holy man and the Anglo-Indian boy. They grow and develop an awareness of themselves and their surroundings. Kim realizes that his progress depends on the cooperation of several people: the Lama, Mukherjee, Colonel Creighton, and Mahbub Ali. The Lama too undergoes a change of character. He realizes that his physical quest for the River of Arrow has clouded his spiritual vision. The River of Arrow is at his feet if he has the faith to see it.

In selecting the Buddhist Lama as a main character, Kipling emphasizes the Middle Way. To the Lama, there is no color, no caste, no sect. He is also the tone of moderation without the extremes of Hinduism and Islam, the two main religious forces on the Indian subcontinent.

In the relationship between Kim and the Lama, Kipling portrays an integral part of Indian spiritual life, the teacher-disciple relationship, or the *guru-chela* interaction. It is not an ordinary relationship between a holy man and a boy; it is a special relationship, as the Lama notes, forged out of a previous association in an earlier life, the result of good karma. *Kim* is indeed a virtuoso performance; it is Kipling at his best.

K. Bhaskara Rao

OTHER MAJOR WORKS

SHORT FICTION: *Quartette*, 1885 (with John Lockwood Kipling, Alice Macdonald Kipling, and Alice Kipling); *In Black and White*, 1888; *The Phantom Rickshaw, and Other Tales*, 1888; *Plain Tales from the Hills*, 1888; *Soldiers Three: A Collection of Stories*, 1888; *The Story of the Gadsbys*, 1888; *Under the Deodars*, 1888; *Wee Willie Winkie, and Other Child Stories*, 1888; *The City of Dreadful Night, and Other Places*, 1890; *The Courting of Dinah Shadd, and Other Stories*, 1890; *Life's Handicap*, 1891; *Mine Own People*, 1891; *Many Inventions*, 1893; *The Jungle Book*, 1894; *The Second Jungle Book*, 1895; *Soldier Tales*, 1896; *The Day's Work*, 1898; *Stalky and Co.*, 1899; *Just So Stories*, 1902; *Traffics and Discoveries*, 1904; *Puck of Pook's Hill*, 1906; *Actions and Reactions*, 1909; *Rewards and Fairies*, 1910; *A Diversity of Creatures*, 1917; *Land and Sea Tales for Scouts and Guides*, 1923; *Debits and Credits*, 1926; *Thy Servant a Dog*, 1930; *Limits and Renewals*, 1932; *Collected Dog Stories*, 1934.

POETRY: *Schoolboy Lyrics*, 1881; *Echoes*, 1884 (with Alice Kipling); *Departmental Ditties*, 1886; *Barrack-Room Ballads, and Other Verses*, 1892; *The Seven Seas*, 1896; *An Almanac of Twelve Sports*, 1898; *Recessional, and Other Poems*, 1899; *The Five Nations*, 1903; *Collected Verse*, 1907; *A History of England*, 1911 (with C. R. L. Fletcher); *Songs from Books*, 1912; *Sea Warfare*, 1916; *Twenty Poems*, 1918; *Rudyard Kipling's Verse, 1885-1918*, 1919; *The Years Between*, 1919; *Q. Horatii Flacci Carminum Librer Quintus*, 1920 (with Charles L. Graves, A. D. Godley, A. B. Ramsay, and R. A. Knox); *Songs for Youth*, 1924; *Sea and Sussex from Rudyard Kipling's Verse*, 1926; *Rudyard Kipling's Verse, 1886-1926*, 1927; *Songs of the Sea*, 1927; *Poems, 1886-1929*, 1929; *Selected Poems*, 1931; *Rudyard Kipling's Verse, 1885-1932*, 1933; *Rudyard Kipling's Verse*, 1940 (definitive edition).

NONFICTION: *American Notes*, 1891; *Letters of Marque*, 1891; *The Smith Administration*, 1891; *A Fleet in Being: Notes of Two Trips with the Channel Squadron*, 1898; *From Sea to Sea*, 1899; *Letters to the Family*, 1908; *The New Army in Training*, 1914; *France at War*, 1915; *The Fringes of the Fleet*, 1915; *Sea Warfare*, 1916; *Letters of Travel, 1892-1913*, 1920; *The Irish Guards in the Great War*, 1923; *A Book of Words*, 1928; *Something of Myself: For My Friends Known and Unknown*, 1937; *Uncollected Prose*, 1938 (2 volumes); *Rudyard Kipling to Rider Haggard: The Record of a Friendship*, 1965 (Morton N. Cohen, editor); *The Letters of Rudyard Kipling*, 1990-2004 (6 volumes; Thomas Pinney, editor); *Writings on Writing*, 1996 (Sandra Kemp, editor); *Kipling's America: Travel Letters, 1889-1895*, 2003 (D. H. Stewart, editor).

MISCELLANEOUS: *The Sussex Edition of the Complete Works in Prose and Verse of Rudyard Kipling*, 1937-1939 (35 volumes).

BIBLIOGRAPHY

Adams, Jad. *Kipling*. London: Haus Books, 2005. Biography sheds light on the inspirations for Kipling's work and addresses sides of his character that have not been widely discussed. Includes index.

Allen, Charles. *Kipling Sahib: India and the Making of Rudyard Kipling*. Boston: Little, Brown, 2007. Biography focuses on Kipling's life from his birth until 1889, including his thirteen years in India, which were the inspiration for much of his writing. Traces the experiences of Kipling's parents in India and describes the Indian culture Kipling was born into as well as the state of the country when he returned in 1882 to begin his literary career by working on a newspaper in Lahore.

Bloom, Harold, ed. *Rudyard Kipling*. New York: Chelsea House, 1987. Collection of essays addresses Kipling's major work, his views on art and life, and his vision of empire. Includes introduction, chronology, and bibliography.

_______. *Rudyard Kipling's "Kim."* New York: Chelsea House, 1987. Collection of nine essays about the novel ranges from general appreciation to detailed critical analysis. Supplemented by the editor's introduction as well as a chronology and a bibliography.

Carrington, Charles. *Rudyard Kipling: His Life and Works*. 3d ed. New York: Macmillan, 1978. Standard biography focuses on Kipling's life and the influences on it rather than on literary critique; material on Kipling's adult life is much stronger than that on his childhood. Appendixes contain information previously suppressed by Kipling's heirs. Includes a chronology of his life and work and a family tree.

Dillingham, William B. *Rudyard Kipling: Hell and Heroism*. New York: Palgrave Macmillan, 2005. Asserts that most biographers and critics have neglected Kipling's deeply pessimistic worldview and his complex code of heroism and focuses on these aspects of Kipling's personality to analyze the writers' life and some of his works, including *Kim*.

Gilmour, David. *The Long Recessional: The Imperial Life of Rudyard Kipling*. New York: Farrar, Straus and Giroux, 2002. Provides an interesting account of Kipling's life and his complex and changing views of the British Empire. Written with an awareness of the rise of terrorism emanating from the postcolonial developing world.

Lycett, Andrew. *Rudyard Kipling*. New York: Weidenfeld & Nicolson, 1999. Exhaustive biography, based in part on newly discovered sources, provides invaluable insight into the life and work of Kipling. Includes bibliographical references and index.

Ricketts, Harry. *Rudyard Kipling: A Life*. New York: Carroll & Graf, 2000. Presents a detailed and lively account of Kipling's life and also analyzes the novels and other literary works the author published during his popular but controversial career.

Rutherford, Andrew, ed. *Kipling's Mind and Art: Selected Critical Essays*. Stanford, Calif.: Stanford University Press, 1964. Collection of essays includes commentary on Kipling's work by several prominent writers and literary critics, including Edmund Wilson, George Orwell, and Lionel Trilling.

Seymour-Smith, Martin. *Rudyard Kipling*. New York: St. Martin's Press, 1989. Provocative and controversial work probes deeply into Kipling's personality and sexuality, arguing that these are the key to an understanding of Kipling's writings.

Tompkins, J. M. S. *The Art of Rudyard Kipling*. Lincoln: University of Nebraska Press, 1965. First published in 1959, this major critical study of Kipling's literary work should be consulted in any discussion of Kipling's art.

D. H. LAWRENCE

Born: Eastwood, Nottinghamshire, England; September 11, 1885
Died: Vence, France; March 2, 1930
Also known as: David Herbert Lawrence; Lawrence H. Davison

PRINCIPAL LONG FICTION

The White Peacock, 1911
The Trespasser, 1912
Sons and Lovers, 1913
The Rainbow, 1915
The Lost Girl, 1920
Women in Love, 1920
Aaron's Rod, 1922
Kangaroo, 1923
"The Ladybird," "The Fox," "The Captain's Doll," 1923
The Boy in the Bush, 1924 (with M. L. Skinner)
The Plumed Serpent, 1926
Lady Chatterley's Lover, 1928
The Escaped Cock, 1929 (best known as *The Man Who Died*)
The Virgin and the Gipsy, 1930
Mr. Noon, 1984 (wr. 1920-1922)

OTHER LITERARY FORMS

D. H. Lawrence was among the most prolific and wide-ranging of modern writers, a fact all the more remarkable considering that he spent so much time on the move, battling chronic tuberculosis, which cut short his life in his forty-fifth year. In addition to his novels, he published more than a dozen books of poetry, collected in *The Complete Poems of D. H. Lawrence* (1964); eight volumes of short fiction, including half a dozen novellas, collected in *The Complete Short Stories of D. H. Lawrence* (1961); and seven plays, collected in *The Complete Plays of D. H. Lawrence* (1965). He also wrote a wide range of nonfiction, including four fine travel books: *Twilight in Italy* (1916), *Sea and Sardinia* (1921), *Mornings in Mexico* (1927), and *Etruscan Places* (1932). *Movements in European History* (1921), published under the pseudonym Lawrence H. Davison, is a subjective meditation on historical cycles and Europe's decline, and *Psychoanalysis and the Unconscious* (1921) is a highly original and influential volume of literary criticism.

Lawrence's religious vision, in the guise of a commentary on the Bible's book of Revelation, is offered in *Apocalypse* (1931). Many other essays on diverse subjects appeared in periodicals during the last two decades of his life and were collected posthumously by Edward McDonald in *Phoenix: The Posthumous Papers of D. H. Lawrence* (1936), and by

Warren Roberts and Harry T. Moore in *Phoenix II: Uncollected, Unpublished, and Other Prose Works* (1968). Lawrence was also a formidable correspondent, and his letters are invaluable aids to understanding the man and the writer. Some 1,257 of the more than 5,500 known letters are available in a collection edited by Harry T. Moore. Several of Lawrence's fictional works—including *Sons and Lovers*, *Lady Chatterley's Lover*, *Women in Love*, and *The Virgin and the Gipsy*—have been adapted to the motion-picture medium, and his life is the subject of the 1981 film *The Priest of Love*.

ACHIEVEMENTS

The running battle against censorship in which D. H. Lawrence engaged throughout most of his career undoubtedly performed a valuable service to subsequent writers and the reading public, though it cost him dearly both emotionally and financially. The essentially symbolic role of sexuality in his writing resembles somewhat that found in Walt Whitman's, but Lawrence's more overt treatment of it—liberating as it was to a generation whose Victorian upbringing had been castigated by the Freudians—led to a general misunderstanding of his work that persisted for almost three decades after his death. The thirty-year suppression of *Lady Chatterley's Lover* backfired, as censorship so often does, attracting the public's attention to the object of the prohibition. Unfortunately this notoriety made the novel, far from Lawrence's greatest, the one most commonly associated with his name in the popular mind. His reputation among more serious readers was not helped by the series of sensationalistic memoirs published by some of his more ardent followers in the 1930's and early 1940's. Championed as a prophet of free love and utopianism, repudiated as a crazed homosexual and protofascist, Lawrence the artist all but disappeared from view.

The appearance of several serious and sympathetic studies of Lawrence in the middle and late 1950's, by presenting a more accurate record of his life and a more discriminating assessment of his work, largely succeeded in salvaging Lawrence's stature as a major writer. Among those most responsible for the Lawrence revival were F. R. Leavis, Harry T. Moore, Edward Nehls, and Graham G. Hough. Subsequent readers have been able to recognize more readily in the best of Lawrence's work what Leavis described as its "marked moral intensity," its "reverent openness before life."

In addition to his prophetic themes, Lawrence's technical innovations are now acknowledged as among the most important in modern fiction. He could convey a "ripping yarn" and portray lifelike characters when he chose, and parts of *Sons and Lovers* and *The Lost Girl*, among many other works, demonstrate his mastery of traditional realism in the representation of his native Midlands. More fundamentally, however, Lawrence's novels are triumphs of mood and sensibility; they seek (as Frank Kermode has said) less to represent life than to enact it. He has no peer in the evocative rendering of place, introducing poetic symbols that carry the meaning without losing sight of their basis in intensely observed, concrete details.

Lawrence's approach to characterization following *The Rainbow* was unconventional in that he avoided "the old stable ego" and pattern-imposed character types in an effort to go beneath the rational and articulate levels of consciousness to the nonhuman being in his characters. As Walter Allen has observed, for Lawrence "the value of people . . . consisted in how far mystery resided in them, how far they were conscious of mystery." The linear, cause-and-effect development of characters controlled by the rational intellect was for him a hindrance. He focused instead on the surging, dynamic forces—sexual impulses, the potency of nature and animals, the terrible allure of death—that in their purest form defy rationality and are communicated by a kind of unmediated intuition.

His prose style was similarly subjective in emphasis. The frequent repetitiveness and inflated rhetoric can be tiresome, but at its best the prose is supple and sensuous, its dynamic rhythms incantatory, a powerful vehicle of Lawrence's vision. Further, he avoided the neat resolution of closure of traditional narratives, typically preferring the "open end" in which the vital forces operating in his characters are felt to be continuously and dynamically in process rather than subdued by the authorial imposition of finality. His comment on the bustling activities of Indian peasants on market day, in *Mornings in Mexico*, epitomizes his fictional method as well as his vitalist doctrine: "In everything, the shimmer of creation and never the finality of the created."

Lawrence's approach to fiction involved considerable risks, and many of his novels are seriously flawed. There are those who cannot read him at all. Nevertheless, the integrity of his vision and the sheer power with which he communicated it have made E. M. Forster's estimate (written shortly after Lawrence's death) stand up: "He was the greatest imaginative novelist of his generation."

BIOGRAPHY

David Herbert Lawrence was born on September 11, 1885, in the Midlands coal-mining village of Eastwood, Nottinghamshire. The noise and grime of the pits dominated Eastwood, but the proximity of fabled Sherwood Forest was a living reminder of what Lawrence would later call "the old England of the forest and agricultural past" on which industrialization had been so rudely imposed. The contrast was to remain an essential element in his makeup. Allied to it was the equally sharp contrast between his parents. Arthur John Lawrence, the father, had worked in the coal pits from the age of seven. Coarse, semiliterate, intensely physical, a hail-fellow popular with his collier mates, he was prone to drink and to near poverty. Lydia Lawrence (née Beardsall), his wife, was a former schoolteacher from a pious middle-class Methodist family, which counted among its forebears a noted composer of Wesleyan hymns. Along with his four siblings, young Lawrence was inevitably caught up in the frequent and sometimes violent strife between his mother and father. Delicate and sickly as a child, he could scarcely have emulated his father—not that he was inclined to do so. Instead, he sided with his mother. She in turn doted on him and encouraged him in his studies as a means of escape from the working-class life, thus further alienating him from his father. Only in later life would Lawrence come to see the dangerous liabilities of this overweening maternal bond and the counterbalancing attractiveness of his father's unassuming strength and vitality.

Lawrence was an outstanding student in school and at the age of twelve won a scholarship to Nottingham High School. After graduation in 1901, he worked for three unhappy months as a clerk in a surgical-appliance factory in Nottingham, until he fell seriously ill with pneumonia. About this time, he met Jessie Chambers, whose family lived on a small farm outside Eastwood. Over the next ten years his close relationship with the "spiritual" Jessie (the "Miriam" of *Sons and Lovers*) and her sympathetic family offered further stimulus to his fondness for the beauties of nature, for reading, and for ideas; eventually, with Jessie's encouragement and partial collaboration, he began to write stories and verse. The Chamberses' way of life and the bucolic scenery of Haggs farm, so tellingly unlike the ambience of Lawrence's own home, would later provide him with materials for his first novel, *The White Peacock.* After his prolonged convalescence from pneumonia, in 1903 he found a position as a "pupil-teacher" at an elementary school in nearby Ilkeston, Derbyshire. Two years there were followed by a third as an uncertified teacher in the Eastwood British School. In 1906, having won a King's Scholarship competition, he began a two-year course of study for his teachers' certificate at Nottingham University College. By 1908, he qualified to teach at Davidson Road School, a boys' elementary school in the London suburb of Croydon, where he remained until 1911.

Meanwhile, Lawrence had published several poems in 1909 in *The English Review,* edited by Ford Madox Hueffer (later Ford), who introduced him to such established writers as H. G. Wells, Ezra Pound, and William Butler Yeats. Soon Lawrence was busily working at two novels, *The White Peacock* and the autobiographical *Paul Morel* (the working title of *Sons and Lovers*). While the former was still in press in December, 1910, his mother died of cancer, an event whose profound impact on him is duly commemorated in his poems and in *Paul Morel,* which he had already begun to rewrite. By this time his relationship with Jessie Chambers had diminished considerably, and he had had several brief affairs with other women. His ill health and his increasing commitment to writing (*The Trespasser,* his second novel, was to appear the following year) induced him to forgo teaching in the winter of 1911-1912. Back in Eastwood, in April, he met and fell in love with Frieda von Richthoven Weekley, the high-spirited daughter of a German baron, wife of a professor of philology at Nottingham University, and at thirty-two the mother of three small children. In May, Lawrence and Frieda eloped to the Continent. There, for the next six months, Lawrence wrote poems, stories, travel sketches (most of which were later collected in *Twilight in Italy*), and his final revision of the autobiographical novel. This writing, particularly the metamorphosis of *Paul Morel* into *Sons and Lovers* (with which Frieda assisted him by discussing her own maternal feelings and the theories of Freud), marked the true beginning of Lawrence's artistic maturity.

The advent of World War I coincided with what in many ways was the most crucial period of his development as a writer. By the end of 1914, Lawrence and Frieda had married, the critical success of *Sons and Lovers* had established his reputation, he had formed important associations with Edward Garnett, John Middleton Murry, and Katherine Mansfield, and he had begun to work on what many now consider his greatest novels, *The Rainbow* and *Women in Love* (originally conceived as a single work, *The Sisters*). The triumph that might have been his soon turned to ashes, however. The official suppression of *The Rainbow* in November, 1916—the charge of "immorality" was leveled on both political and sexual grounds—was followed by a series of nightmarish episodes in which, largely because of Frieda's German origins, the Lawrences were hounded and persecuted as supposed enemy spies. Lawrence was reviled in the "patriotic" English press, and, after *The Rainbow* fiasco, in which many of his literary associates had failed to come to his defense, he found it increasingly difficult to publish his work and hence to make a living. Though he completed *Women in Love* in 1917, it did not appear until 1920 in the United States. Events seemed to conspire against him so that, by the end of the war, he could never again feel at home in his native land. This bitter severance motivated the "savage pilgrimage" that dominated the last decade of his life, driving him feverishly around the globe in search of some "ideal centre" in which to live and work in hope for the future.

Lawrence's travels were as much spiritual as geographical in character, and his quest became the primary focus of his writing after the war. The more than two years he spent in Italy and Sicily (1919-1921) provided him with the materials for the concluding chapters of *The Lost Girl* (which he had begun before the war and set aside to work on *The Sisters*) and for *Aaron's Rod*. Heading for the United States by way of Asia, the Lawrences briefly visited Ceylon and then Australia, where he wrote *Kangaroo* in just six weeks. In September, 1922, they arrived in the United States and soon settled near Taos, New Mexico, on a mountain ranch that was to be "home" for them during most of the next three years. Here Lawrence rewrote *Studies in Classic American Literature* (1923; begun in 1917) and produced such important works as "Eagle in New Mexico" and "Spirits Summoned West" (poems), "The Woman Who Rode Away," "The Princess," "St. Mawr," and half of the travel sketches that comprise *Mornings in Mexico*. During this period Lawrence also made three trips to Mexico, staying there a total of about ten months; his travel experiences, embellished by his rather extensive readings in Aztec history and archaeology, provided the sources for his novel of Mexico, *The Plumed Serpent*, his most ambitious creative undertaking of the postwar years. On the day he finished the novel in Oaxaca, he fell gravely ill with acute tuberculosis and nearly died. After convalescing in Mexico City and on the ranch in New Mexico, he returned with Frieda to Europe in the late fall of 1925, settling first in Spotorno on the Italian Riviera and later in a villa outside Florence.

Lawrence's last years were clouded by the inevitable encroachment of his disease, but he remained remarkably active. He toured the ancient Etruscan ruins; took up painting, producing some strikingly original works; and wrote three complete versions of what would become, in its final form, his most famous novel, *Lady Chatterley's Lover*. The book's banning and confiscation in 1928, reviving the old outcry of "obscenity," prompted several of his most eloquent essays on the subject of pornography and censorship. It was his final battle, save that which could not be won. Lawrence died in Vence, France, on March 2, 1930, at the age of forty-four.

ANALYSIS

D. H. Lawrence occupies an ambiguous position with respect to James Joyce, Marcel Proust, T. S. Eliot, and the other major figures of the modernist movement. While on one hand he shared their feelings of gloom about the degeneration of modern European life and looked to ancient mythologies for prototypes of the rebirth all saw as necessary, on the other he keenly distrusted the modernists' veneration of traditional culture and their classicist aesthetics. The modernist ideal of art as "an escape from personality," as a finished and perfected creation sufficient unto itself, was anathema to Lawrence, who once claimed that his motto was not art for art's sake but "art for my sake." For him, life and art were intertwined, both expressions of the same quest: "To be alive, to be man alive, to be whole man alive: that is the point." The novel realized its essential function best when it embodied and vitally enacted the novelist's mercurial sensibility. His spontaneity, his limitations and imperfections, and his fleeting moments of intuition were directly transmitted to the reader, whose own "instinct for life" would be thereby quickened. Lawrence believed that at its best "the novel, and the novel supremely," could and should perform this important task. That is why he insisted that the novel is "the one bright book of life." One way of approaching his own novels—and the most significant, by general consensus, are *Sons and Lovers*, *The Rainbow*, *Women in Love*, *The Plumed Serpent*, and *Lady Chatterley's Lover*—is to consider the extent to which the form and content of each in turn rises to this vitalist standard.

To be "whole man alive," for Lawrence, involved first of all the realization of *wholeness*. The great enemy of human (and of aesthetic) wholeness, he believed, was modern life itself. Industrialization had cut man off from the past, had mechanized his daily life and transformed human relations into a power struggle to acquire material commodities, thereby alienating man from contact with the divine potency residing in both nature and other men and women. Modern Europe was therefore an accumulation of dead or dying husks, fragmented and spiritually void, whose inevitable expression was mass destruction. For Lawrence, World War I was the apotheosis of modernization.

Contemporary history provided only the end result of a long process of atomization and dispersion whose seeds lay in ancient prehistory. In *Fantasia of the Unconscious* (1922), Lawrence formulates a myth of origins that sheds light on his quest for wholeness in his travels among "primitive" peoples as well as in his novels. He describes a kind of golden age before the Flood, when the pagan world, both geographically and culturally, was a single, unified entity. This *Ur*-culture, unlike the modern fragmented age, had developed a holistic knowledge or "science in terms of life." The primal wisdom did not differentiate among body, mind, and spirit; the objective and the subjective were one, as the reason and the passions were one; man and nature and the cosmos lived in harmonious relation with one another. Men and women all over the earth shared this knowledge. They "wandered back and forth from Atlantis to the Polynesian Continent. . . . The interchange was complete, and knowledge, science, was universal over the earth." Then the glaciers melted, whole continents were drowned, and the monolithic world fragmented into isolated races, each developing its own culture, its own "science." A few refugees from the lost continents fled to the high ground of Europe, Asia, and America. There they "refused to forget, but taught the old wisdom, only in its half-forgotten, symbolic forms. More or less forgotten, as knowledge: remembered as ritual, gesture, and myth-story."

In modern Europe, even these vestiges of the old universal knowledge had largely become extinct, and with them died what was left of the unitary being of man. First Christianity, with its overemphasis on bodiless spirituality, and then modern science, with its excessive dependence on finite reason as the instrument of control over a merely mechanistic world, had killed it. After the war Lawrence hoped, in traveling to lands where Christianity, modern science, and industrialization had not yet fully taken hold, to uncover the traces of the primalknowledge, if only "in its half-forgotten, symbolic forms." By somehow establishing a vital contact with "primitive" men and women and fusing his "white consciousness" with their "dark-blood consciousness," he hoped to usher in the next phase in the development of the human race. His novels would sound the clarion call—awakening the primordial memory by means of "ritual, gesture, and myth-story"—summoning "whole man alive" to cross over the threshold into the New World of regenerated being.

Although this myth of apocalypse and rebirth was fully articulated during Lawrence's "wander years" after the war, it was clearly anticipated in his earlier works. There the horror of the modern world's "drift toward death" and the yearning for some "holy ground" on which to begin anew were keenly felt. The initial experience of fragmentation in Lawrence's life was obviously the primal conflict between his mother and father, which among other things resulted in a confusion in his own sexual identity. In the fiction of this period, the stunting of life by fragmentation and imbalance is evident in the portrayal of such characters as Miriam Leivers in *Sons and Lovers*, Anton Skrebensky in *The Rainbow*, and Gerald Crich in *Women in Love*, just as the quest for vital wholeness is exemplified in the same novels by Paul Morel, Ursula Brangwen, and Rupert Birkin, respectively. If the secondary characters in Lawrence's novels tend in general to be static types seen from without, his protagonists, beginning with Ursula in *The Rainbow* and continuing through Constance Chatterley in *Lady Chatterley's Lover*, are anything but static. Rather, they are volatile, inconsistent, and sometimes enigmatic. In *The Plumed Serpent*, Kate Leslie vacillates between intellectual abstraction and immediate sensuous experience; between egotistic willfulness and utter self-abandonment to another; between withdrawal behind the boundaries of the safe and the known, and the passionate yearning for metamorphosis; and so on. There is a constant ebb and flow in Kate's behavior, even a rough circularity, that creates a spontaneous, improvisatory feeling in her narrative. Lawrence's protagonists are always in flux, realizing by turns the various aspects of their natures, and this dynamism is largely what makes them so alive. They are open to life: in themselves, in their natural environment, and in other vital human beings.

Lawrence believed that the novel was the one form of human expression malleable enough to articulate and dramatize the dynamic process of living. In his essay "Why the Novel Matters," he celebrates the novelist's advantage over the saint, the scientist, and the philosopher, all of whom deal only with parts of the composite being of humankind. The novelist alone, says Lawrence, is capable of rendering the whole of "man alive." He alone, by so doing, "can make the whole man alive [that is, the reader] tremble."

The priestly or prophetic function of the novelist is clearly central to this aesthetic doctrine. Lawrence is one of the very few modern writers to assume this role and to do so explicitly. At times, this very explicitness becomes problematic. His novels are quite uneven; most are marred in varying degrees by hectoring didacticism that is less evident in his short fiction. Nevertheless, he needed the amplitude of an extended narrative to give voice to the several sides of his complex sensibility, as if to discover himself in the process. Perhaps that, as much as anything else, was the object of his quest. Collectively his novels represent a restless search for a form capable of rendering that sensibility fully and honestly.

SONS AND LOVERS

In a letter written a few months after the publication of *Sons and Lovers*, Lawrence made an admission that suggests that "art for my sake" could have been a cathartic as well as a heuristic function. "One sheds one's sickness in books," he wrote, "repeats and presents one's emotions, to be master of them." *Sons and Lovers*, his third novel, was the work that enabled Lawrence to come to terms, at least provisionally, with the traumas of his formative years. The more than two years he spent working and reworking the book amounted to an artistic and psychological rite of passage essential to his development as a man and as a writer.

The novel spans the first twenty-six years in the life of Paul Morel. Because of the obvious similarities between Paul's experiences and Lawrence's, and because the story in part concerns Paul's apprenticeship as an artist—or, more accurately, the obstacles he must overcome to be an artist—the novel has been seen as an example of a subspecies of the bildungsroman, the *Künstlerroman*. Comparison with James Joyce's *A Portrait of the Artist as a Young Man* (1916) suggests, however, how loosely the term applies to Lawrence's novel. Where Joyce scrupulously selects only those scenes and episodes of Stephen Dedalus's life that directly contribute to the young artist's development (his first use of language, his schooling, his imaginative transcendence of sex, religion, and politics, his aesthetic theories), Lawrence's focus is far more diffuse.

The novel opens with a conventional set-piece description of the town of Bestwood (modeled on Eastwood) as it has been affected by the arrival and growth of the mining industry during the last half century. This is followed by an account of the courtship and early married life of Walter and Gertrude Morel, Paul's parents. Even after Paul's birth, the main emphasis remains for many chapters on the mother and father, and considerable space is devoted to their first child, William, whose sudden death and funeral conclude part 1 of the novel. Paul's interest in drawing is mentioned halfway through part 1, but it is not a major concern until he becomes friends with Miriam Leivers in part 2, and there the companionship itself actually receives more attention. Though the comparison does an injustice to the nature of Lawrence's real achievement in the novel, perhaps *Sons and Lovers* more nearly resembles *Stephen Hero* (1944), the earlier and more generally autobiographical version of Joyce's novel, than it does the tightly constructed *A Portrait of the Artist as a Young Man*.

When, in the late stages of revision, Lawrence changed his title from *Paul Morel* to *Sons and Lovers*, his motive was akin to Joyce's when the Irishman discarded *Stephen Hero* and began to rewrite. The motive was form—form determined by a controlling idea. The subject of *Sons and Lovers* is not simply Paul's development but his development as an instance of the pattern suggested by the title; that pattern involves the Morels' unhappy marriage, the fateful experiences of Paul's brother William, Paul's frustrated relationship with Miriam, and his later encounters with Clara and Baxter Dawes, as well as Paul's own maturation. For Lawrence, the pattern clearly had wide application. Indeed, in a letter to Edward Garnett, his editor, written a few days after completing the revised novel, Lawrence claimed that his book sounded "the tragedy of thousands of young men in England."

This claim, along with the change in title and the late revisions designed to underscore a theme already present in the narrative, was probably influenced by the discussions that Lawrence and Frieda had in 1912 regarding Freud's theories, of which Frieda was then an enthusiastic proponent. (There is no evidence of Lawrence's awareness of Freud before this.) In a more general sense, the "tragedy" was rooted historically, as the novel shows, in the disruption of natural human relationships that was one of the by-products of modernization. Directly or indirectly, the characters in the novel are entrapped by the materialistic values of their society, unable even when they consciously reject those values to establish true contact with one another. Instead they tend to treat one another as objects to be possessed or manipulated for the purpose of self-gratification.

Thus Mrs. Morel, frustrated by her marriage to her coal miner husband, transfers her affections to her sons, first to William, the eldest, and then to Paul after William's death. Walter Morel, the father, becomes a scapegoat and an outcast in his own home. Whether consciously or not, Mrs. Morel uses her sons as instruments to work out her own destiny vicariously, encouraging them in pursuits that will enable them to escape the socially confining life that she herself cannot escape, yet resenting it when the sons do begin to make a life away from her. Paul's fixation on his mother—and his hatred of his father—contributes to a confusion of his sexual identity and to his inability to love girls his own age in a normal, healthy way. In the same letter to Edward Garnett, Lawrence characterized this inability to love as a "split," referring to the rupture in the son's natural passions caused by the mother's possessive love.

The split causes Paul to seek out girls who perform the psychological role of mother surrogates: Miriam, an exaggerated version of the spiritual, Madonna-like aspect of the mother image; and the buxom Clara Dawes, who from a Freudian viewpoint represents the "degraded sex object," the fallen woman, equally a projection of the son's prohibited erotic desires for his mother. Because Paul's feeling for Miriam and Clara are thus compartmentalized and unbalanced, both relationships are unfulfilling, a fact that only reinforces his Oedipal bondage. At the same time, part of the responsibility for the unsatisfactory relationships belongs to Miriam and Clara themselves, both of whom exploit Paul to help them fulfill their own private fantasy lives. The world of *Sons and Lovers* is populated by isolated, fragmentary souls not unlike the inhabitants of T. S. Eliot's 1922 *The Waste Land* ("We think of the key, each in his prison/ Thinking of the key, each confirms a prison").

A decade after the appearance of *Sons and Lovers*, Lawrence declared that of all his books, it was the one he would like to rewrite, because in it he had treated his father unfairly. By then, of course, he was overtly committed to finding embodiments of "whole man alive" and, in retrospect, his father seemed to offer such an embodiment. When he wrote *Sons and Lovers*, however, he had not yet fully come to appreciate the importance of his father's unaffected male vitality. Although occasionally Walter Morel appears in a favorable light, the novel generally emphasizes his ineffectuality as a husband and father. The Oedipal conflict on which the story hinges perhaps made this unavoidable. In any event, the struggle to attain wholeness is centered in Paul Morel.

Because Paul's mother is "the pivot and pole of his life, from which he could not escape," her death amounts to the great crisis of the novel. The terrible spectacle of her agony as she lies dying slowly of cancer torments Paul until, by giving her an overdose of morphine, he commits a mercy killing. Unconsciously, the act seems to be motivated by his desire to release her from her debilitating "bondage" as wife and mother, the roles that have made her erotically unattainable to Paul. Her death is followed by an eerie, Poe-like scene in which the shaken Paul, momentarily imagining his mother as a beautiful young sleeping maiden, stoops and kisses her "passionately," as if to waken her like the handsome prince in a fairy tale, only to be horrified by her cold and unresponsive lips. It is a key moment, adumbrating as it does the writer's subsequent shift in allegiances to the "sensuous flame of life" associated with his father. For Paul, however, the loss of his mother induces a period of deep depression (interestingly enough, guilt is not mentioned) in which his uppermost desire is to reunite with his mother in death. This "drift towards death" was what Lawrence believed made Paul's story symptomatic of the times, "the tragedy of thousands of young men in England."

Nevertheless, the novel does not end tragically. Paul, on the verge of suicide, decides instead to turn his back on the "immense dark silence" where his lover/mother awaits him and to head toward the "faintly humming, glowing town"—and beyond it, to the Continent, where he plans to continue his artistic endeavors (just as Lawrence did). Some readers have found this last-minute turnabout implausible, a breakdown in the novel's form, but Lawrence anticipates Paul's "rebirth" by having him realize, after his mother's death, that he must finally sever his ties to both Miriam and Clara. For him to have returned to them then for consolation and affection would have meant that, inwardly, he was still cherishing some hope of preserving the maternal bond, even if only through his mother's unsatisfactory substitutes. When Paul effects a reconciliation between Clara and her estranged husband Baxter Dawes, who has been presented throughout in terms strongly reminiscent of Walter Morel, he is (as Daniel A. Weiss and others have observed) tacitly acting out a reversal of the original Oedipal conflict. If the primary emphasis of *Sons and Lovers* is on the tragic split in the emotional lives of the Morels, its conclusion finds Paul taking the steps necessary to begin to heal the split in himself. Only by so doing would Paul, like Lawrence, be able to undertake a quest for vital wholeness. That quest would become the chief subject of the novels following *Sons and Lovers*.

As sometimes happens to a writer after he has successfully struggled to transform autobiography into art, Lawrence reacted against *Sons and Lovers* almost as soon as he had finished it. The process of reevaluating the influence of his parents, begun in his revisions of the novel and particularly evident in its concluding chapters, continued apace. His nonfiction of the period exhibits a growing hostility to women as spawners of intellectual and spiritual abstraction and the early traces of his interest in the reassertion of the vital male. Lawrence reacted also against certain aspects of the narrative technique used in *Sons and Lovers*. As he worked on his next novel, initially called *The Sisters*, he found that he was no longer interested in "visualizing" or "creating vivid scenes" in which characters revealed themselves through dramatic encounters and dialogue. The conventions of plot and the "furniture" of realistic exposition bored him. Moreover, the traditional methods of characterization were positively a hindrance to the kind of novel he felt he must write.

Lawrence had in fact embarked on a long and difficult struggle to create a new kind of novel, unprecedented in English fiction. When his publisher balked, Lawrence defended his experiment in an important letter that clarifies his intentions not only in what would eventually become *The Rainbow* and *Women in Love* but in most of his subsequent fiction:

> You mustn't look in my novel for the old stable *ego* of the character. There is another *ego*, according to whose action the individual is unrecognizable, and passes through, as it were, allotropic states which it needs a deeper sense than any we've been used to exercise, to discover are states of the same radically unchanged element. (Like as diamond and coal are the same pure single element of carbon.)

What all this suggests, and what is implicit in the novels themselves, is that the conventions of realism, which were developed preeminently in the English novel of the nineteenth century, are inadequate tools for use by a writer whose aim is the transformation of the very society whose values were embodied in realism. The "old-fashioned human element," "the old stable ego," the "certain moral scheme" prescribing "consistency" and linear development—these were relics of positivism, bourgeois humanism, and other ideologies of a dying culture. Lawrence gropes a bit in the attempt to describe their successors, but it is clear enough that the "other ego," the "physic" or nonhuman in humanity, and the "radically unchanged element" whose "allotropic" transformations determine a "rhythmic form" along lines unknown, are references to the mysterious source of vital energies capable (he believed) of regenerating both art and society.

THE RAINBOW

The Rainbow applies these ideas in a most interesting way. It is an elegiac study of the dying culture, written in Lawrence's revolutionary "new" manner. The story spans three generations of the Brangwen family, beginning with the advent of industrialism around 1840 in the rural Erewash valley—signaled by the construction of canals, the collieries, and the railroad—and continuing up to the first decade of the twentieth century. The theme is the destruction of the traditional way of life and the attempt, by the Brangwens, either to accommodate themselves to that loss or to transcend it by discovering a new basis for being.

The novel opens with a rhapsodic prose poem telescoping two hundred years of Brangwens into archetypal male and female figures living in "blood intimacy" with one another and with the land: "The pulse of the blood of the teats of the cows beat into the pulse of the hands of the men. [The men] mounted their horses and held life between the grip of their knees." Despite their "vital connection," however, there are opposing impulses in the male and the female principles that become increasingly important as the story proceeds. The Brangwen men, laboring in the fields of the Marsh Farm, are compared with the rim of a wheel revolving around the still center that is hearth and home; the women, like the axle of the wheel, live in the still center but always direct their gaze outward, beyond the wheel's rim toward the road, the village, the church steeple, "the spoken world" that is encroaching on the horizon. This tension between centripetal and centrifugal forces, the rim and the axle, is fruitful so long as the Brangwens live in harmony with the land, for it is a reflection of the cyclical processes of nature in which the clash of opposites generates change and growth.

With the second generation, however, the principal Brangwen couple, Will and Anna, leaves the land and moves to the industrial town of Beldover, where Will works in a shop that produces machine-made lace. The seasonal cycle is replaced by the Christian liturgical calendar, in Lawrence's view a step toward abstraction. The old male-female opposition, having lost its former function as the means by which men and women participate in the dynamic rhythms of nature, becomes a destructive force. The marriage of contraries loses impetus because it now reflects not nature but the mechanisms that are dividing society. Husband and wife settle into a fixed domestic routine, typically Victorian, of piety (on Will's side) and child rearing (on Anna's). Anna's "outward" impulse is thus sublimated, and, like Gertrude Morel in *Sons and Lovers*, she counts on her children to act out her frustrated quest beyond the pale.

Most important of these children is the oldest daughter, Ursula, who, with her sister Gudrun, will also figure prominently in *Women in Love*. Ursula has been called "the first complete modern woman" (Marvin Mudrick) and, even more sweepingly, "the first 'free soul'" (Keith Sagar) in the English novel. It is Ursula, a member of Lawrence's own generation, who finally breaks out of the old circle of life. As she grows into womanhood she challenges and ultimately rejects traditional views of religion, democracy, education, free enterprise, love, and marriage. She is the first Brangwen female to enter a profession and support herself (as a schoolteacher); she attends the university; she travels to London and the Continent. On several levels, then, her "centrifugal" movement takes her far afield. Despite her explorations, however, she has no sense of who she really is. The traditional order, which formerly provided a living relationship with nature and with other men and women, has all but collapsed. Motivated only by her isolate will and unreciprocated by any meaningful male contrary—as is amply demonstrated by her unsatisfying love affairs with Winifred Inger, her schoolmistress, and the shallow Anton Skrebensky—Ursula's quest becomes a desperate exercise in redundancy and futility, her vital energies randomly dispersed.

The novel ends as it began, symbolically. In the last of a series of "ritual scenes," in which characters are suddenly confronted with the "physic" or nonhuman "ego" that is the mysterious life force, Ursula encounters a herd of stampeding horses. Whether hallucinatory or actual, the horses seem to represent the "dark" potencies that she has tried so long to discover on her quest and that have so far eluded her. Now, terrified, she escapes. Soon after, she falls ill with pneumonia, miscarries a child by Skrebensky, and lies delirious with fever for nearly a fortnight. All this is fitting as the culmination of Ursula's abortive, well-driven quest. Her "drift toward death," more like a plunge finally, is even more representative of her generation's crisis than Paul Morel's was in *Sons and Lovers*. As in the earlier novel, furthermore, Lawrence attempts to end *The Rainbow* on a hopeful note. After her convalescence, Ursula awakes one morning on the shores of what appears to be a new world, "as if a new day had come on the earth." Having survived the deluge, she is granted a vision of the rainbow—a symbol related to but superseding the old closed circle—which seems to offer hope for the regeneration not only of Ursula but also of her world.

On both levels, however, the symbolic promise is less than convincing. Unlike Paul Morel, Ursula has not performed any action or had any insight that suggests that her final "rebirth" is more than wishful thinking. As for the modern world's regeneration, when the novel appeared, in September, 1915, nothing could have been less likely. Lawrence hated the war, but like many other modern writers he saw it as the harbinger of the apocalypse, accelerating the advent of a new age. Before long he realized that he had "set my rainbow in the sky too soon, before, instead of after, the deluge." The furor provoked by the novel must have made the irony of his premature hopefulness all the more painful. In the teeth of that furor and the public persecution waged against Frieda and himself as supposed German spies, Lawrence set about writing *Women in Love*, considered by many today his greatest novel and one of the half dozen or so masterpieces of modern fiction.

WOMEN IN LOVE

Whatever their differences with respect to the emphasis placed on the operations of the "physic," or nonhuman, forces in humanity, *Sons and Lovers* and *The Rainbow* share several important traits that set them apart from most of Lawrence's subsequent novels, beginning with *Women in Love*. For one, they have in common a narrative structure that, by locating the action firmly within a social context spanning generations, subscribes to the novelistic convention of rendering the story of individuals continuous with the larger movements of history. *Women in Love* takes up the story of the "modern" Brangwens about three and one-half years after the end of *The Rainbow* but, in contrast to the earlier novel's sixty-six-year span, concentrates attention onto a series of loosely connected episodes occurring within a ten-month period, from spring to winter of 1909 or 1910.

One result of this altered focus, at once narrower and relatively looser than that of the earlier novels, is that the social background seems far more static than before. The great transformation of society known as modernization has already occurred, and the characters move within a world whose ostensible change is the slow, inward process of decay. The shift of emphasis is evident also in the protagonists' attitudes toward society. The conclusions of the earlier novels—Paul's turning away from death toward the "humming, glowing town," and Ursula's vision of the rainbow offering hope that a corrupt world would "issue to a new germination"—imply that Western civilization could still respond to the most urgent needs of the individual. In *Women in Love* that assumption has completely vanished. Thus, although Lawrence originally conceived of *The Rainbow* and *Women in Love* as a single work and would later describe them as forming together "an organic artistic whole," the latter novel embodies a far darker view of the world. As Lawrence once said, *Women in Love* "actually does contain the results in one's soul of the war: it is purely destructive, not like *The Rainbow*, destructive-consummating."

The phrase "purely destructive" only slightly exaggerates the despairing nature of the novel's apocalyptic vision. Certainly its depiction of modern society as a dying tree "infested with little worms and dry-rot" suggests that the impetus toward death and destruction is so pervasive as to make the war all but inevitable. In the novel, the working class, far from resisting the dehumanizing mechanism of the industrial system, is "satisfied to belong to the great wonderful machine, even whilst it destroyed them." The leisure class is seen as similarly deluded and doomed. Hermione Roddice's chic gatherings at Breadalby, her country estate (modeled on Lady Ottoline Morrell's Garsington), offer no genuine alternative to the dying world but only a static image of the "precious past," where all is formed and final and accomplished—a "horrible, dead prison" of illusory peace. Meanwhile contemporary art has abdicated its time-honored role as naysayer to a corrupt social order. Indeed, in the gay artist Halliday, the promiscuous Minette, and the other decadent bohemians who congregate at the Pompadour Café in London, Lawrence clearly implicates intellectual and artistic coteries such as Bloomsbury in the general dissolution of modern society.

That the pandering of the modern artist to the death-drive of mechanistic society was a general phenomenon and not limited to England is emphasized near the end of the novel with the appearance of Loerke, a German sculptor whose work adorns "a great granite factory in Cologne." Loerke, who asserts on one hand that art should interpret industry as it had formerly interpreted religion and on the other that a work of art has no relation to anything but itself, embodies the amorality of modernist aesthetics from Lawrence's viewpoint. Dominated by "pure unconnected will," Loerke is, like Hermione, sexually perverse, and, like the habitués of the Pompadour, he "lives like a rat in the river of corruption."

All of these secondary characters in *Women in Love* exemplify the results of the displacement of the traditional order by industrialization, or what Lawrence terms "the first great phase of chaos, the substitution of the mechanical principle for the organic." Except for Hermione, they are consistently presented from without, in static roles prescribed for them by a static society. Against this backdrop move the four principal characters: Ursula and Gudrun Brangwen, who are sisters, and Rupert Birkin and Gerald Crich, who are friends. The interweaving relationships of these four, highlighted in scenes of great emotional intensity and suggestiveness, provide the "rhythmic form" of the novel. Notwithstanding their interactions with external society and their long philosophical arguments, they are chiefly presented in terms of a continuous struggle among the elemental energies vying for expression within them. Mark Schorer aptly describes the book as "a drama of primal compulsions." The "drama" concerns the conflict between the mechanical will and the organic oneness of being, between the "flux of corruption" or death and the regenerative forces of life, as these are variously embodied in the four main characters and their constantly shifting relationships.

Birkin, full of talk about spontaneity and "pure being" and the "blood-knowledge" available in sensuality, is clearly a spokesman for certain of Lawrence's favorite ideas. Considering this, it is interesting that from the outset the novel emphasizes his involvement in the death fixation of modern society at large. He has been one of the "mud-flowers" at the Café Pompadour. In addition, he has been for several years involved in an affair with the perverse socialite Hermione, an affair that has degenerated into a hysterical battle of wills, sapping Birkin of his male vitality. As he tells Gerald, he wants above all to center his life on "the finality of love" for one woman and close relationships with a few other friends, but his goal is frustrated by the lingering parody of it represented in Hermione and the London bohemians. It is therefore significant that he is frequently ill and once goes to the south of France for several weeks to recuperate. His sickness is as much spiritual as physical. Dissatisfied with his prosaic career as a school inspector and frustrated in his relationships, he often finds himself "in pure opposition to everything." In this depressed state he becomes preoccupied with death and dissolution, "that dark river" (as he calls it) that seethes through all modern reality, even love. Not until after his violent break with Hermione, during which she nearly kills him, does Birkin begin to find his way back to life.

Unlike Birkin, Gerald does not believe that love can form the center of life. Instead he maintains that there is no center to life but simply the "social mechanism" that artificially holds it together; as for loving, Gerald is incapable of it. Indeed the novel everywhere implies that his inability to love derives from his abdication of vital, integrated being in favor of mere social fulfillment. As an industrial magnate (he is the director of the local coal mines and has successfully modernized them), Gerald advocates what Birkin calls the "ethics of productivity," the "pure instrumentality of mankind," being for him the basis of social cohesion and progress. If society is essentially mechanistic, Gerald's ambition is to be "the God of the machine" whose will is "to subjugate Matter to his own ends. The subjugation itself," Lawrence adds significantly, "was the point." This egotistic obsession is illustrated in a powerful scene in which Gerald rides a young Arab mare up to a railroad track and, while Gudrun and Ursula look on aghast, he violently forces the terrified mare to stay put as the train races noisily by them. The impact of this cruel assertion of will to power registers forcefully on Ursula, who is duly horrified and outraged, and on Gudrun, who is mesmerized by the "unutterable subordination" of the mare to the "indomitable" male.

After abortive affairs with other women, Birkin and Gerald are inevitably attracted to the Brangwen sisters. The protracted ebb and flow of the two relationships is tellingly juxtaposed in a series of scenes richly symbolic of the central dialectic of life and death. Meanwhile, not content with the romantic promise of finding love with a woman only, Birkin proposes to Gerald that they form a vital male bond as of blood brothers pledged to mutual love and fidelity. Whatever its unconscious origins, the intent of the offer is clearly not sexual. As the rest of the novel demonstrates (anticipating a theme that becomes more central and explicit in subsequent novels such as *Aaron's Rod* and *The Plumed Serpent*), Birkin is searching for a kind of pure intimacy in human relationships. He seeks with both men and women a bond of blood and mind and spirit—the integrated wholeness of being that for Lawrence was sacred—that when realized might form the nucleus of a new, vital human community. Because of Gerald's identification with the mechanism of industrial society, Birkin's repeated offer of a *Blutbrüderschaft* amounts to an invitation to a shared rebirth emblematic of epochal transfiguration, an apocalypse in microcosm. Because of that same identification, of course, Gerald, confused and threatened, must refuse the offer. Instead he chooses to die.

The choice of death is brilliantly dramatized in Gerald's impassioned encounters with Gudrun. Despite her earlier identification with the mare he brutally "subordinated," Gudrun might still have offered him the sort of vital relationship that both so desperately need. At any rate, had they been able to pursue their potential for love, the sort of shared commitment to mutual "being" that Birkin offers Gerald and that he eventually discovers with Ursula, regeneration, however painful and difficult, could have been realized. Rather than accept this challenge, however, Gerald falls back on his usual tactics and tries to subjugate Gudrun to his will. After his father's death, he becomes acutely aware of the void in his life and turns at once to Gudrun—walking straight from the cemetery in the rain to her house, up to her bedroom, his shoes still heavy with mud from the grave—not out of love but desperate need: the need to assert himself, heedless of the "otherness" of another, as if in so doing he could verify by sheer force of will that he exists. Because this egotistic passion is a perversion of love as Lawrence saw it, however, and because Gerald's yearning for ontological security is a perversion of the quest for true being, Gerald's anxieties are only made worse by his contact with Gudrun. For her part, Gudrun, unlike the helplessly dominated mare, never yields herself fully to Gerald. In fact, she does all she can to thwart and humiliate him, and their relationship soon becomes a naked battle of wills. It is redundant to say that this is a battle to the death, for, on the grounds that it is fought, the battle itself is death in Lawrencian terms. In the end, Gerald, whose aim all along as "God of the machine" had been to subjugate Matter to his will, becomes literally a frozen corpse whose expression terrifies Birkin with its "last terrible look of cold, mute Matter." Gudrun, headed at the end for a rendezvous with the despicable Loerke, arrives at a like consummation.

Whatever Lawrence might say about the "purely destructive" forces at work in *Women in Love*, in the relationship of Birkin and Ursula he finds a seed of new life germinating, albeit precariously, within the "dark river of dissolution." After the severance of his nearly fatal tie with Hermione, Birkin finds himself for a time in a quandary. Believing as he still does that the only means of withstanding dissolution is to center his life on close human ties, he casts about him to discover precisely the kind of relationship that will best serve or enact his quest for being. The "purely sensual, purely unspiritual knowledge" represented by a primitive statue of an African woman impresses Birkin but finally proves too remote a mystery for him to emulate; in any event, the modern female embodiments of this "mystic knowledge" of the senses are, like Hermione and Gudrun, will-dominated and murderous. A second way is that represented by the proposed bond with Gerald, the "Nordic" machine-god who for Birkin represents "the vast abstraction of ice and snow, . . . snow-abstract annihilation." When these alternatives both reveal themselves as mere "allotropic" variations of the flux of corruption from which he seeks release, Birkin finally hits upon a third way, "the way of freedom." He conceives of it in idealistic terms, as

> the paradisal entry into pure, single being, the individual soul taking precedence over love and desire for union, stronger than any pangs of emotion, a lovely state of free proud singleness, which accepted the obligation of the permanent connection with others, and with the other, submits to the yoke and leash of love, but never forfeits its own proud individual singleness, even while it loves and yields.

It is a difficult and elusive ideal, and when Birkin tries, laboriously, to describe it to Ursula—inviting her to join him in a new, strange relationship, "not meeting and mingling . . . but an equilibrium, a pure balance of two single beings" dynamically counterpoised as two stars are—she mocks him for dissimulating. Why does he not simply declare his love for her without "dragging in the stars"? She has a point, and Lawrence's art only benefits from such moments of self-criticism. Still, these paradoxical images of separateness in union, of a bond that finds its strength in the reciprocal affirmation of "otherness," do express, like the wheel's axle and rim in *The Rainbow*, Lawrence's essential vision of integrated, dynamic relationships. Furthermore, only by actively pursuing such a marriage of opposites, in which the separateness of each partner is necessary to the indissolubility of the bond, can both parties be caught up in something altogether new: "the third," which transcends individual selves in the oneness of pure being. For Lawrence this is the true consummation, springing up from "the source of the deepest life-force."

So polluted had the river of life become in modern Europe, however, that Lawrence could no longer bring himself to believe that this transcendence, ephemeral as it was to begin with, could survive the general cataract of dissolution. Moreover, even when Birkin and Ursula do find fulfillment together, it is not enough; for Birkin, at any rate, the new dispensation must involve other people as well as themselves. For both reasons, the quest for integrated wholeness of being, a mystery into which Birkin and Ursula are only new initiates, becomes translated into a pilgrimage through space. They must depart from the old, dying world and, like Lawrence and Frieda after the war, proceed in search of holy ground. The primary focus of subsequent novels, this quest is defined in *Women in Love* simply as "wandering to nowhere, . . . away from the world's somewheres." As "nowhere" is the translation of the word *utopia*, the social impetus of the search is implicit. "It isn't really a locality, though," Birkin insists. "It's a perfected relation between you and me, and others . . . so that we are free together." With this ideal before him, Lawrence was poised at the crossroads of his career.

In the postwar novels, which present fictionalized versions of his and Frieda's experiences in Italy (*Aaron's Rod*), Australia (*Kangaroo*), and Mexico (*The Plumed Serpent*), the quest translates increasingly into a sociopolitical doctrine projected onto whole societies. The bond between men and the fascination of powerful male leaders became more and more of an obsession in these novels. Lawrence tried mightily to remain faithful to the notion that the regeneration of societies should correspond to the "perfected relations" between individuals. The analogy presented difficulties, however, and the struggle to express his essentially religious vision in political terms proved fatal to his art. There are brilliant moments in all of these novels, especially in *The Plumed Serpent*, yet the alien aspects of the foreign lands he visited finally obscured the central issues in what was, at bottom, a quest for self-discovery. *Women in Love*, still in touch with the real motives of that quest and yielding immediate access to its first (and, as it turned out, finest) fruits, offers the richest rendering of both the modern drift toward death and its Lawrencian antidote, "whole man alive."

However ill defined the object of his protagonists' plans for flight from Europe, ever since the cataclysm of 1914-1918, Lawrence himself had determined to relocate in the United States. Florida, California, upstate New York, New Mexico—all at one time or another figured as proposed sites of his American Dream. In one of these areas, apart from the great urban centers, he would establish a utopian colony to be called Rananim. There he would start over again, free from the runaway entropy of modern Europe. In America, and more particularly aboriginal America, he believed that the Tree of Life remained intact, its potency still issuing "up from the roots, crude but vital." Nevertheless, when the war ended he did not go to America straightaway but headed east, not to arrive in the Western Hemisphere until late in 1922. During this prolonged period of yearning, his vision of America as the New World of the soul, the locus of the regeneration of humankind, took on an increasingly definite form. He was imaginatively committed to it even before settling near Taos, New Mexico, where he and Frieda lived on a mountain ranch for most of the next three years.

After studying the classic works of early American literature, he decided that he would write an "American novel," that is, a novel that would invoke and adequately respond to the American "spirit of place." For Lawrence the continent's daemon was the old "blood-and-vertebrate consciousness" embodied in the Mesoamerican Indian and his aboriginal religion. Because of four centuries of white European domination, that spirit had never been fully realized, yet despite the domination it still lay waiting beneath the surface for an annunciation. The terms of this vision, even apart from other factors having to do with his frustrating contacts with Mable Dodge Luhan and her coterie of artists in Taos, all but made it inevitable that Lawrence would sooner or later situate his American novel in a land where the Indian presence was more substantial than it was in the southwestern United States. The Pueblo Indian religion impressed him deeply with its "revelation of life," but he realized that for a genuine, large-scale rebirth to occur in America, "a vast death-happening must come first" to break the hold of the degenerate white civilization. It was natural enough that he turned his eyes south to Mexico, a land that actually had been caught up in revolution for more than a decade—a revolution moreover in which the place of the Indian (who constituted more than 30 percent of the population) in the national life was a central issue. Reading pre-Columbian history and archaeology, Lawrence found in Aztec mythology a ready-made source of symbols and in the story of the Spanish conquest an important precedent for his narrative of contemporary counterrevolution and religious revival.

THE PLUMED SERPENT

The writing of his *Quetzalcoatl*, the working title of what would become *The Plumed Serpent*, proved unusually difficult, however. *Kangaroo* had taken Lawrence only six weeks to write; *Aaron's Rod* and *The Lost Girl* were also composed in sudden, if fitful, bursts. In contrast, he worked on his "American novel" off and on for nearly two years, even taking the precaution of writing such tales as "The Woman who Rode Away," "The Princess," and "St. Mawr" (all of which have much in common with the novel), and the Mexican travel sketches in *Mornings in Mexico*, as a kind of repeated trial run for his more ambitious project.

One reason the novel proved recalcitrant was that Lawrence became increasingly aware during his three journeys into the Mexican interior that his visionary Mexico and the real thing were far from compatible. The violence of the country appalled him; its revolution, which he soon dismissed as "self-serving Bolshevism," left him cold; and most important, its Roman Catholic Indians were demonstrably uninterested and seemingly incapable of responding to the sort of pagan revival called for by Lawrence's apocalyptic scheme. So committed was he to his American "Rananim," however, that he was unwilling or unable to entertain the possibility of its failure. Rather than qualify his program for world regeneration in the light of the widening breach between his long-cherished dream and the disappointing reality, he elaborated the dream more fully and explicitly than ever, inflating his claims for it in a grandiose rhetoric that only called its sincerity into question. Had he been content with a purely visionary, symbolic tale, a prose romance comparable in motive with William Butler Yeats's imaginary excursions to "Holy Byzantium," such questions would probably not have arisen. Lawrence, however, could not let go of his expectation that in Mexico the primordial spirit of place would answer to his clarion call.

At the same time, the realist in Lawrence allowed evidence to the contrary to appear in the form of his extraordinarily vivid perceptions of the malevolence of the Mexican landscape and its dark-skinned inhabitants. Even these, however, were forced into the pattern of New World apocalypse. In his desperation to have it both ways, doggedly asserting the identity of his own spiritual quest and the course of events in the literal, external world, he contrived a kind of symbolic or mythic formula in which sexual, religious, and political rebirth are not only equated but also presented as mutually dependent. The result, according to most critics, is a complicated muddle in which the parts, some of which are as fine as anything he ever wrote, do not make a whole. For Lawrence, however, the muddle itself would ultimately prove instructive.

In a sense, *The Plumed Serpent* begins where *Women in Love* ends. The flow of Birkin and Ursula's relationship in the earlier novel is directed centrifugally away from England toward a nameless "nowhere" of shared freedom in pure being. In *The Plumed Serpent*, the protagonist, Kate Leslie, having heard the death knell of her spirit in Europe, has arrived at the threshold of the New World of mystery, where a rebirth awaits her "like a doom." That the socialist revolution has addressed only the material needs of Mexicans and left their dormant spirit untouched suggests that Mexico is also in need of rebirth. Disgusted by the tawdry imitation of a modern European capital that is Mexico City, the seat of the failed revolution, Kate journeys westward to the remote lakeside village of Sayula. Sayula also happens to be the center of a new-Aztec religious revival led by Don Ramón Carrasco, who calls himself "the living Quetzalcoatl." The boat trip down the "spermlike" lake to Sayula begins Kate's centripetal movement toward her destiny, and also Mexico's movement toward an indigenous spiritual reawakening; both movements are directed, gradually but inexorably, toward an "immersion in a sea of living blood."

Unlike Birkin and Ursula of *Women in Love*, Kate, a middle-aged Irish widow, wants at first only to be "alone with the unfolding flower of her own soul." Her occasional contacts with the provincial Indians inspire in her a sense of wonder at their "dark" mystery, but at the same time she finds their very alienness oppressive and threatening. She feels that the country wants to pull her down, "with a slow, reptilian insistence," to prevent her "free" spirit from soaring. Since Kate values her freedom and her solitude, she retreats periodically from the "ponderous, down-pressing weight" that she associates with the coils of the old Aztec feathered serpent, Quetzalcoatl.

Don Ramón explains to her that she must submit to this weight on the spirit, for by pulling her down into the earth it may bring her into contact with the deep-rooted Tree of Life, which still thrives in the volcanic soil of primordial Mexico beneath the "paleface overlay" on the surface. This injunction is aimed not only at Kate but also at contemporary Mexico itself, which, beckoned by the pulsating drumbeats and hymns of the Men of Quetzalcoatl, is urged to turn its back on the imported white creeds (Catholicism and Bolshevism) and rediscover its indigenous roots. Only by yielding their hold on the conscious will can the "bound" egos of the Mexicans as well as of Kate achieve a transfiguration, symbolized in the novel by the Morning Star. Indeed, as a representative of white "mental consciousness," Kate is destined to perform an important role in the new dispensation in Mexico. Ramón's aim is to forge a new mode of consciousness emerging from the dynamic tension between the white and dark sensibilities. The new mode is embodied by Ramón himself, in his capacity to "see both ways" without being absorbed by either, just as the ancient man-god Quetzalcoatl united the sky and the earth, and as the Morning Star (associated with Quetzalcoatl) partakes of both night and day, moon and sun, yet remains itself.

Thus described, this doctrine may seem a welcome elaboration of the star-equilibrium theory of human relationships advanced by Birkin in the earlier novel. The transcendent emergence of "the third," at best an elusive idea of divine immanence in *Women in Love*, seems to be clarified by the Aztec cosmogonic symbolism of *The Plumed Serpent*. Undoubtedly the latter novel is the fullest statement of Lawrence's vitalist religion, yet there is something in the very explicitness of the religion in the novel that renders it suspect. As if in tacit acknowledgment of this, Lawrence, impatient with the slow progress of Don Ramón's appeal to the spirit, introduces a more overt form of conquest. When both Kate and Mexico fail to respond unequivocally to the invitation to submit voluntarily, Ramón reluctantly resorts to calling on the assistance of Don Cipriano Viedma, a full-blooded Indian general who commands a considerable army. Although Lawrence attempts to legitimate this move by having Ramón induct Cipriano into the neo-Aztec pantheon as "the living Huitzilopochtli" (the Aztec god of war) and by having Kate envision Cipriano as the Mexican Indian embodiment of "the ancient phallic mystery, . . . the god-devil of the male Pan" before whom she must "swoon," the novel descends into a pathological nightmare from which it never quite recovers.

It is not simply that Cipriano politicizes the religious movement, reducing it to yet another Latin American literary adventure that ends by imposing Quetzalcoatlism as the institutional religion of Mexico; nor is it simply that Cipriano, with Ramón's blessing, dupes Kate into a kind of sexual subservience that puts Gerald Crich's machine-god efforts with Gudrun (in *Women in Love*) to shame. The nadir of the novel is reached when Cipriano performs a public execution, stabbing to death three blindfolded prisoners who have betrayed Ramón. This brutal act is given priestly sanction by Ramón and even accepted by Kate, in her new role as Malintzi, fertility goddess in the nascent religion. "Why should I judge him?" asks Kate. "He is of the gods. . . . What do I care if he kills people? His flame is young and clean. He is Huitzilopochtli, and I am Malintzi." Their "godly" union is consummated at the foot of the altar in the new temple of Quetzalcoatl. At this point, if not before, the threefold quest for "immersion in a sea of living blood" ceases to serve a metaphorical function and becomes all too chillingly literal.

With its rigidified "mystical" doctrine, its hysterical rhetoric, and its cruelly inhuman advocacy of "necessary" bloodshed and supermasculine dominance, *The Plumed Serpent* offers what amounts to a perfect Lawrencian hell but persists in celebrating it as if it were the veritable threshold of paradise. The novel has found a few defenders among critics enamored of "mythic design," but Harry T. Moore is surely correct in calling it "a tremendous volcano of a failure." Though for a short time he thought it his best novel, by March, 1928, Lawrence himself repudiated *The Plumed Serpent* and the militaristic "leader of men" idea that it embodies.

Nevertheless, *The Plumed Serpent* marks a crucial phase in Lawrence's development, for it carries to their ultimate conclusion the most disturbing implications of the ideas that had vexed his mind ever since the war. Submersion in the "dark blood," as the novel demonstrates, could lead as readily to wholesale murder in the name of religion as to vital and spontaneous relations between men and women. By courageously following his chimerical "Rananim" dream through to its end in a horrific, palpable nightmare, Lawrence accepted enormous risks, psychological as well as artistic. The effort nearly cost him his life, bringing on a severe attack of tuberculosis complicated by malaria. In the few years that remained to him, however, he was in a real sense a man reborn, able to return in imagination (in *The Virgin and the Gipsy* and *Lady Chatterley's Lover*, among other works) to his native Midlands, where he could once again take up the quest for "whole man alive," happily unencumbered by the grandiose political imperatives of world regeneration. Purging him of this ideological sickness, the writing of *The Plumed Serpent* proved as salutary to his later career as *Sons and Lovers* had been to his period of greatest accomplishment.

When Lawrence settled in southern Europe after leaving America in late 1925, he began to reshape his spiritual map in ways suggestive of his shifting outlook during his last years. The problem with the United States, he decided, was that everyone was too tense. Americans took themselves and their role in the world far too seriously and were unable to slacken their grip on themselves for fear that the world would collapse as a result. In contrast, the Europeans (he was thinking chiefly of southern Europeans rather than his own countrymen) were freer and more spontaneous because they were not controlled by will and could therefore let themselves go. At bottom, the European attitude toward life was characterized by what Lawrence called "insouciance." Relaxed, essentially free from undue care or fret, Europeans were open to "a sort of bubbling-in of life," whereas the Americans' more forthright pursuit of life only killed it.

Whether this distinction between America and Europe has any validity for others, for the post-America Lawrence it meant a great deal. In *The Plumed Serpent*, his "American novel," instead of realizing the free and spontaneous life flow made accessible by insouciance, he engaged in an almost hysterical striving after life writ large, resorting to political demagoguery and a formalized religion fully armed with rifles as well as rites. Apparently aware in retrospect of his error, he eschewed the strong-leader/submissive-follower relationship as the keynote to regeneration. In its place he would focus on a new relationship: a "sort of tenderness, sensitive, between men and men and men and women, and not the one up one down, lead on I follow, *ich dien* sort of business." Having discovered the virtues of insouciance and tenderness, Lawrence began to write *Lady Chatterley's Lover*, one of his most poignant, lyrical treatments of individual human relations.

Lady Chatterley's Lover

As always in Lawrence, the physical setting offers a crucial barometer of sensibility. In this case the treatment of setting is indicative of the novelist's loss of faith in the "spirit of place" as a valid embodiment of his quest. In comparison with his other novels, *Lady Chatterley's Lover* presents a scene much reduced in richness and complexity. Wragby Hall, the baronial seat of the Chatterleys, is described as "a warren of a place without much distinction." Standing on a hill and surrounded by oak trees, Wragby offers a view dominated by the smokestacks of the mines in and around the Midlands village of Tevershall. Like Shortlands, the Criches' estate in *Women in Love*, Wragby and its residents attempt through formal artifice to deny the existence of the pits from which the family income derives. The attempt is futile, however, for "when the wind was that way, which was often, the house was full of the stench of this sulphurous combustion of the earth's excrement," and smuts settle on the gardens "like black manna from skies of doom." As for Tevershall ("'tis now and 'tever shall be"), the mining village offers only the appalling prospect of "the utter negation of natural beauty, the utter negation of the gladness of life, . . . the utter death of the human intuitive faculty." Clearly Wragby and Tevershall are two sides of the same coin minted by the godless machine age. Between the two is a tiny, ever-diminishing remnant of old Sherwood Forest. The wood is owned by the Chatterleys, and many of its trees were "patriotically" chopped down during the Great War for timber for the allies' trenches.

It is here that Constance (Connie) Chatterley and her lover, Oliver Mellors, the gamekeeper, find—or rather create—life together. As Julian Moynihan has observed, the little wood symbolizes "the beleaguered and vulnerable status to which the vital career has been reduced" at the hands of modern civilization. The old centrifugal impulse for a faraway "nowhere" has yielded to a desperate centripetal flight toward refuge from the industrial wasteland. Try as they might to find sanctuary within the wood, however, the lovers must recognize that there is no longer any room in the world for true sanctuary, much less for a "Rananim." "The industrial noises broke the solitude," Lawrence writes. "The sharp lights, though unseen, mocked it. A man could no longer be private and withdrawn. The world allows no hermits." The geographic focus of the Lawrencian quest is no longer able to provide a modicum of hope and so yields to a new, scaled-down, more intimate image: the human body.

The sterility and spiritual paralysis of the modern world are embodied by Clifford Chatterley, Connie's husband. A paraplegic victim of the war, Clifford is both literally and symbolically deadened to the life of the passions. All his energy is directed to verbal, abstract, or social undertakings in which actual contact is minimal. Clifford believes in the form and apparatus of the social life and is indifferent to private feelings. A director of mines, he sees the miners as objects rather than men, mere extensions of the pit machinery. For him, "the function determines the individual," who hardly matters otherwise. Clifford also writes fashionably shallow stories and entertains other writers and critics to curry favor. He modernizes the coal mines with considerable success. Thus in broad outline he resembles Gerald Crich of *Women in Love*, but in the far simpler world of *Lady Chatterley's Lover*, Lawrence chooses not to cloud matters by giving his antagonist any redeeming qualities. The reader is never invited to sympathize with Clifford's plight. Motoring around Wragby Hall in his mechanical wheelchair, Clifford coolly urges Connie to have a child by another man—the "sex thing" having been of no particular importance to him even before the war—so that he can have an heir to Wragby. By the end of the novel, he turns to his attendant Mrs. Bolton for the only intimacy left to him: a regressive, perverse form of contact. Such heaping of abuse onto Clifford, far in excess of what is needed to establish his symbolic role, undoubtedly detracts from the novel.

So long as she remains with Clifford, Connie finds herself in a condition of static bondage in which her individuality is circumscribed by the function identified in her title. A "lady" by virtue of her marriage, she is not yet truly a woman. Sex for her is merely a "thing" as it is for Clifford, an instrument of tacit control over men. She is progressively gripped by malaise. Physically she is "old at twenty-seven, with no gleam and sparkle in the flesh"; spiritually she is unborn. Her affair with Mellors is of course the means of her metamorphosis, which has been compared (somewhat ironically) with the awakening of Sleeping Beauty at the handsome prince's magical kiss. Less obvious is the overlapping of this fairy-tale pattern with a counterpattern of male transformation such as that found in the tale of the Frog Prince. For Mellors, too, is trapped in a kind of bondage, alone in his precarious refuge in the wood. The "curse" on him is his antipathy to intimate contacts, especially with women, after his disastrous marriage to the promiscuous Bertha Coutts.

The initial encounters between Connie and Mellors in the wood result only in conflict and hostility, as both, particularly Mellors, cling to their socially prescribed roles and resist the challenge of being "broken open" by true contact with another. When they finally do begin to respond to that challenge, however, it is Mellors who takes the lead in conducting Connie through her initiation into the mysteries of "phallic" being. With his "tender" guidance she learns the necessity of letting go her hold on herself, yielding to the "palpable unknown" beyond her conscious will. She discovers the importance of their "coming off together" rather than the merely "frictional" pleasures of clitoral orgasm (a notion acceptable within Lawrence's symbolic context if not widely endorsed by the "how to" manuals of the Masters and Johnson generation, of which Lawrence would no doubt have disapproved). When she tries to get Mellors to tell her that he loves her, he rejects the abstract, overused word in favor of the earthier Anglo-Saxon language of the body and its functions. On one occasion he even introduces her to sodomy so as to "burn out the shames, the deepest, oldest shames, in the most secret places." The result of all this, paradoxically, is that the couple arrives at the state of "chastity." Having broken their ties to the sterile world, they are able to accept an imposed separation until it is possible, after a period of waiting for Mellors's divorce to occur, for them to live together in hope for their future.

In an aside in chapter 9, Lawrence, asserting that it is "the way our sympathy flows and recoils that really determines our lives," affirms that the great function of a novel is precisely to "inform and lead into new places the flow of our sympathetic consciousness" and to "lead our sympathies away in recoil from things gone dead." As a statement of intention, this will do for all of Lawrence's novels. Of course, even the best of intentions do not necessarily lead to artistic achievement. *Lady Chatterley's Lover*, though in many respects a remarkable recovery after the dead end that was the "leadership novels," is nevertheless flawed by the very directness with which it follows the "flow and recoil" idea. For one thing, the deck is too obviously stacked against Clifford. Lawrence never takes him seriously as a man; by making him the stationary target of so much scorn simply for what he represents, Lawrence in effect replicates Clifford's own treatment of people as mere objects or functions.

Because the "recoil" against Clifford as a "thing gone dead" seems facile and almost glib, Connie's counterflow toward Mellors seems also too easy, despite Lawrence's efforts to render her conflicting, vacillating feelings. Another part of the problem lies in the characterization of Mellors, who, after his initial reluctance, proves to be a tiresomely self-satisfied, humorless, "knowing" spokesman for the gospel according to Lawrence. Connie, however, is a marvelous creation, far more complex than even Mellors seems to realize. She is a worthy successor to Lawrence's other intriguing female characters: Gertrude Morel, Ursula and Gudrun Brangwen, Alvina Houghton (of *The Lost Girl*), and Kate Leslie.

At his best, in *Sons and Lovers, The Rainbow,* and especially *Women in Love*, Lawrence manages to enact the flow and counterflow of consciousness, the centrifugal dilation and the centripetal contraction of sympathies, in a far more complex and convincing way than he does in his last novel. Notwithstanding his battles with Mrs. Grundy, the underlying impulse of all his work is unquestionably moral: the passionate yearning to discover, celebrate, and *become* "whole man alive." The desperateness with which he pursued that elusive ideal in both his life and his art sometimes led him to resort to a bullying, declamatory didacticism, which took the chance of alienating his readers' sympathies.

Lawrence's moral vision was most compelling when embodied and rendered in dramatic or symbolic terms rather than externally imposed by "oracular" utterance and rhetorical bombast, but "art for my sake" necessarily involved him in these risks, of which he was fully aware. At a time when aesthetic objectivity and the depersonalization of the artist were the dominant aims of the modernists, Lawrence courageously pursued his vision wherever it might lead.

Through his capacity for outrage against what he considered a dying civilization, his daring to risk failure and humiliation in the ongoing struggle to find and make known the "vital quick" that alone could redeem humanity and to relocate humankind's lost spiritual roots, Lawrence performed the essential role of seer or prophetic conscience for his age. Moreover, because subsequent events in the twentieth century more than confirmed his direst forebodings, his is a voice that readers today cannot afford to ignore. While many are decrying the death of the novel amid the proliferation of the much-ballyhooed "literature of exhaustion," one could do worse than turn to Lawrence to find again the "one bright book of life."

Ronald G. Walker

OTHER MAJOR WORKS

SHORT FICTION: *The Prussian Officer, and Other Stories*, 1914; *England, My England*, 1922; *St. Mawr: Together with "The Princess,"* 1925; *Rawdon's Roof*, 1928; *The Woman Who Rode Away, and Other Stories*, 1928; *Love Among the Haystacks, and Other Stories*, 1930; *The Lovely Lady, and Other Stories*, 1933; *A Modern Lover*, 1934; *The Complete Short Stories of D. H. Lawrence*, 1961.

PLAYS: *The Widowing of Mrs. Holroyd*, pb. 1914; *Touch and Go*, pb. 1920; *David*, pb. 1926; *The Plays*, pb. 1933; *A Collier's Friday Night*, pb. 1934; *The Complete Plays of D. H. Lawrence*, 1965.

POETRY: *Love Poems and Others*, 1913; *Amores*, 1916; *Look! We Have Come Through!*, 1917; *New Poems*, 1918; *Bay*, 1919; *Tortoises*, 1921; *Birds, Beasts, and Flowers*, 1923; *The Collected Poems of D. H. Lawrence*, 1928; *Pansies*, 1929; *Nettles*, 1930; *The Triumph of the Machine*, 1931; *Last Poems*, 1932; *Fire, and Other Poems*, 1940; *Phoenix Edition of Complete Poems*, 1957; *The Complete Poems of D. H. Lawrence*, 1964 (Vivian de Sola Pinto and Warren Roberts, editors).

NONFICTION: *Study of Thomas Hardy*, 1914; *Twilight in Italy*, 1916; *Movements in European History*, 1921; *Psychoanalysis and the Unconscious*, 1921; *Sea and Sardinia*, 1921; *Fantasia of the Unconscious*, 1922; *Studies in Classic American Literature*, 1923; *Reflections on the Death of a Porcupine, and Other Essays*, 1925; *Mornings in Mexico*, 1927; *Pornography and Obscenity*, 1929; *À Propos of Lady Chatterley's Lover*, 1930; *Assorted Articles*, 1930; *Apocalypse*, 1931; *Etruscan Places*, 1932; *The Letters of D. H. Lawrence*, 1932 (Aldous Huxley, editor); *Phoenix: The Posthumous Papers of D. H. Lawrence*, 1936 (Edward McDonald, editor); *The Collected Letters of D. H. Lawrence*, 1962 (2 volumes; Harry T. Moore, editor); *Phoenix II: Uncollected, Unpublished, and Other Prose Works*, 1968 (Moore and Roberts, editors); *The Letters of D. H. Lawrence*, 1979-2000 (8 volumes; James T. Boulton and others, editors); *Selected Critical Writings*, 1998; *Late Essays and Articles*, 2004; *Introductions and Reviews*, 2005.

BIBLIOGRAPHY

Balbert, Peter. *D. H. Lawrence and the Phallic Imagination: Essays on Sexual Identity and Feminist Misreading*. New York: St. Martin's Press, 1989. Collection of essays presents a well-reasoned response to feminist critics who, especially since the 1970's, have accused Lawrence of misogyny. Includes bibliography and index.

Bell, Michael. *D. H. Lawrence: Language and Being*. New York: Cambridge University Press, 1992. Focuses primarily on Lawrence's novels, discussing the development of Lawrence's metaphysics not only in terms of his emotional life but also in terms of Martin Heidegger's metaphysics.

Black, Michael. *D. H. Lawrence: The Early Fiction*. New York: Cambridge University Press, 1986. Analyzes three early novels—*The White Peacock*, *The Trespasser*, and *Sons and Lovers*—and eight short stories. Explains how Lawrence uses imagery that is personal to the author and is often poetic or musical in nature.

Burack, Charles Michael. *D. H. Lawrence's Language of Sacred Experience: The Transfiguration of the Reader*. New York: Palgrave Macmillan, 2005. Maintains that Lawrence structured *Lady Chatterley's Lover*, *The Rainbow*, *The Plumed Serpent*, and *Women in Love* as if they were religious initiation rites intended to evoke new spiritual experiences in their readers.

Ellis, David. *D. H. Lawrence: Dying Game, 1922-1930*. New York: Cambridge University Press, 1997. The third volume of the Cambridge University Press biography of Lawrence links his writings with the incidents of his life. Argues that more than most authors, Lawrence wrote fiction that was closely associated with his daily living. Discusses Lawrence's fiction and revisions during the 1920's, including his work on *Lady Chatterley's Lover.*

Jackson, Dennis, and Fleda Brown Jackson, eds. *Critical Essays on D. H. Lawrence.* Boston: G. K. Hall, 1988. Collection of twenty essays provides various critical insights. Includes articles by scholars and by well-known writers such as Anaïs Nin and Sean O'Casey. All literary genres in which Lawrence wrote are represented by one or more contributions. Also of note is the editors' introduction, which addresses trends in critical and biographical literature about Lawrence.

Kinkead-Weekes, Mark. *D. H. Lawrence: Triumph to Exile, 1912-1922.* New York: Cambridge University Press, 1996. The second volume of the three-volume Cambridge University Press biography covers Lawrence's life from his elopement with Frieda von Richthofen and the publication of *Sons and Lovers* through World War I. Provides a highly detailed account based on previously unavailable Lawrence letters and discusses Lawrence's relationships with Ezra Pound, T. S. Eliot, Wyndham Lewis, Ford Madox Ford, and others.

Moore, Harry T. *The Priest of Love: A Life of D. H. Lawrence.* Rev. ed. New York: Farrar, Straus and Giroux, 1974. In preparing this first objective biography, Moore lived for several years at Lawrence sites and interviewed Lawrence's family and friends. Remains the standard source for accuracy and completeness.

Schneider, Daniel J. *The Consciousness of D. H. Lawrence: An Intellectual Biography.* Lawrence: University Press of Kansas, 1986. Biography aimed at a general audience focuses on Lawrence's philosophical and psychological views. Traces all the major works chronologically and discusses Lawrence's religious nature at all stages of his life.

Worthen, John. *D. H. Lawrence: The Early Years, 1885-1912.* New York: Cambridge University Press, 1991. The first book in a three-volume Cambridge University Press biography, with the other volumes written by David Ellis and Mark Kinkead-Weekes (above). Covers Lawrence's childhood in Nottinghamshire and his years as a teacher in a London suburb. Offers insights into Lawrence's relationships with his mother and with Jessie Chambers, Louie Burrows, Frieda Weekley, and other individuals who influenced his formative years.

_______. *D. H. Lawrence: The Life of an Outsider.* New York: Counterpoint, 2005. Compelling, readable biography by a distinguished Lawrence scholar focuses on Lawrence's perpetual status as an "outsider" and his rebellious nature. Includes photographs.

Wright, T. R. *D. H. Lawrence and the Bible.* New York: Cambridge University Press, 2000. Analyzes Lawrence's use of biblical allusions and themes in arguing that the Bible plays a significant role in almost all of Lawrence's works.

GEORGE MEREDITH

Born: Portsmouth, England; February 12, 1828
Died: Flint Cottage, near Box Hill, Surrey, England; May 18, 1909

PRINCIPAL LONG FICTION

The Shaving of Shagpat, 1855
Farina, 1857
The Ordeal of Richard Feverel, 1859
Evan Harrington, 1861
Emilia in England, 1864 (also known as *Sandra Belloni: Or, Emilia in England*, 1886)
Rhoda Fleming, 1865
Vittoria, 1867
The Adventures of Harry Richmond, 1871
Beauchamp's Career, 1874-1875 (serial), 1876 (book)
The Egoist: A Comedy in Narrative, 1879
The Tragic Comedians, 1880
Diana of the Crossways, 1885
One of Our Conquerors, 1891
Lord Ormont and His Aminta, 1894
The Amazing Marriage, 1895
Celt and Saxon, 1910 (unfinished)

OTHER LITERARY FORMS

Ironically, George Meredith, one of nineteenth century England's greatest novelists, actually considered himself a poet. Regrettably, the several volumes of poetry he published during his lifetime went largely unnoticed. Even though Alfred, Lord Tennyson, praised "Love in the Valley," published in his first volume, *Poems* (1851), dedicated to his then father-in-law, Thomas Love Peacock, it was as a novelist that Meredith achieved recognition in his own time. Undaunted, nevertheless, Meredith continued to write poems and, in keeping with his stated vocation and with his aspiration, both his first and his last published books were collections of poems.

Modern Love and Poems of the English Roadside (1862) represents Meredith's lyric and dramatic power at its height, especially in the sequence of fifty sixteen-line lyrics, *Modern Love*. In these poems, Meredith traces the dissolution of a marriage with an unrestrained candor that is more like the attitudes toward marital relationships of the late twentieth century than the straight-faced, closed-lipped Victorian notions. At the lowest point in the sequence, the persona exclaims, "In tragic life, God wot,/ No villain need be! Passions spin the plot;/ We are betrayed by what is false within." Herein Meredith seems to

George Meredith (Library of Congress)

capture with great precision the essence of tragedy. Meredith's poetic vision is not always dark; light imagery, in fact, plays a significant role in his poetry.

The thinking man appears often in Meredith's works, but he is perhaps most prominent in the 1877 work *On the Idea of Comedy and of the Uses of the Comic Spirit.* This essay is significant enough to be included in many contemporary collections of criticism, especially in those that pertain to drama. Acknowledging that the muse of comedy has never been "one of the most honored of the Muses," Meredith submits that it is the "Comic Spirit" that civilizes humans. By means of thoughtful laughter, the Comic Spirit corrects and checks the foibles of all those who exceed the bounds of temperance and indulge by excessive behavior. Although Meredith opened himself to censure in his own day, his ideas about women and their roles in comedy are particularly interesting to today's readers. Indeed, comedy, "the fountain of common sense," teaches that men and women are social equals and that women are often men's superiors.

ACHIEVEMENTS

In the late nineteenth century, George Meredith achieved the status of a literary dictator or arbiter of taste. The path toward this recognition was, however, a long and arduous one. For years, Meredith received little to no recognition, and he had to wait for the publication of *The Ordeal of Richard Feverel* before he enjoyed the limited appreciation of Algernon Charles Swinburne, Dante Gabriel Rossetti, and others among the Pre-Raphaelites. Not until the appearance of *The Egoist* in 1879 did Meredith's literary reputation reach its zenith.

During his last years, Meredith received many awards and honors, including the succession of Alfred, Lord Tennyson, as the president of the Society of British Authors and election as one of the original members of the Order of Merit. Within twenty years after Meredith's death in 1909, nevertheless, his literary reputation began to suffer a partial eclipse, from which it began to recover in the 1970's. One explanation for Meredith's decline in reputation is simple: His turgid style and complex plots demand more from the average reader than he or she is often willing to give.

C. L. Cline's three-volume edition of *The Letters of George Meredith*, which appeared in 1970, and Phyllis B. Bartlett's two-volume collection of *The Poems of George Meredith* (1978) have done much to reawaken interest in Meredith's work, particularly in his poetry, which seems to appeal to modern readers much more markedly than it had to those of his own time. Even so, the influence of Meredith the novelist on such younger writers as Thomas Hardy was decisive, and Meredith's theory of the Comic Spirit as the civilizing force of all thoughtful persons speaks to all cultures of all times.

BIOGRAPHY

Born the son and grandson of tailors, George Meredith appears to have rejected his humble origins. Indeed, he once threatened that he would "most horribly haunt" any who attempted to reconstruct his biography. Despite his modest heritage, legacies from his mother and an aunt permitted him to attend private schools, St. Paul's Church School, Southsea, and the Moravian School of Neuwied, Germany. His objective in formal training was to become a lawyer, and he was apprenticed to a London solicitor in 1845. Young Meredith soon became dissatisfied with the legal profession, however, and began to seek a career as a journalist, a vocation that he pursued throughout most of his life, since he was never quite able to survive financially as an author of novels and poems.

From at least 1845 until his marriage in 1849 to Mary Ellen Nicolls, a widow and the daughter of Thomas Love Peacock, Meredith appears to have read widely and deeply in the literature of Greece, Rome, Germany, France, and England. The first few years of his marriage appear to have been ones of continued intellectual growth. The Merediths lived either with or near the aspiring young author's famous father-in-law. Meredith made good use of Peacock's extensive and often arcane library, whose shelves included volumes on such Near Eastern religions as Zoroastrianism, a faith that was later to have a profound influence on Meredith's novels and poems.

The first few years of apparent bliss were soon terminated, however, when Mary eloped in 1858 with the painter Henry Wallis to the isle of Capri. Meredith was consequently left alone to rear his son, Arthur; the author later wrote about these unhappy times both in the novel *The Ordeal of Richard Feverel* and in the lyric sequence *Modern Love*. After Mary's death in 1861, Meredith married, within three years, Marie Vulliamy; this match proved to be both enduring and much happier. After serving as war correspondent, he and Marie moved to Flint Cottage, Box Hill, Surrey. Box Hill is where admiring and enthusiastic young authors went to seek Meredith's sage counsel.

ANALYSIS

Although George Meredith's works all emphasize the corrective, civilizing influences of the Comic Spirit, his novels, as well as his poems, forcefully work out a sort of theodicy that is consistently informed by the Near Eastern religion Zoroastrianism. This philosophy that treats the being and government of God and the immortality of the soul displays the theme of the struggle between good and evil in the early work *Farina*.

Surrounded by the trappings of medieval Germany, Farina, the hero of the tale, is left to contend with the evil effects of a bout between a monk and Satan. The monk represents the Zoroastrian god of light or good, Ormuzd, and Satan, the god of darkness or evil, Ahriman.

THE ORDEAL OF RICHARD FEVEREL

In the later, much more successful novel *The Ordeal of Richard Feverel*, this dialectic is seen in the sixth chapter, "The Magian Conflict" (the magi were ancient priests of Zoroaster). In this case, Meredith assigns the roles of the two opposing parties of the struggle to a Tinker and a Yeoman; the witness to this debate is the adolescent Richard Feverel, whose father, Sir Austin, has attempted unsuccessfully to shield him from any introduction to the world's forces of good and evil.

The Tinker, who appears to be a faithful follower of Zoroaster, the ancient prophet of the faith, asserts that the Good Spirit reigns supreme. The Yeoman, whom Meredith playfully calls Speed-the-Plough, protests, because of his recent misfortune of having lost several jobs, that the Evil Spirit dominates. The Yeoman is particularly hostile to Farmer Blaize, with whom Richard and a companion have also had an unpleasant encounter. Farmer Blaize is responsible for the beginning of the Yeoman's misfortunes. Tinker and Yeoman discuss the universal strife between good and evil in Zoroastrian terms, wherein the Good Spirit is supposed to hold dominion for a two-thousand-year period and the Evil Spirit is believed to assume dominion for a like period of two thousand years. Clearly, then, this debate challenges the young Richard to side with Ahriman (darkness) or to join the legions of Ormuzd (light).

Richard later relates the details of this encounter to Adrian Harley, a sort of tutor and confidant of the young Mr. Feverel, who is actually a disciple of the Comic Spirit and whom the narrator addresses as the Wise Youth. Adrian explains to Richard that "I'm perfectly aware that Zoroaster is not dead. You have been listening to a common creed. Drink the Fire-worshippers, if you will." Adrian recognizes the nature of the timeless controversy and applies to it the synecdoche, "Zoroaster," to point out the age of the struggle. Adrian also emphasizes that this struggle is a universal one, the result of a "common creed," regardless of Sir Austin's refusal to acknowledge it.

Adrian's comic toast to the Fire-worshippers is also ironic in that Richard and Tom Bakewell, the plowman, have plotted to burn Farmer Blaize's hayracks. That night, Richard and his friend Ripton Thompson watch the fiery destruction resulting from the match of Tom Bakewell, whose last name is comically appropriate to his role. This "Bakewell Comedy," however, has serious overtones when seen in the light of the Zoroastrian metaphor. The fire of the boys' vision is not a pure one, for there are "dense masses of smoke" amid the flames that leap into the darkness like "snakes of fire." In Zoroastrianism, Ahriman (Evil) is responsible for this corruption of the pure flame.

The chapter's title, "Arson," which initiates the Bakewell Comedy, effectively points out the boys' error. The boys are, like Tom Bakewell, not good Zoroastrians because the fire they are worshiping reflects the evil nature of their revenge. Adrian sees through their conspiracy; however, he does not expose the boys. Rather, in the true manner of the Zoroastrians, he believes that the most effective punishment would be a spiritual, inner conflict. "The farmer's whip had reduced them to bodily contortions; these were decorous compared with the spiritual writhings they had to perform under Adrian's skillful manipulation." Adrian knows the true value of fire to the Zoroastrians: it is a symbol of the inner light of the soul, which glows brightest when fired by Ormuzd. If the soul is possessed by the evil Ahriman, the spiritual light is contaminated and burns, if at all, with a dim, impure glimmer.

Richard's next crucial encounter intensifies the glow of the purer fire burning within him. He meets Lucy Desborough, destined to be his wife. The imagery used to describe this encounter is filled with references to light. Nature herself has provided "a Temple for the flame" of love. From a boat, Richard first sees Lucy pictured in an idyllic scene of radiant sunshine reflecting from the "green-flashing plunges of a weir." Lucy's face is shaded from the sun's illumination mysteriously but compellingly "by a broad straw hat with a flexible brim that left her lips and chin in the sun, and sometimes nodding, sent forth a light of promising eyes." Her hair was "golden where the ray touched" it. Even her name is derived from the Latin word for light: *lux*. Richard's soul is filled with the light of passionate love, but he has another journey to the vision of the celestial light of the Zoroastrians.

Other references to Zoroastrianism abound in the novel. For example, at a later point, Sir Austin yields to the dark force of Ahriman when he chooses to "do nothing" at a time when his son needs his counsel most. Consequently, he turns his son away from him, perhaps forever, thus proving that a father with a "system" for child rearing cannot meet that system on its own terms.

Viewed within the bounds of the magian conflict, *The Ordeal of Richard Feverel* is seen as a novel about the inevitability of the human strife between good and evil, both of which are inextricably mixed within the soul of every human being. Some measure of hope is given the novel, however, when the reader learns that, finally, Richard does view, if but for a moment, the celestial light of Ormuzd through the aid of a truly devoted wife.

It is this hope that raises *The Ordeal of Richard Feverel* to the level of true tragedy, which must in some measure be positive. Although Sir Austin falls victim to Ahriman, his son, Richard, has seen the vision of Ormuzd. By the use of Zoroastrian imagery, Meredith has greatly intensified his conviction that the ultimate destiny of humankind is unity with the light of the spirit or, more realistically for Meredith, unity with the great "Over Reason" of the universe. This unity directs humans along the path of spiritual evolution and is the apex of Meredith's developing doctrine about humanity: blood (perfection of the body), brain (perfection of the mind), and spirit (perfection of the needs of human spiritual consciousness by means of realizing one's intrinsic independence and freedom).

The tone of the first half of *The Ordeal of Richard Feverel* is predominantly one of comic irony; the latter half of the novel, however, assumes tragic dimensions. Meredith's later novels display a much greater reliance upon the comic mood. Even so, the essence of "The Magian Conflict" is never lost; rather, Meredith wields the forces of darkness against those of light to accentuate the balancing, equalizing role of his emerging Comic Spirit, whose seeds have been planted in the wise youth, Adrian Harley. The struggle to reach the evolutionary apex, the light of the spirit, assumes a background role in the novels following *The Ordeal of Richard Feverel* and is treated later most directly in the poetry. In his novels, Meredith becomes increasingly more concerned with the question of how one should meet the vicissitudes of everyday life.

Meredith published his essay *On the Idea of Comedy and of the Uses of the Comic Spirit* in 1877. *Beauchamp's Career* appeared the year before; the novel portrays many of the theories Meredith proposed in his essay. In 1879, Meredith completed *The Egoist*, which the author named "a comedy in narrative." Meredith's last great achievement in the novel genre appeared in 1885 and was titled *Diana of the Crossways*. The novels provide interesting examples of the working out of Meredith's theories centered in the Comic Spirit, and they demonstrate some degree of the use of Zoroastrian imagery. *Beauchamp's Career* employs the Zoroastrian contrast of light and dark to a much greater extent than the other two novels. Meredith draws from Zoroastrianism to a noticeable degree, however, in each of these three novels in order to make the instructive character of his Comic Spirit more emphatic.

BEAUCHAMP'S CAREER

Meredith makes repeated references to fire, sun, and light throughout *Beauchamp's Career*, which undoubtedly reflects his prior use of Zoroastrianism in *The Ordeal of Richard Feverel*. Meredith's dependence upon Zoroastrianism is most pronounced, however, in his characterization of Dr. Shrapnel. Nevil Beauchamp is ambitious and wants to be a politician; he plans to exercise his philanthropic desire to "save the world." He joins a radical political party in order to battle the more conservative Tory Party and to oppose the vehement objections of his Uncle Everard Romfrey, a hater of radicals. After Nevil loses an election for a seat in Parliament, he comes under the tutelage of Dr. Shrapnel, a professed Fire-worshipper.

As "Fire-worshippers" is a name that Zoroastrians were often mistakenly called, when Dr. Shrapnel testifies, "I am a Fire-worshipper," the reader perceives already an element of Meredith's comedy. Dr. Shrapnel, whose name calls to mind a number of images, all of which indicate either potential destruction or active destruction, has obviously become enamored of the mystic, esoteric nature of the religion and hence has adopted certain of its tenets to his own philosophy. Basically Shrapnel's personal doctrine is, in his own words: "That is our republic: each one to his work; all in union! There's the motto for us! *Then* you have music, harmony, the highest, fullest, finest!"

Admittedly, Shrapnel's philosophy is good, or superior in its idealism, and it represents a direct restatement of Meredith's own philosophy (expressed in many of his poems). At this point in the novel, however, the philosophy is stated by an extremist; hence, there is a touch of the comic, which becomes more apparent as the novel progresses. Meredith's infrequent use of the exclamation point and his almost negative use of italics make this particular passage stand out as the radical view of an extremist.

Rosamund Culling, the future wife of Nevil's uncle, thinks of Shrapnel as "a black malignant . . . with his . . . talk of flying to the sun." As may be expected from Rosamund's tone, Dr. Shrapnel has at some time in her company been overzealous in the expression of his republican sentiments. News of Dr. Shrapnel's inflammatory radicalism soon reaches Nevil's Uncle Romfrey, who proceeds to horsewhip Shrapnel to the point of severe injury. Lack of understanding by his fellowman appears to be Shrapnel's failing and provides the occasion for comment from the Comic Spirit, who judges that Shrapnel must suffer for his intemperance, for his imbalance. Compromise should be humankind's objective.

Both in *The Egoist* and in *Diana of the Crossways*, the part played by Zoroastrian imagery is greatly reduced from that it played in *The Ordeal of Richard Feverel* and *Beauchamp's Career*. Meredith's Comic Spirit, however, comes to the front in full array; the increased subordination of Zoroastrian imagery to Meredith's portrayal of his Comic Spirit indicates that Meredith's theories and understanding of the purpose of his literary art were expanding and maturing. In the later novels, Meredith's Zoroastrian and classical images become frequently and inseparably fused, a combination that further exemplifies Meredith's artistry and more significantly indicates that Meredith's philosophy was progressively becoming more distinct. His thinking was beginning to become a cultivated doctrine.

The Egoist

The Egoist characterizes the egocentric element in Meredith's theory of high comedy. Sir Willoughby Patterne, who thinks himself the epitome of goodness and excellence in the world, surrounds himself with admirers and sycophants who satisfy his compulsion to be adored. In creating Patterne, Meredith has taken the next logical step from his production of Beauchamp. Patterne does not merely aspire to goodness and excellence; he actually believes himself to be the embodiment of these qualities.

Patterne attempts to satisfy his ego chiefly by involving himself with three women whom he manipulates with promises of marriage. His first "pretender," Constance Durham, sees through Patterne's facade of greatness with some degree of alacrity and leaves him. The lovely Clara Middleton, however, is not so insightful. She experiences a great deal of emotional turmoil, first in ascertaining the truth of Patterne's pose and then in distinguishing the light of "her sun" from that of Patterne's less self-assured cousin, Vernon Whitford, "a Phoebus Apollo turned Fasting Friar."

Here, Meredith gives more attention to extravagances so that he may better reveal the necessity for the corrective influence of his Comic Spirit. Sir Willoughby Patterne burns; he does not merely reflect. His fire is the product of his own egotism, which burns with an outer brilliance but promises no inner flame. Meredith may well be recalling satirically the Western world's traditional misconception of the importance of fire to the Zoroastrians, who do not worship fire for itself but only as a symbol of the light of the inner spirit.

The character of Vernon presents a striking contrast to that of Patterne. His light is the light of Apollo, who is not only the Greek god of poetry but also the classical god of the sun. Meredith has fused classical allusion with the Zoroastrian importance placed upon fire. Vernon's flame is one of inner strength, for he burns with the light of poetic truth as well as with physical fire. He is also a Fasting Friar, however, a characteristic that raises doubt about the nature of his fire, since Meredith was not an ascetic. In effect, he has achieved in the characterization of Vernon the moderation that Dr. Shrapnel's explosive goals denied him, since Vernon's flame is tempered with some degree of asceticism. Vernon has measured life for what it is, but he has not given up the light of hope for what life can become. Meredith has achieved in his image of the contrast of the two fires the blending of Zoroastrian, classical, and Christian elements.

Laetitia Dale, the third of Patterne's "adorers," presents an interesting foil to Patterne's character. At the beginning of the novel, she is described as a delicate, misled woman, a "soft cherishable Parsee." The Zoroastrian connection is obvious: The Parsees are a modern sect of the Zoroastrians. Indeed, within Meredith's comic framework, Laetitia worships "her sun" much as the Parsees were reputed to worship a "god of fire."

Laetitia gradually becomes a strong, practical Parsee, however, as she, like the other two women in Patterne's egotistic design, begins to see that the source of Patterne's fire is not from within. Patterne is left in the end with Laetitia and is forced to accept her on her own terms. No reader of *The Egoist* can claim its conclusion as romantic or condemn it as pessimistic; rather, Meredith has achieved a noble expression of the corrective power of his Comic Spirit.

DIANA OF THE CROSSWAYS

Meredith creates in *Diana of the Crossways* a character who faces decisions similar to those of the women in *The Egoist*. Even Diana's superior wit and intellect do not prevent her from battling the forces of darkness. Meredith prepares the reader for Diana's struggle in the introductory chapter of the novel. He develops a light image, "rose pink," which "is rebuked by hideous revelations of filthy foul," a likeness of darkness. Meredith opens this novel with a discussion of the same subject he had treated in his other novels. For man to think himself already a part of the celestial light at his present step on the evolutionary ladder is surreptitious folly. The future holds for him only "hideous revelations of filthy foul." The narrator further asserts that it is not within the capacity of man to suppress completely the evil forces of darkness. The duality of good and evil inevitably creeps into life.

Having established an atmosphere of foreboding, the narrator sets out to explore Diana's mental processes. Diana quickly becomes disillusioned by a mismatched marriage. Her husband, Warwick, is a man of limited intelligence. As a consequence, Diana becomes drawn to ideas outside the rigid, Victorian system of mores. Her desires strongly urge her to take leave of her witless, insensitive husband, who has accused her of infidelity. She experiences a night of conflict in which she fights like "the Diana of the pride in her power of fencing with evil."

Meredith's presentation of the strife between good and evil by his mixing of classical mythology with overtones of the Zoroastrian duality creates a sense of the universal nature of Diana's struggle. Diana must decide whether to remain loyal to her marriage vows or to strike out on her own and obey her inner compulsions. She finds the impetus for her escape in Dacier, a character who is associated with devil imagery. Indeed, Dacier is the embodiment of Meredith's assertion that there is "an active Devil about the world."

Dacier is a lure to Diana in her desire to escape. His devilish character, however, is ironically exposed by his sanctimonious friend, Sir Lukin. Lukin declares that no man should be fooled by masks of goodness that seem to cover the bad in the world. Dacier, who presents every indication of virtuous conduct, is compared to the old Jewish Prince of Devils, Asmodeus, who spurs on appetite and uproarious activities of all sorts. Although the name Asmodeus appears in the Apocrypha, it also bears connotations to Eshina-Dewa, a wicked spirit of ancient Persian mythology. This is one of Meredith's clearest fusions of Zoroastrianism with Christianity.

Dacier is thwarted in his evil intentions to seduce Diana. An acceptable guide appears for Diana in Thomas Redworth, a character capable of controlling Diana's energetic impulses. Dacier does obtain a prize, however, in the lovely but naïve Constance Asper. Constance is "all for symbols, harps, effigies, what not" and believes that brains in women are "devilish." Constance is perhaps the ideal mate for *The Egoist*'s Sir Willoughby Patterne, and she presents no problems for Dacier's devious motivations. Constance, along with Dr. Shrapnel and Patterne, has failed to see the smoke for the fire. All three are so enamored of the physical brilliance of the flames that they cannot see the subtle glow of spiritual truth within the heart of the blaze.

In *Diana of the Crossways*, Meredith suggests that the endurance of life is perhaps more replete with task than with play. The individual is forced to make a distinction between good and bad, which life seldom presents in a clear-cut fashion. Constance and Dacier somewhat ironically indulge each other in their ostensibly opposing forces. The subtle comment of the Comic Spirit is that both approach life with attitudes of excess; hence, both have lost contact with the steady movement toward self-improvement. Diana and Redworth offer hope to the reader, however, because they have accepted the moderation that the Comic Spirit has taught them and that is necessary for the future success of the human spirit.

These novels present Meredith's concern with the inevitability of "The Magian Conflict" in the life of each man. They also present Meredith's keen observation that this conflict is never one from which one emerges successfully with ease. The struggle makes man's attempt to choose an acceptable path—a way that is acceptable both to him and to his society—extremely difficult. The conflict is presented in terms of Zoroastrian, Christian, and classical myth; Meredith borrows from each in order to make his presentation of this undeniable, unavoidable battle assume universal dimensions. Meredith's Comic Spirit attempts to aid man in his struggle, but it is not always successful in exposing man's shortcomings, excesses, and refusal to see himself in a true light. In the fullest meaning of Meredith's doctrine, however, the individual is also instrumental in the greater, universal struggle of humankind to move up the evolutionary ladder.

Meredith demonstrates in his attitude toward humankind and nature the belief that humans can achieve their evolutionary destiny by conforming to the lessons and demands of nature. His philosophy is universal in scope and implies a comprehensive fusion of nearly all the ethical ideals that people have gathered from the beginning of time. Although Meredith does not discard all the dogma or the moral ideals of the many religious philosophies he studied, he does select with careful scrutiny those elements that he feels contribute to his own doctrines. Indeed, he demonstrates that he is vitally affected by all the religious thought known to him.

John C. Shields

OTHER MAJOR WORKS

SHORT FICTION: *The Case of General Ople and Lady Camper*, 1890; *The Tale of Chloe*, 1890.

PLAYS: *Bertram: Or, The Castle of St. Aldobrand*, pr., pb. 1816; *Manuel*, pb. 1817; *Fredolfo*, pb. 1819.

POETRY: *Poems*, 1851; *Modern Love and Poems of the English Roadside*, 1862; *Poems and Lyrics of the Joy of Earth*, 1883; *Ballads and Poems of Tragic Life*, 1887; *A Reading of Earth*, 1888; *Poems: The Empty Purse*, 1892; *Odes in Contribution to the Song of French History*, 1898; *A Reading of Life, with Other Poems*, 1901; *Last Poems*, 1909; *The Poetical Works of George Meredith*, 1912 (3 volumes); *The Poems of George Meredith*, 1978 (2 volumes; Phyllis B. Bartlett, editor).

NONFICTION: *On the Idea of Comedy and of the Uses of the Comic Spirit*, 1877; *The Letters of George Meredith*, 1970 (3 volumes; C. L. Cline, editor).

BIBLIOGRAPHY

Beer, Gillian. *Meredith: A Change of Masks*. London: Athlone Press, 1970. Beer attempts one of the first modern appraisals of Meredith's art, seeing him as a novelist anticipating twentieth century concerns and techniques, as well as questioning Victorian certitudes. Includes an index.

Fraser, Robert. "Nineteenth-Century Adventure and Fantasy: James Morier, George Meredith, Lewis Carroll, and Robert Louis Stevenson." In *A Companion to Romance: From Classical to Contemporary*, edited by Corinne Saunders. Malden, Mass.: Blackwell, 2004. Fraser's essay about Meredith and three other British writers is included in this study of romance literature, which charts the genre from its beginnings through the twenty-first century.

Harris, Margaret. "George Meredith at the Crossways." In *A Companion to the Victorian Novel*, edited by William Baker and Kenneth Womack. Westport, Conn.: Greenwood Press, 2002. An introductory overview of the Victorian novel. Contains essays about Meredith and other authors and discussions of the historical and social context of the Victorian novel, the growth of serialization, and the different genres of Victorian fiction.

Jones, Mervyn. *The Amazing Victorian: A Life of George Meredith*. London: Constable, 1999. Jones's biography aims to recover Meredith from obscurity and introduce the author to a new generation of readers. He links Meredith life to his writing and includes a forty-page appendix recounting the plot summaries of all of Meredith's novels.

Muendel, Renate. *George Meredith*. Boston: Twayne, 1986. Chapters on Meredith's poetry, his early fiction, his novels of the 1870's and 1880's, and his last novels. A beginning chapter provides a brief biography. Includes a chronology, notes, and an annotated bibliography.

Roberts, Neil. *Meredith and the Novel*. New York: St. Martin's Press, 1997. Roberts employs twentieth century literary criticism, especially the ideas of literary critic Mikhail Bakhtin, to analyze all of Meredith's novels. Includes bibliographical references and an index.

Shaheen, Mohammad. *George Meredith: A Re-Appraisal of the Novels*. Totowa, N.J.: Barnes & Noble Books, 1981. Shaheen suggests that traditional Meredith criticism has viewed his fiction too much in the light of *The Egoist*. He concentrates on

Meredith's other major works as more representative of the author's true independent mind and specifically explores how character expresses theme for Meredith. Contains a bibliography.

Stevenson, Richard C. *The Experimental Impulse in George Meredith's Fiction.* Lewisburg, Pa.: Bucknell University Press, 2004. Stevenson focuses on the novels he considers most representative of Meredith's experimental fiction—*The Ordeal of Richard Feverel, The Adventures of Harry Richmond, The Egoist, One of Our Conquerors, Lord Ormont and His Aminta*, and *The Amazing Marriage.* He demonstrates how these books feature controversial contemporary themes, innovative narrative structures, representations of human consciousness, and other unconventional elements.

Tague, Gregory. *Ethos and Behavior: The English Novel from Jane Austen to Henry James (including George Meredith, W. M. Thackeray, George Eliot, and Thomas Hardy).* Bethesda, Md.: Academica Press, 2008. *The Ordeal of Richard Feverel* and *The Egoist* are among the novels Tague analyzes in his examination of English didactic literature. His study includes a discussion of the ethical aspects of these novels and the conduct of their fictional characters.

Williams, Ioan, ed. *Meredith: The Critical Heritage.* London: Routledge & Kegan Paul, 1971. A collection of reviews and essays showing the critical reception of Meredith's work from 1851 through 1911. Contains indexes of his work, periodicals, and newspapers.

JEAN RHYS

Ella Gwendolen Rees Williams

Born: Roseau, Dominica Island, West Indies; August 24, 1894
Died: Exeter, England; May 14, 1979
Also known as: Ella Gwendolen Rees Williams

PRINCIPAL LONG FICTION

Postures, 1928 (also known as *Quartet*, 1929)
After Leaving Mr. Mackenzie, 1930
Voyage in the Dark, 1934
Good Morning, Midnight, 1939
Wide Sargasso Sea, 1966

OTHER LITERARY FORMS

Although Jean Rhys (rees) is now remembered primarily for her novels, her first published book was a collection of short stories, *The Left Bank, and Other Stories* (1927). As Ford Madox Ford points out in the preface to the collection, Rhys's heroines are geographically, psychologically, and emotionally of "the Left Bank," not only of Paris—although Rhys captured the Paris of the 1920's as well as anyone—but also of all of the cities of the world. They are underdogs, alone, betrayed, on the edge of poverty; they are women in a man's world.

In addition to *The Left Bank*, Rhys published two other collections of stories: *Tigers Are Better-Looking* (1968) and *Sleep It Off, Lady* (1976). In 1987, *The Collected Short Stories* brought together her work in this genre. At her death, she left an essentially completed first section of an autobiography with Diana Athill, who had edited *Wide Sargasso Sea* and *Sleep It Off, Lady*. Athill published this section and a less complete second section as *Smile Please: An Unfinished Autobiography* in 1979. A collection of Rhys's letters was published in 1984.

ACHIEVEMENTS

When *Wide Sargasso Sea*, her last novel, was published, Jean Rhys was described in *The New York Times* as the greatest living novelist. Such praise is overstated, but Rhys's fiction, long overlooked by academic critics, began in the late twentieth century to undergo a revival, spurred by feminist studies. Rhys played a noteworthy role in the French Left Bank literary scene in the 1920's, and between 1927 and 1939, she published four substantial novels and a number of jewel-like short stories. Although she owes her current reputation in large measure to the rising interest in female writers and feminist themes, her work belongs more properly with the masters of literary impressionism: Joseph Conrad, Ford Madox Ford, Marcel Proust, and James Joyce. She began to publish her writing under the encouragement of her intimate friend Ford Madox Ford, and she continued to write in spite of falling out of favor with his circle. As prizes and honors came to her in her old age after the publication of *Wide Sargasso Sea*, it must have given her grim satisfaction to realize that she had attained entirely by her own efforts a position as a writer at least equal to that of her erstwhile friends.

BIOGRAPHY

Jean Rhys was born Ella Gwendolen Rees Williams in the West Indies on the island of Dominica in 1894, the daughter of a Welsh father and a part-Creole mother. English society classified her as "colored." Her childhood associates were often Creole, and she was surrounded by ideas peculiar to their culture, such as voodoo and witchcraft. At the same time, she attended a convent school and seriously considered the life of a nun. The colonial mentality was strong in Dominica, and the "proper" role for a well-bred young woman was sharply defined: passive, obedient, submissive.

In 1910, Rhys left Dominica and went to live in Cambridge, England, with her aunt, Clarice Rhys Williams. After a short term in a local school, she enrolled in the Royal Academy of Dramatic Art in London. Her father died soon after she arrived in England, and she found herself short of money. The transition from the West Indies to England must have been extremely painful for the sixteen-year-old girl: the climate harsh, the people cold, the social and economic situation threatening. Those who knew her as a young woman testified that she was strikingly beautiful. After a term at the Royal Academy of Dramatic Art, she toured as a minor actor or chorus girl with provincial theater troupes and did modeling. A young woman alone under these circumstances would have seen at first hand how male dominance and financial control in British society combined to exploit the female. Many of Rhys's stories and novels reflect scenes from her career on the stage, and most of them hinge on the theme of male exploitation of women through financial domination.

Near the end of World War I, Rhys married Jean Lenglet (alias Edouard de Neve), an adventurer who had served in the French Foreign Legion and who was probably employed by the French secret service during the war. The newlywed couple lived in Paris, constantly moving from one cheap hotel to another, although de Neve secured temporarily a position with the international mission administering Vienna. A son was born to them in 1919, but he lived only three weeks. A daughter born in 1922 lived but required special medical care.

Rhys tried to earn a living in Paris by modeling and writing. Pearl Adam, the wife of a correspondent for *The Times* of Paris, took an interest in some of Rhys's sketches and introduced her to Ford Madox Ford, then editor of *The Transatlantic Review*. Through him, she entered into the expatriate community of the early 1920's, meeting James Joyce, Ernest Hemingway, and other prominent writers. Shortly after Rhys met Ford in the autumn of 1924, her husband was sent to prison for illegal dealing in antiques. Ford was living at the time with the artist Stella Bowen. Rhys, penniless, moved in with them and soon formed an intimate relationship with Ford. A casual episode in Ford's generally messy life was something much more serious for the young woman; Rhys treats this affair in her first novel, *Quartet*. De Neve never forgave Rhys for her involvement with Ford.

After her divorce from de Neve, Rhys became closely involved with a literary agent, Leslie Tilden Smith. They were eventually married and lived together until his death in 1945. Subsequently, Rhys married her late husband's cousin, Max Hamer, who later served time in prison for mismanagement of his firm's funds. Throughout the 1940's and 1950's, Rhys suffered greatly from poverty, poor health, and family problems. Her books were all out of print. She was not, however, entirely forgotten. The actor Selma Vaz Diaz adapted a dramatic monologue from *Good Morning, Midnight* for stage use in 1949, and eight years later, the British Broadcasting Corporation's third program presented the monologue, which received excellent notices. The publication of *Wide Sargasso Sea* in 1966 and the rapid growth of feminist studies led to a Rhys revival, and the reprinting of all her works followed. Rhys died in May, 1979, in Exeter, England.

Analysis

Jean Rhys's first novel, *Quartet*, reflects closely her misadventures with Ford Madox Ford. The heroine, Marya Zelli, whose husband is in prison, moves in with the rich and respectable Hugh and Lois Heidler. Hugh becomes Marya's lover, while Lois punishes her with petty cruelties. The central figure is a woman alone, penniless, exploited, and an outsider. In her next novel, *After Leaving Mr. Mackenzie*, the central figure, Julia Martin, breaks off with her rich lover, Mr. Mackenzie, and finds herself financially desperate. *Voyage in the Dark* tells the story of Anna Morgan, who arrives in England from the West Indies as an innocent young girl, has her first affair as a chorus girl, and descends through a series of shorter and shorter affairs to working for a masseuse. In *Good Morning, Midnight*, the alcoholic Sasha Jensen, penniless in Paris, remembers episodes from her past that have brought her to this sorry pass.

All four of these novels show a female character subject to financial, sexual, and social domination by men and "respectable" society. In all cases, the heroine is passive, but "sentimental." The reader is interested in her feelings rather than in her ideas and accomplishments. She is alienated economically from any opportunity to do meaningful and justly rewarding work. She is an alien socially, either from a foreign and despised colonial culture or from a marginally respectable social background. She is literally an alien or foreigner in Paris and London, which are cities of dreadful night for her. What the characters fear most is the final crushing alienation from their true identities, the reduction to some model or type imagined by a foreign man. They all face the choice of becoming someone's gamine, *garçonne*, or femme fatale, or of starving to death, and they all struggle against this loss of personal identity. After a silence of more than twenty years, Rhys returned to these same concerns in her masterpiece, *Wide Sargasso Sea*. While the four early novels are to a large degree autobiographical, *Wide Sargasso Sea* has a more literary origin, although it, too, reflects details from the author's personal life.

WIDE SARGASSO SEA

Wide Sargasso Sea requires of the reader a familiarity with Charlotte Brontë's *Jane Eyre* (1847). In Brontë's novel, Jane is prevented from marrying Rochester by the presence of a madwoman in the attic, his insane West Indian wife, who finally perishes in a fire that she sets, burning Rochester's house and blinding him, but clearing the way for Jane to wed him. The madwoman in *Jane Eyre* is depicted entirely from the exterior. It is natural that the mad West Indian wife, when seen only through the eyes of her English rival and of Rochester, appears completely hideous and depraved. Indeed, when Jane first sees the madwoman in chapter 16 of the novel, she cannot tell whether it is a beast or a human being groveling on all fours. Like a hyena with bloated features, the madwoman attacks Rochester in this episode.

Wide Sargasso Sea is a sympathetic account of the life of Rochester's mad wife, ranging from her childhood in the West Indies, her Creole and Catholic background, and her courtship and married years with the deceitful Rochester to her final descent into madness and captivity in England. Clearly, the predicament of the West Indian wife resembles that of Rhys herself in many ways. In order to present the alien wife's case, Rhys writes a "countertext," an extension of Brontë's novel that fills in the "missing" testimony, the issues over which Brontë glosses.

Wide Sargasso Sea consists of two parts. Part 1 is narrated by the girl growing up in Jamaica who is destined to become Rochester's wife. The Emancipation Act has just been passed (the year of that imperial edict was 1833), and the blacks on the island are passing through a period of so-called apprenticeship that should lead to their complete freedom in 1837. This is a period of racial tension and anxiety for the privileged colonial community. Fear of black violence runs high, and no one knows exactly what will happen to the landholders once the blacks are emancipated. The girlish narrator lives in the interface between the privileged white colonists and the blacks. Although a child of landowners, she is impoverished, clinging to European notions of respectability, and in constant fear. She lives on the crumbling estate of her widowed mother. Her closest associate is Christophine, a Martinique *obeah* woman, or Voodoo witch. When her mother marries Mr. Mason, the family's lot improves temporarily, until the blacks revolt, burning their country home, Coulibri, and killing her half-witted brother. She then attends a repressive Catholic school in town, where her kindly colored "cousin" Sandi protects her from more hostile blacks.

Part 2 is narrated by the young Rochester on his honeymoon with his bride at her country home. Wherever appropriate, Rhys follows the details of Brontë's story. Rochester reveals that his marriage is merely a financial arrangement. After an uneasy period of passion, Rochester's feelings for his bride begin to cool. He receives a letter of denunciation accusing her of misbehavior with Sandi and revealing that madness runs in the family. To counter Rochester's growing hostility, the young bride goes to her former companion, the *obeah* woman Christophine, for a love potion. The nature of the potion is that it can work for one night only. Nevertheless, she administers it to her husband. His love now dead, she is torn from her native land, transported to a cruel and loveless England, and maddeningly confined. Finally, she takes candle in hand to burn down Rochester's house in suicidal destruction.

In Brontë's novel, the character of the mad wife is strangely blank, a vacant slot in the story. Her presence is essential, and she must be fearfully hateful, so that Jane Eyre has no qualms about taking her place in Rochester's arms, but the novel tells the reader almost nothing else about her. Rhys fills in this blank, fleshing out the character, making her live on a par with Jane herself. After all, Brontë tells the reader a great deal about Jane's painful childhood and education; why should Rhys not supply the equivalent information about her dark rival?

It is not unprecedented for a writer to develop a fiction from another writer's work. For example, T. H. White's *Mistress Masham's Repose* (1946) imagines that some of Jonathan Swift's Lilliputians were transported to England, escaped captivity, and established a thriving colony in an abandoned English garden, where they are discovered by an English schoolgirl. Her intrusion into their world is a paradigm of British colonial paternalism, finally overcome by the intelligence and good feeling of the girl. This charming story depends on Swift's fiction, but the relationship of White's work to Swift's is completely different from the relationship of Rhys's work to Brontë's. Rhys's fiction permanently alters one's understanding of *Jane Eyre*. Approaching Brontë's work after Rhys's, one is compelled to ask such questions as, Why is Jane so uncritical of Rochester? How is Jane herself like the madwoman in the attic? Rhys's fiction reaches into the past and alters Brontë's novel.

Rhys's approach in *Wide Sargasso Sea* was also influenced by Ford Madox Ford and, through Ford, Joseph Conrad. In the autumn of 1924, when Rhys first met Ford, he was writing *Joseph Conrad: A Personal Remembrance*, which was published later that year. Some thirty years earlier, when Conrad was just beginning his career as a writer, his agent had introduced him to Ford in hopes that they could work in collaboration, since Conrad wrote in English (a language he had adopted only as an adult) with great labor. Ford and Conrad produced *The Inheritors* (1901) and *Romance* (1903) as coauthors. During their years of association, Ford had some hand in the production of several works usually considered Conrad's sole effort, although it has never been clear to what degree Ford participated in the creation of the fiction of Conrad's middle period.

About 1909, after Ford's disreputable ways had become increasingly offensive to Conrad's wife, the two men parted ways. Immediately after Conrad's death in 1924, however, Ford rushed into print his memoir of the famous author. His memoir of Conrad is fictionalized and hardly to be trusted as an account of their association in the 1890's, but it sheds a great deal of light on what Ford thought about writing fiction in 1924, when he was beginning his powerful Tietjens tetralogy and working for the first time with Rhys. Ford claimed that he and Conrad invented literary impressionism in English. Impressionist fiction characteristically employs limited and unreliable narration, follows a flow of associated ideas leaping freely in time and space, aims to render the impression of a scene vividly so as to make readers see it as if it were before their eyes, and artfully selects and juxtaposes seemingly unrelated scenes and episodes so that readers must construct the connections and relationships that make the story intelligible. These are the stylistic features of Rhys's fiction as well as of Ford's *The Good Soldier* (1915), Conrad's *Heart of Darkness* (1902), Henry James's *The Turn of the Screw* (1898), and Joyce's *Ulysses* (1922).

An "affair"—the mainspring of the plot in an impressionist novel—is some shocking or puzzling event that has already occurred when the story begins. The reader knows what has happened but does not understand fully why and how it happened. The story proceeds in concentric rings of growing complication as the reader finds something that appeared at first to be clear-cut becoming more and more intricate. In Conrad's *Lord Jim* (1900), the affair is the scandalous abandonment of the pilgrim ship by the English sailor. In *The Good Soldier*, it is the breakup of the central foursome, whose full infidelity and betrayal are revealed only gradually. Brontë's *Jane Eyre* provided Rhys with an impressionist "affair" in the scene in which the mad West Indian wife burns Rochester's house, blinding him and killing herself. Like Conrad's Marlow, the storyteller who sits on the veranda mulling over Jim's curious behavior, or *The Good Soldier*'s narrator Dowell musing about the strange behavior of Edward Ashburnham, Rhys takes up the affair of Rochester and reworks it into ever richer complications, making the initial judgments in *Jane Eyre* seem childishly oversimplified. "How can Jane simply register relief that the madwoman is burned out of her way? There must be more to the affair than that," the secondary fiction suggests.

One of the most important features of literary impressionism is the highly constructive activity that it demands of the reader. In a pointillist painting, small dots of primary colors are set side by side. At a certain distance from the canvas, these merge on the retina of the eye of the viewer into colors and shapes that are not, in fact, drawn on the canvas at all. The painting is constructed in the eyes of each viewer with greater luminosity than it would have were it drawn explicitly. In order to create such a shimmering haze in fiction, Ford advises the use of a limited point of view, which gives the reader dislocated fragments of remembered experience. The reader must struggle constantly to fit these fragments into a coherent pattern. The tools for creating such a verbal collage are limited, "unreliable" narration, psychological time shifts, and juxtaposition. Ford observes that two apparently unrelated events can be set side by side so that the reader will perceive their connection with far greater impact than if the author had stated such a connection openly. Ford advises the impressionist author to create a verbal collage by unexpected selection and juxtaposition, and *Wide Sargasso Sea* makes such juxtapositions on several levels. On the largest scale, *Wide Sargasso Sea* is juxtaposed with *Jane Eyre*, so that the two novels read together mean much more than when they are read independently. This increase of significance is what Ford called the "unearned increment" in impressionist art. Within *Wide Sargasso Sea*, part 1 (narrated by the West Indian bride) and part 2 (narrated by Rochester) likewise mean more in juxtaposition than when considered separately. Throughout the text, the flow of consciousness of the storytellers cunningly shifts in time to juxtapose details that mean more together than they would in isolation.

Because *Wide Sargasso Sea* demands a highly constructive reader, it is, like *The Good Soldier* or *Heart of Darkness*, an open fiction. When the reader completes *Jane Eyre*, the mystery of Rochester's house has been revealed and purged, the madwoman in the attic has been burned out, and Jane will live, the reader imagines, happily ever after. *Jane Eyre* taken in isolation is a closed fiction. Reading *Wide Sargasso Sea* in juxtaposition to *Jane Eyre*, however, opens the latter and poses questions that are more difficult to resolve: Is Jane likely to be the next woman in the attic? Why is a disabled man a gratifying mate for Jane? At what price is her felicity purchased?

The doppelgänger, twin, or shadow character runs throughout Rhys's fiction. All of her characters seem to be split personalities. There is a public role, that of the approved "good girl," that each is expected to play, and there is the repressed, rebellious "bad girl" lurking inside. If the bad girl can be hidden, the character is rewarded with money, love, and social position. The bad girl will sometimes put in an appearance, however, when the character drinks too much or gets excited or angry. When the dark girl appears, punishment follows, swift and sure. This is the case with Marya Zelli in *Quartet*, Julia Martin in *After Leaving Mr. Mackenzie*, Anna Morgan in *Voyage in the Dark*, and Sasha Jensen in *Good Morning, Midnight*. It is also the case in Brontë's *Jane Eyre*. The education of Jane Eyre consists of her learning to repress those dark, selfish impulses that Victorian society maintained "good little girls" should never feel. Jane succeeds in stamping out her "bad" self through a stiff British education, discipline, and self-control. She kills her repressed identity, conforms to society's expectations, and gets her reward—a crippled husband and a burned-out house. Rhys revives the dark twin, shut up in the attic, the naughty, wild, dark, selfish, bestial female. She suggests that the struggle between repressed politeness and unrepressed self-interest is an ongoing process in which total repression means the death of a woman's identity.

Todd K. Bender

OTHER MAJOR WORKS

SHORT FICTION: *The Left Bank, and Other Stories*, 1927; *Tigers Are Better-Looking*, 1968; *Sleep It Off, Lady*, 1976; *The Collected Short Stories*, 1987.

NONFICTION: *Smile Please: An Unfinished Autobiography*, 1979; *The Letters of Jean Rhys*, 1984 (also known as *Jean Rhys: Letters, 1931-1966*).

BIBLIOGRAPHY

Angier, Carole. *Jean Rhys*. New York: Viking Press, 1985. Biography treats Rhys's fiction as essentially autobiographical. Far from viewing the author as a feminist, Angier presents Rhys as an intensely lonely individualist and solipsist without a program or external loyalties. Depicts her lifelong attempt to understand herself as being governed by a tragic and pessimistic view of human nature and the world.

_______. *Jean Rhys: Life and Work*. Boston: Little, Brown, 1990. Major work of Rhys scholarship combines detailed biographical study with sections devoted to interpretations of the novels. Includes voluminous notes and an extensive bibliography.

Davidson, Arnold E. *Jean Rhys*. New York: Frederick Ungar, 1985. Draws heavily on a number of critical sources to support a feminist interpretation of Rhys's fiction and provides a useful approach to the major works. Includes bibliography and index.

Dell'Amico, Carol. *Colonialism and the Modernist Movement in the Early Novels of Jean Rhys*. New York: Routledge, 2005. Describes how Rhys's novels published before *Wide Sargasso Sea*, or the so-called European texts, address issues of colonialism and imperialism. Argues that Rhys viewed imperialism as a condition of homelessness for both the colonized and the urban colonizers.

James, Louis. *Jean Rhys*. London: Longman, 1978. Focuses primarily on *Wide Sargasso Sea* but also provides an informative short introduction to Rhys's life and the full range of her work. Includes bibliography.

Lonsdale, Thorunn. "Literary Allusion in the Fiction of Jean Rhys." In *Caribbean Women Writers*, edited by Mary Condé and Thorunn Lonsdale. New York: St. Martin's Press, 1999. Focuses on the many critically neglected intertextual references to nineteenth and twentieth century European and American literature in Rhys's novels and short stories.

Maurel, Sylvie. *Jean Rhys*. New York: St. Martin's Press, 1998. Examines Rhys's writings from the perspectives of feminist criticism and literary theory while providing close readings of the texts and of their language. Includes bibliography and index.

Savory, Elaine. *Jean Rhys*. New York: Cambridge University Press, 1998. Presents critical readings of all of Rhys's works, drawing on previously unpublished sources. Argues that Rhys's writings should be approached from a Caribbean perspective and discusses Rhys's representation of race, gender, social class, and nationality.

Simpson, Anne B. *Territories of the Psyche: The Fiction of Jean Rhys*. New York: Palgrave Macmillan, 2005. Offers a psychoanalytic reading of Rhys's novels and short stories, describing how these works explore the dynamics of the human psyche. Includes bibliography and index.

Thomas, Sue. *The Worlding of Jean Rhys*. Westport, Conn.: Greenwood Press, 1999. Views Rhys's works as "Dominican autoethnography" and emphasizes how Rhys's Creole background is reflected in her writings. Includes analyses of all five novels.

VIRGINIA WOOLF

Born: London, England; January 25, 1882
Died: The River Ouse, near Rodmell, Sussex, England; March 28, 1941
Also known as: Adeline Virginia Stephen

Principal long fiction

The Voyage Out, 1915
Night and Day, 1919
Jacob's Room, 1922
Mrs. Dalloway, 1925
To the Lighthouse, 1927
Orlando: A Biography, 1928
The Waves, 1931
Flush: A Biography, 1933
The Years, 1937
Between the Acts, 1941
Melymbrosia, 1982 (wr. 1912; revised 2002)

Other literary forms

To say that Virginia Woolf lived to write is no exaggeration. Her output was both prodigious and varied; counting her posthumously published works, it fills more than forty volumes. Beyond her novels, her fiction encompasses several short-story collections. As a writer of nonfiction, Woolf was similarly prolific, her book-length works including *Roger Fry: A Biography* (1940) and two influential feminist statements, *A Room of One's Own* (1929) and *Three Guineas* (1938). Throughout her life, Woolf also produced criticism and reviews; the best-known collections are *The Common Reader: First Series* (1925) and *The Common Reader: Second Series* (1932). In 1966 and 1967, the four volumes of *Collected Essays* were published. Additional books of essays, reviews, and sketches continue to appear, most notably the illuminating selection of autobiographical materials, *Moments of Being* (1976). Her letters—3,800 of them survive—are available in six volumes; when publication was completed, her diaries stood at five. Another collection, of Woolf's essays, also proved a massive, multivolume undertaking.

Achievements

From the appearance of her first novel in 1915, Virginia Woolf's work was received with respect—an important point, since she was extremely sensitive to criticism. Descendant of a distinguished literary family, member of the avant-garde Bloomsbury Group, herself an experienced critic and reviewer, she was taken seriously as an artist. Nevertheless, her early works were not financially successful; she was forty before she earned a living from her writing. From the start, the rather narrow territory of her novels precluded broad popularity, peopled as they were with sophisticated, sexually reserved, upper-middle-class characters, finely attuned to their sensibilities and relatively insulated from the demands of mundane existence. When in *Jacob's Room* she first abandoned the conventional novel to experiment with the interior monologues and lyrical poetic devices that characterize her mature method, she also began to develop a reputation as a "difficult" or "highbrow" writer, though undeniably an important one. Not until the brilliant fantasy *Orlando* was published did she enjoy a definite commercial success. Thereafter, she received both critical and popular acclaim; *The Years* was even a bona fide best seller.

During the 1930's, Woolf became the subject of critical essays and two book-length studies; some of her works were translated into French. At the same time, however, her novels began to be judged as irrelevant to a world beset by growing economic and political chaos. At her death in 1941, she was widely regarded as a pioneer of modernism but also reviewed by many as the effete, melancholic "invalid priestess of Bloomsbury," a stereotype her friend and fellow novelist E. M. Forster dismissed at the time as wholly inaccurate; she was, he insisted, "tough, sensitive but tough."

Over the next twenty-five years, respectful attention to Woolf's work continued, but in the late 1960's, critical interest accelerated dramatically and has remained strong. Two reasons for this renewed notice seem particularly apparent. First, Woolf's feminist essays *A Room of One's Own* and *Three Guineas* became rallying documents in the growing women's movement; readers who might not otherwise have discovered her novels were drawn to them via her nonfiction and tended to read them primarily as validations of her feminist thinking. Second, with the appearance of her husband Leonard Woolf's five-volume autobiography from 1965-1969, her nephew Quentin Bell's definitive two-volume biography of her in 1972, and the full-scale editions of her own diaries and letters commencing in the mid-1970's, Woolf's life has become one of the most thoroughly documented of any modern author. Marked by intellectual and sexual unconventionality, madness, and suicide, it is for today's readers also one of the most fascinating; the steady demand for memoirs, reminiscences, and photograph collections relating to her has generated what is sometimes disparagingly labeled "the Virginia Woolf industry." At its worst, such insatiable curiosity is morbidly voyeuristic, distracting from and trivializing Woolf's achievement; on a more responsible level, it has led to serious, provocative reevaluations of the political and especially the feminist elements in her work, as well as to redefinitions of her role as an artist.

BIOGRAPHY

Daughter of the eminent editor and critic Sir Leslie Stephen and Julia Jackson Duckworth, both of whom had been previously widowed, Virginia Woolf was born Adeline Virginia Stephen in 1882 into a solidly late Victorian intellectual and social milieu. Her father's first wife had been William Makepeace Thackeray's daughter, James

Russell Lowell was her godfather, and visitors to the Stephens' London household included Henry James, George Meredith, and Thomas Hardy. From childhood on, she had access to her father's superb library, and she benefited from her father's guidance and commentary on her rigorous, precocious reading. Nevertheless, unlike her brothers, she did not receive a formal university education, a lack she always regretted and that partly explains the anger in *Three Guineas*, in which she proposes a "university of outsiders." (Throughout her life she declined all academic honors.)

In 1895, when Woolf was thirteen, her mother, just past fifty, suddenly died. Altruistic, self-sacrificing, totally devoted to her demanding husband and large family, the beautiful Julia Stephen fulfilled the Victorian ideal of womanhood and exhausted herself doing so; her daughter would movingly eulogize her as Mrs. Ramsay in *To the Lighthouse*. The loss devastated Woolf, who experienced at that time the first of four major mental breakdowns in her life, the last of which would end in death.

Leslie Stephen, twenty years his wife's senior and thus sanguinely expecting her to pilot him comfortably through old age, was devastated in another way. Retreating histrionically into self-pitying but deeply felt grief, like that of his fictional counterpart, Mr. Ramsay, he transferred his intense demands for sympathetic attention to a succession of what could only seem to him achingly inadequate substitutes for his dead wife: first, his stepdaughter Stella Duckworth, who herself died suddenly in 1897, then, Virginia's older sister Vanessa. The traditional feminine role would eventually have befallen Virginia had Leslie Stephen not died in 1904. Writing in her 1928 diary on what would have been her father's ninety-sixth birthday, Woolf reflects that, had he lived, "his life would have entirely ended mine. . . . No writing, no books;—inconceivable."

On her father's death, Woolf sustained her second incapacitating breakdown, but she also gained, as her diary suggests, something crucial: freedom. That freedom took an immediate and, to her parents' staid friends and relatives, shocking form. Virginia, Vanessa, and their brothers Thoby and Adrian abandoned the Stephen house in respectable Kensington to set up a home in the seedy bohemian district of London known as Bloomsbury. There, on Thursday evenings, a coterie of Thoby Stephen's Cambridge University friends regularly gathered to talk in an atmosphere of free thought, avant-garde art, and sexual tolerance, forming the nucleus of what came to be called the Bloomsbury Group. At various stages in its evolution over the next decade, the group included such luminaries as biographer Lytton Strachey, novelist E. M. Forster, art critic Roger Fry, and economist John Maynard Keynes. In 1911, they were joined by another of Thoby's Cambridge friends, a colonial official just returned from seven years in Ceylon, Leonard Woolf; Virginia Stephen married him the following year. Scarcely twelve months after the wedding, Virginia Woolf's third severe breakdown began, marked by a suicide attempt; her recovery took almost two years.

The causes of Woolf's madness have been much debated and the treatment she was prescribed—bed rest, milk, withdrawal of intellectual stimulation—much disputed, especially since Woolf apparently never received psychoanalytic help, even though the Hogarth Press, founded by the Woolfs in 1917, was one of Sigmund Freud's earliest English publishers. A history of insanity ran in the Stephen family; if Virginia was afflicted with a hereditary nervous condition, it was thought, then, that must be accepted as unalterable. On the other hand, the timing of these three breakdowns prompts speculation about more subtle causes. About her parents' deaths she evidently felt strong guilt; of *To the Lighthouse*, the fictionalized account of her parents' relationship, she would later say, "I was obsessed by them both, unhealthily; and writing of them was a necessary act." Marriage was for her a deliberately sought yet disturbing commitment, representing a potential loss of autonomy and a retreat into what her would-be novelist Terence Hewet envisions in *The Voyage Out* as a walled-up, firelit room. She found her own marriage sexually disappointing, perhaps in part because she had been molested both as a child and as a young woman by her two Duckworth stepbrothers.

In the late twentieth century, feminist scholars especially argued as a cause of Woolf's madness the burden of being a greatly talented woman in a world hostile to feminine achievement, a situation Woolf strikingly depicts in *A Room of One's Own* as the plight of William Shakespeare's hypothetical sister. Indeed, the young Virginia Stephen might plunder her father's library all day, but by teatime she was expected to don the role of deferential Victorian female in a rigidly patriarchal household. Once she settled in Bloomsbury, however, she enjoyed unconventional independence and received much sympathetic encouragement of her gifts, most of all from her husband.

Leonard Woolf, himself a professional writer and literary editor, connected his wife's madness directly with her genius, saying that she concentrated more intensely on her work than any writer he had ever known. Her books passed through long, difficult gestations; her sanity was always most vulnerable immediately after a novel was finished. Expanding on his belief that the imagination in his wife's books and the delusions of her breakdowns "all came from the same place in her mind," some critics have gone so far as to claim her madness as the very source of her art, permitting her to make mystical descents into inner space from which she returned with sharpened perception.

It is significant, certainly, that although Woolf's first publication, an unsigned article for the newspaper *The Guardian*, appeared just two months after her 1904 move to Bloomsbury, her first novel, over which she labored for seven years, was only completed shortly after her marriage; her breakdown occurred three months after its acceptance for publication. Very early, therefore, Leonard Woolf learned to keep a daily record of his wife's health; throughout their life together, he would be alert for those signs of fatigue or erratic behavior that signaled approaching danger and the need for her customary rest cure. Rational, efficient, uncomplaining, Leonard Woolf has been condemned by some disaffected scholars as a pseudosaintly nurse who benignly badgered his patient into crippling dependence. The compelling argument against this extreme interpretation is Virginia Woolf's astonishing productivity after she recovered from her third illness. Although there were certainly periods of instability and near disaster, the following twenty-five years were immensely fruitful as she discarded traditional fiction to move toward realizing her unique vision, all the while functioning actively and diversely as a fine critic, too.

After Woolf's ninth novel, *The Years*, was finished in 1936, however, she came closer to mental collapse than she had been at any time since 1913. Meanwhile, a larger pattern of breakdown was developing in the world around her as World War II became inevitable. Working at her Sussex home on her last book, *Between the Acts*, she could hear the Battle of Britain being fought over her head; her London house was severely damaged in the Blitz. Strangely, however, that novel was her easiest to write; Leonard Woolf, ever watchful, was struck by her tranquillity during this period. The gradual symptoms of warning were absent this time; when her depression began, he would recall, it struck her "like a sudden blow." She began to hear voices and knew what was coming. On February 26, 1941, she finished *Between the Acts*. Four weeks later, she went out for one of her usual walks across the Sussex downs, placed a heavy stone in her pocket, and stepped into the River Ouse. Within minutes Leonard Woolf arrived at its banks to find her walking stick and hat lying there. Her body was recovered three weeks later.

ANALYSIS

In one of her most famous pronouncements on the nature of fiction—as a practicing critic, she had much to say on the subject—Virginia Woolf insists that "life is not a series of gig lamps symmetrically arranged; but a luminous halo, a semi-transparent envelope surrounding us from the beginning of consciousness to the end." In an ordinary day, she argues, "thousands of ideas" course through the human brain; "thousands of emotions" meet, collide, and disappear "in astonishing disorder." Amid this hectic interior flux, the trivial and the vital, the past and the present, are constantly interacting; there is endless tension between the multitude of ideas and emotions rushing through one's consciousness and the numerous impressions scoring on it from the external world. Thus, even personal identity becomes evanescent, continually reordering itself as "the atoms of experience . . . fall upon the mind." It follows, then, that human beings must have great difficulty communicating with one another, for of this welter of perceptions that define individual personality, only a tiny fraction can ever be externalized in word or gesture. Yet, despite—in fact, because of—their frightening isolation as unknowable entities, people yearn to unite both with one another and with some larger pattern of order hidden behind the flux, to experience time standing still momentarily, to see matches struck that briefly illuminate the darkness.

Given the complex phenomenon of human subjectivity, Woolf asks, "Is it not the task of the novelist to convey this varying, this unknown and uncircumscribed spirit . . . with as little mixture of the alien and external as possible?" The conventional novel form is plainly inadequate for such a purpose, she maintains. Dealing sequentially with a logical set of completed past actions that occur in a coherent, densely detailed physical and social environment, presided over by an omniscient narrator interpreting the significance of it all, the traditional novel trims and shapes experience into a rational but falsified pattern. "Is life like this?" Woolf demands rhetorically. "Must novels be like this?"

In Woolf's first two books, nevertheless, she attempted to work within conventional modes, discovering empirically that they could not convey her vision. Although in recent years some critics have defended *The Voyage Out* and *Night and Day* as artistically satisfying in their own right, both novels have generally been considered interesting mainly for what they foreshadow of Woolf's later preoccupations and techniques.

The Voyage Out

The Voyage Out is the story of Rachel Vinrace, a naïve and talented twenty-four-year-old amateur pianist who sails from England to a small resort on the South American coast, where she vacations with relatives. There, she meets a fledgling novelist, Terence Hewet; on a pleasure expedition up a jungle river, they declare their love. Shortly thereafter, Rachel falls ill with a fever and dies. The novel's exotic locale, large cast of minor characters, elaborate scenes of social comedy, and excessive length are all atypical of Woolf's mature work. Already, however, many of her later concerns are largely emerging. The resonance of the title itself anticipates Woolf's poetic symbolism; the "voyage out" can be the literal trip across the Atlantic or up the South American river, but it also suggests the progression from innocence to experience, from life to death, which she later depicts using similar water imagery. Her concern with premature death and how survivors come to terms with it prefigures *Jacob's Room*, *Mrs. Dalloway*, *To the Lighthouse*, and *The Waves*. Most significant is her portrayal of a world in which characters are forever striving to overcome their isolation from one another. The ship on which Rachel "voyages out" is labeled by Woolf an "emblem of the loneliness of human life." Terence, Rachel's lover, might be describing his creator's own frustration when he says he is trying "to write a novel about Silence, the things people don't say. But the difficulty is immense."

Moments of unity amid seemingly unconquerable disorder do occur, however. On a communal level, one such transformation happens at a ball being held to celebrate the engagement of two English guests at the resort's small hotel. When the musicians go home, Rachel appropriates the piano and plays Mozart, hunting songs, and hymn tunes as the guests gradually resume dancing, each in a newly expressive, uninhibited way, eventually to join hands in a gigantic round dance. When the circle breaks and each member spins away to become individual once more, Rachel modulates to Bach; her weary yet exhilarated listeners sit quietly and allow themselves to be soothed by the serene complexity of the music. As dawn breaks outside and Rachel plays on, they envision "themselves and their lives, and the whole of human life advancing nobly under the direction of the music." They have transcended their single identities temporarily to gain a privileged glimpse of some larger pattern beyond themselves.

If Rachel through her art briefly transforms the lives of a small community, she herself privately discerns fleeting stability through her growing love for Terence. Even love is insufficient, however; although in the couple's newfound sense of union "divisions disappeared," Terence feels that Rachel seems able "to pass away to unknown places where she had no need of him." In the elegiac closing scenes of illness (which Woolf reworked many times and which are the most original as well as moving part of the novel), Rachel "descends into another world"; she is "curled up at the bottom of the sea." Terence, sitting by her bedside, senses that "they seemed to be thinking together; he seemed to be Rachel as well as himself." When she ceases breathing, he experiences "an immense feeling of peace," a "complete union" with her that shatters when he notices an ordinary table covered with crockery and realizes in horror that in this world he will never see Rachel again. For her, stability has been achieved; for him, the isolating flux has resumed.

Night and Day

Looking back on *The Voyage Out*, Woolf could see, she said, why readers found it "a more gallant and inspiring spectacle" than her next and least known book *Night and Day*. This second novel is usually regarded as her most traditional in form and subject—in its social satire, her obeisance to Jane Austen. Its dancelike plot, however, in which mismatched young couples eventually find their true loves, suggests the magical atmosphere of William Shakespeare's romantic comedies as well. References to Shakespeare abound in the book; for example, the delightfully eccentric Mrs. Hilbery characterizes herself as one of his wise fools, and when at the end she presides over the repatterning of the couples in London, she has just arrived from a pilgrimage to Stratford-upon-Avon. Coincidentally, *Night and Day* is the most conventionally dramatic of Woolf's novels, full of dialogue, exits and entrances; characters are constantly taking omnibuses and taxis across London from one contrived scene to the next.

Like *The Voyage Out, Night and Day* does point to Woolf's enduring preoccupations. It is, too, a novel depicting movement from innocence to maturity and escape from the conventional world through the liberating influence of love. Ralph Denham, a London solicitor from a large, vulgar, middle-class family living in suburban Highgate, would prefer to move to a Norfolk cottage and write. Katharine Hilbery measures out her days serving tea in her wealthy family's beautiful Chelsea home and helping her disorganized mother produce a biography of their forebear, a great nineteenth century poet. Her secret passions, however, are mathematics and astronomy. These seeming opposites, Ralph and Katharine, are alike in that both retreat at night to their rooms to pursue their private visions. The entire novel is concerned with such dualities—public selves and private selves, activity and contemplation, fact and imagination; but Woolf also depicts the unity that Ralph and Katharine can achieve, notwithstanding the social and intellectual barriers separating them. At the end, as the couple leaves Katharine's elegant but constraining home to walk in the open night air, "they lapsed gently into silence, travelling the dark paths side by side towards something discerned in the distance which gradually possessed them both."

The sustained passages of subtle interior analysis by which Woolf charts the couple's growing realization of their need for each other define her real area of fictional interest, but they are hemmed in by a tediously constrictive traditional structure. Except for her late novel, *The Years*, also comparatively orthodox in form, her first two books took the longest to finish and underwent the most extensive revisions, undoubtedly because she was writing against her grain. Nevertheless, they represented a necessary apprenticeship; as she would later remark of *Night and Day*, "You must put it all in before you can leave out."

Jacob's Room

Woolf dared to leave out a great deal in the short experimental novel she wrote next. Described in conventional terms, *Jacob's Room* is a bildungsroman, or "novel of formation," tracing its hero's development from childhood to maturity: Jacob Flanders is first portrayed as a small boy studying a tide pool on a Cornish beach; at twenty-six, he dies fighting in World War I. In structure, style, and tone, however, *Jacob's Room* defies such labeling. It does not move in steady chronological fashion but in irregular leaps. Of the fourteen chapters, two cover Jacob's childhood, two, his college years at Cambridge, the remainder, his life as a young adult working in London and traveling abroad. In length, and hence in the complexity with which various periods of Jacob's existence are treated, the chapters range from one to twenty-eight pages. They vary, that is, as the process of growth itself does.

Individual chapters are likewise discontinuous in structure, broken into irregular segments that convey multiple, often simultaneous perspectives. The ten-page chapter 8, for example, opens with Jacob's slamming the door of his London room as he starts for work in the morning; he is then glimpsed at his office desk. Meanwhile, on a table back in his room lies his mother's unopened letter to him, placed there the previous night by his lover, Florinda; its contents and Mrs. Flanders herself are evoked. The narrator then discourses on the significance of letter writing. Jacob is next seen leaving work for the day; in Greek Street, he spies Florinda on another man's arm. At eight o'clock, Rose Shaw, a guest at a party Jacob attended several nights earlier, walks through Holburn, meditating bitterly on the ironies of love and death. The narrator sketches London by lamplight. Then, Jacob is back in his room reading by the fire a newspaper account of the Prime Minister's speech on Home Rule; the night is very cold. The narrator abruptly shifts perspective from congested London to the open countryside, describing the snow that has been accumulating since midafternoon; an old shepherd crossing a field hears a distant clock strike. Back in London, Jacob also hears the hour chiming, rakes out his fire, and goes to bed. There is no story here in any conventional sense, no action being furthered; in the entire ten pages, only one sentence is direct dialogue. What Woolf delineates is the *texture* of an ordinary day in the life of Jacob and the world in which he exists. Clock time moves the chapter forward, while spatially the chapter radiates outward from the small area Jacob occupies. Simultaneously, in the brief reference to the Prime Minister, Woolf suggests the larger procession of modern history that will inexorably sweep Jacob to premature death.

Such indirection and understatement characterize the whole novel: "It is no use trying to sum people up," the narrator laments. "One must follow hints." Thus, Jacob is described mainly from the outside, defined through the impressions he makes on others, from a hotel chambermaid to a Cambridge don, and by his surroundings and possessions. Even his death is conveyed obliquely: Mrs. Flanders, half asleep in her Yorkshire house, hears "dull sounds"; it cannot be guns, she thinks, it must be the sea. On the next page, she stands in her dead son's London room, holding a pair of Jacob's old shoes and asking his friend pathetically, "What am I to do with these, Mr. Bonamy?" The novel ends.

To construct Jacob's ultimately unknowable biography out of such fragments, Woolf evolves not only a new structure but a new style. Long, fluid sentences contain precise physical details juxtaposed with metaphysical speculations on the evanescence of life and the impossibility of understanding another person. Lyrical descriptions of nature—waves, moths, falling snow, birds rising and settling—are interspersed to suggest life's beauty and fragility. Images and phrases recur as unifying motifs: Jacob is repeatedly associated with Greek literature and myth and spends his last fulfilling days visiting the Parthenon. Most important, Woolf begins to move freely in and out of her characters' minds to capture the flow of sense impressions mingling with memory, emotion, and random association, experimenting with that narrative method conveniently if imprecisely labeled "stream of consciousness."

Jacob's Room is not a mature work, especially with its intrusive narrator, who can be excessively chatty, archly pedantic, and sententious. Woolf protests the difficulties of her task ("In short, the observer is choked with observations") and cannot quite follow the logic of her new method; after an essaylike passage on the necessity of illusion, for example, she awkwardly concludes, "Jacob, no doubt, thought something in this fashion." Even the lovely passages of poetic description at times seem self-indulgent. The book definitely shows its seams. Woolf's rejection of traditional novel structure, however, and her efforts to eliminate "the alien and the external" make *Jacob's Room* a dazzling advance in her ability to embody her philosophical vision: "Life is but a procession of shadows, and God knows why it is that we embrace them so eagerly, and see them depart with such anguish, being shadows."

MRS. DALLOWAY

Within three years, Woolf had resolved her technical problems superbly in *Mrs. Dalloway*. The intruding narrator vanishes; though the freedom with which point of view shifts among characters and settings clearly posits an omniscient intelligence, the narrator's observations are now subtly integrated with the thoughts of her characters, and the transitions between scenes flow organically. Woolf's subject is also better suited to her method: Whereas *Jacob's Room* is a story of youthful potential tragically cut off, *Mrs.*

Dalloway is a novel of middle age, about what people have become as the result of choices made, opportunities seized or refused. Jacob Flanders had but a brief past; the characters in *Mrs. Dalloway* must come to terms with theirs, sifting and valuing the memories that course through their minds.

The book covers one June day in the life of Clarissa Dalloway, fifty-two years old, an accomplished London political hostess and wife of a Member of Parliament. A recent serious illness from which she is still recovering has made her freshly appreciate the wonder of life as she prepares for the party she will give that evening. Peter Walsh, once desperately in love with her, arrives from India, where he has had an undistinguished career; he calls on her and is invited to the party, at which another friend from the past, Sally Seton, formerly a romantic and now the conventional wife of a Manchester industrialist, will also unexpectedly appear. Running parallel with Clarissa's day is that of the mad Septimus Warren Smith, a surviving Jacob Flanders, shell-shocked in the war; his suicide in the late afternoon delays the arrival of another of Clarissa's guests, the eminent nerve specialist Sir William Bradshaw. Learning of this stranger's death, Clarissa must confront the inevitability of her own.

Mrs. Dalloway is also, then, a novel about time itself (its working title at one point was *The Hours*). Instead of using chapters or other formal sectioning, Woolf structures the book by counterpointing clock time, signaled by the obtrusive hourly tolling of Big Ben, against the subjective flow of time in her characters' minds as they recover the past and envision the future. Not only does she move backward and forward in time, however; she also creates an effect of simultaneity that is especially crucial in linking Septimus's story with Clarissa's. Thus, when Clarissa Dalloway, buying flowers that morning in a Bond Street shop, hears "a pistol shot" outside and emerges to see a large, official automobile that has backfired, Septimus is standing in the crowd blocked by the car and likewise reacting to this "violent explosion" ("The world has raised its whip; where will it descend?"). Later, when Septimus's frightened young Italian wife Rezia guides him to Regents Park to calm him before their appointment with Bradshaw, he has a terrifying hallucination of his dead friend Evans, killed just before the Armistice; Peter Walsh, passing their bench, wonders, "What awful fix had they got themselves in to look so desperate as that on a fine summer morning?" This atmosphere of intensely populated time and space, of many anonymous lives intersecting briefly, of the world resonating with unwritten novels, comic and tragic, accounts in part for the richly poignant texture of nearly all Woolf's mature work.

In her early thinking about *Mrs. Dalloway*, Virginia Woolf wanted to show a "world seen by the sane and the insane, side by side." Although the novel definitely focuses on Clarissa, Septimus functions as a kind of double, representing her own responses to life carried to an untenable extreme. Both find great terror in life and also great joy; both want to withdraw from life into blissful isolation, yet both want to reach out to merge with others. Clarissa's friends, and indeed she herself, sense a "coldness" about her, "an impenetrability"; both Peter and Sally believe she chose safety rather than adventure by marrying the unimaginative, responsible Richard Dalloway. The quiet attic room where she now convalesces is described as a tower into which she retreats nunlike to a virginal narrow bed. Yet Clarissa also loves "life; London; this moment of June"—and her parties. Though some critics condemn her party giving as shallow, trivial, even corrupt (Peter Walsh could make her wince as a girl by predicting that she would become "the perfect hostess"), Clarissa considers her parties a form of creativity, "an offering," "her gift" of bringing people together. For Septimus, the war has destroyed his capacity to feel; in his aloneness and withdrawal, he finds "an isolation full of sublimity; a freedom which the attached can never know"—he can elude "human nature," "the repulsive brute, with the blood-red nostrils." Yet just watching leaves quivering is for him "an exquisite joy"; he feels them "connected by millions of fibres with his own body" and wants to reveal this unity to the world because "communication is health; communication is happiness."

Desperate because of his suicide threats, Septimus's wife takes him to see Sir William Bradshaw. At the center of the novel, in one of the most bitter scenes in all of Woolf's writing (certainly one with strong autobiographical overtones), is Septimus's confrontation with this "priest of science," this man of "lightning skill" and "almost infallible accuracy" who "never spoke of 'madness'; he called it not having a sense of proportion." Within three minutes, he has discreetly recorded his diagnosis on a pink card ("a case of complete breakdown . . . with every symptom in an advanced stage"); Septimus will be sent to a beautiful house in the country where he will be taught to rest, to regain proportion. Rezia, agonized, understands that she has been failed by this obtuse, complacently cruel man whom Woolf symbolically connects with a larger system that prospers on intolerance and sends its best young men to fight futile wars. Septimus's suicide at this point becomes inevitable.

The two stories fuse when Bradshaw appears at the party. Learning of the reason for his lateness, Clarissa, deeply shaken, withdraws to a small side room, not unlike her attic tower, where she accurately imagines Septimus's suicide: "He had thrown himself from a window. Up had flashed the ground; through him, blundering, bruising, went the rusty spikes. . . . So she saw it." She also intuits the immediate cause: Bradshaw is "capable of some indescribable outrage—forcing your soul, that was it"; seeing him, this young man must have said to himself, "they make life intolerable, men like that." Thus, she sees, "death was defiance," a means to preserve one's center from being violated, but "death was an attempt to communicate," and in death, Septimus's message that all life is connected is heard by one unlikely person, Clarissa Dalloway. Reviewing her own past as she has reconstructed it this day, and forced anew to acknowledge her own mortality, she realizes that "he had made her feel the beauty." Spiritually regenerated, she returns to her party "to kindle and illuminate" life.

TO THE LIGHTHOUSE

In her most moving, complexly affirmative novel, *To the Lighthouse*, Woolf portrays another woman whose creativity lies in uniting people, Mrs. Ramsay. For this luminous evocation of her own parents' marriage, Woolf drew on memories of her girlhood summers at St. Ives, Cornwall (here transposed to an island in the Hebrides), to focus on her perennial themes, the difficulties and joys of human communication, especially as frustrated by time and death.

The plot is absurdly simple: An expedition to a lighthouse is postponed, then completed a decade later. Woolf's mastery, however, of the interior monologue in this novel makes such a fragile plot line quite sufficient; the real "story" of *To the Lighthouse* is the reader's gradually increasing intimacy with its characters' richly depicted inner lives; the reader's understanding expands in concert with the characters' own growing insights.

Woolf again devises an experimental structure for her work, this time of three unequal parts. Approximately the first half of the novel, titled "The Window," occurs during a single day at the seaside home occupied by an eminent philosopher, Mr. Ramsay, his wife, and a melange of children, guests, and servants, including Lily Briscoe, an amateur painter in her thirties, unmarried. Mrs. Ramsay's is the dominant consciousness in this section. A short, exquisitely beautiful center section, "Time Passes," pictures the house succumbing to time during the family's ten-year absence and then being rescued from decay by two old women for the Ramsays' repossession. Periodically interrupting this natural flow of time are terse, bracketed, clock-time announcements like news bulletins, telling of the deaths of Mrs. Ramsay, the eldest son Andrew (in World War I), and the eldest daughter Prue (of childbirth complications). The final third, "The Lighthouse," also covers one day; the diminished family and several former guests having returned, the lighthouse expedition can now be completed. This section is centered almost entirely in Lily Briscoe's consciousness.

Because Mr. and Mrs. Ramsay are both strong personalities, they are sometimes interpreted too simply. Particularly in some readings by feminist critics, Mr. Ramsay is seen as an insufferable patriarch, arrogantly rational in his work but almost infantile emotionally, while Mrs. Ramsay is a Victorian earth mother, not only submitting unquestioningly to her husband's and children's excessive demands but actively trying to impose on all the other female characters her unliberated way of life. Such readings are sound to some extent, but they undervalue the vivid way that Woolf captures in the couple's monologues the conflicting mixture of motives and needs that characterize human beings of either sex. For example, Mrs. Ramsay is infuriated that her husband blights their youngest son James's anticipation of the lighthouse visit by announcing that it will storm tomorrow, yet his unflinching pursuit of truth is also something she most admires in him. Mr. Ramsay finds his wife's irrational habit of exaggeration maddening, but as she sits alone in a reverie, he respects her integrity and will not interrupt, "though it hurt him that she should look so distant, and he could not reach her, he could do nothing to help her." Lily, a shrewd observer who simultaneously adores and resists Mrs. Ramsay, perceives that "it would be a mistake . . . to simplify their relationship."

Amid these typical contradictions and mundane demands, however, "little daily miracles" may be achieved. One of Woolf's finest scenes, Mrs. Ramsay's dinner, provides a paradigm (though a summary can scarcely convey the richness of these forty pages). As she mechanically seats her guests at the huge table, Mrs. Ramsay glimpses her husband at the other end, "all in a heap, frowning": "She could not understand how she had ever felt any emotion of affection for him." Gloomily, she perceives that not just the two of them but everyone is separate and out of sorts. For example, Charles Tansley, Mr. Ramsay's disciple, who feels the whole family despises him, fidgets angrily; Lily, annoyed that Tansley is always telling her "women can't paint," purposely tries to irritate him; William Bankes would rather be home dining alone and fears that Mrs. Ramsay will read his mind. They all sense that "something [is] lacking"—they are divided from one another, sunk in their "treacherous" thoughts. Mrs. Ramsay wearily recognizes that "the whole of the effort of merging and flowing and creating rested on her."

She instructs two of her children to light the candles and set them around a beautiful fruit centerpiece that her daughter Rose has arranged for the table. This is Mrs. Ramsay's first stroke of artistry; the candles and fruit compose the table and the faces around it into an island, a sheltering haven: "Here, inside the room, seemed to be order and dry land; there, outside, a reflection in which things wavered and vanished, waterily." All the guests feel this change and have a sudden sense of making "common cause against that fluidity out there." Then the maid brings in a great steaming dish of *boeuf en daube* that even the finicky widower Bankes considers "a triumph." As the guests relish the succulent food and their camaraderie grows, Mrs. Ramsay, serving the last helpings from the depths of the pot, experiences a moment of perfect insight: "There it was, all around them. It partook . . . of eternity." She affirms to herself that "there is a coherence in things, a stability; something, she meant, that is immune from change, and shines out . . . in the face of the flowing, the fleeting." As is true of so much of Woolf's sparse dialogue, the ordinary words Mrs. Ramsay then speaks aloud can be read both literally and symbolically: "Yes, there is plenty for everybody." As the dinner ends and she passes out of the room triumphantly—the inscrutable poet Augustus Carmichael, who usually resists her magic, actually bows in homage—she looks back on the scene and sees that "it had become, she knew . . . already the past."

The burden of the past and the coming to terms with it are the focus of part 3. Just as "a sort of disintegration" sets in as soon as Mrs. Ramsay sweeps out of the dining room, so her death has left a larger kind of wreckage. Without her unifying artistry, all is disorder, as it was at the beginning of the dinner. In a gesture of belated atonement for quarreling with his wife over the original lighthouse trip, the melodramatically despairing Mr. Ramsay insists on making the expedition now with his children James and Cam, although both hate his tyranny and neither wants to go. As they set out, Lily remains behind to paint. Surely mirroring the creative anxiety of Woolf herself, she feels "a painful but exciting ecstasy" before her blank canvas, knowing how ideas that seem simple become "in practice immediately complex." As she starts making rhythmic strokes across the canvas, she loses "consciousness of outer things" and begins to meditate on the past, from which she gradually retrieves a vision of Mrs. Ramsay that will permit her to reconstruct and complete the painting she left unfinished a decade ago, one in which Mrs. Ramsay would have been, and will become again, a triangular shadow on a step (symbolically echoing the invisible "wedge-shaped core of darkness" to which Mrs. Ramsay feels herself shrinking during her moments of reverie). Through the unexpectedly intense pain of recalling her, Lily also comprehends Mrs. Ramsay's significance, her ability "to make the moment something permanent," as art does, to strike "this eternal passing and flowing . . . into stability." Mrs. Ramsay is able to make "life stand still here."

Meanwhile, Mr. Ramsay and his children are also voyaging into the past; Cam, dreamily drifting her hand in the water, begins, as her mother did, to see her father as bravely pursuing truth like a tragic hero. James bitterly relives the childhood scene when his father thoughtlessly dashed his hopes for the lighthouse visit, but as they near the lighthouse in the present and Mr. Ramsay offers his son rare praise, James too is reconciled. When they land, Mr. Ramsay himself, standing in the bow "very straight and tall," springs "lightly like a young man . . . on to the rock," renewed. Simultaneously, though the boat has long since disappeared from her sight and even the lighthouse itself seems blurred, Lily intuits that they have reached their goal and she completes her painting. All of them have reclaimed Mrs. Ramsay from death, and she has unified them; memory can defeat time. "Yes," Lily thinks, "I have had my vision." Clearly, Woolf had achieved hers too and transmuted the materials of a painful past into this radiant novel.

Although Woolf denied intending any specific symbolism for the lighthouse, it resonates with almost infinite possibilities, both within the book and in a larger way as an emblem of her work. Like the candles at the dinner party, it can be a symbol of safety and stability amid darkness and watery flux, its beams those rhythmically occurring moments of illumination that sustain Mrs. Ramsay and by extension everyone. Perhaps, however, it can also serve as a metaphor for human beings themselves as Woolf portrays them. The lighthouse signifies what can be objectively perceived of an individual—in Mrs. Ramsay's words, "our apparitions, the things you know us by"; but it also signals invisible, possibly tragic depths, for, as Mrs. Ramsay knew, "beneath it is all dark, it is all spreading, it is unfathomably deep."

THE WAVES

In *The Waves*, widely considered her masterpiece, Woolf most resolutely overcomes the limits of the traditional novel. Entirely unique in form, *The Waves* cannot perhaps be called a novel at all; Woolf herself first projected a work of "prose yet poetry; a novel and a play." The book is a series of grouped soliloquies in varying combinations spoken by six friends, three men and three women, at successive stages in their lives from childhood to late middle age. Each grouping is preceded by a brief, lyrical "interlude" (Woolf's own term), set off in italic type, that describes an empty house by the sea as the sun moves across the sky in a single day.

The texture of these soliloquies is extremely difficult to convey; the term "soliloquy," in fact, is merely a critical convenience. Although each is introduced in the same straightforward way ("Neville said," "Jinny said"), they obviously are unspoken, representing each character's private vision. Their style is also unvarying—solemn, formal, almost stilted, like that of choral figures. The author has deliberately translated into a rigorously neutral, dignified idiom the conscious and subconscious reality her characters perceive but cannot articulate on their own. This method represents Woolf's most ambitious attempt to capture the unfathomable depths of separate human personalities, which defy communication in ordinary life—and in ordinary novels. The abstraction of the device, however, especially in combination with the flow of cosmic time in the interludes, shows that she is also concerned with depicting a universal pattern that transcends mere individuals. Thus, once more Woolf treats her theme of human beings' attempts to overcome their isolation and to become part of a larger stabilizing pattern; this time, however, the theme is embodied in the very form of her work.

It would be inaccurate, however, to say that the characters exist only as symbols. Each has definable qualities and unique imagery; Susan, as an example, farm-bred and almost belligerently maternal, speaks in elemental images of wood smoke, grassy paths, flowers thick with pollen. Further, the characters often evoke one another's imagery; the other figures, for example, even in maturity picture the fearful, solitary Rhoda as a child rocking white petals in a brown basin of water. They are linked by intricately woven threads of common experience, above all by their shared admiration for a shadowy seventh character, Percival. Their gathering with him at a farewell dinner before he embarks on a career in India is one of the few actual events recorded in the soliloquies and also becomes one of those miraculous moments of unity comparable to that achieved by Mrs. Ramsay for her dinner guests; as they rise to leave the restaurant, all the characters are thinking as Louis does: "We pray, holding in our hands this common feeling, 'Do not move, do not let the swing-door cut to pieces this thing that we have made, that globes itself here.'" Such union, however, is cruelly impermanent; two pages later, a telegram announces Percival's death in a riding accident. Bernard, trying to make sense of this absurdity, echoes the imagery of encircling unity that characterized their thoughts at the dinner: "Ideas break a thousand times for once that they globe themselves entire."

It is Bernard—identified, significantly, throughout the book as a storyteller—who is given the long final section of *The Waves* in which "to sum up," becoming perhaps a surrogate for the author herself. (As a young man at school, worrying out "my novel," he discovers how "stories that follow people into their private rooms are difficult.") It is he who recognizes that "I am not one person; I am many people," part of his friends as they are part of him, all of them incomplete in themselves; he is "a man without a self." Yet it is also he who on the novel's final page, using the wave imagery of the universalizing interludes, passionately asserts his individuality: "Against you I will fling myself, unvanquished and unyielding, O Death!" Life, however obdurate and fragmented, must be affirmed.

The Waves is without doubt Woolf's most demanding and original novel, her most daring experiment in eliminating the alien and the external. When she vowed to cast out "all waste, deadness, and superfluity," however, she also ascetically renounced some of her greatest strengths as a novelist: her wit and humor, her delight in the daily beauty, variety, and muddle of material existence. This "abstract mystical eyeless book," as she at one point envisioned it, is a work to admire greatly, but not to love.

The six years following *The Waves* were a difficult period for Woolf both personally and artistically. Deeply depressed by the deaths of Lytton Strachey and Roger Fry, two of her oldest, most respected friends, she was at work on an "essay-novel," as she first conceived of it, which despite her initial enthusiasm became her most painfully frustrating effort—even though it proved, ironically, to be her greatest commercial success.

THE YEARS

In *The Years*, Woolf returned to the conventional novel that she had rejected after *Night and Day*; she planned "to take in everything" and found herself "infinitely delighting in facts for a change." Whereas *The Waves* had represented the extreme of leaving out, *The Years* suggests the opposite one of almost indiscriminate putting in. Its very subject, a history of the Pargiter clan spanning fifty years and three generations, links it with the diffuse family sagas of John Galsworthy and Arnold Bennett, whose books Woolf was expressly deriding when she demanded, "Must novels be like this?"

Nevertheless, *The Years* is more original than it may appear; Woolf made fresh use of her experimental methods in her effort to reanimate traditional form. The novel contains eleven unequal segments, each standing for a year; the longest ones, the opening "1880" section and the closing "Present Day" (the 1930's), anchor the book; the nine intermediate sections cover the years between 1891 and 1918. Echoing *The Waves*, Woolf begins each chapter with a short panoramic passage describing both London and the countryside. Within the chapters, instead of continuous narrative, there are collections of vignettes, somewhat reminiscent of *Jacob's Room*, depicting various Pargiters going about their daily lives. Running parallel with the family's history are larger historical events, including Edward VII's death, the suffrage movement, the Irish troubles, and especially World War I. These events are usually treated indirectly, however; for example, the "1917" section takes place mainly in a cellar to which the characters have retreated, dinner plates in hand, during an air raid. It is here that Eleanor Pargiter asks, setting a theme that suffuses the rest of the novel, "When shall we live adventurously, wholly, not like cripples in a cave?"

The most pervasive effect of the war is felt in the lengthy "Present Day" segment, which culminates in a family reunion, where the youngest generation of Pargiters, Peggy and North, are lonely, cynical, and misanthropic, and their faltering elders are compromised either by complacency or failed hopes. Symbolically, Delia Pargiter gives the party in a rented office, not a home, underscoring the uprooting caused by the war. Yet the balancing "1880" section is almost equally dreary: The Pargiters' solid Victorian house shelters a chronically ailing mother whose children wish she would die, a father whose vulgar mistress greets him in hair curlers and frets over her dog's eczema, and a young daughter traumatized by an exhibitionist in the street outside. One oppressive way of life seems only to have been superseded by another, albeit a more universally menacing one.

The overall imagery of the novel is likewise unlovely: Children recall being scrubbed with slimy washcloths; a revolting dinner of underdone mutton served by Sara Pargiter includes a bowl of rotting, flyblown fruit, grotesquely parodying Mrs. Ramsay's *boeuf en daube* and Rose's centerpiece; London is populated with deformed violet-sellers and old men eating cold sausages on buses. Communication in such a world is even more difficult than in Woolf's earlier books; the dialogue throughout is full of incomplete sentences, and a central vignette in the "Present Day" section turns on one guest's abortive efforts to deliver a speech toasting the human race.

Despite these circumstances, the characters still grope toward some kind of transforming unity; Eleanor, the eldest surviving Pargiter and the most sympathetic character in the novel, comes closest to achieving such vision on the scale that Lily Briscoe and Clarissa Dalloway do. At the reunion, looking back over her life, she wonders if there is "a pattern; a theme recurring like music . . . momentarily perceptible?" Casting about her, trying to connect with her relatives and friends but dozing in the process, she suddenly wakes, proclaiming that "it's been a perpetual discovery, my life. A miracle." Answering by implication her question posed fifteen years earlier during the air raid, she perceives that "we're only just beginning . . . to understand, here and there." That prospect is enough, however; she wants "to enclose the present moment . . . to fill it fuller and fuller, with the past, the present and the future, until it shone, whole, bright, deep with understanding."

Even this glowing dream of eventual unity is muted, however, when one recalls how Eleanor's embittered niece Peggy half pities, half admires her as a person who "still believed with passion . . . in the things man had destroyed," and how her nephew North, a captain in the trenches of World War I, thinks, "We cannot help each other, we are all deformed." It is difficult not to read the final lines of this profoundly somber novel ironically: "The sun had risen, and the sky above the houses wore an air of extraordinary beauty, simplicity and peace."

BETWEEN THE ACTS

Woolf's final work, *Between the Acts*, also deals with individual lives unfolding against the screen of history, but her vision and the methods by which she conveys it are more inventive, complex, and successful than in *The Years*. Covering the space of a single day in June, 1939, as world war threatens on the Continent, *Between the Acts* depicts the events surrounding a village pageant about the history of England, performed on the grounds of Pointz Hall, a country house occupied by the unhappily married Giles and Isa Oliver. The Olivers' story frames the presentation of the pageant, scenes of which are directly reproduced in the novel and alternate with glimpses of the audience's lives during the intervals between the acts. The novel's title is hence richly metaphorical: The acts of the drama itself are bracketed by the scenes of real life, which in turn can be viewed as brief episodes in the long pageant of human history. Equally ambiguous, then, is the meaning of "parts," connoting clearly defined roles within a drama but also the fragmentation and incompleteness of the individuals who play them, that pervasive theme in Woolf's work.

In *The Years*, Woolf had focused on the personal histories of her characters; history in the larger sense made itself felt as it impinged on private lives. This emphasis is reversed in *Between the Acts*. Though the novel has interesting characters, Woolf does not provide much information about their backgrounds, nor does she plumb individual memory in her usual manner. Instead, the characters possess a national, cultural, communal past—finally that of the whole human race from the Stone Age to the present. That Woolf intends her characters to be seen as part of this universal progression is clear from myriad references in the early pages to historical time. For example, from the air, the "scars" made by the Britons and the Romans can be seen around the village as can the Elizabethan manor house; graves in the churchyard attest that Mrs. Haines's family has lived in the area "for many centuries," whereas the Oliver family has inhabited Pointz Hall for "only something over a hundred and twenty years"; Lucy Swithin, Giles's endearing aunt, enjoys reading about history and imagining Piccadilly when it was a rhododendron forest populated by mastodons, "from whom, presumably, she thought . . . we descend."

The pageant itself, therefore, functions in the novel as more than simply a church fund-raising ritual, the product of well-meaning but hapless amateurs (though it exists amusingly on that level too). It is a heroic attempt by its author-director, the formidable Miss La Trobe, to make people see themselves playing parts in the continuum of British history. Thus, the audience has an integral role that blurs the lines "between the acts"; "Our part," says Giles's father, Bartholomew, "is to be the audience. And a very important part too." Their increasing interest in the pageant as they return from the successive intermissions signals their growing sense of a shared past and hence of an identity that both binds and transcends them as individuals.

The scenes of the pageant proceed from bathos to unnerving profundity. The first player, a small girl in pink, announces, "England am I," then promptly forgets her lines, while the wind blows away half the words of the singers behind her. Queen Elizabeth, splendidly decorated with six-penny brooches and a cape made of silvery scouring pads, turns out to be Mrs. Clark, the village tobacconist; the combined applause and laughter of delighted recognition muffle her opening speech. As the pageant progresses from a wicked though overlong parody of Restoration comedy to a satiric scene at a Victorian picnic, however, the audience becomes more reflective; the past is now close enough to be familiar, triggering their own memories and priming them for the last scene, Miss La Trobe's inspired experiment in expressionism, "The Present Time. Ourselves." The uncomprehending audience fidgets as the stage remains empty, refusing to understand that they are supposed to contemplate their own significance. "Reality too strong," Miss La Trobe mutters angrily from behind the bushes, "Curse 'em!" Then, "sudden and universal," a summer shower fortuitously begins. "Down it rained like all the people in the world weeping." Nature has provided the bridge of meaning Miss La Trobe required. As the rain ends, all the players from all the periods reappear, still in costume and declaiming fragments of their parts while flashing mirrors in the faces of the discomfited audience. An offstage voice asks how civilization is "to be built by orts, scraps and fragments like ourselves," then dies away.

The Reverend Streatfield, disconcerted like the rest of the audience, is assigned the embarrassing role of summing up the play's meaning. Tentatively, self-consciously, he ventures, "To me at least it was indicated that we are members of one another. . . . We act different parts; but are the same. . . . Surely, we should unite?" Then he abruptly shifts into a fund-raising appeal that is drowned out by a formation of war planes passing overhead. As the audience departs, a gramophone plays a valedictory: "Dispersed are we; we who have come together. But let us retain whatever made that harmony." The audience responds, thinking "There is joy, sweet joy, in company."

The qualified optimism of the pageant's close, however, is darkened by the bleak, perhaps apocalyptic postscript of the framing story. After the group disperses, the characters resume their usual roles. Lucy Swithin, identified earlier as a "unifier," experiences a typically Woolfian epiphany as she gazes on a fishpond, glimpsing the silver of the great carp below the surface and "seeing in that vision beauty, power and glory in ourselves." Her staunchly rational brother Bartholomew, a "separatist," goes into the house. Miss La Trobe, convinced that she has failed again, heads for the local pub to drink alone and plan her next play; it will be set at midnight with two figures half hidden by a rock as the curtain rises. "What would the first words be?"

It is the disaffected Giles and Isa, loving and hating each other, who begin the new play. In a remarkable ending, Woolf portrays the couple sitting silently in the dark before going to bed: "Before they slept, they must fight; after they had fought they would embrace." From that embrace, they may create another life, but "first they must fight, as the dog fox fights the vixen, in the heart of darkness, in the fields of night." The "great hooded chairs" in which they sit grow enormous, like Miss La Trobe's rock. The house fades, no longer sheltering them; they are like "dwellers in caves," watching "from some high place." The last lines of the novel are, "Then the curtain rose. They spoke."

This indeterminate conclusion implies that love and hate are elemental and reciprocal, and that such oppositions on a personal level are also the polarities that drive human history. Does Woolf read, then, in the gathering European storm, a cataclysm that will bring the pageant of history full circle, back to the primitive stage of prehistory? Or, like W. B.

Yeats in "The Second Coming," does she envision a new cycle even more terrifying than the old? Or, as the faithful Lucy Swithin does, perhaps she hopes that "*all* is harmony could we hear it. And we shall."

Eight years earlier, Virginia Woolf wrote in her diary, "I think the effort to live in two spheres: the novel; and life; is a strain." Miss La Trobe, a crude alter ego for the author, is obsessed by failure but always driven to create anew because "a vision imparted was relief from agony . . . for one moment." In her brilliant experimental attempts to impart her own view of fragmented human beings achieving momentary harmony, discovering unity and stability behind the flux of daily life, Woolf repeatedly endured such anguish, but after *Between the Acts* was done, the strain of beginning again was too great. Perhaps the questions Virginia Woolf posed in this final haunting novel, published posthumously and unrevised, were answered for her in death.

Kristine Ottesen Garrigan

OTHER MAJOR WORKS

SHORT FICTION: *Two Stories*, 1917 (one by Leonard Woolf); *Kew Gardens*, 1919; *The Mark on the Wall*, 1919; *Monday or Tuesday*, 1921; *A Haunted House, and Other Short Stories*, 1943; *Mrs. Dalloway's Party*, 1973 (Stella McNichol, editor); *The Complete Shorter Fiction of Virginia Woolf*, 1985.

NONFICTION: *The Common Reader: First Series*, 1925; *A Room of One's Own*, 1929; *The Common Reader: Second Series*, 1932; *Three Guineas*, 1938; *Roger Fry: A Biography*, 1940; *The Death of the Moth, and Other Essays*, 1942; *The Moment, and Other Essays*, 1947; *The Captain's Death Bed, and Other Essays*, 1950; *A Writer's Diary*, 1953; *Letters: Virginia Woolf and Lytton Strachey*, 1956; *Granite and Rainbow*, 1958; *Contemporary Writers*, 1965; *Collected Essays, Volumes 1-2*, 1966; *Collected Essays, Volumes 3-4*, 1967; *The Flight of the Mind: The Letters of Virginia Woolf, Vol. I, 1888-1912*, 1975 (Nigel Nicolson, editor; also known as *The Letters of Virginia Woolf, Vol. I: 1888-1912*); *The London Scene: Five Essays*, 1975; *Moments of Being*, 1976 (Jeanne Schulkind, editor); *The Question of Things Happening: The Letters of Virginia Woolf, Vol. II, 1912-1922*, 1976 (Nicolson, editor; also known as *The Letters of Virginia Woolf, Vol. II: 1912-1922*); *A Change of Perspective: The Letters of Virginia Woolf, Vol. III, 1923-1928*, 1977 (Nicolson, editor; also known as *The Letters of Virginia Woolf, Vol. III: 1923-1928*, 1978); *Books and Portraits*, 1977; *The Diary of Virginia Woolf*, 1977-1984 (5 volumes; Anne Olivier Bell, editor); *A Reflection of the Other Person: The Letters of Virginia Woolf, Vol. IV, 1929-1931*, 1978 (Nicolson, editor; also known as *The Letters of Virginia Woolf, Vol. IV: 1929-1931*, 1979); *The Sickle Side of the Moon: The Letters of Virginia Woolf, Vol. V, 1932-1935*, 1979 (Nicolson, editor; also known as *The Letters of Virginia Woolf, Vol. V: 1932-1935*); *Leave the Letters Til We're Dead: The Letters of Virginia Woolf, Vol. VI, 1936-1941*, 1980 (Nicolson, editor); *The Essays of Virginia Woolf*, 1987-1994 (4 volumes); *Carlyle's House, and Other Sketches*, 2003 (David Bradshaw, editor).

BIBLIOGRAPHY

Barrett, Eileen, and Patricia Cramer, eds. *Virginia Woolf: Lesbian Readings*. New York: New York University Press, 1997. Part 2 of this collection of conference papers focuses on Woolf's novels, with lesbian interpretations of *The Voyage Out*, *Mrs. Dalloway*, *To the Lighthouse*, *Orlando*, *The Waves*, *The Years*, and *Between the Acts*.

Beja, Morris, ed. *Critical Essays on Virginia Woolf.* Boston: G. K. Hall, 1985. Collection is divided into two sections: reviews of Woolf's major works and essays on Woolf's art and artistic vision. The various interpretations reflect the editor's premise that Woolf, although claimed by several ages and schools of criticism, was unique and thus cannot be pigeonholed in any specific way.

Blair, Emily. *Virginia Woolf and the Nineteenth-Century Domestic Novel*. Albany: State University of New York Press, 2007. Describes the influence of nineteenth and early twentieth century literature, particularly its descriptions of femininity, on Woolf's work and compares her novels to those of Elizabeth Gaskell and Margaret Oliphant.

Briggs, Julia. *Virginia Woolf: An Inner Life*. Orlando, Fla: Harcourt, 2005. Biography focuses on Woolf's work in relation to her fascination with the workings of the mind. Traces the creation of each of Woolf's books, from *The Voyage Out* through *Between the Acts*, combining literary analysis with details of Woolf's life.

Goldman, Jane. *The Cambridge Introduction to Virginia Woolf.* New York: Cambridge University Press, 2006. Provides a wealth of information designed to help students and other readers better understand Woolf's writings, including biographical details and discussions of the novels. One section places Woolf's life and work within historical, political, and cultural context, including information about the Bloomsbury Group; another section focuses on critical reception of the works from the 1940's through the 1990's and includes contemporary reviews.

_______. *The Feminist Aesthetics of Virginia Woolf: Modernism, Post-impressionism, and the Politics of the Visual*. New York: Cambridge University Press, 2001. Feminist reading of Woolf's works focuses on the influence of literary and artistic modernism and places the works within their historical and cultural context.

Gordon, Lyndall. *Virginia Woolf: A Writer's Life*. New York: W. W. Norton, 1985. Biography looks not only at Woolf's life in Bloomsbury but also at her works, including her unfinished memoirs, the drafts of novels, and some lesser-known and unpublished pieces. Divides Woolf's life into three phases: her childhood, her time of literary apprenticeship and recurring illness, and her mature period of artistic achievement.

King, James. *Virginia Woolf.* New York: W. W. Norton, 1995. Literary biography relates Woolf's life to her works, showing how the chief sources of material for her writing were her life, her family, and her friends.

Lee, Hermione. *Virginia Woolf.* New York: Alfred A. Knopf, 1997. Detailed biography describes Woolf's complex family relationships, her lifelong battle with mental illness, and her relationship to the Bloomsbury Group.

Marder, Herbert. *The Measure of Life: Virginia Woolf's Last Years*. Ithaca, N.Y.: Cornell University Press, 2000. Biography focuses on the events of the final decade of Woolf's life and analyzes the changes in her writings during this period.

Reid, Panthea. *Art and Affection: A Life of Virginia Woolf.* New York: Oxford University Press, 1996. Biography draws on the vast amount of material available about Woolf and her circle to examine Woolf's desires to write and to be loved. Especially strong in providing a psychological explanation for Woolf's artistic choices, such as her decision to abandon conventional representation in her fiction.

Roe, Sue, and Susan Sellers, eds. *The Cambridge Companion to Virginia Woolf.* New York: Cambridge University Press, 2000. Collection of essays by leading scholars addresses Woolf's life and work from a wide range of intellectual perspectives. Includes analyses of her novels and discussions of Woolf in relation to modernism, feminism, and psychoanalysis.

BIBLIOGRAPHY

Selection

Every effort has been made to include studies published in 2000 and later. Most items in this bibliography contain a listing of secondary sources, making it easier to identify other critical commentary on novelists, movements, and themes.

Theoretical, thematic, and historical studies

Altman, Janet Gurkin. *Epistolarity: Approaches to a Form.* Columbus: Ohio State University Press, 1982. Examines the epistolary novel, explaining how novelists use the letter form to develop characterization, further their plots, and develop meaning.

Beaumont, Matthew, ed. *Adventures in Realism.* Malden, Mass.: Blackwell, 2007. Fifteen essays explore facets of realism, which was critical to the development of the novel. Provides a theoretical framework for understanding how novelists attempt to represent the real and the common in fiction.

Brink, André. *The Novel: Language and Narrative from Cervantes to Calvino*. New York: New York University Press, 1998. Uses contemporary theories of semiotics and narratology to establish a continuum between early novelists and those of the postmodern era in their conscious use of language to achieve certain effects. Ranges across national boundaries to illustrate the theory of the development of the novel since the seventeenth century.

Brownstein, Rachel. *Becoming a Heroine: Reading About Women in Novels*. New York: Viking Press, 1982. Feminist survey of novels from the eighteenth century through the latter half of the twentieth century. Examines how "becoming a heroine" defines for women a sense of value in their lives. Considers novels by both men and women, and discusses the importance of the traditional marriage plot.

Bruzelius, Margaret. *Romancing the Novel: Adventure from Scott to Sebald.* Lewisburg, Pa.: Bucknell University Press, 2007. Examines the development of the adventure novel, linking it with the medieval romance tradition and exploring readers' continuing fascination with the genre.

Cavallaro, Dani. *The Gothic Vision: Three Centuries of Horror, Terror, and Fear.* New York: Continuum, 2005. Study of the gothic novel from its earliest manifestations in the eighteenth century to the early twenty-first century. Through the lenses of contemporary cultural theories, examines readers' fascination with novels that invoke horror, terror, and fright.

Doody, Margaret Anne. *The True Story of the Novel.* New Brunswick, N.J.: Rutgers University Press, 1996. Traces the roots of the novel, traditionally thought to have been developed in the seventeenth century, to classical Greek and Latin texts that exhibit characteristics of modern fiction.

Hale, Dorothy J., ed. *The Novel: An Anthology of Criticism and Theory, 1900-2000.* Malden, Mass.: Blackwell, 2006. Collection of essays by theorists and novelists. Includes commentary on the novel form from the perspective of formalism, structuralism, poststructuralism, Marxism, and reader response theory. Essays also address the novel through the lenses of sociology, gender studies, and feminist theory.

_______. *Social Formalism: The Novel in Theory from Henry James to the Present.* Stanford, Calif.: Stanford University Press, 1998. Emphasizes the novel's special ability to define a social world for readers. Relies heavily on the works of contemporary literary and cultural theorists. Provides a summary of twentieth century efforts to identify a theory of fiction that encompasses novels of many kinds.

Hart, Stephen M., and Wen-chin Ouyang, eds. *A Companion to Magical Realism.* London: Tamesis, 2005. Essays outlining the development of Magical Realism, tracing its roots from Europe through Latin America to other regions of the world. Explores the political dimensions of the genre.

Hoffman, Michael J., and Patrick D. Murphy, eds. *Essentials of the Theory of Fiction.* 2d ed. Durham, N.C.: Duke University Press, 1996. Collection of essays by influential critics from the late nineteenth century through the twentieth century. Focuses on the essential elements of fiction and the novel's relationship to the world it depicts.

Lodge, David. *The Art of Fiction: Illustrated from Classic and Modern Texts.* New York: Viking Press, 1993. Short commentaries on the technical aspects of fiction. Examples from important and minor novelists illustrate literary principles and techniques such as point of view, suspense, character introduction, irony, motivation, and ending.

Lynch, Deirdre, and William B. Walker, eds. *Cultural Institutions of the Novel.* Durham, N.C.: Duke University Press, 1996. Fifteen essays examine aspects of long fiction produced around the world. Encourages a redefinition of the genre and argues for inclusion of texts not historically considered novels.

Moretti, Franco, ed. *The Novel.* 2 vols. Princeton, N.J.: Princeton University Press, 2006. Compendium exploring the novel from multiple perspectives, including as an anthropological, historical, and sociological document; a function of the national tradition from which it emerges; and a work of art subject to examination using various critical approaches.

Priestman, Martin, ed. *The Cambridge Companion to Crime Fiction.* New York: Cambridge University Press, 2003. Essays examine the nature and development of the genre, explore works by writers (including women and ethnic minorities) from several countries, and establish links between crime fiction and other literary genres. Includes a chronology.

Scaggs, John. *Crime Fiction.* New York: Routledge, 2005. Provides a history of crime fiction, explores key subgenres, and identifies recurring themes that suggest the wider social and historical context in which these works are written. Suggests critical approaches that open crime fiction to serious study.

Shiach, Morag, ed. *The Cambridge Companion to the Modernist Novel.* New York: Cambridge University Press, 2007. Essays explaining the concept of modernism and its influence on the novel. Detailed examination of works by writers from various countries, all influenced by the modernist movement. Includes a detailed chronology.

Vice, Sue. *Holocaust Fiction.* New York: Routledge, 2000. Examines controversies generated by novels about the Holocaust. Focuses on eight important works, but also offers observations on the polemics surrounding publication of books on this topic.

Zunshine, Lisa. *Why We Read Fiction: Theory of Mind and the Novel.* Columbus: Ohio State University Press, 2006. Applies theories of cognitive psychology to novel reading, explaining how experience and human nature lead readers to constrain their interpretations of a given text. Provides numerous examples from well-known novels to illustrate how and why readers find pleasure in fiction.

BRITISH FICTION
(INCLUDING AUSTRALIAN, CANADIAN, SCOTTISH, AND IRISH FICTION)

Ahern, Stephen. *Affected Sensibilities: Romantic Excess and the Genealogy of the Novel, 1680-1810.* New York: AMS Press, 2007. Explores the rise and rapid demise of various forms of fiction that feature excessive sensibility. Considers amatory fiction, sentimental fiction, and gothic narratives produced during the eighteenth century.

Crowe, Marian E. *Aiming at Heaven, Getting the Earth: The English Catholic Novel Today.* Lanham, Md.: Rowman & Littlefield, 2007. Surveys works of four twentieth century Catholic novelists. Introductory chapters provide detailed examination of the theory of the English Catholic novel, its history, and practices current in the last half of the twentieth century.

Damrosch, Leopold, Jr., ed. *Modern Essays on Eighteenth-Century Literature.* New York: Oxford University Press, 1988. Overview of critical commentary on important eighteenth century figures and literary works. Selections represent critical approaches popular during the 1970's and 1980's.

David, Deirdre, ed. *The Cambridge Companion to the Victorian Novel.* New York: Cambridge University Press, 2001. Eleven essays offer thematic analyses of issues important for understanding Victorian fiction. Discusses Victorian publishing practices and examines issues of gender, sexuality, race, aesthetics, religion, and science.

Eagleton, Terry. *The English Novel: An Introduction.* Malden, Mass.: Blackwell, 2005. Surveys English fiction by concentrating on the work of major authors. Considers novels from various theoretical perspectives, giving primacy to Marxist readings that stress the historical and sociological aspects of fiction.

ECW's Biographical Guide to Canadian Novelists. Oakville, Ont.: ECW Press, 1993. Brief sketches of the careers of forty-nine Canadian novelists, providing information on major works and principal literary interests.

James, Louis. *The Victorian Novel.* Malden, Mass.: Blackwell, 2006. Overview of the historical and social context in which Victorian novels were written. Also examines this fiction in relationship to historical, religious, and biographical works produced contemporaneously. Includes a chronology.

Kenyon, Olga. *Women Novelists Today: A Survey of English Writing in the Seventies and Eighties*. New York: St. Martin's Press, 1988. Extensive critical commentary on six important English women novelists. Introductory chapter examines the effect of the feminist movement on women novelists and reviews the importance of techniques such as realism in English fiction.

Levine, George. *The Realistic Imagination: English Fiction from Frankenstein to Lady Chatterley*. Chicago: University of Chicago Press, 1981. Examines the concept of realism and its application in important nineteenth century novels. Provides an overview of the development of fiction during this period.

McKeon, Michael. *The Origins of the English Novel, 1600-1740*. New ed. Baltimore: Johns Hopkins University Press, 2001. Theoretically based assessment of the cultural, political, and philosophical conditions in England that gave rise to the novel in the eighteenth century. Considers a number of important precursors to novelists Samuel Richardson and Henry Fielding.

MacLulich, Thomas D. *Between Europe and America: The Canadian Tradition in Fiction*. Toronto, Ont.: ECW Press, 1988. Explores the sources of Canadian fiction to identify its unique characteristics. Traces the development of that lineage from the nineteenth century through the twentieth century.

Nolan, Emer. *Catholic Emancipations: Irish Fiction from Thomas Moore to James Joyce*. Syracuse, N.Y.: Syracuse University Press, 2007. Traces the development of the Irish novel from 1820 into the twentieth century, concentrating on the influence of Catholicism on the production of fiction.

Norton, Rictor, ed. *Gothic Readings: The First Wave, 1764-1840*. London: Leicester University Press, 2000. Sketches the careers of important Gothic novelists, provides samples from their works, and discusses the development of the genre. Includes commentary on Gothic fiction from eighteenth and nineteenth century critics and readers.

O'Gorman, Francis, ed. *The Victorian Novel*. Malden, Mass.: Blackwell, 2002. Excerpts from dozens of influential twentieth century studies of Victorian fiction. Organized thematically; includes materials on formalist approaches, feminist readings, issues involving realism, historical approaches to fiction, postcolonial readings, discussions focusing on language and form, the impact of science on the novel, and the importance of publication practices.

Parrinder, Patrick. *Nation and Novel: The English Novel from Its Origins to the Present Day*. New York: Oxford University Press, 2006. Historical account of English fiction as a representation of the concept of nationhood and character. Organized chronologically. Includes significant critical commentary on important novels and novelists. Heavily reliant on theoretical studies of fiction and culture.

Peters, Joan Douglas. *Feminist Metafiction and the Evolution of the British Novel.* Gainesville: University Press of Florida, 2002. Uses feminist theory to reexamine the development of English fiction, demonstrating the key role women writers played in shaping the genre. Also discusses novels written by men that feature female protagonists.

Powell, Kersi Tarien. *Irish Fiction: An Introduction.* New York: Continuum, 2004. Handbook designed to introduce readers to Irish fiction. Explores themes common among most Irish writers and examines key novels that have shaped the genre.

Pykett, Lyn, ed. *Reading Fin de Siècle Fictions.* London: Longman, 1996. Twelve essays on writers who flourished between 1880 and 1910, applying contemporary critical theories to analyze individual works. Attempts to explore changes that transformed the novel during this period in English literary history.

Reed, Walter L. *An Exemplary History of the Novel: The Quixotic Versus the Picaresque.* Chicago: University of Chicago Press, 1981. Systematic study of the novel that examines its unique qualities and contrasts it with older forms of discourse. Offers close readings of several texts, explaining how the English novel fits within the larger developments in European fiction.

Richetti, John, ed. *The Cambridge Companion to the Eighteenth Century Novel.* New York: Cambridge University Press, 1996. Focuses on the cultural and historical context in which the novel developed. Chapters explore the work of major figures, the role of women writers, and the rise of gothic fiction.

_______, et al., eds. *The Columbia History of the British Novel.* New York: Columbia University Press, 1994. Collection of essays tracing the development of English fiction from the seventeenth century through the twentieth century. Explores important recurring themes and also writers not normally identified as the most notable. Contains brief biographies of one hundred novelists.

Ter Horst, Robert. *The Fortunes of the Novel: A Study in the Transposition of a Genre.* New York: Peter Lang, 2003. Reviews the rise of the English novel from its roots in early Spanish prose fiction, especially the work of Miguel de Cervantes, through the novels of Daniel Defoe, Sir Walter Scott, and Charles Dickens. Focuses on the preoccupation of novelists with economic issues, broadly defined.

Van Sant, Ann Jessie. *Eighteenth-Century Sensibility and the Novel.* New York: Cambridge University Press, 1993. Thematic analysis of eighteenth century fiction, focusing on the concept of sensibility and the use of the sensual (both visual and tactile) as a technique in novels.

Willmott, Glenn. *Unreal Country: Modernity in the Canadian Novel in English.* Montreal: McGill-Queen's University Press, 2002. Attempts to identify the critical and cultural dimensions of a specifically Canadian literature. Relies on theories of modernism for establishing the theoretical framework in which individual novels are examined.

Laurence W. Mazzeno

Glossary of Literary Terms

absurdism: A philosophical attitude, pervading much of modern drama and fiction, that underlines the isolation and alienation that humans experience, having been thrown into what absurdists see as a godless universe devoid of religious, spiritual, or metaphysical meaning. Conspicuous in its lack of logic, consistency, coherence, intelligibility, and realism, the literature of the absurd depicts the anguish, forlornness, and despair inherent in the human condition. Counter to the rationalist assumptions of traditional humanism, absurdism denies the existence of universal truth or value.

allegory: A literary mode in which a second level of meaning, wherein characters, events, and settings represent abstractions, is encoded within the surface narrative. The allegorical mode may dominate an entire work, in which case the encoded message is the work's primary reason for being, or it may be an element in a work otherwise interesting and meaningful for its surface story alone. Elements of allegory may be found in Jonathan Swift's *Gulliver's Travels* (1726) and Thomas Mann's *Der Zauberberg* (1924; *The Magic Mountain*, 1927).

anatomy: Literally the term means the "cutting up" or "dissection" of a subject into its constituent parts for closer examination. Northrop Frye, in his *Anatomy of Criticism* (1957), uses the term to refer to a narrative that deals with mental attitudes rather than people. As opposed to the novel, the anatomy features stylized figures who are mouthpieces for the ideas they represent.

antagonist: The character in fiction who stands as a rival or opponent to the *protagonist*.

antihero: Defined by Seán O'Faoláin as a fictional figure who, deprived of social sanctions and definitions, is always trying to define himself and to establish his own codes. Ahab may be seen as the antihero of Herman Melville's *Moby Dick* (1851).

archetype: The term "archetype" entered literary criticism from the psychology of Carl Jung, who defined archetypes as "primordial images" from the "collective unconscious" of humankind. Jung believed that works of art derive much of their power from the unconscious appeal of these images to ancestral memories. In his extremely influential *Anatomy of Criticism* (1957), Northrop Frye gave another sense of the term wide currency, defining the archetype as "a symbol, usually an image, which recurs often enough in literature to be recognizable as an element of one's literary experience as a whole."

atmosphere: The general mood or tone of a work; atmosphere is often associated with setting but can also be established by action or dialogue. A classic example of atmosphere is the primitive, fatalistic tone created in the opening description of Egdon Heath in Thomas Hardy's *The Return of the Native* (1878).

bildungsroman: Sometimes called the "novel of education," the bildungsroman focuses on the growth of a young *protagonist* who is learning about the world and finding his or her place in life; typical examples are James Joyce's *A Portrait of the Artist as a*

Young Man (1914-1915, serial; 1916, book) and Thomas Wolfe's *Look Homeward, Angel* (1929).

biographical criticism: Criticism that attempts to determine how the events and experiences of an author's life influence his or her work.

bourgeois novel: A novel in which the values, preoccupations, and accoutrements of middle-class or bourgeois life are given particular prominence. The heyday of the bourgeois novel was the nineteenth century, when novelists as varied as Jane Austen, Honoré de Balzac, and Anthony Trollope both criticized and unreflectingly transmitted the assumptions of the rising middle class.

canon: An authorized or accepted list of books. In modern parlance, the literary canon comprehends the privileged texts, classics, or great books that are thought to belong permanently on university reading lists. Recent theory—especially feminist, Marxist, and poststructuralist—critically examines the process of canon formation and questions the hegemony of white male writers. Such theory sees canon formation as the ideological act of a dominant institution and seeks to undermine the notion of canonicity itself, thereby preventing the exclusion of works by women, minorities, and oppressed peoples.

character: Characters in fiction can be presented as if they were real people or as stylized functions of the plot. Usually characters are a combination of both factors.

classicism: A literary stance or value system consciously based on the example of classical Greek and Roman literature. While the term is applied to an enormous diversity of artists in many different periods and in many different national literatures, "classicism" generally denotes a cluster of values including formal discipline, restrained expression, reverence for tradition, and an objective rather than a subjective orientation. As a literary tendency, classicism is often opposed to *Romanticism*, although many writers combine classical and romantic elements.

climax/crisis: The term "climax" refers to the moment of the reader's highest emotional response, whereas "crisis" refers to a structural element of plot, a turning point at which a resolution must take place.

complication: The point in a novel when the *conflict* is developed or when the already existing conflict is further intensified.

conflict: The struggle that develops as a result of the opposition between the *protagonist* and another person, the natural world, society, or some force within the self.

contextualist criticism: A further extension of *formalist criticism*, which assumes that the language of art is constitutive. Rather than referring to preexistent values, the artwork creates values only inchoately realized before. The most important advocates of this position are Eliseo Vivas (*The Artistic Transaction*, 1963) and Murray Krieger (*The Play and Place of Criticism*, 1967).

conventions: All those devices of stylization, compression, and selection that constitute the necessary differences between art and life. According to the Russian Formalists, these conventions constitute the "literariness" of literature and are the only proper concern of the literary critic.

deconstruction: An extremely influential contemporary school of criticism based on the works of the French philosopher Jacques Derrida. Deconstruction treats literary works as unconscious reflections of the reigning myths of Western culture. The primary myth is that there is a meaningful world that language signifies or represents. The deconstructionist critic is most often concerned with showing how a literary text tacitly subverts the very assumptions or myths on which it ostensibly rests.

defamiliarization: Coined by Viktor Shklovsky in 1917, this term denotes a basic principle of Russian Formalism. Poetic language (by which the Formalists meant artful language, in prose as well as in poetry) defamiliarizes or "makes strange" familiar experiences. The technique of art, says Shklovsky, is to "make objects unfamiliar, to make forms difficult, to increase the difficulty and length of perception. . . . Art is a way of experiencing the artfulness of an object; the object is not important."

detective story: The so-called classic detective story (or mystery) is a highly formalized and logically structured mode of fiction in which the focus is on a crime solved by a detective through interpretation of evidence and ratiocination; the most famous detective in this mode is Arthur Conan Doyle's Sherlock Holmes. Many modern practitioners of the genre, however, such as Dashiell Hammett, Raymond Chandler, and Ross Macdonald, have de-emphasized the puzzlelike qualities of the detective story, stressing instead characterization, theme, and other elements of mainstream fiction.

determinism: The belief that an individual's actions are essentially determined by biological and environmental factors, with free will playing a negligible role. (See *naturalism.*)

dialogue: The similitude of conversation in fiction, dialogue serves to characterize, to further the *plot*, to establish *conflict*, and to express thematic ideas.

displacement: Popularized in criticism by Northrop Frye, this term refers to the author's attempt to make his or her story psychologically motivated and realistic, even as the latent structure of the mythical motivation moves relentlessly forward.

dominant: A term coined by Roman Jakobson to refer to that which "rules, determines, and transforms the remaining components in the work of a single artist, in a poetic canon, or in the work of an epoch." The shifting of the dominant in a *genre* accounts for the creation of new generic forms and new poetic epochs. For example, the rise of *realism* in the mid-nineteenth century indicates realistic conventions becoming dominant and *romance* or fantasy conventions becoming secondary.

doppelgänger: A double or counterpart of a person, sometimes endowed with ghostly qualities. A fictional character's doppelgänger often reflects a suppressed side of his or her personality. One of the classic examples of the doppelgänger motif is found in

Fyodor Dostoevski's novella *Dvoynik* (1846; *The Double*, 1917); Isaac Bashevis Singer and Jorge Luis Borges, among others, offer striking modern treatments of the doppelgänger.

epic: Although this term usually refers to a long narrative poem that presents the exploits of a central figure of high position, the term is also used to designate a long novel that has the style or structure usually associated with an epic. In this sense, for example, Herman Melville's *Moby Dick* (1851) and James Joyce's *Ulysses* (1922) may be called epics.

episodic narrative: A work that is held together primarily by a loose connection of self-sufficient episodes. *Picaresque novels* often have episodic structure.

epistolary novel: A novel made up of letters by one or more fictional characters. Samuel Richardson's *Pamela: Or, Virtue Rewarded* (1740-1741) is a well-known eighteenth century example. In the nineteenth century, Bram Stoker's *Dracula* (1897) is largely epistolary. The technique allows for several different points of view to be presented.

euphuism: A style of writing characterized by ornate language that is highly contrived, alliterative, and repetitious. Euphuism was developed by John Lyly in his *Euphues, the Anatomy of Wit* (1578) and was emulated frequently by writers of the Elizabethan Age.

existentialism: A philosophical, religious, and literary term, emerging from World War II, for a group of attitudes surrounding the pivotal notion that existence precedes essence. According to Jean-Paul Sartre, "Man is nothing else but what he makes himself." Forlornness arises from the death of God and the concomitant death of universal values, of any source of ultimate or a priori standards. Despair arises from the fact that an individual can reckon only with what depends on his or her will, and the sphere of that will is severely limited; the number of things on which he or she can have an impact is pathetically small. Existentialist literature is antideterministic in the extreme and rejects the idea that heredity and environment shape and determine human motivation and behavior.

exposition: The part or parts of a fiction that provide necessary background information. Exposition not only provides the time and place of the action but also introduces readers to the fictive world of the story, acquainting them with the ground rules of the work.

fantastic: In his study *The Fantastic* (1970), Tzvetan Todorov defines the fantastic as a *genre* that lies between the "uncanny" and the "marvelous." All three genres embody the familiar world but present an event that cannot be explained by the laws of the familiar world. Todorov says that the fantastic occupies a twilight zone between the uncanny (when the reader knows that the peculiar event is merely the result of an illusion) and the marvelous (when the reader understands that the event is supposed to take place in a realm controlled by laws unknown to humankind). The fantastic is thus essentially unsettling, provocative, even subversive.

feminist criticism: A criticism advocating equal rights for women in political, economic, social, psychological, personal, and aesthetic senses. On the thematic level, the feminist reader should identify with female characters and their concerns. The object is to provide a critique of phallocentric assumptions and an analysis of patriarchal ideologies inscribed in a literature that is male-centered and male-dominated. On the ideological level, feminist critics see gender, as well as the stereotypes that go along with it, as a cultural construct. They strive to define a particularly feminine content and to extend the *canon* so that it might include works by lesbians, feminists, and women writers in general.

flashback: A scene in a fiction that depicts an earlier event; it may be presented as a reminiscence by a character in the story or may simply be inserted into the narrative.

foreshadowing: A device to create suspense or dramatic irony in fiction by indicating through suggestion what will take place in the future.

formalist criticism: Two particularly influential formalist schools of criticism arose in the twentieth century: the Russian Formalists and the American New Critics. The Russian Formalists were concerned with the conventional devices used in literature to defamiliarize that which habit has made familiar. The New Critics believed that literary criticism is a description and evaluation of its object and that the primary concern of the critic is with the work's unity. Both schools of criticism, at their most extreme, treated literary works as artifacts or constructs divorced from their biographical and social contexts.

genre: In its most general sense, this term refers to a group of literary works defined by a common form, style, or purpose. In practice, the term is used in a wide variety of overlapping and, to a degree, contradictory senses. Tragedy and comedy are thus described as distinct genres; the novel (a form that includes both tragic and comic works) is a genre; and various subspecies of the novel, such as the *gothic* and the *picaresque*, are themselves frequently treated as distinct genres. Finally, the term "genre fiction" refers to forms of popular fiction in which the writer is bound by more or less rigid conventions. Indeed, all these diverse usages have in common an emphasis on the manner in which individual literary works are shaped by particular expectations and conventions; this is the subject of genre criticism.

genre fiction: Categories of popular fiction in which the writers are bound by more or less rigid conventions, such as in the *detective story*, the *romance*, and the *Western*. Although the term can be used in a neutral sense, it is often used dismissively.

gothic novel: A form of fiction developed in the eighteenth century that focuses on horror and the supernatural. In his preface to *The Castle of Otranto* (1765), the first gothic novel in English, Horace Walpole claimed that he was trying to combine two kinds of fiction, with events and story typical of the medieval romance and character delineation typical of the realistic novel. Other examples of the form are Matthew Gregory

Lewis's *The Monk: A Romance* (1796; also known as *Ambrosio: Or, The Monk*) and Mary Wollstonecraft Shelley's *Frankenstein: Or, The Modern Prometheus* (1818).

grotesque: According to Wolfgang Kayser (*The Grotesque in Art and Literature*, 1963), the grotesque is an embodiment in literature of the estranged world. Characterized by a breakup of the everyday world by mysterious forces, the form differs from fantasy in that the reader is not sure whether to react with humor or with horror and in that the exaggeration manifested exists in the familiar world rather than in a purely imaginative world.

Hebraic/Homeric styles: Terms coined by Erich Auerbach in *Mimesis: The Representation of Reality in Western Literature* (1953) to designate two basic fictional styles. The Hebraic style focuses only on the decisive points of narrative and leaves all else obscure, mysterious, and "fraught with background"; the Homeric style places the narrative in a definite time and place and externalizes everything in a perpetual foreground.

historical criticism: In contrast to *formalist criticism*, which treats literary works to a great extent as self-contained artifacts, historical criticism emphasizes the historical context of literature; the two approaches, however, need not be mutually exclusive. Ernst Robert Curtius's *European Literature and the Latin Middle Ages* (1940) is a prominent example of historical criticism.

historical novel: A novel that depicts past historical events, usually public in nature, and features real as well as fictional people. Sir Walter Scott's Waverley novels established the basic type, but the relationship between fiction and history in the form varies greatly depending on the practitioner.

implied author: According to Wayne Booth (*The Rhetoric of Fiction*, 1961), the novel often creates a kind of second self who tells the story—a self who is wiser, more sensitive, and more perceptive than any real person could be.

interior monologue: Defined by Édouard Dujardin as the speech of a character designed to introduce the reader directly to the character's internal life, the form differs from other kinds of monologue in that it attempts to reproduce thought before any logical organization is imposed on it. See, for example, Molly Bloom's long interior monologue at the conclusion of James Joyce's *Ulysses* (1922).

irrealism: A term often used to refer to modern or postmodern fiction that is presented self-consciously as a fiction or a fabulation rather than a mimesis of external reality. The best-known practitioners of irrealism are John Barth, Robert Coover, and Donald Barthelme.

local colorists: A loose movement of late nineteenth century American writers whose fiction emphasizes the distinctive folkways, landscapes, and dialects of various regions. Important local colorists include Bret Harte, Mark Twain, George Washington Cable, Kate Chopin, and Sarah Orne Jewett. (See *regional novel*.)

Marxist criticism: Based on the nineteenth century writings of Karl Marx and Friedrich Engels, Marxist criticism views literature as a product of ideological forces determined by the dominant class. However, many Marxists believe that literature operates according to its own autonomous standards of production and reception: It is both a product of ideology and able to determine ideology. As such, literature may overcome the dominant paradigms of its age and play a revolutionary role in society.

metafiction: This term refers to fiction that manifests a reflexive tendency, such as Vladimir Nabokov's *Pale Fire* (1962) and John Fowles's *The French Lieutenant's Woman* (1969). The emphasis is on the loosening of the work's illusion of reality to expose the reality of its illusion. Other terms used to refer to this type of fiction include "irrealism," "postmodernist fiction," "antifiction," and "surfiction."

modernism: An international movement in the arts that began in the early years of the twentieth century. Although the term is used to describe artists of widely varying persuasions, modernism in general was characterized by its international idiom, by its interest in cultures distant in space or time, by its emphasis on formal experimentation, and by its sense of dislocation and radical change.

motif: A conventional incident or situation in a fiction that may serve as the basis for the structure of the narrative itself. The Russian Formalist critic Boris Tomashevsky uses the term to refer to the smallest particle of thematic material in a work.

motivation: Although this term is usually used in reference to the convention of justifying the action of a character from his or her psychological makeup, the Russian Formalists use the term to refer to the network of devices that justify the introduction of individual *motifs* or groups of motifs in a work. For example, "compositional motivation" refers to the principle that every single property in a work contributes to its overall effect; "realistic motivation" refers to the realistic devices used to make a work plausible and lifelike.

multiculturalism: The tendency to recognize the perspectives of those traditionally excluded from the canon of Western art and literature. In order to promote multiculturalism, publishers and educators have revised textbooks and school curricula to incorporate material by and about women, members of minority groups, persons from non-Western cultures, and homosexuals.

myth: Anonymous traditional stories dealing with basic human concepts and antinomies. According to Claude Lévi-Strauss, myth is that part of language where the "formula *tradutore, tradittore* reaches its lowest truth value. . . . Its substance does not lie in its style, its original music, or its syntax, but in the story which it tells."

myth criticism: Northrop Frye says that in myth "we see the structural principles of literature isolated." Myth criticism is concerned with these basic principles of literature; it is not to be confused with mythological criticism, which is primarily concerned with finding mythological parallels in the surface action of the *narrative*.

narrative: Robert Scholes and Robert Kellogg, in *The Nature of Narrative* (1966), say that by "narrative" they mean literary works that include both a story and a storyteller. The term "narrative" usually implies a contrast to "enacted" fiction such as drama.

narratology: The study of the form and functioning of *narratives*; it attempts to examine what all narratives have in common and what makes individual narratives different from one another.

narrator: The *character* who recounts the *narrative*, or story. Wayne Booth describes various dramatized narrators in *The Rhetoric of Fiction* (1961): unacknowledged centers of consciousness, observers, narrator-agents, and self-conscious narrators. Booth suggests that the important elements to consider in narration are the relationships among the narrator, the author, the characters, and the reader.

naturalism: As developed by Émile Zola in the late nineteenth century, naturalism is the application of the principles of scientific *determinism* to fiction. Although it usually refers more to the choice of subject matter than to technical conventions, those conventions associated with the movement center on the author's attempt to be precise and scientifically objective in description and detail, regardless of whether the events described are sordid or shocking.

New Criticism: See *formalist criticism.*

novel: Perhaps the most difficult of all fictional forms to define because of its multiplicity of modes. Edouard, in André Gide's *Les Faux-monnayeurs* (1925; *The Counterfeiters*, 1927), says the novel is the freest and most lawless of all *genres*; he wonders if fear of that liberty is the reason the novel has so timidly clung to reality. Most critics seem to agree that the novel's primary area of concern is the social world. Ian Watt (*The Rise of the Novel*, 2001) says that the novel can be distinguished from other fictional forms by the attention it pays to individual characterization and detailed presentation of the environment. Moreover, says Watt, the novel, more than any other fictional form, is interested in the "development of its characters in the course of time."

novel of manners: The classic examples of this form might be the novels of Jane Austen, wherein the customs and conventions of a social group of a particular time and place are realistically, and often satirically, portrayed.

novella, novelle, nouvelle, novelette, novela: Although these terms often refer to the short European tale, especially the Renaissance form employed by Giovanni Boccaccio, the terms often refer to that form of fiction that is said to be longer than a short story and shorter than a novel. "Novelette" is the term usually preferred by the British, whereas "novella" is the term usually used to refer to American works in this *genre*. Henry James claimed that the main merit of the form is the "effort to do the complicated thing with a strong brevity and lucidity."

phenomenological criticism: Although best known as a European school of criticism practiced by Georges Poulet and others, this so-called criticism of consciousness is also propounded in the United States by such critics as J. Hillis Miller. The focus is less on individual works and *genres* than it is on literature as an act; the work is not seen as an object but rather as part of a strand of latent impulses in the work of a single author or an epoch.

picaresque novel: A form of fiction that centers on a central rogue figure, or picaro, who usually tells his or her own story. The plot structure is normally *episodic*, and the episodes usually focus on how the picaro lives by his or her wits. Classic examples of the mode are Henry Fielding's *The History of Tom Jones, a Foundling* (1749; commonly known as *Tom Jones*) and Mark Twain's *Adventures of Huckleberry Finn* (1884).

plot/story: "Story" refers to the full *narrative* of *character* and action, whereas "plot" generally refers to action with little reference to character. A more precise and helpful distinction is made by the Russian Formalists, who suggest that "plot" refers to the events of a narrative as they have been artfully arranged in the literary work, subject to chronological displacement, ellipses, and other devices, while "story" refers to the sum of the same events arranged in simple, causal-chronological order. Thus story is the raw material for plot. By comparing the two in a given work, the reader is encouraged to see the narrative as an artifact.

point of view: The means by which the story is presented to the reader, or, as Percy Lubbock says in *The Craft of Fiction* (1921), "the relation in which the narrator stands to the story"—a relation that Lubbock claims governs the craft of fiction. Some of the questions the critical reader should ask concerning point of view are the following: Who talks to the reader? From what position does the narrator tell the story? At what distance does he or she place the reader from the story? What kind of person is he or she? How fully is he or she characterized? How reliable is he or she? For further discussion, see Wayne Booth, *The Rhetoric of Fiction* (1961).

postcolonialism: Postcolonial literature emerged in the mid-twentieth century when colonies in Asia, Africa, and the Caribbean began gaining their independence from the European nations that had long controlled them. Postcolonial authors, such as Salman Rushdie and V. S. Naipaul, tend to focus on both the freedom and the conflict inherent in living in a postcolonial state.

postmodernism: A ubiquitous but elusive term in contemporary criticism, "postmodernism" is loosely applied to the various artistic movements that followed the era of so-called high modernism, represented by such giants as James Joyce and Pablo Picasso. In critical discussions of contemporary fiction, the term "postmodernism" is frequently applied to the works of writers such as Thomas Pynchon, John Barth, and Donald Barthelme, who exhibit a self-conscious awareness of their modernist predecessors as well as a reflexive treatment of fictional form.

protagonist: The central *character* in a fiction, the character whose fortunes most concern the reader.

psychological criticism: While much modern literary criticism reflects to some degree the impacts of Sigmund Freud, Carl Jung, Jacques Lacan, and other psychological theorists, the term "psychological criticism" suggests a strong emphasis on a causal relation between the writer's psychological state, variously interpreted, and his or her works. A notable example of psychological criticism is Norman Fruman's *Coleridge, the Damaged Archangel* (1971).

psychological novel: A form of fiction in which *character*, especially the inner lives of characters, is the primary focus. This form, which has been of primary importance at least since Henry James, characterizes much of the work of James Joyce, Virginia Woolf, and William Faulkner. For a detailed discussion, see *The Modern Psychological Novel* (1955) by Leon Edel.

realism: A literary technique in which the primary convention is to render an illusion of fidelity to external reality. Realism is often identified as the primary method of the novel form: It focuses on surface details, maintains a fidelity to the everyday experiences of middle-class society, and strives for a one-to-one relationship between the fiction and the action imitated. The realist movement in the late nineteenth century coincides with the full development of the novel form.

reception aesthetics: The best-known American practitioner of reception aesthetics is Stanley Fish. For the reception critic, meaning is an event or process; rather than being embedded in the work, it is created through particular acts of reading. The best-known European practitioner of this criticism, Wolfgang Iser, argues that indeterminacy is the basic characteristic of literary texts; the reader must "normalize" the text either by projecting his or her standards into it or by revising his or her standards to "fit" the text.

regional novel: Any novel in which the character of a given geographical region plays a decisive role. Although regional differences persist across the United States, a considerable leveling in speech and customs has taken place, so that the sharp regional distinctions evident in nineteenth century American fiction have all but disappeared. Only in the South has a strong regional tradition persisted to the present. (See *local colorists*.)

rhetorical criticism: The rhetorical critic is concerned with the literary work as a means of communicating ideas and the means by which the work affects or controls the reader. Such criticism seems best suited to didactic works such as satire.

roman à clef: A fiction wherein actual people, often celebrities of some sort, are thinly disguised.

romance: The romance usually differs from the novel form in that the focus is on symbolic events and representational characters rather than on "as-if-real" characters and events. Richard Chase says that in the romance, character is depicted as highly stylized, a function of the plot rather than as someone complexly related to society. The romancer is more likely to be concerned with dreamworlds than with the familiar world, believing that reality cannot be grasped by the traditional novel.

Romanticism: A widespread cultural movement in the late eighteenth and early nineteenth centuries, the influence of which is still felt. As a general literary tendency, Romanticism is frequently contrasted with *classicism.* Although many varieties of Romanticism are indigenous to various national literatures, the term generally suggests an assertion of the preeminence of the imagination. Other values associated with various schools of Romanticism include primitivism, an interest in folklore, a reverence for nature, and a fascination with the demoniac and the macabre.

scene: The central element of *narration*; specific actions are narrated or depicted that make the reader feel he or she is participating directly in the action.

science fiction: Fiction in which certain givens (physical laws, psychological principles, social conditions—any one or all of these) form the basis of an imaginative projection into the future or, less commonly, an extrapolation in the present or even into the past.

semiotics: The science of signs and sign systems in communication. According to Roman Jakobson, semiotics deals with the principles that underlie the structure of signs, their use in language of all kinds, and the specific nature of various sign systems.

sentimental novel: A form of fiction popular in the eighteenth century in which emotionalism and optimism are the primary characteristics. The best-known examples are Samuel Richardson's *Pamela: Or, Virtue Rewarded* (1740-1741) and Oliver Goldsmith's *The Vicar of Wakefield* (1766).

setting: The circumstances and environment, both temporal and spatial, of a *narrative.*

spatial form: An author's attempt to make the reader apprehend a work spatially in a moment of time rather than sequentially. To achieve this effect, the author breaks up the *narrative* into interspersed fragments. Beginning with James Joyce, Marcel Proust, and Djuna Barnes, the movement toward spatial form is concomitant with the *modernist* effort to supplant historical time in fiction with mythic time. For the seminal discussion of this technique, see Joseph Frank, *The Widening Gyre* (1963).

stream of consciousness: The depiction of the thought processes of a *character,* insofar as this is possible, without any mediating structures. The metaphor of consciousness as a "stream" suggests a rush of thoughts and images governed by free association rather than by strictly rational development. The term "stream of consciousness" is often used loosely as a synonym for *interior monologue.* The most celebrated example of stream of consciousness in fiction is the monologue of Molly Bloom in James Joyce's *Ulysses* (1922); other notable practitioners of the stream-of-consciousness technique include Dorothy Richardson, Virginia Woolf, and William Faulkner.

structuralism: As a movement of thought, structuralism is based on the idea of intrinsic, self-sufficient structures that do not require reference to external elements. A structure is a system of transformations that involves the interplay of laws inherent in the system itself. The study of language is the primary model for contemporary structuralism. The structuralist literary critic attempts to define structural principles that operate intertextually throughout the whole of literature as well as principles that operate in *genres* and in individual works. One of the most accessible surveys of structuralism and literature available is Jonathan Culler's *Structuralist Poetics* (1975).

summary: Those parts of a fiction that do not need to be detailed. In *Tom Jones* (1749), Henry Fielding says, "If whole years should pass without producing anything worthy of . . . notice . . . we shall hasten on to matters of consequence."

thematics: According to Northrop Frye, when a work of fiction is written or interpreted thematically, it becomes an illustrative fable. Murray Krieger defines thematics as "the study of the experiential tensions which, dramatically entangled in the literary work, become an existential reflection of that work's aesthetic complexity."

tone: The dominant mood of a work of fiction. (See *atmosphere.*)

unreliable narrator: A narrator whose account of the events of the story cannot be trusted, obliging readers to reconstruct—if possible—the true state of affairs themselves. Once an innovative technique, the use of the unreliable narrator has become commonplace among contemporary writers who wish to suggest the impossibility of a truly "reliable" account of any event. Notable examples of the unreliable narrator can be found in Ford Madox Ford's *The Good Soldier* (1915) and Vladimir Nabokov's *Lolita* (1955).

Victorian novel: Although the Victorian period extended from 1837 to 1901, the term "Victorian novel" does not include the later decades of Queen Victoria's reign. The term loosely refers to the sprawling works of novelists such as Charles Dickens and William Makepeace Thackeray—works that frequently appeared first in serial form and are characterized by a broad social canvas.

vraisemblance/verisimilitude: Tzvetan Todorov defines vraisemblance as "the mask which conceals the text's own laws, but which we are supposed to take for a relation to reality." Verisimilitude refers to a work's attempts to make the reader believe that it conforms to reality rather than to its own laws.

Western novel: Like all varieties of *genre fiction*, the Western novel—generally known simply as the Western—is defined by a relatively predictable combination of *conventions*, *motifs*, and recurring themes. These predictable elements, familiar from many Western films and television series, differentiate the Western from *historical novels* and idiosyncratic works such as Thomas Berger's *Little Big Man* (1964) that are also set in the Old West. Conversely, some novels set in the contemporary West are regarded as Westerns because they deal with modern cowboys and with the land itself in the manner characteristic of the *genre.*

Charles E. May

Guide to Online Resources

Web Sites

The following sites were visited by the editors of Salem Press in 2009. Because URLs frequently change, the accuracy of these addresses cannot be guaranteed; however, long-standing sites, such as those of colleges and universities, national organizations, and government agencies, generally maintain links when sites are moved or updated.

American Literature on the Web

http://www.nagasaki-gaigo.ac.jp/ishikawa/amlit

Among this site's features are several pages providing links to Web sites about specific genres and literary movements, southern and southwestern American literature, minority literature, literary theory, and women writers, as well as an extensive index of links to electronic text collections and archives. Users also can access information for five specific time periods: 1620-1820, 1820-1865, 1865-1914, 1914-1945, and since 1945. A range of information is available for each period, including alphabetical lists of authors that link to more specific information about each writer, time lines of historical and literary events, and links to related additional Web sites.

Books and Writers

http://www.kirjasto.sci.fi/indeksi.htm

This broad, comprehensive, and easy-to-use resource provides access to information about hundreds of authors throughout the world, extending from 70 B.C.E to the twenty-first century. Links take users from an alphabetical list of authors to pages featuring biographical material, lists of works, and recommendations for further reading about individual authors; each writer's page also includes links to related pages on the site. Although brief, the biographical essays provide solid overviews of the authors' careers, their contributions to literature, and their literary influences.

The Canadian Literature Archive

http://www.umanitoba.ca/canlit

Created and maintained by the English Department at the University of Manitoba, this site is a comprehensive collection of materials for and about Canadian writers. It includes an alphabetical listing of authors with links to additional Web-based information. Users also can retrieve electronic texts, announcements of literary events, and videocasts of author interviews and readings.

A Celebration of Women Writers

http://digital.library.upenn.edu/women

This site presents an extensive compendium of information about the contributions of women writers throughout history. The "Local Editions by Authors" and "Local Editions by Category" pages include access to electronic texts of the works of numerous writers, including Louisa May Alcott, Djuna Barnes, Grazia Deledda, Edith Wharton, and Virginia Woolf. Users can also access biographical and bibliographical information by browsing lists arranged by writers' names, countries of origin, ethnicities, and the centuries in which they lived.

Contemporary Writers

http://www.contemporarywriters.com/authors

Created by the British Council, this site offers "up-to-date profiles of some of the U.K. and Commonwealth's most important living writers (plus writers from the Republic of Ireland that we've worked with)." The available information includes biographies, bibliographies, critical reviews, news about literary prizes, and photographs. Users can search the site by author, genre, nationality, gender, publisher, book title, date of publication, and prize name and date.

Internet Public Library: Native American Authors

http://www.ipl.org/div/natam

Internet Public Library, a Web-based collection of materials, includes this index to resources about writers of Native American heritage. An alphabetical list of authors enables users to link to biographies, lists of works, electronic texts, tribal Web sites, and other online resources. The majority of the writers covered are contemporary Indian authors, but some historical authors also are featured. Users also can retrieve information by browsing lists of titles and tribes. In addition, the site contains a bibliography of print and online materials about Native American literature.

LiteraryHistory.com

http://www.literaryhistory.com

This site is an excellent source of academic, scholarly, and critical literature about eighteenth, nineteenth, and twentieth century American and English writers. It provides numerous pages about specific eras and genres, including individual pages for eighteenth, nineteenth, and twentieth century literature and for African American and postcolonial literature. These pages contain alphabetical lists of authors that link to articles, reviews, overviews, excerpts of works, teaching guides, podcast interviews, and other materials. The eighteenth century literature page also provides access to information about the eighteenth century novel.

Literary Resources on the Net

http://andromeda.rutgers.edu/~jlynch/Lit

Jack Lynch of Rutgers University maintains this extensive collection of links to Internet sites that are useful to academics, including numerous Web sites about American and English literature. This collection is a good place to begin online research about the novel, as it links to hundreds of other sites with broad ranges of literary topics. The site is organized chronically, with separate pages for information about the Middle Ages, the Renaissance, the eighteenth century, the Romantic and Victorian eras, and twentieth century British and Irish literature. It also has separate pages providing links to Web sites about American literature and to women's literature and feminism.

LitWeb

http://litweb.net

LitWeb provides biographies of more than five hundred world authors throughout history that can be accessed through an alphabetical listing. The pages about each writer contain a list of his or her works, suggestions for further reading, and illustrations. The site also offers information about past and present winners of major literary prizes.

The Modern Word: Authors of the Libyrinth

http://www.themodernword.com/authors.html

The Modern Word site, although somewhat haphazard in its organization, provides a great deal of critical information about writers. The "Authors of the Libyrinth" page is very useful, linking author names to essays about them and other resources. The section of the page headed "The Scriptorium" presents "an index of pages featuring writers who have pushed the edges of their medium, combining literary talent with a sense of experimentation to produce some remarkable works of modern literature." The site also includes sections devoted to Samuel Beckett, Umberto Eco, Gabriel García Márquez, James Joyce, Franz Kafka, and Thomas Pynchon.

Novels

http://www.nvcc.edu/home/ataormina/novels/default.htm

This overview of American and English novels was prepared by Agatha Taormina, a professor at Northern Virginia Community College. It contains three sections: "History" provides a definition of the novel genre, a discussion of its origins in eighteenth century England, and separate pages with information about genres and authors of nineteenth century, twentieth century, and postmodern novels. "Approaches" suggests how to read a novel critically for greater appreciation, and "Resources" provides a list of books about the novel.

Outline of American Literature

http://www.america.gov/publications/books/outline-of-american-literature.html

This page of the America.gov site provides access to an electronic version of the ten-chapter volume *Outline of American Literature*, a historical overview of prose and poetry from colonial times to the present published by the U.S. Department of State. The work's author is Kathryn VanSpanckeren, professor of English at the University of Tampa. The site offers links to abbreviated versions of each chapter as well as access to the entire publication in PDF format.

Voice of the Shuttle

http://vos.ucsb.edu

One of the most complete and authoritative places for online information about literature, Voice of the Shuttle is maintained by professors and students in the English Department at the University of California, Santa Barbara. The site provides thousands of links to electronic books, academic journals, association Web sites, sites created by university professors, and many, many other resources about the humanities. Its "Literature in English" page provides links to separate pages about the literature of the Anglo-Saxon era, the Middle Ages, the Renaissance and seventeenth century, the Restoration and eighteenth century, the Romantic age, the Victorian age, and modern and contemporary periods in Britain and the United States, as well as a page focused on minority literature. Another page on the site, "Literatures Other than English," offers a gateway to information about the literature of numerous countries and world regions.

ELECTRONIC DATABASES

Electronic databases usually do not have their own URLs. Instead, public, college, and university libraries subscribe to these databases, provide links to them on their Web sites, and make them available to library card holders or other specified patrons. Readers can visit library Web sites or ask reference librarians to check on availability.

Canadian Literary Centre

Produced by EBSCO, the Canadian Literary Centre database contains full-text content from ECW Press, a Toronto-based publisher, including the titles in the publisher's Canadian fiction studies, Canadian biography, and Canadian writers and their works series, *ECW's Biographical Guide to Canadian Novelists*, and *George Woodcock's Introduction to Canadian Fiction*. Author biographies, essays and literary criticism, and book reviews are among the database's offerings.

Literary Reference Center

EBSCO's Literary Reference Center (LRC) is a comprehensive full-text database designed primarily to help high school and undergraduate students in English and the humanities with homework and research assignments about literature. The database contains massive amounts of information from reference works, books, literary journals, and other materials, including more than 31,000 plot summaries, synopses, and overviews of literary works; almost 100,000 essays and articles of literary criticism; about 140,000 author biographies; more than 605,000 book reviews; and more than 5,200 author interviews. It also contains the entire contents of Salem Press's MagillOnLiterature Plus. Users can retrieve information by browsing a list of authors' names or titles of literary works; they can also use an advanced search engine to access information by numerous categories, including author name, gender, cultural identity, national identity, and the years in which he or she lived, or by literary title, character, locale, genre, and publication date. The Literary Reference Center also features a literary-historical time line, an encyclopedia of literature, and a glossary of literary terms.

MagillOnLiterature Plus

MagillOnLiterature Plus is a comprehensive, integrated literature database produced by Salem Press and available on the EBSCO*host* platform. The database contains the full text of essays in Salem's many literature-related reference works, including *Masterplots*, *Cyclopedia of World Authors*, *Cyclopedia of Literary Characters*, *Cyclopedia of Literary Places*, *Critical Survey of Long Fiction*, *Critical Survey of Short Fiction*, *World Philosophers and Their Works*, *Magill's Literary Annual*, and *Magill's Book Reviews.* Among its contents are articles on more than 35,000 literary works and more than 8,500 writers, poets, dramatists, essays, and philosophers, more than 1,000 images, and a glossary of more than 1,300 literary terms. The biographical essays include lists of authors' works and secondary bibliographies, and almost four hundred overview essays offer information about literary genres, time periods, and national literatures.

NoveList

NoveList is a readers' advisory service produced by EBSCO. The database provides access to 155,000 titles of both adult and juvenile fiction as well information about literary awards, book discussion guides, feature articles about a range of literary genres, and "recommended reads." Users can search by author name, book title, or series title or can describe the plot to retrieve the name of a book, information about the author, and book reviews; another search engine enables users to find titles similar to books they have enjoyed reading.

Rebecca Kuzins

CATEGORY INDEX

SUBJECT INDEX